Patagonia

timeout.com/patagonia

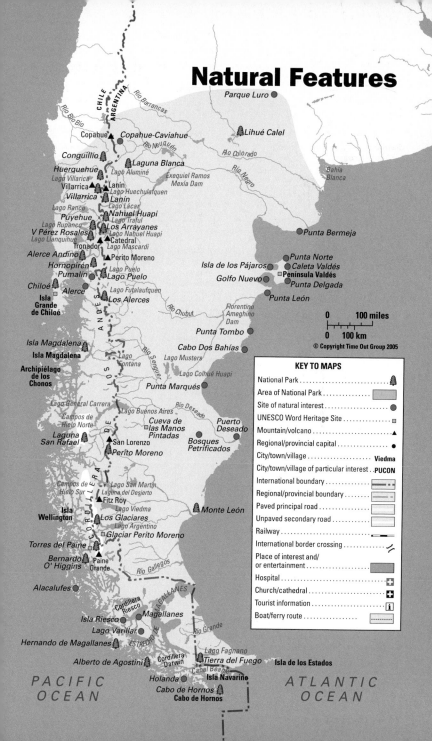

Published by **Time Out Guides Ltd**, a wholly owned subsidiary of Time Out Group Ltd.

Time Out and the Time Out logo are trademarks of Time Out Group Ltd.

© **Time Out Group Ltd 2005**
Previous edition 2002

10 9 8 7 6 5 4 3 2

This edition first published in Great Britain in 2005 by Ebury Publishing
Ebury Publishing is a division of The Random House Group Ltd,
20 Vauxhall Bridge Road, London SW1V 2SA

Random House Australia Pty Limited 20 Alfred Street, Milsons Point,
Sydney, New South Wales 2061, Australia
Random House New Zealand Limited 18 Poland Road, Glenfield, Auckland 10,
New Zealand

Random House South Africa (Pty) Limited Isle of Houghton, Corner Boundary
Road & Carse O'Gowrie, Houghton 2198, South Africa

Random House UK Limited Reg. No. 954009

Distributed in USA by Publishers Group West
1700 Fourth Street, Berkeley, California 94710

Distributed in Canada by Penguin Canada Ltd
10 Alcorn Avenue, Toronto, Ontario, Canada M4V 3B2

For further distribution details, see www.timeout.com

ISBN 1904978460 (until January 2007)
ISBN 9781904978466 (after January 2007)

A CIP catalogue record for this book is available from the British Library

Colour reprographics by Icon, Crowne House, 56-58 Southwark Street, London
SE1 1UN

Printed and bound by Firmengruppe APPL, aprinta druck, Wemding, Germany

Papers used by Ebury Publishing are natural, recyclable products made from
wood grown in sustainable forests

Time Out Guides Limited
Universal House
251 Tottenham Court Road
London W1T 7AB
Tel + 44 (0)20 7813 3000
Fax + 44 (0)20 7813 6001
Email guides@timeout.com
www.timeout.com

Editorial

Editor Matt Chesterton
Managing Editor Mark Rebindaine
Consultant Editor Joshua Goodman
Copy Editor Ros Sales
Listings Checker Gabriela Moltó
Proofreader Rob Dimery
Indexer Jonathan Cox

Editorial/Managing Director Peter Fiennes
Series Editor Ruth Jarvis
Deputy Series Editor Lesley McCave
Business Manager Gareth Garner
Guides Co-ordinator Holly Pick
Accountant Kemi Olufuwa

Design

Art Director Buenos Aires Gonzalo Gil, Tribalwerks
Designer Sofia Sanchez Barrenechea, Tribalwerks

Art Director London Scott Moore
Art Editor Tracey Ridgewell
Digital Imaging Dan Conway

Picture Desk

Picture Editor Jael Marschner
Deputy Picture Editor Tracey Kerrigan
Picture Researcher Helen McFarland

Advertising

Sales Director Mark Phillips
International Sales Manager Ross Canadé
International Sales Executive Simon Davies
Advertising Sales (Buenos Aires) Mark Rebindaine
Advertising Assistant Lucy Butler

Marketing

Marketing Director Mandy Martinez
Marketing & Publicity Manager, US Rosella Albanese

Production

Production Director Mark Lamond
Production Controller Marie Howell

Time Out Group

Chairman Tony Elliott
Managing Director Mike Hardwick
Group Financial Director Richard Waterlow
Group Commercial Director Lesley Gill
Group General Manager Nichola Coulthard
Group Circulation Director Jim Heinemann
Group Art Director John Oakey
Online Managing Director David Pepper
Group Production Director Steve Proctor
Group IT Director Simon Chappell

Contributors

Introduction Matt Chesterton, Chris Moss. **History** Chris Moss (*The historical Hall of Fame; Butch and the Sundance myth* Joshua Goodman; *The truth is down there* Matt Chesterton). **Patagonia Today** Joshua Goodman (*Penguin power* Matt Chesterton). **Wild Patagonia** Garry Hill (*Catch the condor* Lucy Hawking). **Arts & Culture** Chris Moss. **Eating & Drinking** Estefania Giganti, Chris Moss (*The wine box* Matt Chesterton). **Festivals & Events** Matt Chesterton. **National Parks & Trekking** Joshua Goodman, Anna Norman. **Adventure & Water Sports** Harry Hastings **Fishing & Hunting** Harry Hastings. **Golf** Harry Hastings. **Ranching** Joshua Goodman. **Skiing** Harry Hastings. **Getting Started (Argentina)** Chris Moss, Cathy Runciman. **The North** Declan McGarvey, Mark Rebindaine, Cathy Runciman (*Art in the right place* Matt Chesterton). **The Lake District 1** Fiona McCann, Garry Hill, Kristin James Henley, Mark Rebindaine (*Full steam ahead* Steve Crossan, Amy Rennison). **Central Patagonia** Joshua Goodman, Mark Rebindaine (*The long, unwinding road* Harry Hastings). **The Atlantic Coast** Joshua Goodman, Declan McGarvey, Mark Rebindaine. **The Deep South 1** Anna Norman, Max Sloman. **Getting Started (Chile)** Chris Moss. **The Lake District 2** Chris Moss (*Idle Days in Patagonia* Fiona McCann). **Chiloé** Chris Moss. **The Southern Highway** Joshua Goodman (*How to take the high road* Tasha Kosviner). **Sea Routes South** Gabriela Moltó, Chris Moss. **The Deep South 2** Anna Norman, Max Sloman (*Campfire blues* Joshua Goodman). **Antarctica** Brian Hagenbuch, Mark Rebindaine (*Cool cruising* Matt Chesterton). **Falklands/Malvinas/Other South Atlantic islands** Brian Hagenbuch, James Peck (*Forgotten Army* Declan McGarvey). **Directory** Declan McGarvey (*Buenos Aires; Santiago* Brian Hagenbuch).

Maps Nexo Servicios Gráficos, Luis Sáenz Peña 20, Piso 7 'B', Buenos Aires (www.nexolaser.com.ar)

Photography by: pages 3, 12, 31, 101, 127, 131, 133, 134, 135, 136, 225 Declan McGarvey; pages 5, 9, 52, 54, 67, 70, 145, 149, 151, 153 Anna Norman; pages 7, 11, 17, 20, 22, 23, 47, 56, 70, 98, 100, 112, 115, 116, 119, 120, 122, 142, 150, 155, 157, 166, 169, 199, 200, 203, 204, 211, 217, 221, 226, 227 Joshua Goodman; pages 10, 51 Archivo General de la Nación; pages 14, 29, 30, 35, 40, 71, 72, 109, 111, 192 Gonzalo Gil; pages 24, 27, 83, 85, 89, 91, 93, 95, 96, 103, 104, 105, 108, 200, 229 Fiona McCann; page 28 Greg Rosati; pages 29, 70, 139 Tillman Jaeger; page 32 BP Malen; page 32 Daniel Feldman; pages 38, 62, 81, 90, 107 Francisco Ciavaglia; pages 44, 46, 56, 58, 59, 116 Maita Barrenechea; page 48 Deborah Brunswick; page 57 Javier Verstraten; page 60 Carlos Sanchez; page 71 Muestra Itinerante de Dinosaurios de la Patagonia; pages 75, 81, 165, 166, 176, 178, 181, 183, 184, 188, 194, 197, 215 Patricio Sutton; pages 101, 129, 157, 158, 159, 160, 161 Sofia Sanchez Barrenechea; page 173 Andina del Sud; page 187 Jeff Edvalds (Yankee Way Lodge); page 191 Stefán Bastulin Cortese; page 208 Cruceros Marítimos Skorpios (Chile); page 212 Kristin Henley; page 224 Zelfa Silva. The following images were supplied by the featured establishments: pages 59, 64, 126.

The Editor would like to thank: Carlos Fernández Balboa, Ian Barnett, Maita Barrenechea, Claudio Bertonatti (Fundación Vida Silvestre), Felipe Deves, Luis Gryngarten, Julieta Houcade, Karina (PROCHILE), Paul McTavish, Hugo Navarrete, José and Estela Pais, Alejandra Riera, Martín Saubidet, Zelfa Silva, Helen Vigors, Rodrigo de Zavalía and everyone at Tribalwerks.

Contents

Introduction

Next time someone tells you that all they need is a little space, suggest Patagonia. Of course there are many other motives for visiting the southernmost regions of Argentina and Chile: seas full of shipwrecks and whales; land that is home to dinosaurs, steppe and ice fields, to native Mapuche and Welsh settlers; to wild winds and wilder mythologies. But despite a recent tourist boom, one word still echoes down the three centuries of exploration south of the 40th parallel – empty.

Big and beautiful are close runners-up. Any guide to Patagonia risks being superlative about the peaks, repetitive about the parks and hyperbolic about the lakes. There's so much space, so many views, scores of natural wonders and countless glaciers, volcanoes and valleys. Apologies in advance – especially if you read the book from cover to cover while touring the whole region (for which you'll need about three years).

Along with space, Patagonia now has luxury hotels, fishing lodges and spas, an increasing number of paved roads, an emerging cuisine of its own and delicious wines. But this is still the undeveloped world in two developing countries, so be prepared for cancelled flights, fluctuating currencies and makeshift infrastructure. Try not to get too worked up about it – this is pioneering country and challenges are part of the package.

Raw and romantic as it is, Patagonia is not only for the dreamer. Should you overdose on penning poems while gazing at the views, take up some oars, skis, crampons or just plain old trekking boots and get stuck into the ups and downs of the Andes or the bays and fjords of the Pacific and Atlantic coasts. Or, if you prefer, drive it, cruise it, bike it or ride it. The world hasn't shrunk here yet – movement alone is a thrill.

For earlier generations, Patagonia was a remote, impenetrable, often dangerous place, and no doubt part of its appeal is this history of struggle against distance and the elements. In these ultra-connected times Patagonia is only a flight (or two) away, but still far removed from the cramped, clock-watching environments of most modern urbanites.

So make the most of your time here. Later, you'll miss the hidden islands and the silent lakes; the creak of ice walls and the rat-a-tat of woodpeckers; the blink-or-you'll-miss-them creatures and the sleep-for-eight-hours-and-miss-nothing central plains.

But the memories will last. Writers, artists and scientists, from Charles Darwin to Bruce Chatwin, have spent centuries trying to sort through these impressions – to explain the hold this strange and compelling region has on the human heart and mind. One can brood over Patagonia for decades.

ABOUT TIME OUT GUIDES

Time Out Patagonia is one of an expanding series of travel guides produced by the people behind London and New York's successful listings magazines. Our guides are all written and updated by local experts who have striven to provide you with all the most up-to-date information you'll need to explore the region, whether you're a regular or first-time visitor.

THE LOWDOWN ON THE LISTINGS

Above all, we've tried to make this book as useful as possible. Addresses, telephone numbers, websites, opening times or closed periods and prices have all been included. And, as far as possible, we've given details of facilities, services and events, checked and correct as we went to press. However, owners and managers can change their arrangements at any time, and often do, and seasonal closures in Patagonia vary from year to year. Before

you go out of your way, we'd strongly advise you to phone to check opening times and other particulars. While every effort has been made to ensure the accuracy of the information contained in this guide, the publishers cannot accept responsibility for any errors it may contain.

PRICES AND PAYMENT

The prices we've supplied should be treated as guidelines, not gospel, especially in the light of currency fluctuations. Prices have been converted to US dollars for consistency and ease of understanding. Both the Argentinian and Chilean peso have been relatively stable over the past few years, but expect the unexpected.

In main tourist towns we have noted where hotels, bars and restaurants accept the following credit cards: American Express (AmEx), Diners Club (DC), MasterCard (MC) and Visa (V). MasterCard and Visa are the most widely accepted cards.

Hotels & restaurants

Hotels

All prices have been given to us directly by the hotel and are accurate at time of going to press. If prices vary wildly from those we've quoted, ask whether there's a good reason. Note that for hotels in smaller destinations we have listed the price for a double room as the best indication of the hotel's price bracket. In some places (lodges, *estancias*) only all-inclusive packages are offered and this is indicated. See also *p231* **Accommodation**.

Restaurants

Within this guide we have denoted the price range of each restaurant we mention with between one and four dollar symbols. These correspond approximately to the following price brackets, for a full meal with drinks per person (excluding tip).

$	under US$5
$$	between US$5 and US$12
$$$	between US$12 and US$20
$$$$	above US$20

THE LIE OF THE LAND

Patagonia is as much a concept as an officially defined region. We have taken Patagonia to cover the entire southern section of Argentina and Chile from about the same latitude downwards. This guide covers destinations in Argentinian Patagonia first, then Chilean Patagonia. Each section starts with an explanation of the lie of the land and a summary of its major features and attractions. Patagonia's most important national parks are covered in special feature boxes.

TELEPHONE NUMBERS

All phone numbers in this guide give the full local area code, separated by a space from the main six or seven digit number. To make a local call simply dial the main six- or seven-digit number. You'll need to dial the full number, including area code, if you are calling a venue from another area. To call Chile or Argentina from abroad, first enter the appropriate country code (56 for Chile, 54 for Argentina) followed by the rest of the number but dropping the initial zero. Argentinian cellular phone numbers have 15 after the area code; in Chile they begin with 09 and have no area code.

ESSENTIAL INFORMATION

For all the practical information you might need for visiting the area before and during your trip, including visa and customs information, disabled access, emergency telephone numbers, transport options, car hire and a list of useful websites, turn to the Directory chapter at the back of the guide.

LET US KNOW WHAT YOU THINK

We hope that you enjoy *Time Out Patagonia*, and we'd like to know what you think of it. We welcome tips for places that you consider we should include in future editions of the guide. You can email us at guides@timeout.com.

Advertisers

bue

destino **buenos aires**
destination

www.bue.gov.ar

BUE FOR YOU **ON LINE MAPS** MUST-SEE PLACES PHOTOGALLERY CULTURAL AGENDA BUSINESS AGENDA

gobBsAs

In Context

Museo Paleontologico
Egidio Feruglio. *See p131.*

History

A story of ice and fire, geological cataclysms and social upheavals, war and peace and the dream of prosperity.

ONCE UPON A TIME IN THE SOUTH

Long before there were landowners in Patagonia, there was land – it just hasn't always been where it is today. Up until some 130 million years ago South America was a province of the supercontinent known as Gondwanaland, a composite landmass that also included what is now India, Australia and Antarctica. Then, the continents split and South America drifted some 4,800 kilometres (3,000 miles) westwards to its current latitude.

The first living things to make Patagonia their home were the dinosaurs who roamed the region around 230 million years ago. Fossils from the Triassic, Jurassic and Cretaceous periods show this activity continued up to 65 million years ago, long after South America had broken off from Gondwanaland. In Neuquén,

Argentina – a prehistoric subtropical basin – palaeontological finds demonstrate the evolution of distinct species in the already separate continent. Recent dramatic finds include the sauropod (small head, long neck and tail, pea-brain) *Argentinosaurus*, currently recognised as the biggest dinosaur ever to have walked the earth, and the *Gigantosaurus*, a huge carnivore from around 100 million years ago. The 1997 discovery of thousands of dinosaur eggs near Volcán Auca Mahuida proves that the region once teemed with lizard life (*see p78* **Fossil fever**).

Then, around 100 million years ago, the Andes began to emerge from volcanic fissures when two tectonic masses – the South American and the Nazca plates – collided. The mountains we see today are the product of a second period of cataclysmic vulcanisation that took place from 15 million to around four million years ago.

The common perception is of a single high mountain chain; but the long Andean barrier (called the Cordillera de los Andes in Spanish) is in fact three separate ranges, forged by the constant, ongoing convergence of the plates. In Patagonia, from north to south the Andes gradually descend to a mean height of 2,000 metres (6,562 feet), with frequent low passes gouged by glaciers during the ice age. The mountains get lower and lower as the continent tapers and curves towards the east at Tierra del Fuego. The relative youth of the Andes – lesser hills in the Argentinian pampas are 15 times older – is borne out by the predominance of cone-shaped volcanic peaks, many still spewing smoke. A seismic fault runs the length of the Andes and quakes have always been a feature, and are still a threat, on both flanks of the mountains, sometimes accompanied by tsunamis (tidal waves) on the Pacific coast.

COOL FOR (SABRE-TOOTHED) CATS

Suddenly, around four million years ago, it got very, very cold. It is possible that the volcanic violence of areas like the Andes caused a sudden change – blocking out the sun – or that, during some cyclic cooling of the planet, the highest peaks supported larger glaciers that spread out like great tongues of ice. Another theory is that a mile-wide asteroid slammed into Patagonia 3.3 million years ago causing a sudden, rapid cooling.

Whatever the cause of the ice age, the fact remains that from the initial period of global cooling right up to just 115,000 years ago, the Patagonian region was subject to a constant cycle of freezing and melting. Periodically buried beneath enormous ice-fields up to 1,200 metres (3,937 feet) thick, the landscape gradually acquired its present shape.

The entombing of everything in ice is still evoked by glaciers, turquoise lakes and the sedimentary moraines that punctuate the lower levels of the cordillera. Hills of glacial sediment (drumlins) are visible in the southern extremes of Chilean Patagonia while, a little further north, the Chilean archipelago is a dramatic landscape of fjords and icecaps that have changed little since the Andes forced their way through the earth's crust.

After the dinosaurs had been wiped out, life in Patagonia took on different forms. Although the really big boys had left, the Pleistocene era, between around two million and 10,000 years ago, was still a time of giants – including large sabre-toothed cats that fed on even bigger prey. These included the glyptodon, the largest of the

ancient armadillos, and the milodon, a ground sloth with the appearance of a giant bear and twice the size of a modern man (*see p212* **Bruce and the giant sloth**).

THEY BOLDLY WENT

As the ice and snow turned to mud and slush, the Patagonian steppes began to take on the tawny, parched hue for which they are famous. And in this dust, for the first time, were footprints. Whether the presence of humans in Patagonia was the southern conclusion to a migration across the frozen Bering Strait from Siberia to Alaska around 25-40,000 years ago or a combination of this and the later seaborne arrival of other groups from Australia or Polynesia is not yet proven; several distinct waves of migration may have contributed to the peopling of Patagonia. For many years, the Bering theory was widely accepted, but similar patterns in blood groups, head shapes, etymology and cultural norms have all been used to deduce a link between indigenous Americans and Australians. There is even culinary evidence to support this claim, say some, as the Chilean speciality of *curanto* (a stew of shellfish and potatoes baked on hot stones in a shallow pit) is akin to certain Polynesian dishes in character and preparation (*see p192* **Seafood special**).

What is known for certain is that by 12,000 BC migration had extended throughout the Americas, and on both sides of the Andes bands of nomadic hunters fed on the large Pleistocene mammals. The end of the ice age signalled the demise of many of these species, and those groups that had not dedicated their efforts to fishing turned to the fruits and berries that grew in the more fertile lands. As these early Patagonians adapted to their environment, they settled in family-based societies, cultivated maize and potatoes and domesticated the guanaco camelids that still populate the area.

> **'The Mapuche are the only indigenous group in southern South America to survive colonisation.'**

An array of indigenous communities evolved in Patagonia, separated and defined by its diverse geographies. By the the 16th century, when the first Europeans arrived by sea, there were some 400,000 inhabitants, the majority in the more temperate lands of northern Patagonia. The two most important groups were the Mapuche and Tehuelche, the former straddling the Andes in settled communities, the latter a tall and rugged nomadic people who roamed the

The historical Hall of Fame

Argentinosaurus
(c100 million-c65 million years ago)
Weighing in at 100 tons and taller than a
six-storey building, Argentina's answer to
the brontosaurus is the largest animal ever
to have walked the earth.

Hernão de Magalhães
(c1480-1521) Aka Ferdinand Magellan.
The Portuguese-born explorer was the first
European to discover the region, as part
of his epic round-the-world voyage of 1520.
The names of Patagonia and Tierra del Fuego
are both linked to this voyage.

Orélie-Antoine de Tounens
(1825-78) In 1860, this eccentric Frenchman
won the trust of local tribes and proclaimed
himself sovereign of the independent but non-
existent Kingdom of Araucanía. His present-
day successor, Prince Philippe Boiry, continues
to lead a shadow government from Paris.

Jemmy Button
(c1830-c1864) The English name given to
one of four Yamana natives Darwin bought
for the price of a button and cruelly paraded
before King William IV in England. Repatriated
on a later voyage a few years later, fully
clothed and duly Christianised, he eventually
won revenge against his former kidnappers
by killing a party of Anglican missionaries.

Lewis Jones
(1836-1904) The force behind the creation of
a mini-Welsh homeland centred in present-
day Trelew. Although Jones's first
contingent of 1865 slept in caves,
through sheer graft
the Welsh became
prosperous farmers
and merchants.

Thomas Bridges
(1842-99) Bridges' roots are
humble – the Anglican missionary
who settled Ushuaia was named
by a priest who found him
abandoned under a bridge in
Scotland on St Thomas' day.
A champion and protector
of Tierra del Fuego's
aborigines, the original
version of his Yamana-
English dictionary is in
the British Museum.

Julio Roca
(1843-1914, *pictured*) Leader of the
1870s military campaigns that wiped out
the indigenous tribes of northern Patagonia
and propelled him into the presidency in
1880. History books still euphemistically
refer to the massacre as the Conquest
of the Desert.

Francisco 'Perito' Moreno
(1852-1919) The father of Argentina's
national parks system first visited Patagonia
in 1873. He earned the 'Perito' nickname
– Spanish for expert – for his skill as a
geographer and naturalist.

Julio Popper
(1857-93) The Romanian-born gold-hunter
was lured to Tierra del Fuego in 1886 by
a revamped version of the 17th-century El
Dorado legend. He got so lucky that he began
minting his own currency and had to create a
private army to ward off his multiple enemies.

Padre Alberto de Agostini
(1883-1960) Salesian missionary, mountain
climber and Patagonia's unofficial patron
saint, De Agostini was sent to Patagonia from
Italy in 1910. His final ascent, aged 60, was
of Mount Sarmiento. His photos, maps and
23 books are among the best produced
about the region.

Antoine de Saint-Exupéry
(1900-1944) He's one of the best loved
writers of the 20th century but the author of
The Little Prince considered himself first and
foremost an aviator. In 1929, Saint-Exupéry
inaugurated the Patagonian air mail service
between Bahia Blanca and Comodoro
Rivadavia, an experience captured in
his bestselling novella, *Night Flight*.

Néstor Kirchner
(1950-) The former Santa
Cruz governor was the first
Patagonian to be made
president of Argentina. Fiercely
proud of his roots (he loves his
nickmane 'El Pinguino'), Kirchner
passed the presidential baton
to his wife, Cristina, in
December 2007,
ensuring Patagonia
another four years as the
'second seat' of power.

open plains in skin and fur; then there were the Alacaluf and Chonos in the Chilean archipelago and a number of indigenous Fuegian groups who settled in the far south.

The Mapuche ('people of the earth') were a hardy, brave tribe which, around the 14th century, absorbed or displaced several other groups in the Lake District areas of Chile and Argentina. By the 16th century, the Mapuche had shaken off their semi-nomadic habits and turned to harvesting crops in the rich volcanic soil. Theirs was a non-hierarchical, non-centralising society based on kinship and built around the family unit or *lov*.

The Mapuche had (and indeed still have) a reputation as warriors and for internecine squabbles and witchcraft. Their main rivals for territory and occasional enemies in skirmishes were the Tehuelche, though the Spanish conquerors were to become their most hated foe. The speedy adoption of the horse by the Mapuche, as well as other imports like goats, sheep and foreign crops, allowed them to prosper while the Tehuelche dwindled in significance. The Mapuche are the only indigenous group in southern South America to survive colonisation, though other tribal cultures endure in mixed-blood populations like the Alacaluf in Aisén.

In the far south, the low mountains did not impose natural frontiers and interaction between small, nomadic civilisations was fairly fluid. Here dwelt the Yamana (or Yahgan) canoe people, the Haush and the Selk'nam – sometimes called Ona – exploiting the marine resources and forests in sub-zero temperatures and occasionally fighting over scarce land and scant resources. These groups may have given Tierra del Fuego its fiery name, as their camp fires, dotted along the coastline, were seen from the water by Magellan and his crew in 1520.

Broadly speaking, the further south you ventured the more primitive was the indigenous culture; but even among the Fuegian tribes there were complex religious beliefs, sophisticated cosmologies and numerous rites to observe. The Hain, for instance, a Selk'nam ceremony, was designed to celebrate a boy's passage into manhood and was a major community occasion; one ceremony involved a tribesman dressing up as a conehead, tying his genitals with guanaco tendon to look like a young woman and being decorated with feathers. Girls, on the other hand, were painted red when they first menstruated and told to keep quiet for several days.

There are records of such rites from the early 20th century, but by then all the tribes had been almost completely crushed by European colonisation. The Selk'nam, too, were doomed.

The process, however, had been long and complicated and between the 16th and 19th centuries the indigenous peoples of Patagonia did their utmost to escape or resist domination.

PUTTING PATAGONIA ON THE MAP

In the eyes of most Spanish conquistadors (and, by extension, their royal sponsors) Patagonia was simply not worth the trip – too distant, too empty, too backward and, most crucially, not enough to loot. After their arrival in the Americas in 1492, the empire-builders kept busy sizing up Mexico, Peru and the north – but there was a bit of space in the itinerary for escapades in the far south.

The Río de la Plata in Argentina was a natural entrance for Juan Diaz de Solis's explorations of 1516 – he was actually looking for a sea route linking the Atlantic and Pacific oceans – but it took him no further than a meeting with a violently hostile tribe in Uruguay who killed and ate him.

More successful was a Portuguese sailor in the employ of the Spanish crown – Hernão de Magalhães (known as Hernando de Magallanes in Spanish or Ferdinand Magellan in English). He made landfall in 1520 at what is now San Julián in the Argentine province of Santa Cruz and baptised the then unimaginably remote lands as Patagonia (*see p21* **The name game**). Magellan had gallows erected there to deal with mutineers, which British pirate Francis Drake would later make use of for the same purpose. On that same voyage, Magellan discovered the strait at the 52nd parallel that still bears his name, thus opening up the waters round Patagonia, not to mention new routes to the Spice Islands and Asia and the rest of the world. (Magellan himself was killed by natives on Mactan Island in the Philippines, but one of his subordinates, Sebastián Elcano, completed the record-breaking circumnavigation of the globe in September 1522.)

Though Magellan had been bankrolled by the Spanish court, news of his discoveries inspired more independent-minded explorers. French, Dutch, British, Spanish and Portuguese sailors had eyes on the south whether for legitimate trade or for the sacking of other nation's possessions. The circulation of a gold-plated myth describing a beautiful city of riches called Trapalanda and another tall tale about a fantastic City of the Caesars further fuelled the imaginations of seagoing freebooters.

Francis Drake sailed to Patagonia in 1578, an incursion that prompted the Spaniards to attempt to seal off the southern straits; the Viceroy of Peru sent Pedro Sarmiento de Gamboa, an accomplished navigator and cartographer, to patrol the Pacific Ocean and Magellan Strait, but bad weather, mutiny and a clash with British corsair Edward Fenton turned the massive expedition into a titanic disaster. Meanwhile Drake, searching for a fast route to the Spanish colonies of the Pacific, voyaged on up the west coast of South America to California and became the second sailor to go round the world. He left a trail of terror and destruction in his wake and earned himself a knighthood in the process.

If the golden age of piracy was over by the end of the 17th century, there were still pressing reasons for exploring the Patagonian seas, and whalers, jibbers, navies and explorers kept the two oceans positively frothing with activity. The competing imperial powers of Britain, Spain, Portugal, Holland and France fought for dominion over the seas and fast, safe routes to the Spice Islands. Few could serve their desires better than a slice of terra firma from which to manage their affairs.

The sea has left an important historical legacy in Patagonia. Towns like Puerto Deseado, Punta Arenas and Valdivia were crucial stopover ports from these first voyages until the building of the Panama Canal in the early 20th century provided a more economical and less tempestuous sea route.

HOW THE SOUTH WAS WON

The impassibility of large stretches of the cordillera meant that Spanish expeditions were compelled to approach the Chilean and Argentinian territories from different angles. On the Argentinian mainland, a process of colonisation was set in motion by the creation of a mule highway that linked it to Alto Peru (the mine-rich lands now part of Bolivia). The end of this road was the city of Santa María de Buenos Aires, founded by Juan de Garay in 1580, which remained a backwater of the empire until the late 18th century. All eyes looked north for silver, wine, cloth and foodstuffs.

> ## 'Roman Catholicism followed hot on the heels of colonisation by sword.'

Meanwhile Chile was approached overland from the northern heartlands of imperial Spanish America. The man who had massacred the Incas in Peru, Francisco Pizarro, gave permission to his faithful protégé Pedro de Valdivia to colonise Chile. In 1541, he founded Santiago de la Nueva Extremadura and over the next decade led expeditions southwards beyond the Biobío river, founding Valdivia in 1552. But the Mapuche (who were called Araucanos by the Spaniards), led by cacique

(chieftain) Lautaro, were indomitable in their defence of the lands south of the Biobío, and in 1553 massacred Valdivia and his entire army. Legend has it that the Mapuche, with a macabre line in poetic justice, disembowelled Valdivia's corpse and stuffed it with gold.

As elsewhere in the Americas, Roman Catholicism followed hot on the heels of colonisation by sword and tyranny. Arriving in 1593 in southern Chile the Jesuits sought to Christianise the Mapuche – who had complex rites and beliefs – but their peaceful efforts in fact served to legitimise the military campaigns.

In 1598 Martín García de Oñez de Loyola, the regional governor for the Spanish Empire in Chile, was captured by the Mapuche, and his head used in ceremonies for years afterwards.

By the 17th century, the colonial authorities and the indigenous groups were in a state of permanent war – the former well armed, but the latter, bearing spears and bows and arrows, well versed in the art of guerrilla warfare and resolute in the defence of their land. Spain wanted to enslave the natives using a feudal regime called the *encomienda*, a system that had proven highly successful in Peru. But in 1622, a royal decree stated that 'the royal patrimonial Indians' of Chilean Araucania were not '*encomendable*' – thus admitting that the Spaniards were incapable of enslaving the Mapuche. With the Spaniards momentarily defeated, Spanish women and children were integrated into Mapuche settlements.

The Chilean south became known as *la frontera*, a barrier between European America and native America. Where intermarriage took place, mestizo populations emerged, but a society of landowning *criollos* (ethnic Spaniards born in the colonies) had also evolved. While there was a standoff – and some trade and intermarriage – between colonial and native forces, war was not the only spectre hanging over the Mapuche people. The introduction of European diseases like smallpox, typhus and measles, famines caused by crop burning and the production of alcohol all had deleterious effects on the indigenous population.

In the 1770s a Jesuit, Thomas Falkner, wrote a book in which he warned the Spaniards of the vulnerability of Patagonia to ambitions from other nations with strong naval forces. The only hub of any kind in Argentinian Patagonia was San Julián, the port used by Magellan and Drake for regrouping and repairing their ships and resting. The Spaniards decided to fortify this outpost and create new forts at San José in Chubut and at Carmen de Patagones. Evil weather, barren land, scurvy and native uprisings proved insurmountable obstacles to establishing the first two forts and only

Settlers were drawn to Patagonia's unspoilt beauty.

Carmen, founded in 1780 by Antonio de Viedma, was to last. Apart from this tiny township, until the mid-19th century, European presence in Patagonia was limited to maritime outposts at places like Puerto Deseado, Valdivia and Chiloé; the key military forts built by the Spanish armies were in the fertile (and virtually empty) pampas, well north of Patagonia's limits.

PEOPLING PATAGONIA

Patagonia was eventually to acquire a new importance when the lands of the south became two nations. Argentina declared independence in 1816, Chile in 1818, but as the thrust of the independence movement was northward – no new nation was likely to succeed until the mining areas and key cities like Lima and Potosí were liberated – there was no urgent need to explore the south.

Argentina did, however, turn its attention to Carmen de Patagones, considered then, as it is now, to be the gateway to Patagonia. Populated in the main by first- and second-generation Spanish immigrants, its mainly royalist citizens were reluctant to accept the new *criollo* government and in 1827, 150 soldiers, under

the command of Felipe Pereyra, along with a motley militia of gauchos, pirates and slaves, were sent down to stamp the new government's authority on the region.

Apart from this single 'official' outpost, the colonisation of Patagonia was spasmodic and often carried out not by central decree but by independent incursions into indigenous territory – these ranged from small colonies of Europeans and religious orders to assorted bandits, gold-hunters and scientists.

Chile's most important gesture was to found Punta Arenas, in 1848, where convicts and banished military men established a small colony. Two decades later, British and Yugoslav settlers arrived to work as butchers, hoteliers, shopkeepers and to serve the needs of the busy refuelling port.

Among the first Europeans to successfully settle in Patagonia were the Welsh. Their ambition was to free themselves from English oppression and to find a safe haven in which to practise their non-conformist religion and speak their native tongue. In May 1865, 153 men, women and children sailed from Liverpool

Puerto San Julián
Where Magellan and Drake hung out.
See p141.

Parque Cruz de Froward
The history of Punta Arenas is written on
this cemetery's tombstones. See p219.

Estancia Harberton
The family farm of the Bridges, the first
missionary settlers in Ushuaia. See p163.

Villa El Chocón
The centre of dinosaur valley. See p75.

Churches of Chiloé
Christianity, Chiloé-style. See p188.

aboard the *Mimosa* – at the invitation of
Guillermo Rawson, then a minister in Bartolomé
Mitre's government – in search of a new home.
Met by Lewis Jones, who had led the planning
of the colony and enthused his compatriots with
stories of arable lands in an idyllic setting, these
colonists were dismayed to see not so much
green valleys and leeks as sand and savages.

Obstacles included a lack of food and water,
parched earth and, given the considerable agro-
challenge, the fact that many of the settlers
were in fact miners, not farmers. A measure of
support came from the Argentinians (who flew
their own flag over the colony to make sure the
Welsh didn't view their Promised Land as a
political entity), and there were generally good
relations with the local Tehuelche natives.

Towns were founded and further shiploads
of Welsh, in 1874 and 1911, strengthened the
colony. During this time, the Welsh had an
enlightening moment when they found the Río
Chubut ran higher than the surrounding land
– thus providing easy, unpowered irrigation –
and also explored up the Chubut valley to the
foothills of the Andes. There were always
challenges – some gold-hunting Welsh had their
genitals cut off and stuffed in their mouths by
a group of less than friendly Mapuches, and a
massive flood in 1899 set development back
years – but the Welsh persevered and
eventually prospered in Chubut province.

From the late 19th century on, Europeans
came in numbers to settle in Patagonia. Chile,
faced with a southern geography of islands
and fjords, as well as the formidable Mapuche
presence, was keen to tempt immigrants from
overseas. On paper, Chile claimed all the south

from Osorno to Cape Horn, but it was only in
the 1840s, during the presidency of Manuel
Bulnes, that measures were taken to incorporate
Patagonia officially into the nation.

In the Chilean Lake District, the most
important settlers were the Germans, seduced
into taking farming lands within sight of
Mapuche townships by Bernardo Philippi and
Vicente Pérez Rosales. While researching flora
and fauna for a Berlin museum, Philippi was
commissioned by Chile to survey the lands
around Osorno and Llanquihue; vacant areas
were subsequently designated state property.
Philippi was sent to Germany to gather farmers
and Pérez Rosales, Chile's leading naturalist,
coordinated the settlement. The first German
settlers alighted in Puerto Montt in 1852 and
continued to arrive up until 1880.

During a series of military campaigns
between 1860 and 1900, the government pushed
the frontier – and the railway – south and swept
away traditional Mapuche lands and properties.
Settlers were given 40 hectares apiece and the
remaining lands were auctioned off. Germans
took large swathes of lands throughout the
Lake District, while Valdivia grew into Chile's
main industrial city. Some land was set aside
for Mapuche reservations. From 1895, Chiloé
was also allotted to European settlers, and
attracted newcomers from Britain, France
and Spain, as well as Germany.

> **'The Welsh colonists were
> dismayed to see not so
> much green valleys and
> leeks as sand and savages.'**

Others crashed the party without an
invitation. On 17 November 1860, French dandy
and adventurer Orélie-Antoine de Tounens
proclaimed, with the support of the local
Mapuches, the foundation of a constitutional
hereditary monarchy in the Valdivia area –
as King of Araucania and Patagonia, his plan
was to unite and 'civilise' the natives.

The Chilean government, viewing Orélie
as a potential threat to sovereignty, had him
arrested; French consular appeals, claiming the
self-anointed monarch was merely insane, led
to his release – so long as he returned to France.
After writing his memoirs in Paris, Orélie sailed
back to Patagonia and the monarchy was re-
established between 1869 and 1871, until the
same colonel who had arrested him a decade
earlier chased him out of Chile. The monarch
attempted to return once more to his kingdom
in 1874, without success, and he died in France
in September 1878. A series of successors –

none tied to the first king by blood – have maintained the claim to the throne of Araucania and Patagonia from Paris, and continue to do so through the courts (legal, not royal) to this day.

> **'During a series of military campaigns between 1860 and 1900, the government swept away Mapuche lands and properties.'**

Free-spirited North Americans were also attracted to the south – not least because their own Wild West was being quickly tamed. Joining the Argentinian gaucho and Chilean *huaso* cowboys on the open ranges, outlaws James Ryan and Harry Place, aka Butch Cassidy and the Sundance Kid, spent four years ranching, breaking horses and keeping a low profile in Cholila, near El Bolsón. Between land surveys and business meetings, they managed, some say, in 1905, to rob a bank in Río Gallegos, but when word got round they bolted to find a new home, ending up in Uruguay or Bolivia (*see p23* **Butch and the Sundance myth**).

Other Americans, along with Europeans and Chileans, went south to seek out Julio Popper, a Romanian who created the Lavaderos de Oro del Sur company and generated all the PR for one of the most short-lived gold rushes in history. Some managed to combine their mining activities with ethnographic studies of the local population.

THE MISSIONARY POSITION

Both geographically and historically, the remote lands of Tierra del Fuego are distinct from the mainland. During the surveying expeditions led by Australian-born navigator Philip Parker King in 1826-30, four Yamana from Tierra del Fuego were arrested in retaliation for their tribe's seizure of a whaling ship. They were taken to England and spent several months at court, learning English and table manners and being paraded in front of King William IV and Queen Adelaide. The nicknames given to the three men were York Minster, Jemmy Button (the price the earlier captors had paid for him) and Boat Memory (in allusion to the stolen boat), who died of smallpox while in Britain. The sole female was given the moniker Fuegia Basket.

When Charles Darwin sailed as official – and unpaid – naturalist during the voyages Captain Robert FitzRoy undertook in the 1830s, one of their duties was to return the three surviving natives. After rewarding excursions into Patagonia in search of shells, fossils and wildlife, the raw data of Darwin's subsequent

The truth is down there

Rich in myth and legend, Patagonia also does a brisk trade in tall stories and conspiracy theories. And in an environment where even the unembellished truth can come in the guise of petrified forests, volcanic causeways and dinosaur footprints, it isn't hard to see why.

The usual reaction, therefore, to a story about UFOs buzzing the pampas or a ghost ship sighted off the coast of Chile, is: 'What, *again*?' Something more exotic is required to pique the interest.

In 2004 Argentinian journalist Abel Basti achieved just that. He published a book entitled *Bariloche: Nazi Guía-Turística*, written and structured in pastiche travel guide style. Like most 'alternative' histories, it has a premise that is at once preposterous and intriguing: namely, that, far from dying in a Berlin bunker, Adolf Hitler and some of his closest cohorts fled Germany in a submarine, making it safely to Argentina and settling down to an ill-earned retirement in San Carlos de Bariloche. Thanks to the numerous documents and photographs unearthed by Basti, interested tourists can, in the course of exploring one of Patagonia's most picturesque towns, visit the cafés where the Fuhrer allegedly took afternoon tea, the butcher's where Martin Bohrmann allegedly bought his sausages, and so on.

In fact, Basti's book is only the newest take on the Hitler-in-Patagonia thesis – and arguably the least wacky. Believers in the 'Antarctic Reich' theory contend that Hitler left Argentina in the early 1950s and moved to Neuschwabenland, an SS colony founded beneath the Antarctic icecap. Here, it is conjectured, Hitler lived out his natural life among the penguins. To keep himself busy he resumed his unpromising artistic career and completed a series of Antarctic icescapes.

While some if not all of the above can be safely consigned to the X-Files, one thing is certain: contemporary Patagonian myths are commonly no less outlandish than their ancient equivalents. So when you hear that Osama Bin Laden is running a microbrewery in El Bolsón, be sceptical – but not surprised.

Estancia Anita: site of a 1920s uprising.

theory of natural selection, the ship reached Isla Navarino in December 1832, where a Briton, the Reverend Richard Matthews, was trying to establish a mission at the very bottom of the continent. Darwin and FitzRoy left their 'civilised' natives there in order to help out, but Matthews found the locals, en masse, to be unruly and deeply antipathetic to his cause. He left and, when another ship visited Tierra del Fuego in 1859, again to sow the seeds of Christianity, the missionaries were beaten to death, one report claiming Jemmy Button as the instigator of this violent insurrection.

'From the 1870s on, Argentina began to take an interest in its unpopulated south.'

Notwithstanding the massacre of these clergymen, a mission was finally established at Ushuaia by Thomas Bridges in the 1870s. Bridges and his superior, the Rev Wait H Stirling, were ambitious to 'save the Indians', but while there were some achievements – not least Bridges' Yamana-English dictionary – the indigenous Fuegians were doomed. In 1879, the Salesian society, a missionary order founded in Turin in the 1840s, sent its first missionaries south to Patagonia. Hoping to protect the Fuegians, they made a deal with the region's sheep famers: they would shelter those indigenous souls rounded up by Indian-hunters, asking in return one pound sterling towards the mission's costs. Yet the plan backfired. Many Fuegians died after coming into contact with European diseases such as tuberculosis and syphillis, as well as out of sheer boredom.

FLYING FLAGS
The Welsh, the Germans, Butch, Sundance, Orélie and all those who make up the ragbag immigration history of 19th-century Patagonia had arrived in a land nominally belonging to

nation states, but in reality something of a free-for-all. From the 1870s on, Argentina began to take an interest in its unpopulated, uncolonised south. Francisco Pascasio Moreno, a noted naturalist, led expeditions to the Andean regions of Río Negro and Santa Cruz between 1876 and 1879. While Moreno tried hard to maintain a balance between national interests, a humanitarian approach to the indigenous inhabitants and ecological concerns, the military men close to government showed no such sensitivity. The key campaign that led to the near eradication of native Patagonians and the expansion of the Argentinian state was the so-called Conquista del Desierto in 1879-80, led by General Julio A Roca. Advancing against the Tehuelche, the rich pampas and their fringes were seized by Argentinian armies as far as Río Negro and huge tracts of land were opened up for economic development.

In 1884, Roca, now installed as Argentina's president, created the five provinces of Patagonia (Neuquén, Río Negro, Chubut, Santa Cruz and Tierra del Fuego; La Pampa was demarcated in 1996). There was, Roca insisted, a need to establish cities in the region – for political as well as economic reasons – as Carmen de Patagones was still the only significant conurbation at the time. The way was opened for the laying of a railway line from Bahía Blanca to Bariloche (the aptly named Roca line) and Esquel.

Unsurprisingly, the Argentine conquest of territory awakened Chile to its own claims in the south. The two nations signed a 'high peaks watershed' treaty in 1881, recognising the traditional frontier of the Andes and establishing a linear frontier in Tierra del Fuego, but in 1896, disputes arose over the details of the treaty. It was eventually settled in 1902, with Great Britain – by far the biggest foreign investor in Argentina and Argentinian Patagonia – as arbitrator. Britain gave Argentina the eastern half of Tierra del Fuego to protect its own sheep farming interests.

OIL AND OTHER FUTURES
On 13 December 1907, a team drilling for artesian water on behalf of the Argentine Ministry of Agriculture struck oil near the town of Comodoro Rivadavia in Chubut province. Once the bidding was open, dominant players emerged: the state oil firm, YPF (Yacimientos Petroleros Fiscales) – famed in oil circles as 'the only oil firm able to lose money' – and a German company called Astra.

While some got rich from the black gold, those dependent on the staple Patagonian product, wool, found their jobs in danger following a slump in the market after the end of World War I. Inspired by events in Russia and fired up by anarchist Antonio Soto, Argentinian, Chilean and Spanish workers in Santa Cruz rose up in 1920 and 1921 against the *estancia*-owners, demanding jobs and justice. President Hipólito Yrigoyen sent in armed forces commanded by Colonel Héctor Benigno Varela to crush the uprising – hundreds of labourers were killed in the ensuing massacre.

Comodoro Rivadavia became, and remains, Argentina's main oil town, attracting migrant workers from the rest of the country and from Chiloé. There are a proven 3.1 billion barrels of reserves and about 400,000 barrels of oil are produced every day; natural gas and coal – at Río Turbio – are other significant energy reserves in Argentina. Across the border the first Chilean oil well flowed in 1945, in northern Tierra del Fuego, and offshore drilling in the '70s in the same region brought money and people to the far south. But far from making Patagonians rich, oil has been at the centre of numerous strikes in recent years. In the 1990s and right up to 2002, oil workers in Neuquén and Santa Cruz have blocked roads with burning tyres to protest wage cuts and job losses caused by deregulation of the industry and the sale of YPF to Spanish giant Repsol.

Apart from economic migration as a result of oil, immigration to Patagonia has been scant in the 20th century. Among the most notorious new settlers – not to be confused with their 19th-century compatriots – were the German Nazis invited by Juan Perón after World War II. Alpine landscapes, far from prying eyes, were seen as ideal for these fascist friends, though the 1994 arrest of Erich Priebke (accused of killing 335 civilians in Rome) in Bariloche and his subsequent extradition proved otherwise. Argentines and Chileans have been tempted south by tax breaks, with fishing on the coast and manufacturing industries in Argentine Tierra del Fuego providing jobs. But apart from Comodoro Rivadavia, meat and wool packing centre Rio Gallegos and historically important Punta Arenas, Patagonia remains one of the world's empty places.

That has not stopped Argentina and Chile from falling out over who owns the biggest slices of it. During the Videla and Pinochet dictatorships of the 1970s, in Argentina and Chile respectively, a rising tide of nationalism provoked border tensions and led to renewed interest in the south. In 1978, work was begun on Chile's Carreterra Austral (or Southern Highway), linking the scattered, water-bound villages of archipelagic Patagonia to the rest of the country, in an attempt to tie the scattered communities of northern Patagonia to the nation. Atrocities were committed in Patagonia

The name game

Ferdinand Magellan may have been the world's greatest navigator, but when it came to finding the words to match the occasion he was no Neil Armstrong. According to Italian writer Antonio Pigafetta, who accompanied the explorer on his landmark voyage of 1520, Magellan's first words upon glimpsing a Tehuelche tribesman were: 'My God! Look at the size of those feet!'. While not the most incisive contribution to the field of anthropology, Magellan's outburst is thought to have given Patagonia its name. The Spanish swiftly dubbed the Teheulches '*patagones*', an idiom that can loosely be translated as 'bigfoots'.

Another possibility, unearthed by Bruce Chatwin in his travelogue *In Patagonia*, is that the name 'Patagon' is linked to a character in Primaleon, a 16th-century Spanish chivalric romance of the kind lampooned by Cervantes in *Don Quixote*. It features a dog-headed monster called the Grand Patagon. It's likely that Magellan was at least acquainted with the story.

The indigenous tribespeople Magellan encountered had more dignified ways of describing themselves and their environment. 'Mapuche' means 'people of the earth' and their place names still litter the landscape throughout the Lake Districts. It's a refreshing change in countries where streets and towns tend to be named for heroes or presidents. If you get bored, count how many streets are called San Martín or O'Higgins.

There's a sobering aspect to the name game – the lexicon of a people can endure long after they themselves have vanished from history. You'll see the Tehuelche nomad word for place, *aike*, in the far south, often as part of an *estancia*'s name or as in the park Pali-Aike: 'place of the devil'. But the Tehuelche are long gone, their culture erased by the European settlers in their inexorable drive south.

If you need further proof that history has a sense of irony, try this. In order to survive many Tehuelche learnt Welsh from the early settlers of their region who themselves were fleeing the religious intolerance of 19th-century Britain. Their descendants still participate in the annual Eisteffodd festival.

Oil fuelled Patagonia's economic growth.

– where the military men thought few would notice – and among the most infamous was the shooting of political prisoners at the Rawson prison in Trelew in August 1972, a massacre often cited as the beginning of the terror period.

Chile and Argentina came close to war in a dispute over three islands in the Beagle Channel. It took the restoration of democracy in 1983, following that other sovereignty clash between Argentina and Britain, the Falklands/Malvinas War, to get politicians discussing the problem. In 1984 the issue was resolved, thanks largely to the peacemaking of the late Pope Jean Paul II.

In 1986, in an attempt to embrace the provinces of the south, Argentina's first post-junta president, Raúl Alfonsín, proposed making Viedma in Río Negro the country's federal capital. Although not without precedent – Brazil had turned to its undiscovered interior regions by founding Brasilia in 1960 – the Viedma proposal was not welcomed by BA's hedonistic politicians, and disappeared without trace.

'Apart from economic migration, immigration to Patagonia has been scant in the 20th century.'

During the 1990s, several minor border disputes were tabled. These related to the Laguna del Desierto in Santa Cruz and the continental ice fields, hazy geographical regions for both nations, as glacial movement can force the course of a river to change, sending water flowing from one country back into another and making nonsense of the traditional frontier of a watershed. Arbitration and litigation continue.

International news from Patagonia over the last two decades has usually reported on the depletion of the ozone layer and its dangers for residents of Tierra del Fuego, including sheep suffering from skin cancer and blindness.

Regional economic crises and large-scale unemployment, partially caused by a decrease in world trade in wool, are just two of the economic challenges facing the region. The arrival of ageing hippies from Buenos Aires and Santiago over the past 20 years, as well as the recent land grabs by foreign millionaires have made Patagonia fashionable as a romantic retreat for escapists and dilettante ranchers, but have limited significance for locals. The current tourism boom is seen as offering the best sustainable economic future for the Patagonian population. How to exploit this seemingly limitless market while maintaining the region's unique and precious ecology will likely be the most pressing question of the next decade.

Butch and the Sundance myth

Everyone knows the story. A couple of handsome, charming rogues defy US law enforcement and build a career based around unorthodox bank withdrawals. When they're not breaking hearts or blowing up mail trains they find time to lark around on bicycles to Burt Bacharach songs.

Or perhaps we say: everyone's seen the movie. Since 1969, for most people Butch and Sundance means Newman and Redford, and their story that as told by screenwriter William Goldman. But while the outlaws' sojourn in Patagonia is touched on only briefly in the film, it is in some ways the most interesting part of the story – for the historian at least, if not the filmgoer.

Their arrival in Cholila (*see p106*) in 1901 is well documented. But whether James Ryan and Harry Place, aka Butch Cassidy and the Sundance Kid, came to Patagonia to ranch or to rob remains a mystery.

In any case, there's no doubting that the '*gringos locos*', as locals dubbed them and Sundance's wife Ethel Place, revelled in their southern hideout, in a hidden valley snug against the Andes. In a letter sent to the US under an assumed name, Cassidy had this to say about his new home: 'I visited the best cities and best parts of South America till I got here. And this part of the country looked so good that I located, and I think for good.' It's a sentiment at odds with the film's depiction of the outlaws as bored and restless self-exiles.

Despite their chequered past, Cassidy and Sundance are remembered fondly here as jovial, law-abiding citizens, skilled horsemen and serious farmers, at one point managing several hundred cattle and sheep. Their now rotting Abe Lincoln-style log cabin (*pictured*) even once played host to Chubut's governor – hardly the sort of inconspicuous behaviour you'd expect from the world's most sought-after bandits. At the time, its relative luxury in a region of corrugated-iron homes was a tip-off to the pursuing Pinkerton detective agency.

No surprise then, that local historian Raúl Cea, whose father was employed by the bandit-farmers, doubts the duo was capable of pulling off the most notorious feat attributed to them during their southern-hemisphere sabbatical: the 1905 hold-up of the Banco de Tarapaca y Argentino some 1,200 kilometres (750 miles) away by horseback, in Río Gallegos. In a symposium on the subject, held in Esquel in 1999, Cea and a group of scholars from around the world unanimously cleared the two of the crime, conjecturing instead that another pair of US thugs then living in the area, probably William Wilson and Robert Evans, were responsible for the robbery.

It's a convincing thesis, with only one catch: it just ain't Hollywood.

Patagonia Today

Economic collapse, a tourism explosion and two presidents – who says life is dull in the country?

If you've come to Patagonia expecting an ecological wonderland, think again. The lingering perception of the region as some sort of prelapsarian Eden notwithstanding, the wild landscapes that inspired five centuries-worth of travellers, from Magellan to Chatwin, has been thoroughly tamed in the past quarter-century by the advent of globalisation and mass tourism. Other out-of-the-way corners of the world have gone through similar changes, but few so swiftly. As recently as 1976, wildlife biologist William Conway, writing in *National Geographic*, commented that most people would still ask, 'Where is Patagonia?' whenever the subject of his research there was broached.

No single event, however, has shaped contemporary Patagonia more than Argentina's most recent economic collapse. On 4 January

2002, Argentina devalued its peso, the overdue coda to a decade-long policy, carried forward by President Carlos Menem, of liberalising and opening up the country's state-heavy economy. Like the proverbial deck of cards, the economic model praised by the West and the International Monetary Fund (IMF) collapsed under the weight of corruption, mismanagement and weak civil oversight. Virtually overnight, the currency dropped to a quarter of its previous one-to-one parity with the US dollar. For the country as a whole the consequences were disastrous. Unemployment rose to over 20 per cent and half of the population tumbled below the poverty line.

For Patagonia, however, the harshest effects of the slump were short-lived. No sooner did the pot-banging middle-class protestors put down their casseroles than visitors began pouring in to the country's tourist destinations. Argentina and Patagonia went from being Latin America's most expensive destinations to its cheapest.

Closely mirroring its appeal to foreign travellers, Patagonia has also become a huge draw for Argentinians. The boom in tourism has fanned the flames of the old idea that Patagonia is a land rich in opportunities, un *país aparte* (a country unto itself) where *está todo por hacer* (everything remains to be done). The reality, of course, is more complex, but there's no denying the many dreams borne from despair. For the hordes of *porteño* residents of Buenos Aires and young families from the interior who've poured into the region, Patagonia's well-oxygenated, peaceful environment is synonymous with a fresh start. Hard statistics about internal migration are hard to come by, but one need look no further than the skyrocketing population growth of a place like El Calafate, which in one year went from being a sleepy town of 40,000 residents to a bustling commercial centre of 100,000, to sense the dramatic forces at work.

A frontier spirit links, albeit tenuously, these new immigrants with the pioneers of generations past. But unlike previous waves, like the one in the politically febrile 1970s that saw idealistic *porteños* decamp to El Bolsón, the *idée fixe* of the new generation of arrivals is commerce rather than peace, love and harmony. Instead of long hair, they brandish the indelible influence of their urban upbringing – tattoos, pierced tongues and bass-thumping *cumbia villera* music that would send most Grateful Dead fans into cardiac arrest. Joining them in the migratory putsch has been a noticeable number of foreign jetsetters, for whom a ranch or condo in Patagonia is the in thing.

The result is that Patagonia has shed some of its indigenous charm, supplanting it with many of the same unsettling juxtapositions endemic to the rest of the country. Once idyllic Bariloche is now ringed on all sides by *villas miserias*, or shantytowns, and crime has appeared for the first time. Farther south, the pint-sized paradise of El Chaltén is starting to resemble a trailer park, so unhinged has it been by the explosive growth of tourism. Meanwhile, Patagonia's traditional rural culture continues to erode, the victim of lacklustre wool prices and the growth of synthetic apparel. Especially in the interior of Patagonia, farms and even entire towns are disappearing at an alarming rate. By one count, half of Santa Cruz's 1,200 farms have been abandoned in recent years.

Most first-time visitors, however, will be oblivious to these metamorphoses. Compared to over-congested Europe, Patagonia still has plenty of wide-open landscapes to ooh and ahh

about. And indeed, not all the changes are unwelcome. Along with heaps of capital, *porteños* and their ilk have injected fresh ideas into a tourist industry that was in desperate need of a face-lift. Whether it's a flyover of the Hielos Continentales or just a flight between Ushuaia and Bariloche, a range of activities and services that just a few years ago would have been unthinkable are now commonplace. The quality of lodging has also improved greatly.

Chile, for its part, is taking its neighbour's new-found celebrity on the pages of the world's travel magazines in its stride. Despite fears that this considerably more expensive destination would suffer, the austral 2005 summer was a banner tourist season for the country. Confident of their now two-decade head start catering to more fickle, quality-conscious foreign tourists, Chile has yet to suffer the consequences of Argentina's status as the newest in-destination. On the contrary, Chileans have been among the first foreigners to take advantage of the bargains to be had across the border.

'It's no surprise that tourists aren't the only ones arriving in droves.'

One reason Chile escaped contagion from Argentina's economic malaise is a reputation for efficiency that its larger neighbour never enjoyed. The economy, which had been stabilised by the hard hand of General Augusto Pinochet during his dictatorial rule from 1973 to 1990, led the region last decade with average annual growth rates of 6.8 per cent. Although it has often dipped since then, the economy was still expanding at a respectable 6.1 per cent in 2007. Meanwhile, the country's first socialist president in three decades, the popular Ricardo Lagos, solidified Chile's open-for-business reputation even while doggedly pursuing, within a Chilean context, justice for Pinochet's victims. In 2003, Chile became the first South American country to broker a NAFTA-like free-trade accord with the US. Similar accords have been drafted with the EU and Asian countries. Lagos's successor in January 2006 was former defence minister, Michelle Bachelet – Chile's first female head of state and the daughter of one of Pinochet's victims.

In Argentina, where even the weak dollar seems strong, it's no surprise that tourists aren't the only ones arriving in droves. The currency imbalance has also been a huge magnet for foreign investment in forestry, fisheries, chemicals and other resource-intensive, export-driven industries. By far the most dynamic industry, however, has been mining – an industry virtually unknown to Argentina less than a decade ago. Thanks to a doubling in the international price of gold and soaring demand for precious metals from China, the world's leading mining companies have focused their attention on Patagonia's huge untapped supply of subterranean wealth. Over the next five years the country is expected to receive US$4.5 billion in investment in the sector, triple the level of just a few years earlier. Patagonia figures prominently in the rush and the country's biggest gold mine currently under production, Cerro Vanguardia, is located in Santa Cruz province.

It's more than bullion the companies are after. Taking advantage of southern Chile's abundant hydro-power, a Canadian conglomerate wants to spend $2.7 billion – a foreign investment record for the country – to dam three rivers and flood 1,600 hectares (24,000 acres) of pristine woodland in Aisén to fuel an aluminium smelter. Meanwhile both countries are counting on Patagonia's cornucopia of fossil fuels to stem a looming energy crisis. With Argentina's economy expanding at breakneck speed – 8.6 per cent growth in 2007 after an aggregate 17 per cent the previous two years – revitalised assembly lines and industrial plants have been draining the country's energy supplies. The government has scrambled to impose rations on manufacturers and unilaterally cut off gas exports to Chile, which depends on its neighbour for 30 per cent of its generating capacity. But the long-term energy deficit can only be solved by new investments.

After decades of neglect, Patagonians on the whole revel in the attention and promise of jobs from Santiago and Buenos Aires. Indeed, much of Patagonia's Atlantic coast – cities like Comodoro Rivadavia, Río Gallegos and Ushuaia in Tierra del Fuego – owe their existence to an industrialisation drive dating back to the Perón era. In the minds of the blue-collar transplants of these grim, industrial towns, many of whom were lured from Argentina's poorer northern provinces by the promise of jobs, Patagonia's big skies were always silhouetted with smokestacks, not smoking volcanoes.

But there's concern that protection for the region's fragile environment won't keep pace with the frenzied expansion of the industrial frontier. The environmental pressures on Patagonia are greater now than they've ever been in its almost two-century history of human settlement. Although still largely an anomaly in an increasingly polluted planet, conservationists warn that it might only take one cyanide leak or another man-made forest fire like the one that set Torres del Paine National Park ablaze in 2005 (*see p218* **Campfire blues**) to tip the environment's delicate balance.

Indeed, neither of the two countries have environmental records to be proud of. Chile's much-touted economic miracle, during the Pinochet years, was by many accounts an ecological disaster. In a rush to become the world's leading salmon producer, Chilean authorities largely turned a blind eye to the waste and disease generated by hatcheries in Chiloé. From 1985 to 1995 the country clear-cut some 1.8 million hectares (4.5 million acres) of old-growth forest (90 per cent of whose species are unique to Chile) to make way for non-native, industrial tree farms. Argentina's protection of its ecosystem isn't much better, though damage to its share of Patagonia has been partly limited by more space and neglect (until now) of the export potential of its resources.

> **'Chile's "economic miracle", during the Pinochet years, was by many accounts an ecological disaster.'**

With environmental protection budgets already overstretched, most conservation efforts have come from private, often foreign-led, initiatives. The most ambitious – and controversial – figure in that regard is American conservationist Douglas Tompkins, who has brought under protection more than 800,000 hectares (two million acres) of virgin forest and coastal land on both sides of the Andes (*see p138* **Hermit or hero?**). As mistrust of Tompkins' motives has subsided in Chile, he's become a role model for local land-trust initiatives as well. Sebastian Piñera, owner of LAN airlines and a recently declared presidential candidate, cited Tompkins' leadership in his recent acquisition of 18 per cent of Chiloé, which he plans to set aside for conservation. Meanwhile, as part of a rare reversal in fortunes in 2004, US investment bank Goldman Sachs donated a Rhode Island-sized, old-growth forest to a consortium of wildlife conservation groups after repossessing the property from a moribund logging operation it was financing in Tierra del Fuego.

As is always the case with Patagonia, the choice between conservation and progress is a highly politicised one. But with two Patagonian presidents, first Néstor and then Cristina Kirchner, running the show, the region has been thrust on to centre stage for the first time. The Kirchners' loyalty to Patagonia is supreme. After taking office Kirchner *hombre* – born in Río Gallegos – funnelled a windfall of tax dollars to the region in the form of public works like the paving of Santa Cruz's portion of the mythical Ruta 40 and the linking of southern Chubut and Santa Cruz to the nation's power grid. More than ever, natural wealth and industry are coalescing to fulfil US geologist Bailey Willis's prophecy, made during a 1911-1915 survey, that Patagonia would become the prized jewel in Argentina's crown.

Or maybe Uncle Sam's? SOS Patagonia is the name of one of a plethora of websites that has sprung up in the wake of Argentina's crisis to feed a paranoid public's fear that Patagonia could go the way of California and be annexed by the US. One conspiracy theory circulating holds that Argentina's creditors, who were defaulted on to the tune of US$100 billion, are demanding repayment for their worthless bonds in the form of huge swathes of unused, federally owned land. Sadly, the idea isn't as far-fetched as it sounds. To lure back investors the last time Argentina defaulted, President Menem, at the outset of his presidency, repaid creditors by blindly surrendering control of the state's telephone, electricity and gas networks.

Adding to local resentment, both main oil companies in Argentina and Patagonia, YPF and Perez Companc, are now foreign-owned. The region's biggest landholder, with more than one million hectares (400,000 acres) of sheep-grazing land, is the Italian textile magnate Luciano Benetton. Despite Patagonia's strong immigrant roots, newcomer foreign landholders aren't as welcomed as they once were. Some of the rejection is self-inflicted. English multimillionaire Joseph Lewis angered residents in El Bolsón when he bought a nearby 14,000-hectare (5,600-acre) ranch, fenced off access to a long-time swimming hole, renamed the property 'Hidden Lake', and then built for himself a garish, Beverly Hills-style mansion that flaunted local traditions.

True to character, Patagonians aren't taking these perceived threats to their sovereignty and home-grown culture lying down. In Esquel, in the Argentinian province of Chubut, activists took to the streets in 2003 after learning that an American mining company was planning to build an open-cast gold mine just outside the city limits. The protests eventually forced a non-binding referendum and 80 per cent of the town's 30,000 residents rejected the mine and its promise of a huge cash injection into the depressed local economy.

The successful campaign, which garnered international media attention, is emblematic of the upsurge in militant grass-roots movements in post-meltdown Argentina. However, closely linked to this and other novel exercises in direct democracy has been a strong undercurrent of reactionary xenophobia, which politicians have been quick to exploit. Taking its cue from Patagonia's real estate boom, Argentina's Congress is debating a bill to restrict the sale of land to foreigners. And even as attacks on Tompkins subside in Chile, would-be patriot activists in Argentina are just getting started. In the near future, it could be that North American millionaires will have to look elsewhere for that dream retirement ranch.

To be fair, most Patagonians have no more sympathy for divisive ideologues on the left than they do for the first-world economic gurus they blame for bringing Argentina to its knees in the first place. But from the president down, populist policies have proven an irresistibly effective, if short-sighted, tool for taming Argentina's turbulent political climate.

'Equally unpredictable is the impact all the frenzied development will have on Patagonia.'

Not surprisingly, one of the few politicians who's dared to defy the left-veering mainstream is another hard-headed Patagonian, Jorge Sobisch, governor of Neuquén province. Sobisch, as head of conservative provincial party Movimiento Popular Neuquino, was a candidate in the 2007 national presidential elections. Although he was never likely to win, stranger political fortunes have been made before in the weird world of Patagonian politics. Back in 2002, no one gave Néstor Kirchner a snowball's chance of thriving in the hellish world of Argentinian politics – and yet now with Mrs K in charge there is talk of a dynasty being formed (*see p28* **Mr & Mrs**).

Equally unpredictable is the impact all the frenzied development will have on Patagonia as it absorbs more and more of the West's virtues and vices. There are already concerns that the accommodation and tourist boom may turn out to be a bubble, with supply outstripping demand. A number of new hotels in El Calafate – very much the poster child of Patagonian urban expansion – have struggled to attract guests in recent years; some will be forced to close. For tourists, this swing back to 'business as usual' could be a blessing; market forces will ensure that only the best companies survive. For locals, particularly those who have come to the region in search of employment, it's an ill wind.

One thing is for sure: the region, especially on the Argentinian side, is poised to change more in the coming ten years than it has in any decade previously. Making sure progress is as sustainable as it is inevitable is a battle that should be urgently waged.

Mr & Mrs

Succession has long been a source of angst for rulers. Who will take over? Will they praise or bury me? But Néstor Kirchner, ex-president of Argentina, was never a man given to agonising. His solution to the problem was simple. He simply turned over in bed one night and asked his wife if she fancied the job. After several months of 'careful consideration' (read: opinion polls), Cristina Kirchner, neé Fernández, said yes – and on 8 October 2007 became Argentina's first woman president.

She won't be the first female Argentinian head of state: that dubious honour will always belong to poor Isabel Perón, who inherited the job after her husband, Juan Domingo, the founder of the Peronist movement, died in 1974. Ill-prepared for the responsibility and faced with a country on the verge of civil war, Isabel was ousted on 24 March 1976 and fled to Spain.

But that was the 1970s. Whatever problems Argentina may face in the coming years, it is safe to assume that a military coup will not be one of them. Néstor Kirchner, with his tub-thumping, populist style, was a divisive figure – but with approval ratings that rarely dipped below the 60 per cent mark, it's the kind of divisiveness most politicos would kill for – and he handed Mrs K, born in La Plata but Patagonian by marriage, a country in surprisingly good shape.

Foreign commentators puzzle over how an electorate that won't trust a woman to run a barbecue could consider trusting one to run a country. But that's to confuse cultural quirks with raw politics. A more serious charge levelled by the anti-Kirchner Argentinian punditocracy is that *familia* Kirchner is laying the foundations for a democratic dynasty.

It's an important accusation, albeit one that Mr K, with an oratorical style that not so much favours the bludgeon over the rapier as the shoulder-held bazooka over the bludgeon, blasted away at with contempt. Cristina prefers to point to her record. No political ingenue, she has been active in the Peronist party since the 1970s and has represented first Santa Cruz in Patagonia (1995 to 2005) and then Buenos Aires province (2005-2007) in Congress. Like Hillary Clinton, she is probably smarter than her husband and is certainly better dressed.

Which brings us to a side of Cristina that attracts more comment than any other; her glamour. With a fondness for shopping that would have given Imelda Marcos a run for her AmEx card, Cristina's elegance and beauty have done her no harm at all. Mrs Thatcher was known for 'handbagging' her opponents. Cristina, on the other hand, would be unlikely to risk tarnishing her Gucci accessories on a mere political opponent. George W Bush once described Mrs K as 'the most beautiful senator in the world', and there's little doubt that the fanciability factor is an important weapon in Cristina's armoury.

This combination of beauty and brains has inevitably led to comparisons with Eva Perón, the first wife of the man who founded the political movement that has dominated Argentinian politics since – and to which the Kirchners belong. The media love to ruminate over these vital matters: Is Cristina the new Evita? Is she playing party politics or sexual politics? Does Andrew Lloyd Webber have his pen poised?

But Evita, for all her Dior dresses and pearls, was a street-fighting demagogue of the sort that has gone out of fashion. She pushed her husband's programme of big-government paternalism with zeal and accepted the adulation of 'her' people as any former second-rate actress would. Cristina, on the other hand, gives the impression of craving power over pop stardom, and of sticking closely to the pragmatic policies her husband – now the country's First Gentleman – adopted during his presidency.

Elephant seal.

Wild Patagonia

From massive whales to manic woodpeckers, Patagonia teems with all creatures great and small.

Patagonia has been shaped by time and tide – by the Ice Age, the Andes, and the Pacific and Atlantic oceans. Some 140 million years ago it was a vast temperate forest, as testified by the petrified trunks found in Santa Cruz and Chubut. But the geological upheaval of the birth of the Andes first buried the lushness in a grave of ash, and then kick-started the climatological processes that affect present-day Patagonia.

The mountainous east coast of Chile is wet and tree-covered, receiving the full boon of Pacific rains. Continuing east, the Argentinian mountains grab the rest of the moisture, leaving the slopes densely forested and green. All that is then left for the flat easterly steppe and distant Atlantic coast is a constant, dry, deathly wind desiccating anything impertinent enough to try to live there. Tierra del Fuego, despite its extreme position at the meeting of the oceans, is luckier. The southern Andes are far lower and the weather is cold but mitigated by rainfall.

These three natural worlds – mountain, steppe and coast – spread across Patagonia and are home to vastly differing ecosystems. Creepers drape ancient trees and rare deer wander in the forests of the mountains that reach down to the primeval, humid Fuegian woods. On the coast, marine birds and mammals live in huge colonies, screaming and fighting along the rocky shoreline.

SIGNATURE FAUNA

Certain animals' presence somehow defines the particular nature of Patagonia. They are found in every corner and play an important part in the ecology, history and mystery of Patagonia.

Don't miss
Wildlife

Magellanic woodpecker
Noisiest, liveliest tree-climber straight out of the cartoon, with a red punk hairstyle.

Alerce
The dinosaur of the woods – as old, as noble and as high as a tree can get.

Southern right whale
The supreme marine spectacle of the South Atlantic coast.

Calafate
The berry that makes people come back to Patagonia – according to a local myth.

Emperor penguin
The biggest of them all, with an incredible silken sheen to its coat. Reason enough to fork out for an Antarctic adventure.

More commonly known by its indigenous name as the choique, Darwin's rhea is a large, ostrich-like flightless bird that grows up to human adult chest height. Dull brown in colour and long in the neck and leg, its range extends across Patagonia, though you're more likely to see them on farms being bred for their tasty meat. They and their larger cousin the greater rhea (or ñandú) were widely hunted by the gauchos and native populations who caught the escaping animals – which can run at almost 50 kilometres (31 miles) per hour when roused – using their *boleadoras* or 'flying balls'.

> **'After the noisy exuberance of the coast and cordillera, the steppe comes like a long, empty pause.'**

Another long-legged resident, the Chilean flamingo, is remarkably common in the heights, plains and shorelines of Patagonia. Seeing their bright pink plumage amid the autumnal hues of the steppe and foothills makes a stark and beautiful contrast. You will find them near any nutritive, microbe-rich lake, but especially around Lago Argentino and Peninsula Valdés.

A relative of the African camel, the guanaco is the most widespread of the South American camel species (which also include the llama, alpaca and vicuña). This elegant creature served the indigenous population well for thousands of years as a source of transport,

food and clothing. Its fine russet fur, though not as thick as that of the llama or the vicuña, provides excellent insulation. An adult can look – and spit – you in the eye, as they reach almost two metres (seven feet) tall, making the guanaco Patagonia's largest native herbivore. Nonetheless, they can run like the wind, easily leaping over high fences and bounding away more like a gazelle than a camel. They can also swim. Despite such talents and multiple conservation efforts, the guanaco's range and population are shrinking as a result of persistent illegal hunting.

Finally, the most famous but most elusive residents, striking a note of excitement and danger, are the small populations of pumas roaming the steppe and woodlands. Reddish brown, sleek and about as long as a man is tall – Patagonian puma are bigger than those found in other habitats – they are solitary, nocturnal hunters. These increasingly rare big cats play a vital role as head of the Patagonian food chain-feeding on mara (a resident rodent and Patagonia's only unique species), choique, European hare, sheep and even guanaco.

SURVIVING THE STEPPE
Darwin said of the steppe, 'Death instead of life, seemed here the predominant spirit', and after the noisy exuberance of the coast and verdant green and turquoise of the Andean mountain range, or cordillera, the steppe comes like a long, empty pause. Life is hard and nature a tough survivor. The constant wind bends everything to its will, colours are muted – dull grassy tans, greys and browns – and dust covers everything with a gritty coat.

But there is life here too. Under the cover of tough grasses live lizards, two species of armadillo, burrowing owls and even skunks. Running over the plains are the aforementioned mara, a variety of wild chinchilla called vizcacha and the ubiquitous guanaco. Carnivores such as the grey fox, the black-chested buzzard and the occasional puma also manage to eke out a living on the plains.

The central steppe receives so little rain that it officially qualifies as desert; it is composed of vast plains of small, hardy plants and shrubs. Vegetation managing to survive in this environment has had to adapt to the climate; small shiny leaves limit the drying effect of sun and wind, and low and domed or thin and spiky shapes offer as little resistance to the wind as possible. Plants are often unappetisingly spiny to fend off animal visitors, and all have very deep root systems.

The plains are dominated by several species of coarse grass of the coirón family that grow in clumps, spreading quickly in spring and seeding in early summer. In the slightly more sheltered north these are interspersed with small bushes, whereas in the more exposed southerly parts shorter grasses and pin-cushion plants dominate. After the long grey shiver of winter, during spring and summer plants such as mata negra, neneo, jarilla, calafate and coirón poa bloom, and the floor is a carpet of small pink, yellow and white blossoms.

The animals of the steppe are difficult to see and impossible to approach. All are far too used to being prey to spears and guns and their response to human presence is a very sensible high-speed sprint. Your best bet for getting a good look at any animal you chance upon is to stay in your vehicle. As predators hunt at night you're unlikely to catch them out and about.

The herbivores are a little more sociable than the meat-eaters. Look out for mara on the plains around Torres del Paine. They look like a cross between a guinea pig and a hare and grow up to 80 centimetres (31 inches) long. In fact they are often called 'the Patagonian hare' even though they're truly a rodent and hop around like a hyperactive kangaroo.

The resident guanaco herds are perfectly adapted to the life of the steppe. They, unlike their modern replacement – the sheep – know how to feed off the native plants without destroying them. Their tread is light enough not to disturb the soil and so doesn't expose the light, dusty covering to the danger of erosion. One environmental disaster to visit the steppe was the overgrazing by sheep during the 1950s. In 1952 the sheep population topped 22 million. Damage caused to the ecological balance still has an effect and has led to a decline in sheep farming throughout the region. The current size of the Patagonian flock is 5.5 million.

LIVING THE HIGH LIFE

Reaching almost to the ocean, the 120,000 square kilometres (46,332 square miles) of temperate Valdivian rainforests on the slopes of the Andes are unique. Their isolation means that over 95 per cent of the tree species are endemic – they are only found in this one zone. Furthermore, soil and weather conditions promote one of the fastest tree growth rates in the world.

The most celebrated indigenous tree species, however, is the slow-growing giant alerce – a conifer compared to the larch by European botanists. Akin in girth and grandeur to the sequoia redwood trees of North America, it is the second longest-living thing on the planet, regularly reaching birthdays up in the two and three thousands. The trees are home to other unique species including the Patagonian toad and rare chimaihuén (more commonly known as *monito del monte* or 'little hill monkey'), a small nocturnal marsupial. Red and white blooms of the climbing copihue, yellow amancay – a type of narcissus – and the flowering notro tree add colour to the forest.

The lakes and foothills on both sides of the cordillera enjoy a climate pleasantly balanced between the tropical downpours and freezing winters of the nearby mountains and the aridity of the steppe. Glaciers left behind by retreating icecaps melted into their own hollows and left behind enormous puddles. In lakes like Pehoé and Argentino this glacial melt-water is 99 per cent pure; it contains almost no minerals and is effectively sterile: not even the tiniest microbes can survive in water so lacking in essential nutrients. Their startling opaqueness and colour – turquoise milk is one way to describe it – is a result of this purity and the presence of glacial sediments. The water is so

Argentina's Atlantic coastline is a playground for marine wildlife.

Catch the condor

The skies over Argentina are alive with twitchers, clutching well-thumbed guides to the birds of South America while eagerly gazing out of the aeroplane window as though a condor might appear on the descent to Ezieza airport. Birding holidays to Argentina and in particular Patagonia are big news these days. With over 1,000 species to choose from, ornithologists either of the casual or fanatic variety are unlikely to be disappointed by the range and diversity of Argentina's birdlife.

To catch a glimpse of certain feathered friends, timing is everything. Migrating birds (flycatchers, waders and lots of seabirds) return from such regions as Alaska and Canada to South America in the spring (September onwards) – though several hundred species, from the ubiquitous buff-necked ibises, lapwings and ducks, through hawks and buzzards, to all manner of forest-dwelling tweeters can be seen (and heard) year round.

If you're the kind of ornimaniac who needs to see everything, start at the ocean and work your way inland. The eastern seaboard of Argentinian Patagonia, the harsh, unspoilt coastline that stretches from the Río Negro province in the north to the Magellan strait in the south, is home to some 1.8 million Magellanic penguins, many of whom live at Isla de los Pájaros (Bird Island), off Península Valdés. On a windy day, the black-browed albatross with its 250-centimetre (97.5-inch) wingspan wheels over the penguins' heads. A slightly smaller bird, the southern giant petrel, while less graceful than the poetic flight of the albatross, glides effortless on very little wind. Beating its wings only occasionally, it towers, vulture-like in the sky.

In the woodlands on the lower Andean slopes, the lucky bird-watcher may see

– or hear – the Magellanic woodpecker, a black-and-white monster up to 43 centimetres (17 inches) long. In Chile a common sight on the hills and vales is the boisterous, honking buff-necked ibis, while the soundtrack of the Valdivian undergrowth is provided by the cheeky chucao, aka 'huet-huet', clucking his name as he dodges nosy trekkers.

Down by the water, away from obscuring branches, you will spot the prolific lake trout and river birds such as the ringed kingfisher, while you may see an Andean condor soaring overhead on the thermals. Zipping in and out of the fast-flowing, pale aquamarine rivers is the torrent duck, a bird only found in swift rivers and streams near forested areas.

Many marine birds and waders are found off Chile, where they share the skies and islands with pelicans, skuas and terns. Dolphins and penguins (Magellanic and the smaller Humboldt variety) are also everyday sightings, even in the busy shipping channel between Chiloé and the mainland. Slightly inland, Valdivia is a prime spot for seeing large colonies of black-necked swans, as well as great grebes and several types of coot. Further south still, on and around the South Atlantic islands and on the Antarctic peninsular, all the penguin species as well as petrels and bigger albatrosses can be spotted in pristine environments.

An increasing number of international travel companies organise all-inclusive birdwatching tours to Patagonia. Two UK firms with a strong reputation are: **Birdquest** (01254 826317, www.birdquest. co.uk); and **Ornitholidays** (01794 519445, www. ornitholidays.co.uk). In the United States try International Expeditions (0800 6334734, www. voyagers.com).

lifeless that bodies lost to it never decompose, lying perfectly preserved in the icy depths.

This area has some of the richest national parks and nature reserves (*see pp48-53* **National Parks**) in Argentina and Chile. The low hills and edges of the lakes are covered with almost untouched woodlands of coihue, lenga, ñire and rauli – all of the nothofagus or 'false beech' family. If you're really lucky you might see a puma (they are out there), though you're more likely to see sheep, cows, rheas and flamingos – as well as guanacos munching away on the native trees. Look out, too, for the bushes you might recognise as wild roses, which were imported from Europe in the early 20th century as garden ornaments and have taken over the local habitat like a plague.

'The water is so lifeless that bodies lost to it never decompose, lying perfectly preserved in the icy depths.'

Mountain highlights have to be the remote forests of awesome, wrinkled old alerce (Chile and Argentina both have national parks named after this tree, and Parque Pumalín is another key reserve) and the pretty cinnamon-coloured arrayán (or myrtle) forests – spectacular and dense in Península Quetrihué, Argentina's PN Los Alerces and PN Chiloé. Also worth special mention are the mysterious and timeless araucaria – a type of monkey-puzzle tree – further north and the turning of the seasons. The autumnal palette is magical.

Woodland mammals are very timid. You are unlikely to catch even a fleeting glimpse of the huemul and pudú deer, puma, mountain cats, foxes or river otters. The native pudú is the world's smallest deer, about the size of a spaniel and notoriously bashful. In contrast its larger cousin the huemul, or Andean deer, was relatively bold around man. This can't have helped their survival prospects at all and the species, at first massively hunted and now losing out to the introduced red deer, is on the verge of extinction, though there are some protected areas where you may be able to get up close.

BESIDE THE SEASIDE

The wealth of marine life along the long Atlantic coast is due to the cold Malvinas current and its mineral and fish-rich waters. The bleak, cliff-hung coasts and hard volcanic outcrops between the Magellan Strait and Península Valdés are home to the largest concentration of marine wildlife on any continental coastline: 150 colonies of marine birds and 75 of seals and sea lions, 1.6 million

Magellanic penguins, 80,000 southern sea lions, 40,000 elephant seals, over 2,000 southern right whales, and 2,000 dolphins. It is home to the largest continental penguin colony and the only continental colonies of elephant seals. Península Valdés has the densest concentration and widest mix of marine wildlife: if you're short on time, make it a definite destination.

Along the shoreline bask South American sea lions and fur seals, gallivanting around by rotating their front flippers. Punta Pirámides, Punta Norte and Punta Loma house colonies of sea lions, especially around December and January when they come ashore to mate. Look out for the larger males with their chestnut-coloured mane. The much less common fur seal has colonies on Isla Escondida (Chubut) and Cabo Blanco (Santa Cruz).

The massive elephant seals of Península Valdés are not so at ease on land, forced as they are to heave themselves around with a clumsy hitching motion. The enormous males, bigger (four to five metres or 13-16 feet) and heavier than a fully loaded Transit van, come ashore in August to begin their territorial sparring. These bouts can be vicious as they compete for the right to mate with the much smaller females who arrive later at the beginning of September.

Making their presence felt by the racket they generate are the Magellanic penguins. The knee-high male birds come ashore to re-establish their nests in early September and to await the arrival of their mates a couple of weeks later. These plucky little creatures have almost no fear of man and you can get close – but beware of that beak, they will attack if they feel threatened. Old naturalists making studies of the colony used to delight in swapping stories of combined tinnitus and bleeding shins.

Although Punto Tombo has the largest population (currently 40,000 breeding pairs), the smaller colony at Cabo dos Bahías has a much more varied mix of wildlife and lacks Punto Tombo's population of biting flies. At Isla Pingüino near Puerto Deseado you can find the only rockhopper penguin colony on the continent (500 breeding pairs).

Out to sea, the 'must see' is the southern right whale. Growing up to 14 metres (46 feet) long and weighing up to 35,000 kilogrammes (77,263 pounds) they are common between May and December with a peak in September and October. From shore you might catch a glimpse of the V-shaped plume of their exhalation, but take a boat really to understand these gentle giants as they 'tail', splashing the water with that enormous fluke, or 'breach' by lifting almost their entire body out of the water, returning with an almighty crash. The original global population of over 100,000 has been

Resources

Organisations

Fundación Vida Silvestre Argentina
011 4331 3631, www.vidasilvestre.org.ar
**Aves Argentinas – Asociación
Ornitológica del Plata**
011 4312 8958, www.avesargentinas.org.ar
**CODEFF Comité Nacional de Pro-Defensa
de la Fauna y Flora (Chile)**
02 274 7461, www.codeff.cl
UNORCH Unión de Ornitólogos de Chile,
02 236 8178, www.unorch.cl

Recommended books

**A Guide to the Birds and Mammals
of Coastal Patagonia**
Graham Harris
Birds of Tierra del Fuego
Ricardo Clark
Patagonia, the Laws of the Forest
Santiago G de la Vega
Guías de campo de Aves de Patagonia
Liliana Cerutti and Gabriela Poleman
Guía de Campo de las Aves de Chile
Jorge M Araya

decimated by hunting and the 2,000-odd whales coming to breed off Península Valdés represent a significant share of an estimated current worldwide total of 5,000 whales.

Prowling the busy shoreline is the fearsome killer whale, known locally as the orca. During February and March around Punta Norte, if you're patient and very lucky, you might catch the spectacle of one of these nine-metre (30-feet) mammals driving itself up on to the beach, in an incredible demonstration of raw power, in order to snatch a young elephant seal cub right from the flippers of its family.

Less threatening are the five species of dolphin dancing around the bays. Most common are Fitzroy's dolphin (with a dark upper surface, light underneath and a two-tone dorsal fin) and the distinctive black-and-white Commerson's dolphin; both are very acrobatic and playful. Other residents include Peale's dolphin (mostly around the Magellan Strait), and the bottlenose and common dolphin.

LIFE ON EARTH AT THE WORLD'S END

Remote and somewhat isolated by the Magellan Strait, the mix of species is different in Tierra del Fuego to Patagonia as a whole. The climate is similar to that of the Alaskan panhandle; tempestuous, rainy, foggy. Appalling is one way to describe it – but all that rain does allow the existence of dense temperate rainforests, with the trees growing right to the edge of the sea, and inland freshwater lakes.

There are 545 plant species in the region, around 40 of which are unique to Tierra del Fuego. On the ground lie carpets of lichen, moss and fern and in poorly drained areas you can find peat bogs – lichens, limeworts, ferns and reeds growing 1.8 metres (six feet) above the ground on thick, dome-shaped mats of sphagnum moss. There are wildflowers, gentians and orchids and five types of tree, including the Antarctic beech that grows in the valleys and with cypress on steep slopes.

A huge amount of damage has been done by the irresponsible introduction of foreign species. An invasion of rabbits had to be dealt with by the introduction of myxomatosis but the invasion of the Canadian muskrats and beavers goes on unchecked. Still there is room for endemic species like the tucotuco, a small hairless vole that constructs massive underground tunnel complexes and never drinks, the avatorda – a wild goose with a reddish head that still survives in the northern part of Isla Grande – and the Fuegian fox.

'The fearsome orca snatches an elephant seal cub from the flippers of its family.'

Over the coast fly myriad marine birds, including oystercatchers and albatrosses and inland you can catch sight of condors and coscoroba swans. Too fat to fly but still feathered is the chunky flightless steamer duck, so named for its splashing runs across the water's surface when threatened. Around the coast and across in Punta Arenas are colonies of Magellanic penguins. Surprisingly, on its most southerly tip, Tierra del Fuego is home to its own exotic species of parrots and canaries, the most southerly of their kind in the world.

Like most of the world's great wildernesses, Patagonia faces a daunting array of ecological challenges (*see p126* **On the green team**). These range from the legacy of overgrazing to present-day pressures on remote towns to generate employment and revenue by chopping down virgin forests for the paper, furniture and construction industries. More insidious threats are the fires lit by farmers near protected environments and the proximity of exotic eucalyptus, willow, poplar and pine trees. The national parks and a number of local and international NGOs and pressure groups are working with the tourist industry to ensure the region has a sustainable future as one of the planet's most unspoilt environments.

Arts & Culture

Voices in the wilderness.

Unlike the regions of the northern Andes, Patagonia is not an ethnic milieu, producing native words, sounds and pictures. Some will find the culture scene naïve and inchoate or too drenched in the voyeuristic gaze of travellers; others will embrace it as patchy, pragmatic and postmodern.

The arts in Patagonia, then, are an irregular collage of ancient indigenous culture, grassroots community activity, and the impressionistic and occasionally profound ponderings of visiting painters, photographers and writers. Much of the latter is found on gallery walls and shelves far from the region – but in some cities and towns, a home-grown scene is evolving.

NATIVE ARTISTS

The indigenous peoples of Patagonia left no written records and five centuries of genocide, colonisation and mass European immigration have limited our understanding of their forms of cultural expression. The **Cueva de las Manos Pintadas** (Cave of the Painted Hands) in Santa Cruz (*see p113*), which dates back about 12 centuries, is an early example of pictographic art. The Tehuelche also left other cave paintings, most of them simple records of their main activity: hunting. Most indigenous societies produced tools and pottery, much of it bereft of artistic invention, though pre-Mapuche groups like the seventh-century Pitren community in the Biobio area and the Vergel, near Temuco, in the tenth century, produced some impressive ceramics. In Temuco's **Museo Regional de la Auracanía** (*see p168*) you can see how early artistry has been handed down to contemporary sculptors and jewellers. The skills and patterns of primitive arts survive in examples of weavings and other handicrafts – though often in highly bastardised forms.

Something for those long coach journeys...

Ethnological surveys of extinct groups such as the Selk'nam as well as literature from the only extant indigenous community, the Mapuche, show that ritual was central to community life. Ornate masks and robes were used by Fuegian groups, whose dramas tied the seasons to the stages of human life. Most oral traditions were rich in mythological explanations of creation, the climate and social mores and many societies used music.

LITERARY EXPLORATIONS

If indigenous groups were too busy surviving, Europeans soon made up for the lack of literature. The theme of the 'indio' inspired one of Chile's most important works, La Auracana, by Alonso de Ercilla y Zúñiga (1533-94). This first epic poem written in South America is an exercise in tolerance and understanding, analysing the relationship between Spaniards and Auracanians (Mapuches).

Mariners invented the very notion of Patagonia and treated the 'blank space' at 'the end of the world' as ideal for spinning tales. The first recorded mention of 'Patagonia' is in the journal of Antonio Pigafetta, a sailor who journeyed with Magellan in the 16th century. In English it was John Byron (grandfather of Lord Byron), another voyager, who brought the word home. His book, The Narrative of John Byron containing an Account of the Great Distresses suffered, 1768, is a salty thriller and a valuable record of the customs of the Alacaluf people.

During the 19th century, Patagonia came into its own, especially for naturalists. Charles Darwin's famed travelogue Voyage of the Beagle

(1845) is either a tale of gripping discovery or taxonomist's porn, depending on your viewpoint. Darwin notes, often in the same paragraph, details about rock formations, Argentinian politics, rides across the steppes and the 'boisterous' seas as he sails down and up both sides of Patagonia. One local boy who inherited Darwin's scientific passion for nature was Francisco Pascasio Moreno. In his magnum opus Viaje a la Patagonia Austral (1876) and other key works, Moreno catalogues the geology, flora and fauna of Patagonia's diverse landscapes.

'Not all Patagonian writing is lyrical and whimsical.'

The final member of the nature lit trinity is William Henry Hudson, the Thoreau of the pampas. Born to ranch-owning English parents, he was an obsessive birdwatcher in his youth, and in later life gave lectures at the Royal Society. His Idle Days in Patagonia (1893) is a minor classic and though he only gets as far as the Rio Negro (further down and he would have encountered hostile Tehuelche nomads), there is a profound sense of remoteness and of the subtle wonders of the apparently drab desert. Like Darwin before him, Hudson is moved by the wonder of the vast and of the minute.

Another expat pioneer and missionary, Thomas Bridges, compiled his Yámana-English dictionary in the 1890s, a landmark in Patagonian ethnography. The Bridges left their family album in the form of a fat tome by Lucas, son of the preacher man, called The Uttermost Part of the

Earth (1933). There's something unmistakably Patagonian about the book – it goes on and on – but it is a lively and valuable account of the European encounter with Fuegian natives.

The only top-flight literary authors with a Patagonian connection have been of native stock – and from Chile. Biggest star of all is Nobel laureate Pablo Neruda, raised in Temuco. For most, he is a poet who specialised in love and existential abstractions but he had a lot of time for his geography too. The ice-fields of the south are described as 'the blue mother-of-blue; blue's secret, blue solitude; blue's aerie, lapis lazuli blue; the blue spine of my country'. The young Neruda met, and was encouraged by another Nobel prizewinner, Lucila Godoy Y Alcayaga, better known as Gabriela Mistral.

Patagonia is an old favourite of travel writers. George Chaworth Musters's *At home with the Patagonians* (1871) and Lady Florence Dixie's *Across Patagonia* (1880) blend personal reflection with amateur sociology; Bailey Willis's *A Yankee in Patagonia* mixes anecdotes about his life in the region with his mining ambitions.

Not all Patagonian writing is lyrical and whimsical. Osvaldo Bayer's three-volume *Los Vengadores de la Patagonia Trágica* (1972-4),

banned by the military at the time, was the first Argentinian history book that had to be published abroad. It describes the Anarchist uprising of 1920-21 and its bloody suppression.

THE CHATWIN INDUSTRY

British author Bruce Chatwin is generally considered the first post-war writer to put the region on the literary map – if you were born in the US, Australasia or Europe any time after 1950, chances are you first heard the word Patagonia in connection with this much-praised writer born in Sheffield, educated at Marlborough and trained at Sotheby's. He made his name with a travelogue of short, anecdotal chapters. Called *In Patagonia*, it was first published in 1977, won instant acclaim, and is a worldwide bestseller.

In spinning his yarn, Chatwin chooses the company of adventurers and mystics, citing WH Hudson, Darwin and sailor James Weddell, along with urbanites Conan Doyle and Edgar Allan Poe. While literary embellishments add to the read, they make for a somewhat colonial treatment of the region. Chatwin's description of the seduction of Jemmy Button, the Selk'nam who was kidnapped by Fitzroy runs: 'A tall

The things people say

'These plains are pronounced by all most wretched and useless. They are characterised by negative possessions; – without habitations, without water, without trees, without mountains... Why, then, and the case is not peculiar to myself, do these arid wastes take so firm possession of the memory?'
Charles Darwin *Voyage of the Beagle*

'Hundreds of peaks, snowy massifs fantastically covered with ice, bold needles of granite and clayey schists have not only never been scaled but are still today shrouded in the mystery of their rugged, tempestuous heights.'
Padre Alberto de Agostini *Andes Patagónicos*

'It has a look of antiquity, of desolation, of eternal peace, of a desert that has been a desert from of old and will continue a desert for ever.'
WH Hudson *Idle Days in Patagonia*

'I knew I was nowhere, but the most surprising thing of all was that I was still in the world after all this time... I thought: Nowhere is a place.'
Paul Theroux *The Old Patagonian Express*

'Hahshi was a lonely, noisy imp, chocolate-brown in colour, like damp, rotten wood. He was said to come out of dead trees and generally to haunt the vicinity of long-burnt forests.'
Lucas Bridges *Uttermost Part of the Earth*

'Tea towels from Wales hung on the walls alongside completed jigsaws of Welsh landscapes; an outsize kettle was permanently on the hob. The flickering picture of gaudy blondes hosting game shows was the only hint that this was Argentina.'
Miranda France 'Cake fighting in Patagonia' in *Bad Times in Buenos Aires*

'I pictured a low timber house with a shingled roof, caulked against storms, with blazing log fires inside and the walls lined with the best books, somewhere to live when the rest of the world blew up.'
Bruce Chatwin *In Patagonia*

'Antarctica was a cultural void, a space in the imagination... Despite everything I had gone through to get where I was – the years of preparation and anxiety – it seemed to me then that the external journey meant nothing at all.'
Sara Wheeler *Terra Incognita*

Mapuche singer **Beatriz Pichi Malen**.

person in costume beckoned him and he leapt aboard. The pink man handed the uncle a disk that shimmered like the moon and the canoe spread a white wing and flew down the channel towards the source of pearl buttons.'

But most criticism has been levelled at Chatwin for simply inventing stories to make his book work – when John Pilkington went south to write his own book (*An Englishman in Patagonia*, 1991), he met Patagonians portrayed by Chatwin – as lost dreamers at best, but sometimes as mere fools – who had contemplated suing the author.

If flawed, *In Patagonia* is nonetheless a benchmark for travel writers and a model even for fiction writers. As for those who live in Patagonia, they have generally forgiven the excesses of the rather pompous young man who came to visit in the '70s – not least because his book has brought thousands of tourists.

Since Chatwin's startling success, Patagonia has become a prime target for journos keen to get a book out. Among the best are Sara Wheeler's Chile travelogue *Travels in a Thin Country* (1994), marred slightly by backpacker introspection (her Antarctica book *Terra Incognita* (1997) is also highly readable), and Hank Wangford's saddle-and-spurs themed *Lost Cowboys from Patagonia to the Alamo* (1995).

THE MUSIC OF THE SOUTH

In Fernando Solanas's film *El Viaje* (1990), Argentina's funk-pop star, Fito Paez, sings a song titled 'Ushuaia'. The same country's folk rocker hero, León Gieco, made an album called *From Ushuaia to La Quiaca*, exploring folksy forms from across the country. Both artists' songs are testimony to the south's importance as a symbol of national, non-metropolitan identity.

But these are exceptions to the rule. A lot of the rock produced by Argentinian and Chilean bands is a variation on UK archetypes – Pink Floyd, The Cure, Madness, the Stones – with a Latin twist and Spanish lyrics, known

in Argentina as *rock nacional*. Places like Puerto Montt, Bariloche, Valdivia and Comodoro Rivadavia will get bands coming down from the capitals to play – they may be legends for the locals, but chances are you'll never have heard of them. During summer in the main resorts, you'll catch rock and folk at one-off gigs and festivals. In winter, music mostly hibernates, although Ushuaia is leading the field bringing dance music – suddenly hugely popular – south, organising mountain raves and dance parties.

Argentina and Chile are slowly waking up to world music. Ethnic-minded musicians have had not so much to preserve their indigenous heritage as unearth and, even, reinvent it. In Argentina, the challenge has been taken up by singer Beatriz Pichi Malen, from Buenos Aires province, but with her roots in Mapuche culture. Her shows and album, *Plata*, are an insightful introduction to the earthy, evocative and often spooky sounds of northern Patagonia. She is frequently invited to perform gigs in towns like Santa Rosa, Puerto Madryn and Neuquén.

The Mapuche use music to understand nature, divinity and each other. Instruments like the *kultrún* (a skin-covered drum), the *trutruca* (a bamboo pole with an ox horn on the end) and the *pifúlka* (one-note flute) echo the sounds of wind, harvest, seasons and spirits. Music accompanies dances such as the women's ostrich (rhea) dance, but also has a shamanic role in Mapuche communities, conferring on musicians considerable status – when a *kultrún* player dies, the instrument is pierced (to let the life out of it) and buried with her.

In southern Chile a minor furore has been caused by different views of the indigenous tradition. In Puerto Montt, Jaime Barria and his band Bordemar have fused a classical sound akin to Bach and elements of European folk with native rhythms, claiming this as the authentic regional sound. Meanwhile, across the water in Ancud, Chiloé, Marcos Uribe maintains that there is a true roots music still alive within the local Huilliche culture. Armazón, fronted by Uribe's partner, Neddiel Muñoz, allow modern instruments, so long as they throw the strange, mantra-like native lyrics into relief. Indigenous politics are also to the fore: 'We, the Huilliche, keep on existing/and the foreign demon coming from/other lands vanishes.' Between gigs, Armazón are now exploring the musical traditions of the extinct Fuegian natives.

RE-SEEING PATAGONIA

If the Cave of the Painted Hands was the first excursion into abstraction, it hasn't spawned a legacy of blank canvases and installations. Patagonia has long been a favourite of landscape photographers. Bookstores are crammed with large-format books of gorgeous images of Paine, Fitz Roy, remote *estancias*, big skies and all the fauna that flourishes in the south.

Among the best snappers are Argentinian Marcos Zimmermann, whose black-and-white photos of solitary ice sculptures and parched terrain are bleakly beautiful, and, for richly toned panoramas, look for work by David Neilson and Axel Bos. In Argentina's provinces and Chile's regions, young artists turn out contemporary sculpture and insightful painting that manage to exploit local materials and topography – rocks, bones, cave symbols, the wind – but which have the self-analytical edge only Patagonian-born artists can achieve.

Some painters have taken the obvious natural attributes of Patagonia and reworked them. Andrea Juan, from Buenos Aires, combines

video, painting, printmaking and photography techniques to capture the ice-melt caused by global warming, while the unearthly splendour of powerful Patagonian landscapes lends itself to Helmut Ditsch's hyper-real paintings.

Patagonia's culture is nothing if not random. In any one year, there are Welsh Eisteddfods in Chubut, fashion shows at the glaciers, rock gigs in Ushuaia, at least one local novel inspired by maritime history and one travel book or coffee-table photo book being published. Urban centres have artsy scenes – film and theatre are big in Valdivia, classical music is major in Puerto Varas, Frutillar and Bariloche (the local Camarata are world class) and folk festivals are common all over (though the music is often from the north). Ushuaia, meanwhile, is a centre for jazz fans and El Bolsón is a mini cultural magnet.

Shooting the south

Patagonia feels like a film. Perhaps it's the psychological transfer from watching American road movies with big skies and straight roads, but the rolling landscape seems to offer up mysteries and myths begging to be shot.

The best directors aren't overwhelmed by the landscape. One of the earliest cinematic incursions into Patagonia was Lucas Demare's *Plaza Huincul: Pozo Uno* (1960). Demare was born in Neuquén and his film about the hardships suffered by oil riggers anticipates the neo-realist movement brewing in Italy at the time. *La Patagonia rebelde* (1974), Hector Olivera's film adaptation of Osvaldo Bayer's three-volume account of the massacre of *estancia* labourers in 1921-2, was a similarly gritty portrayal of the region and foreshadowed the dark years of the 1976-83 dictatorship.

In recent years some of the strongest films have managed to maintain this realist line while using the landscape and setting as a source of hope and inspiration. Pablo Trapero's *Mundo grúa* (*Crane World*, 1999) was hailed as a new way of looking at contemporary Argentina. The simple and bittersweet story of Rulo, an unemployed fiftysomething heading to Comodoro Rivadavia to look for work ripples with understated emotion and argument rare in a film tradition given to melodrama and literalness.

Two films that have explored the same idea by pitting a small man against a big universe in order to redeem him are Carlos Sorín's

Historias mínimas (2002) and *Bombón el perro* (2004), distinctive for their muted, controlled approach to the visual backdrop. *Historias mínimas* won the Special Prize at San Sebastian 2002 and a Second Coral Award at the Havana Film Festival. Another award-winning film, Gregorio Cramer's *Invierno mala vida* (*Winter Land*, 1997) does something similar, but draws more explicitly on the suggestive, mythical quality of the empty steppe – there's even a sheep that wears a golden fleece. Brazilian Walter Salles's Che Guevara biopic, *The Motorcycle Diaries* (2004), makes good use of Río Negro and the lake district, hinting at the fun as well as the drama of travel on the open road. The Argentinian sections are ultimately more memorable than the heavy-handed scenes in Peru and the Amazon.

Some films, though, have pushed too far either the setting or allegorical potential of Patagonia. A Hollywood-style narrative of flight and freedom was imposed on Río Negro for Marcelo Piñeyro's *Caballos Salvajes* (1995). The attempt fails, mainly because the cheesy plot about a bank clerk who goes along with a bank robber's plan to escape, because he's, er, bored of his job, is far-fetched. This is a bad TV film, laden with clichés. A crude appropriation of the American road-movie narrative it is proof (if any was really needed) that, culturally and historically, Patagonia isn't merely a displaced southern branch of the American West and needs its own film treatment.

Eating & Drinking

Why slam in the lamb when you can roast it for six hours?

Unlike the first Europeans to settle the region, scores of whom succumbed to famine and scurvy, you won't go hungry in modern-day Patagonia. Just don't expect your palate to be dazzled every time you stop for lunch. Set against most of the world's wild underpopulated territories, Patagonia holds up well in gastronomic terms. Several of the region's specialities should be on every foodie's must-eat-once-before-I-die list. But this isn't Provence and nor does it pretend to be.

So what's on the menu? Breakfast might be yesterday's baguettes sliced and toasted, or, if you're lucky, butter *medialunas* (croissants) and jam. Coffee is usually expresso-style in Argentina, but in Chile you'll be given a family-size tin of Nescafé instant powder and told to make it yourself. Lunch in the provinces is likely to consist of local fast food (*minutas*): steak sandwiches, empanadas (a kind of pasty,

usually meat but sometimes cheese, chicken or seafood), Spanish omelette, salads and chips. It's all rather basic, but with a half-bottle of red and the right lighting you'll be fuelled up for the next round of glaciers and mountains.

At dinner the three Ps of Argentinian cuisine – *parrillas* (BBQ), pasta and pizza – dominate that country's small towns, while Chileans find their southern restaurants overwhelmed by *salmón a la plancha*. That's grilled salmon; and though it's a nice treat once in a while, it can become rather like fishy beans-on-toast, so you should explore the menu. Fortunately, the shellfish, which come piled up high on your plate, are tasty enough to eat as served.

Classic desserts across these – for South America – cool regions are often apple and fruit pies, using the forest fruits that grow so prolifically in Andean regions. Sugar cravings can easily be sated by the cakes and pastries served up for the Argentinian equivalent of afternoon tea – the *merienda* – and the Chilean *once* (meaning elevenses but served at 5-6pm) which is often a hot drink and a custardy slice of German-style fruit *küchen*. Argentinian desserts come with a sinful dollop of cream and *dulce de leche* (ultra-sweet milk jam).

If scanning the average restaurant menu in Patagonia is more likely to bring on déjà vu than hunger pangs, things are improving, in part spurred by the influx of affluent European and North American tourists (read, fussy eaters), but also thanks to the influence of the burgeoning 'world cuisine' scene in Buenos Aires and Santiago. Slick, sometimes exclusive, eateries are popping up in the remotest of locations. Even some large hotels are kicking out the mass-market stodge. The excellent restaurants at **Antumalal** hotel (*see p174*) and **Design Suites Bariloche** (*see p103*) are just two trying to move forward.

PLEASURES OF THE FLESH

Everyone knows that Argentinian beef is sublime. But many connoisseurs of *carne* hold that Patagonian lamb is even better. The meat is lean, almost cholesterol-free and so common that many tuck in for breakfast. The most

traditional way of cooking lamb is *al asador*. The animal, strung up on a cross over an open fire, is browned slowly – it can take up to six hours to reach perfection. It may not be the most dignified end for the animal but the results are exceptional. Colonial influences die hard: the British legacy can be seen in the hearty stews and the use of mint sauce.

Several other meats figure on Patagonian menus. Deer, brought to the region by German settlers, and boar, also introduced, are common wild meats, along with the native guanaco. In places like La Pampa you can even hunt for the beasts that end up on your plate.

Native birds are another option. The flightless – and thus easy to catch – choique is used to prepare meatballs and breaded cutlets, or eaten smoked. Meat smoking is a tradition of German settlers in the region (who in Chile use the same technique for salmon), and they are also famous for their cheeses and sausages.

A large chunk of Patagonia is in Argentina so barbecued beef is everywhere: in all big restaurants, small-town *parrillas* (restaurants specialising in grilled meat) and hotels. Meat – plentiful, cheap and good – is always a safe bet in Argentina, and usually good round cattle-town Osorno in Chile. Out of the towns

The wine box

Early adopters, listen up. If your main interest in New World wine relates to the 'new' part, look south. And we don't mean Pasadena.

Wine buffs will be happy too. The quality as well as the quantity of Patagonian wine is on an upwards curve. According to experts the only surprise is that it's taken so long. Growing conditions, particularly in the Río Negro and Neuquen regions of Argentina, are great for grapes: chalky soil; sunny days and chilly nights; the famous and constant Patagonian winds, and an irrigation system of pure Andean snow-melt that has been switched on since the end of the last ice age. Climatic conditions are so predictable that the bugbear of every French grower, the dreaded 'bad year', is virtually unheard of south of the 42nd parallel.

Regarded as a fledgling industry, they have, in fact, been making wine in Patagonia for almost a century. The grand old man of the region's wineries is **Bodegas Humberto Canale**, founded in 1913 in General Roca, Río Negro. Highly recommended are the 2002 pinot noir and the 2004 Black River Torrontés. Phone to arrange a tour of the vineyard (02941 430415, www.bodegahcanale.com).

Bodega Noemia (not open for tours), also in Río Negro, is a much smaller operation, with a cultivating area of only 1.5 hectares (3.7 acres). Its methods are unswervingly traditional; no machines are used at any stage of the process. Look out for its 2003 J Alberto and 2001 Río Negro, both malbecs.

Infinitus (not open for tours), property of Domaine Vistalba who also owns the Fabre Montmayou vineyard in Mendoza, is another producer with a low-tech ethos and a strong reputation abroad. Unless you're as snobbish as Miles from *Sideways*, you'll enjoy its 2001 merlot, declared Best Merlot in Argentina by the English Wine Society.

The new kid on the hock is Neuquén producer **Bodega del Fin del Mundo**, whose first vines were planted in 1999. Unusually for an Argentinian company, it has a marketing strategy that comes close to living up to the product. Look out for its two most recent award winners, the Special Blend and the Pinot Noir Reserva, both 2003. To arrange a tour of the vineyard, call in advance (0299 4855004) or check out their classy website at www.bodegadelfindelmundo.com.

in the real countryside, at one of the region's *estancias*, you can enjoy a cut of the freshest meat that has been slow-roasted to perfection while you were out riding or just lazing around.

CATCH OF THE DAY

With water, water everywhere, fish and seafood make the menu at most restaurants; for seafood specialities visit a *marisqueria*. Wild as well as farmed trout flourish in the rivers and lakes of the Andes. Smoked in salads, grilled or cooked quickly, the flavour is usually fantastic.

The Pacific coast has the widest selection of seafood and, confusingly, it's where the best Atlantic salmon is found, as well as sea-run trout. As a voyeur shopping treat, visit the **Feria Libre** food market in Temuco (*see p168*) – a bustling place where you can see and smell all manner of molluscs and sea beasts.

From both oceans come king prawns, crab, oysters (the best are from San Antonio Oeste) and mussels. Top of the seafood league is the king crab, a coveted crustacean found in just a few parts of the world. Eaten fresh, with just salt and lemon, it lives up to its name.

GETTING YOUR GREENS

Even if meat and fish reign in Patagonia, vegetables are also everywhere, especially in summer. There's no serious vegetarian cause in either Chile or Argentina and cooked meats like ham and salami are often treated as non-meats. If you really are squeamish about eating flesh, there's a healthy cheese scene in the dairy areas of the Lake Districts, fresh greens, carrots and calabashes from local homesteads and grocers,

plus apples, tomatoes and other fruit 'n' veg standards. Potatoes are often said to have originated in Chiloé (though Peru claims otherwise), so try the different types there.

On menus, herbivores should look for *tortilla* (omelette), varieties of *tarta* (pie – often filled with spinach or Swiss chard, squash, cheese, onions), non-meat empanadas and fondues. When ordering, politely insist '*no como carne*' ('I don't eat meat'). If nothing else it will get the waiter's eyebrows working.

> ### 'New Patagonian cuisine is resuscitating Mapuche ingredients and recipes.'

Berries flourish in the microclimate around El Bolsón, and local cultivation methods meet certified organic standards. The area is literally covered with them: boysenberries, raspberries, cherries and blackcurrants. Most species were introduced by the British, although there are several native edible native Patagonian berries too, including michai, murtilla, sauco and calafate. They are the base of delicious jams, bittersweet sauces, chutneys, ice-creams and yoghurts.

Over time few native dishes have survived, but new Patagonian cuisine is resuscitating Mapuche ingredients and recipes. One example is the *charquikán*: a method of drying meat that conserves it for a long period of time. Other interesting dishes include *cochayuyo* (seaweed soup) and *curanto* (meaning hot stone), from the island of Chiloé (*see p192* **Seafood special**).

Lamb *al asador*: looks terrifying, tastes amazing.

In Andean lakeside towns you'll find lots of Swiss, German and Austrian restaurants offering fondue, raclette or goulash. Chocolate shops are also a constant presence in the south, as well as European-style tea houses. The Welsh community deserves a special mention for their generous Welsh teas, served with fruit cake, in towns like Gaiman and Trevelin.

OUT ON THE PISCO

Patagonians like a drink and the latest local phenomenon to spread south is wine (*see p41* **The wine box**). With so many Germans around, there's a bit of a beer fest going on too. One famous brewey is **Cervecería El Bolsón** (*see p106*), which also has its own brewpub and leads the National Hop Festival (*see p45*). In the Chilean Lake District and beyond, Valdivia's Kunstmann brewery competes with the national heavyweights Cristal and Escudo.

Chile's most typical and ancient beverage is pisco, made by distilling grapes till they turn into a potently intoxicating brew. However, avoid any conversations about pisco's origins; it's a topic that Peruvians and Chileans take so seriously that it almost caused a war. The history books support Peru's claim, but it's enormously popular in Chile; 99 per cent of pisco production is drunk locally. Top tipples are Pisco Sour (pisco, lemon, sugar and beaten egg white) and Vaina, a softer drink prepared with old wine, eggs and cinnamon. Chicha – a kind of ciderish apple drink – is popular in Chiloé. Chilean bars and eateries also do a roaring trade in natural juices, but in general Chileans drink more beer and spirits than wining-dining Argentines, for whom decorum is vastly important. That's why the latter are often seen drinking *mate* – a tropical tea supped from a gourd through a metal straw, and shared around a group. It's an important ritual all over Argentina and while hardly drunk at all in central and northern Chile, it's a popular habit in the frontier-hopping Patagonian populations.

PRACTICALITIES

Credit cards are accepted in most of the biggish restaurants in tourist towns and in hotel restaurants, but rarely in smaller villages or off the beaten track. Many places add a cover charge of around US50¢ per person and you should add a tip of about 10 per cent to the bill. Booking is only necessary in very trendy or upmarket restaurants, and if you go out to eat at 8.30pm, don't be surprised if you're the only one there; locals dine late. Usual restaurant opening hours are noon to three, and then again from 8pm to midnight or later. You can expect friendly, informal service, though little English will be spoken in small villages.

The menu

Basics

Carta/menú/lista menu; **la cuenta** the bill; **desayuno** breakfast; **almuerzo** lunch; **cena** dinner; **entrada** starter; **plato principal** main course; **postre** dessert; **casero** home-made; **pan** bread; **agua** water; **cerveza** beer.

Cooking styles & techniques

A la parrilla barbecues; **a la plancha** cooked on griddle; **al asador** strung up and roasted; **al horno** baked; **frito** fried; **jugoso** rare; **a punto** medium; **bien cocido** well done.

Carne y aves (Meat & poultry)

Albóndigas meatballs; **tira de asado** rack of ribs; **bife de chorizo** rump/sirloin; **bife de lomo** tenderloin; **cerdo** pork; **chivito** kid; **chorizo** sausage; **ciervo** deer; **conejo** rabbit; **cordero** lamb; **jamón** ham (**cocido** boiled, **crudo** Parma-style); **lechón** suckling pig; **milanesa** breaded cutlet; **morcilla** blood sausage; **pato** duck; **pollo** chicken; **riñones** kidneys; **vacio** flank.

Pescados & mariscos (Fish & seafood)

Anchoa anchovy; **almeja** clam; **bacalao** cod; **camarón** prawn; **cangrejo** crab; **centolla** king crab; **choro** mussel; **corvina** bass; **lenguado** sole; **mejillón** mussel; **merluza** hake; **ostra** oyster; **pulpo** octopus; **rabas** squid rings; **trucha** trout.

Verduras, arroz & legumbres (Vegetables, rice & pulses)

Arroz rice; **berenjena** aubergine/egg plant; **calabaza** pumpkin/squash; **cebolla** onion; **chaucha** green beans; **choclo** sweetcorn; **palmito** palm heart; **palto** avocado; **papa** potato; **puerro** leek; **zanahoria** carrot.

Fruta (Fruit)

Aná pineapple; **cereza** cherry; **frambuesa** raspberry; **frutilla** strawberry; **manzana** apple; **naranja** orange; **pomelo** grapefruit.

Postres (Desserts)

Budín de pan bread pudding; **helado** ice-cream; **küchen** custard and fruit cake; **miel** honey; **queso** cheese.

Local specialities

Alfajor cornflower biscuits; **curanto** fish stew; **dulce de leche** milk jam; **medialunas** croissants (**de manteca** sweet and buttery, **de grasa** saltier, made with oil).

Festivals & Events

Eat, drink, be merry and then eat some more.

South Americans live according to a simple, but nonetheless refreshing, credo, which states that any doubts about how to react to a given situation can be resolved by throwing a party, preferably a big one. Invitation list? Waste of paper; just invite everyone. Age restrictions? Nope, bring your toddlers and your maiden aunt. Foreigners? More the merrier.

Patagonians, while not so instinctively hedonistic as their comrades in, say, Buenos Aires or Rio de Janeiro, are no exception. Every historical anniversary, every industry and every town or village has its fiesta and nothing and no one is too mundane to be celebrated. So if you thought the Day of the Fox was a bad airport thriller you'd be wrong – it's actually a spring festival in Rio Gallegos.

The method and tenor of celebration varies according to place and occasion, but betting on food, booze and music won't lose you money.

Outdoors is better than indoors. A competition to find the prettiest local lass (the '*reina*' or queen) always draws the crowds. Don't expect canapés and finger food. A big fire, a few dead sheep, some sliced bread and we're good to go.

Listed below are some of the better known festivals and events in the Patagonian calendar. Exact dates and frequency vary, however, so on arrival in any town ask at the tourist office or cultural centres and bookshops.

Summer

Whatever happens, expect people. Schools close between December and March and hordes of Santiago and Buenos Aires residents flee their broiling cities to get a bit of space and fresh air. Planes and buses are booked up, so plan ahead, and the same applies for restaurants around Christmas and New Year.

Fiesta Nacional de la Cereza

Los Antiguos, Santa Cruz. **Location** *see p116.*
Date early Jan.
Argentina's national cherry capital marks the harvest in style, with folkloric bands, displays of gaucho horsemanship, a crafts fair and the election of this year's 'Queen of the Cherry'. Barbecues and stalls selling local specialities keep the masses well fed. No prizes for guessing what's for dessert.

Fiesta del Río

Viedma, Chubut. **Location** *see p120.* **Date** mid Jan.
Lots of messing about on the river culminates in a mad paddle to the finish line in the Río Negro Regata, the world's longest kayak race – it starts 500 kilometres (311 miles) away in Neuquén.

Fiesta Provincial del Asado

Cholila, Chubut. **Location** *see p106.* **Date** late Jan.
The former stomping ground of Butch Cassidy and Sundance plays host to one of Argentina's biggest and best barbecue festivals. Three days are set aside for live music, competitions and, of course, enormous portions of roasted cattle. Vegetarians should give this one a wide berth. One lucky local will earn the right to call herself 'Miss Barbecue' for the remainder of the year.

Fiesta Nacional del Trekking

El Chaltén, Santa Cruz. **Location** *see p151.*
Date 1st wk in Feb.
This well-attended hiker's hoedown in Argentina's trekking capital features competitive events over various distances and terrains. Some of the races are for lone rangers, others for groups and there are also mountain bike scrambles. One eagerly anticipated event is the 'Axeman of the Year' championship in which would-be Paul Bunyans attempt to fillet a tree trunk in as short a time as possible. Lazybones can chill out to live music from local bands.

Semanas Musicales de Frutillar

Frutillar, Región X, Chile. **Location** *see p185.*
Date 1st wk in Feb.
Since 1967 the cream of Chile's classical music fraternity has been decamping to the idyllic shores of Lake Llanquihue for this prestigious week-long festival. Concerts take place in a specially constructed amphitheatre on the lake-shore and have, in recent years, attracted over 400 musicians from Chile and all over the world. If you've ever wondered what it would be like to listen to Beethoven with a volcano in your peripheral vision, this is a must. (For more details check out the website at www. semanasmusicales.cl.)

Fiesta Nacional del Tren a Vapor

El Maitén, Chubut. **Location** *see p109.* **Date** mid Feb.
La Trochita (the Old Patagonian Express) is the star of the show in this celebration of the good old days when steam trains chuffed their way across Patagonia. It's not all nostalgia – competition is fierce to be voted this year's 'Queen of Steam'.

Festival Costumbrista Chilote

Castro, Chiloé. **Location** *see p191.*
Date 3rd weekend in Feb.
Chiloé is proud of its fiestas and this is one of its major celebrations of folk tradition. Villages and towns in Chiloé and along the Southern Highway also host parties of dance, music and food at around this time of year.

National Hop Festival

El Bolsón, Río Negro. **Location** *see p106.*
Date late Feb.
Marking the harvest of beer's most important ingredient, hippie enclave El Bolsón hosts a National Hop Festival. There are competitions for mountain bikers, kayakers and lumberjacks, as well as live music, craft fairs, the nail-biting election of the 'Queen of Hop' and, of course, barrels and barrels of the locally brewed belly wash. Cheers!

Autumn

Catholic saints of all stripes make up the holiday schedule year round and carnival and Easter are major events – in Chiloé, for example, they celebrate **La Quema de Judas** (The Burning of Judas). If you're near the Andes, don't miss the spectacular party thrown in the woods by the greatest hostess of all, mother nature – otoño is where the swathes of green turn red, russet, gold, yellow and orange.

On the Atlantic coast May marks the beginning of the whale breeding season, though your best chance of spotting one of these leviathans in their natural environment is in September or October.

Lluvias de Teatro

Valdivia, Región X, Chile. **Location** *see p176.*
Date mid June.
Theatre fans with a grasp of Spanish should try to catch this excellent theatre festival. Drama is big in this university town and the standard here is at least as high as in Santiago.

Winter

This might not seem like the most obvious time to take a holiday in the south, but it isn't Siberian cold; even in Tierra del Fuego the winds lighten and in mountain resorts snow often comes with days of sunshine. The ski season kicks off across Patagonia on 15 June.

Fiesta Nacional de la Noche más Larga del Año

Ushuaia, Tierra del Fuego. **Location** *see p158.*
Date 21 June.
Gloomy Europeans think of the winter solstice as the year's shortest day: something to be endured rather than enjoyed. Nocturnal Argentinians, on the other hand, prefer to regard it as the year's longest

night and whoop it up accordingly. The place to be is Ushuaia, the world's most austral city, where the entire community takes part in a torch-lit procession, followed by a huge fireworks display and live music from some of the country's top acts.

Festival Folklórico Internacional
Punta Arenas, Chile. **Location** *see p216*.
Date late July.
This is a major winter gathering of Chilean folk and roots bands, taking place over three days in July. For more information on tickets and line-ups, see www.festivalenlapatagonia.cl.

Fiesta Nacional del Montañés
San Martín de los Andes, Neuquén. **Location** *see p87*.
Date mid Aug.
First held in 1981, this is San Martín's top winter festival, involving the whole community in chilly season activities. Tourists will enjoy watching the cross-country skiing races; but for locals the blue-ribbon event is the trunk-chopping challenge.

Ushuaia Sled Dog Race
Ushuaia, Tierra del Fuego. **Location** *see p158*.
Date mid Aug.
Every dog, they say, has his day – but none come bigger than this. In this annual event competitors drive their hounds across the island's frozen valleys, willed on by the crowds. Also at this time of year Ushuaia hosts the Marcha Blanca, a 1,000 strong cross-country skiing challenge. Some people, it seems, will do anything to keep warm.

Fiesta Nacional de la Nieve
San Carlos de Bariloche, Neuquén. **Location** *see p98*.
Date late Aug.
Argentina's most important winter festival is a showcase for Cerro Catedral, its most popular ski resort. The whole of Bariloche comes out to play, lighting up the mountainside in a torchlit procession that casts huge flickering shadows on the pristine pistes. It's quite a sight; and the gravitas of the occasion is diminished only momentarily by the inevitable wacky races, usually waiters in tuxedos and snow shoes scrambling down the hill while trying to keep their trays upright. At midnight there's a fireworks display and the newly chosen 'Queen of Snow' poses for the cameras.

Spring

The snow is thawing, migrant birds are flocking back and foreign tourists starting to trickle in. Blossoms liven up the landscapes and the far south gets its first warm sunshine.

Tetratlón Chapelco
San Martín de los Andes, Neuquén. **Location** *see p87*. **Date** early Sept.
No waiter races, log chopping showdowns or snow queens here – this is a genuinely competitive event and one of the highpoints of the Argentinian

sporting calendar. Just thinking about it is pretty gruelling. Entrants have to complete a circuit of over 60 kilometres (37 miles), the first stretch on skis, the second on mountain bikes, the third in a kayak and then a final sprint to the line on nothing but weary legs. If you're brave or insane enough to consider giving it a whirl, check for details on www.interpatagonia.com (click on 'Agenda').

Eisteddfod
Trelew, Chubut. **Location** *see p131*. **Date** mid Sept.
One of the key events in the year for Patagonia's Welsh-descended communities, Trelew's Eisteddfod adapts traditional Welsh music, dance and poetry. The competition is taken very seriously and has attracted entrants from the motherland in recent years. An international choral festival is held the same month, also in Trelew.

Festival Internacional de Cine
Valdivia, Región X, Chile. **Location** *see p176*.
Date Oct.
Valdivia, one of the south's few cultural meccas, hosts this annual film festival. It showcases arthouse flicks from around the world plus shorts and features produced by the Chilean film industry.

Oktoberfest
Hotel Termas de Puyehue, Región X, Chile.
Location *see p182*. **Date** Oct.
Held, unsurprisingly, each October, Hotel Termas de Puyehue's Oktoberfest celebrates the region's German heritage – or, rather, one important aspect of it. You haven't known pleasure till you've drunk a cold beer while immersed in a hot spring.

Festival favourites **Jazmin de Luna**.

Outdoor Pursuits

National Parks & Trekking

Rivers deep, mountains high – or just a gentle stroll in the woods.

Most people come to Patagonia in search of adventure, nature and the great outdoors. In an area roughly the size of Spain and Portugal combined, with the most stunning landscapes – ancient glaciers, awe-inspiring peaks, a pristine coastline and shimmering lakes – situated in the 31 protected *parques nacionales* (PN), the area has plenty to offer. And although Patagonia's ever-increasing popularity means more people, it has also resulted in an increase in agencies running excursion opportunities, with ice-trekking, climbing and rafting now par for the course for many people.

That these extensive areas of spectacular beauty exist at all is in great part due to the vision of naturalist and explorer Francisco Pascasio Moreno (*see p51* **Environmental warrior**), who donated the land that was to beome Argentina's first national park, **PN Nahuel Huapi**. Shortly afterwards, across the Andes at roughly the same latitude in Chile,

a similar initiative led to the creation of **PN Vicente Pérez Rosales**. Since then, diverse landscapes have been fenced off from non-sustainable agricultural uses and protected from commercial development. Owing to the abundance of recreational opportunities, park authorities in Argentina made the Andes a conservation priority – which is why, up until October 2004, the country didn't have a protected area along its extensive Atlantic coastline. The creation of **PN Monte León** (*see p143*) has helped preserve 616 square kilometres (238 square miles) of Patagonia's beaches, cliffs and marine wildlife (the park's shores are home to a colony of 60,000 Magellanic penguins, and are visited by the southern right whale) as well as important paleontological sites. In addition to the national parks, there are also other protected areas run by provincial conservation authorities and private trusts and foundations. Some natural

Chile's **Parque Torres del Paine** puts most of its rivals in the shade. *See p49.*

locations, such as the **Monumento Nacional Bosque Petrificado** (*see p115*), are national monuments, a step below official national park status. Still others, such as **Península Valdés** (*see p128*), are internationally recognised and protected by UNESCO as World Heritage Sites.

THE NATIONAL PARKS SYSTEMS

Of the two countries' park systems, Chile's **CONAF** (Corporación Nacional Forestal/ www.conaf.cl) is the better funded, though the quality of information and service varies from park to park. Rangers, called *guardaparques* or *guardafauna*, collect entrance fees, up to US$17 in the case of **PN Torres del Paine**, and enforce park rules. They're also responsible for distributing leaflets, usually in Spanish, on flora and fauna, as well as being the best source for information on camping and recreation activities. Increasingly, private concessionaires inside parks run excursions to particular landmarks like glaciers and waterfalls. Their detailed website is an extremely useful guide to Chile's protected areas.

In Argentina, *guardaparques* employed by the equivalent organisation, **Administración de Parques Nacionales** or APN (www. parquesnacionales.gov.ar), perform similar functions with equal measures of good humour and knowledge. But the organisation is less well funded, partly due to the difficulty of charging for entrance at key tourist destinations situated inside park boundaries, such as at the Fitz Roy range. Nonetheless, leaflets are usually available at park entrances.

WHICH PARK AND WHERE?

The most popular trekking centre in Argentina is the Lake District – around Bariloche and San Martín de los Andes in National Parks **Lanín** and **Nahuel Huapi**. Nearby, the drier, more rugged climate of El Bolsón and adjacent **PN Los Alerces**, near Esquel, also attract large numbers of Argentinian hikers. Farther south, the majestic Fitz Roy range near El Chaltén, the country's official trekking capital, in the northern part of **PN Los Glaciares**, is more popular with foreigners.

In Chile, **PN Torres del Paine** is by far the busiest trekking centre. But the volcanic plateaux and dense bamboo and araucaria forests near Puerto Montt and the Chilean Lake District also attracts large numbers of tourists. Experienced hikers and serious mountaineers tend to gravitate towards the relatively unexplored Patagonian ice cap (about the size of the US state of Connecticut); the perennially cloud-covered San Lorenzo, Patagonia's third highest mountain; the icy island outcrops of the Cordillera Darwin off Cape Horn; and the off-trail

Top ten Treks

Río Anay, PN Chiloé
Keep the ocean in sight on this two-to-three-day trek. *See p190.*

Volcán Lanín, PN Lanín
A bird's-eye view of Patagonia. Only for the experienced. *See p85.*

Puyehue volcanic plateau, PN Puyehue
The closest earth-dwellers can get to walking on the moon. *See p180.*

Cerro San Lorenzo, near PN Perito Moreno
Treks around the base of this legendary massif are ideal for 'off the beaten track' trail-blazers.

Lucas Bridges Heritage Trail, Tierra del Fuego
Retrace the footsteps of this early pioneer in a three-day back country hike. *See p161.*

Paine Circuit, PN Torres del Paine
Varied scenery and excellent wildlife spotting – this trek lives up to its international reputation. *See p214.*

Around Fitz Roy, PN Los Glaciares
The peaks that inspired Patagonia Inc are among the region's most breathtaking. *See p152.*

Dientes Circuit, Isla Navarino
Brave the Fuegian winds on Patagonia's toughest and most rewarding hike above the tree line. *See p218.*

Cascadas Trail, Parque Pumalín
Three to four hours through lush woods with a waterfall at the end. Excellent proving ground for novices. *See p197.*

Cochamó to Llanada Grande to Puelo
Hop over the Argentinian–Chilean border in five to seven days.

hikes through the Tierra del Fuego archipelago. For a round-up of the main attraction in each park, *see p53* **National Parks at a glance**.

Patagonia is undoubtedly one of the great trekking capitals of the world, and although the long-kept secret is now out, it's still far

Outdoor Pursuits

less populated than most other major trekking destinations. Except on the more popular trails of a few easily accessed and well-publicised national parks – **Torres del Paine**, **Nahuel Huapi** and **Los Glaciares**, for example – many trails are still surprisingly empty.

WHEN TO GO AND FINDING YOUR WAY

With such remoteness comes responsibility. Getting lost is easy in Patagonia. And if you do, rescue searches are unreliable. For self-reliant trekkers, well versed in the use of a compass and topographical maps, that's probably one of the region's most alluring features. But for the rest of us mere mortals, it's necessary to take certain precautions.

Marked trails, where they exist, are usually inferior to those in the United States and Europe, above the tree line consisting of little more than an isolated, low-lying cairn every few kilometres. Even on better-known trails like the seven-day **Torres del Paine** circuit (which is quickly approaching congestion) it's possible to get lost in areas of dense forest; and since many mountainous areas in Patagonia are still unsettled, you're unlikely to run into anything more civilised than an abandoned shack should you lose your bearings.

Every hiker, therefore, should take along a map, available at shops close to popular trekking destinations. Although the region boasts few native sherpas or porters, the services of English-speaking mountain guides are easy to hire via tourist offices and the better hotels. Otherwise, topographical and satellite maps of varying detail and quality are available in each country's capital from the military mapmaking agencies – for those who know how to use them. In Buenos Aires you need to go to the **Instituto Geográfico Militar** in Buenos Aires (Avenida Cabildo 381, 011 4576 5545, www.igm.gov.ar, open 9am-2pm Mon-Fri); in Santiago visit the **Instituto Geográfico Militar** (Nueva Santa Isabel 1640, 02 460 6825, www.igm.cl, open 9am-6pm Mon-Fri). Mountain clubs, called *clubes de montaña* or Club Andino are found in several towns on both sides of the Andes and sell cheap maps of lesser known trails as well as providing advice to trekkers. One of Latin America's most prestigious mountain clubs is in Patagonia – the **Club Andino Bariloche** (*see p101*).

Patagonia's weather is extremely capricious: four seasons in a single hour is how locals describe the region's abrupt climatic changes. Indeed, it's not uncommon at more southerly latitudes to experience blinding snow squalls in the middle of summer, or mini heat waves in the dead of winter. Take foul weather gear even if the sky is blue when setting out. The region's infamous winds can convert even the sturdiest of tents into kites during storms, especially when above the tree line. But for all that, Patagonia is actually one of the world's most benign environments for hikers. It lies at a lower altitude than the Andean high plains, enjoys a climate free of tropical diseases, and is without dangerous predators. The most bothersome pest is the *tábano*, a blood-sucking, trekker-hating horsefly that takes over the humid forests in January and February and is a serious irritation.

On the upside, pristine mountain streams and glacier-fed rivers provide some of the cleanest freshwater you can drink anywhere in the world. That said, worrywarts might be advised to use iodine tablets or filtering systems when travelling on trails frequented by livestock. Fires at most parks are strictly prohibited owing to the risk of spreading blazes from strong winds.

Most national parks fill up between December and February, when temperatures are highest and the sun sets as late as 11pm. And since it's the busy holiday season, spaces at hotels and *refugios* (mountain refuges), especially in Torres del Paine, fill up quickly. In Argentina, near El Bolsón and Bariloche, otherwise tranquil camp sites enjoy/suffer frequent incursions from Argentinian teenagers set on drinking and playing guitars until the wee hours of the morning.

To avoid disturbances, nature lovers should come at the beginning and end of the summer: November and March/April. The weather remains agreeable, by Patagonian standards, from October through May, though transport and accommodation are significantly harder to come by then. Temperatures drop significantly in winter but winds also abate greatly so weather patterns tend to be more stable. For experienced trekkers with flexible schedules, nothing beats clambering into a pair of snowshoes and heading off into the hills in nobody else's footprints other than those of a few guanacos and pumas.

WHAT TO BRING AND OTHER TIPS

One of Patagonia's best-kept secrets is the wide range of wild trekking that is available across ostensibly private property. Except in a few isolated cases, *estancia* owners allow trekkers to cross their fences provided they respect the general rules of taking no more than photographs and leaving only footprints. Out of courtesy, however, it's always best to ask permission before pitching your tent. For experienced trekkers this is an especially attractive way to see otherwise inaccessible areas in remote Central Patagonia.

Environmental warrior

'Perito' Moreno is a name you can't fail to come into contact with when travelling around Patagonia. Not only does the region's most famous glacier commemorate Moreno, so too do a town and a national park. And for every place named after him there are a handful of places named by him, including Cerro Fitz Roy and Lago Argentino. Just scratching the surface of the history of modern Patagonia reveals his crucial influence; yet Moreno's story is rarely told.

Francisco Pascasio Moreno, born in Buenos Aires in 1852, was fascinated with natural history from childhood, and at the age of 21 undertook his first field trip – to northern Patagonia – where he busied himself collecting fossils and making anthropological studies of the indigenous tribes that had settled there. In 1875 he became the first Argentinian to reach Lago Nahuel Huapi, the first of many achievements to follow in a lifetime of Patagonian exploration.

Moreno's expeditions can hardly be compared with today's – with little infrastructure or government support (forget about guidebooks or coaches), plus poor relations with the natives and frequent illness, these were real Boy's Own-style adventures. Reports tell of Moreno fleeing up the Limay river on a raft after being held prisoner by an indigenous tribe, and on another occasion of being attacked by a puma at the spot where La Leona (a misnomer, since *leona* means lioness) now sits.

But Moreno was more than an explorer: he was also something of a diplomatic champion for Patagonia. He pushed for scientific collaboration internationally, delivering a legendary lecture on Patagonian exploration to the Royal Geographical Society in London in 1899. During Argentina's boundary dispute with Chile he was designated the country's 'Perito' (official national expert), and was rewarded for his patriotic efforts by the gift of an area of land bordering Lago Nahuel Huapi, which he donated back to the government to have it protected by law. And so the national parks system was born. Moreno went on to establish the National Parks Service and the world-renowned Museo de La Plata. Lesser-known achievements include his work helping street kids, his creation of the Argentinian Boy Scouts association, and his untiring efforts to preserve and record the dying cultures of the brutally treated indigenous tribes.

Shortly before Moreno's death in 1919 he wrote: 'I'm sixty-six years old and I don't have a cent!... I, who have given my nation 1,800 leagues and the National Park, where the men of tomorrow will rest to gather new strengths to serve it, will not leave my children a metre of land.' Yet Moreno's legacy lives on in Argentina's national parks system. The privilege of being able to trek across these great tracts of pristine landscape is in large part thanks to this extraordinary man.

Unless you have prior permission from Argentina's National Guard or Chile's Carabineros, avoid any hike that takes you across the two countries' extremely porous border. Cases of foreign hikers being detained for entering or leaving Argentina illegally around Laguna del Desierto, near El Chaltén, have been reported. Increasingly, however, some cross-border hikes – such as that from **Cochamo** in Chile to **Lago Puelo** in Argentina – do now enjoy official approval and require little more than getting your passport stamped at the border outpost. Assuming

navigating skills aren't a problem, the biggest challenge on most of these hikes is finding a reliable means of transport to get to and from the trek. Although farmers are usually willing to give ramblers a lift, there are many isolated places where vehicles don't pass for several weeks at a time; so if you're planning to hitchhike bring abundant supplies or arrange a ride in the nearest town in advance.

Most serious trekkers will bring all their equipment from home. But in case the freedom of the hills suddenly calls, or you just need a replacement buckle for your backpack's belt

It's as if the ice age never ended at Argentina's **Parque Nacional Los Glaciares**. *See p49.*

strap, a number of hunting, fishing and outdoor equipment stores exist near major trekking areas, including Bariloche, Ushuaia, Puerto Natales, Puerto Montt and El Calafate. Some of these stores also rent out equipment, but stocks of kit for hire are limited and usually of inferior quality. If you go on a guided trek arranged through local tourist agencies, or are staying in a high-end lodge or *estancia*, all the required gear will be laid on.

If you need to buy a sleeping bag, jacket or other basic gear, instead of opting for an expensive imported brand, consider buying national products. Several manufacturers make high-quality copies using the same raw materials. Trusted names include: Ansilta, Lippi, Nunatak – the harder-to-find favourite of local mountaineers – and Outside. **Ecrin** (Mendoza 1679, 011 4784 4799) in Buenos Aires and **Patagonia Sport** (Almirante Simpson 77, 02 222 9140) in Santiago are two good shops with specialist equipment and helpful staff.

Standard camping gear – ankle-high waterproof boots, ten-degree sleeping bag, thermal ground mat, rain and cold-weather gear – will suffice for most hikes. Other essentials include a wide-brimmed hat and strong sun protection, to block the UV rays pouring through the hole in the ozone layer. Especially handy when splashing through humid rain forests in Chile, or through peat bogs in Tierra del Fuego, are a pair of gaiters, called *polainas* in Spanish, to protect your lower leg.

For food and other basic supplies, most supermarkets will suffice. The single hardest supply to find in Patagonia is white gas, known as *bencina blanca* in Chile and *solvente* or sometimes *nafta blanca* in Argentina. Hardware stores, followed by supermarkets and pharmacies, are your best bet. Otherwise, for users of MSR-style cookers, the alternative is any high-grade petrol found at service stations. Generic canisters for 'Camping Gaz'-style cookers are harder to find outside major cities.

National Parks at a glance

Argentina has 36 national parks, 11 of which are in Patagonia. In Chile there are 31 national parks – 19 in Patagonia.
This list is organised by province or region.

Argentina

PN Lihué Calel, La Pampa The Hills of Life: easy hikes, cave paintings and mountain fauna are the draw. See p72.

PN Nahuel Huapi, Río Negro & Neuquén The oldest, the biggest and most visited of all, with everything from lakeside hotels and skiing to Andean mountaineering. See p100.

PN Los Arrayanes, Neuquén Take a hike through idyllic arrayán forests. See p95.

PN Lanín, Neuquén The striking 3,790-metre (12,400-foot) volcano is the centrepiece of this majestic wilderness. See p90.

PN Laguna Blanca, Neuquén Birder's paradise of waterlands, where the beautiful black-necked swan breeds. See p79.

PN Los Alerces, Chubut Rivers, swimmable lakes and ancient forests. See p110.

PN Lago Puelo, Chubut Beautiful lake, idyllic camping and thrilling walks. See p107.

PN Los Glaciares, Santa Cruz Six thousand sq km (2,300 sq miles) of stunning glacial drama. Don't miss it. See p150.

PN Perito Moreno, Santa Cruz Not to be confused with the glacier, this little-known gem is bustling with bird life and nature trails. Remote, but pure escapism. See p117.

PN Monte León, Santa Cruz Argentina's newest park, created to protect the coastline and the wildlife that lives there. See p143.

PN Tierra del Fuego Rich in variety – tundra, peat bogs, frozen peaks, dense beech forest. Look out for giant woodpeckers. See p160.

Chile

PN Huerquehue, Araucanía Small, black-sand beaches are unforgettable. The Tres Lagos trail past transparent waters is highly recommended. See p172.

PN Villarrica, Araucanía For the best approach, take the trail to the crater of the volcano – Villarrica's smooth slopes make excellent ski runs. See p172.

PN Nahuelbuta, Araucanía Self-guided, interpretative trails and views of the Pacific are ideal for families. See p169.

PN Tolhuaca, Araucanía The celebrity neighbours of the park are the Tolhuaca thermal baths, though the waterfall, on the Río Malleco, is a beauty. See p169.

PN Conguillío, Araucanía The preferred park of locals for its araucaria trees, decent camping and skiing. See p169.

PN Puyehue, Los Lagos The kingdom of hot springs: Hotel Termas de Puyehue for luxury, Aguas Calientes for lesser budgets – plus Antillanca, one of southern Chile's best ski resorts. See p180.

PN Vicente Pérez Rosales, Los Lagos Don't miss: Salto de Petrohué, elegantly rustic Peulla lodge and majestic Lago Todos los Santos. Nearby is Mount Fuji's twin: Osorno volcano. See p183.

PN Alerce Andino, Los Lagos Pristine, millennial forests and lagunas of every colour – the perfect Kodak moment. Excellent fishing as well. See p195.

PN Chiloé, Los Lagos Rain, rain and more rain – but local traditions, meals of curanto and forests overlooking beaches make getting wet worthwhile. See p190.

PN Hornopirén, Los Lagos Ancient alerce forests, glaciers and volcanoes all are part of this park by the Pacific. See p195.

PN Isla Guamblin, Los Lagos No visitor infrastructure or rangers, just protected marine wildlife and flora.

PN Isla Magdalena, Aisén Magellanic penguins, dense woods and hidden bays.

PN Laguna San Rafael, Aisén Accessible only by plane or boat, the 5,500-metre-long (18,500-feet) San Rafael glacier and evergreen forests are a dream trip. See p207.

PN Queulat, Aisén Detour from the Southern Highway to look over Ventisquero Colgante for icebergs and more icebergs.

PN Bernardo O'Higgins, Magallanes Chile's largest park and the Hielo Continental Sur draws scientists and a few adventurous tourists. Don't miss Pío XI, the southern hemisphere's biggest glacier. See p213.

PN Torres del Paine, Magallanes Southern Chile's most visited PN and a trekking mecca. Breathtaking landscapes and an undeniable sense of adventure. See p214.

PN Pali Aike, Magallanes Volcanic cones, caves and strange lava formations create a lunar landscape.

PN Alberto de Agostini, Magallanes Ice-coated mountains rise from the Beagle Channel; access by boat only. See p219.

PN Cabo de Hornos, Magallanes Circumvent the continent's tip and the sense of achievement is sublime.

Outdoor Pursuits

Adventure & Water Sports

Dive deep, climb high, gallop hard – and then throw yourself off a bridge.

Thanks to its vast range of landscapes and climates, Patagonia has become a nirvana for thrill seekers and adrenaline junkies hell-bent on finding the next rush. Activities on offer are many and varied, with opportunities to jump, dive, pedal and paddle in some of the most unspoilt environs in the world. A number of local companies and excursions are listed in this guide, but there's no shortage of specialists and private agents on-site at each tourist hub, offering information on seasonal activities and local weather conditions. For a general overview of activities, the commercial website www.enjoy-patagonia.org offers plenty of advice.

SADDLE UP OR SOAR AWAY

Many parts of the flattish steppe are ideal cycling environments and though the winds add their own dimension to non-mechanised sports, you can't complain about the hills. Distance cyclists will enjoy the long open stretches and big skies – take water and sun cream. There's also rugged mountain-bike terrain everywhere – national parks like PN Los Alerces in Argentina and PN Villarrica in Chile have official routes and the mud-and-gravel roads through the Seven Lake circuits in both countries are ideal for off-road conditions. You can hire or buy bikes locally, but quality may not be up to your expectations for a major challenge. But as a way to explore the local countryside, bikes hired from local towns will do just fine. Long-distance all-terrain cyclists rate the challenge of Chile's Southern Highway, where the absence of traffic and variety of hills and landscapes make the 1,200-kilometre (746-mile) strip ideal for biking. Bariloche-based www.bikeway.com.ar offers a range of trips and advice for Patagonian pedallers.

Horse riding is extremely popular throughout the cordillera and while all Argentina is horse-mad – you can saddle up and get out into the

There's no better way to see Patagonia than from the saddle.

wilds at just about every *estancia* – southern Chile is also the land of the *baqueano* or Chilean gaucho (or *huaso*). Areas like Cochamo, near Puerto Varas, have 20 times more pathways for horses as they do roads for cars. The bridleways vary from ox-cart tracks and rutted roads round, say, Puyehue to open beaches at Chiloé. In Tierra del Fuego you can ride along the paths used by Ushuaia prison convicts or view shipwrecks from the saddle A number of specialist operators arrange rides on the steppe or in the mountains, from half a day to seven days. The price usually includes camping or nights at *refugios* or hotels.

Those who want to go mechanised can travel as passengers or pilots in four-wheel-drive vehicles – Península Valdés is just one of many great 4x4 centres. Alternatively, there are trial and quad bikes for hire in many towns, particularly those near dune-lined beaches. There is a growing interest in bungee jumping, especially around Cerro Catedral in Bariloche, and sandboarding on the Atlantic coast near the beach resorts. The vast sandbanks and dunes at Puerto Madryn and Puerto Pirámides make it an ideal spot, and fanatical local kids are just waiting for Extreme Sports to jet in and make the scene happen.

For airborne fun, there's paragliding around Bariloche and at Cerro Piltriquitrón, El Bolsón and in Chapelco, San Martín de los Andes; and in Chile, paragliding is offered at Antillanca ski resort. Ballooning excursions are rarer, but there are trips over the Moreno glacier, across the steppe, in La Pampa, and round PN Nahuel Huapi – it's a great way to see Patagonia from the air and needs no expertise. There is hang-gliding and parachuting too, again concentrated round Bariloche. Aeroclubs, operating out of local airports or aerodromes, offer fly-overs of mountainous regions or volcanoes in light aircraft, and – in some cases – arrange gliding and parachuting activities.

Many specialist, higher-risk activities are done by groups of experienced non-tourist visitors. Climbing the pinnacles at Fitz Roy or caving in Antarctica are not to be undertaken lightly, though both Chile and Argentina have clubs of Andinists and speleological associations. If you're an expert yourself, and can speak some Spanish, you should be able to arrange to join an expedition.

Patagonia's volcanoes, while requiring general fitness, are regularly climbed by guided groups and descent is often by toboggan, as at Volcán Lanin. Extreme winter sports are options at all the larger ski resorts – from wild off-piste adventures to heli-skiing for the pros. Canyoning is big around Lago Todos Los Santos, Chile and in El Bolsón's Río Azul.

Canopying has also grown in popularity, primarily at Cerro Lopez, Bariloche. Vertigo sufferers can forget it, but if heights are no problem, there's at least one company that caters specifically to tree enthusiasts. Contact **Canopy Adventure Tour** (02944 15 607191, www.canopybariloche.com).

THE LIFE AQUATIC

Chilean and Argentinian Patagonia boast thousands of kilometres of coastline, dotted with beaches, coves and inlets, fjords, rocky cliffs and islands – many ideal for just about any water sport you can think of (though some are protected marine wildlife reserves and not for sports). The network of rivers and lakes inland, nuzzled up against both sides of the Andes, can satisfy most water-sport enthusiasts. The only thing that may put you off taking a dip are the water temperatures, which fluctuate between 0ºC and 20ºC (32ºF and 68ºF). Therefore many activities keep you either inside a kayak or canoe or on top of a board, and swimming is best done in the heated pools of the region's best hotels and cabins (most open to non-residents for a charge).

On the Atlantic coast, the main water-sport centres are in Chubut province. Around the resort of **Las Grutas** (*see p123*), the waters are clear and bearably warm, and thus excellent for scuba diving, water-skiing and, with enough swell, a little surfing. Further down the coast, **Puerto Madryn** (*see p124*) is the main scuba centre, and more of a year-round destination. You can share your dive with the local marine life, though as this is sometimes frowned upon it's a good idea to stick with a reputable eco-tourism company. To dive with compressed air in Chile or Argentina you'll need to take your internationally recognised paperwork, if you have done courses; some companies cater for absolute beginners, but only to depths of 10 metres (33 feet). The water gets chillier in these parts, but breezes pick up, creating ideal windsurfing and sailing conditions. Surfers can catch a wave here, and as far south as Playa Unión, also a mecca for windsurfing.

Water activities in Chile are inland: in the lakes region, around Lagos Lanalhue, Lleu Lleu, and at the Icalma Lagoon. Further south, Villarrica, Caburga, vast Llanquihue and gusty Todos los Santos lakes are established favourites with windsurfers.

On the Argentinian side of the Andes, every aquatic sport is offered on or around Lago Nahuel Huapi, including scuba diving to see rocky moraines sculpted by the elements, and it's also another good windsurf spot. Lago Traful makes an attractive dive location to see the Bosque Sumergido (submerged forest),

Outdoor Pursuits

30 metres (98.5 feet) under the surface. These are trees that have been buried underwater since a major seismic movement ditched a chunk of cypress-covered land into the lake. Even eerier, but fascinating, is diving to see shipwrecks off the coast. The major ship graveyard is around Cape Horn, where conditions make pleasure diving impossible, but there are other zones where you can arrange to see the ghostly remains from centuries of maritime misadventure: Puerto Madryn, Puerto Deseado and even off the Falkland Islands (Islas Malvinas); or in Chile around Punta Arenas and off Valdivia and Chiloé, where shellfish divers are at work all year round.

With a backbone like the Andes running down Patagonia, the rivers that spill off the high peaks are world class for white-water enthusiasts, and superb for rafting. Preferred rivers in Chile are Liucura, Trancura and Petrohue in the Lake District; further south are the Futaleufú and Baker, which bisect the Carreterra Austral (Southern Highway) and which, since the Biobío became the scene of a dam-building controversy, are increasingly viewed as the top high-grade challenges. Rios Aluminé and Manso in Argentina are also key destinations for rafters. Information and possible itineraries are available at www. patagoniarafting.com.

For those looking for a more laid-back option, kayaking or canoeing is a great way to see some of Patagonia's most beautiful areas. In Argentina the lakes, lagoons and rivers around El Bolsón and Bariloche are popular, and in areas along the coast, such as Playa Costanera near Comodoro Rivadavia, you can rent out kayaks for exploring coves and bays. Rios Ruca Choroi and Aluminé are perfect for those after stronger rapids. The longest kayak regatta in the world takes place each January in Argentina, with paddlers covering 500 kilometres (311 miles) in stages from Neuquén to Viedma down the Rio Negro.

Opposite Chiloé are the fjords and rivers of the Palena province, home to Parque Pumalín and all manner of waterways. Sea kayaks are the only way to explore the jagged edges of this section of the mainland as cliff walls are sheer and canals too narrow for excursion boats. This is a a non-expert activity; basic training is provided.

AROUND THE HORN

Sailing enthusiasts can follow in the wake of early voyagers battling storms, currents and icebergs though the tricky waterways at the tip of the continent. Charter yachts and cruises voyage into waterways around the islands off Tierra del Fuego, to Cape Horn or beyond to the South Atlantic islands or Antarctica. They can be taken from Ushuaia in Argentina, or Punta Arenas or Puerto Williams in Chile. Most tours begin in October and continue through May.

Landlubbers who like the idea if not the wind and wetness of seafaring adventures, can take lake excursions, such as those on Lago Argentino and Lago Viedma. Gentler ocean trips are available from Puerto Madryn, Puerto Deseado and Ushuaia. From the latter you can head out into the Beagle Channel. From Puerto Natales in Chile, boats go north; from Puerto Montt they head south. One of the most popular trips is to the Laguna San Rafael, an isolated lake located deep in the heart of the glacier-riven canals.

PROTECTION AND PRECAUTION

Chile and Argentina have good safety records, but you should select activities and locations according to your skill. You don't need to bring kit – only swimwear for a dip in summer – as equipment can be hired or will be provided by organising agencies. For information on Patagonia's other water-based activity, fishing, *see pp57-59*.

Fishing & Hunting

It's about communing with nature – and then trying to hoick it out of the water.

Patagonia is, among other things, God's gift to the fly-fishing fraternity, and one of the most beautiful and solitary places on earth to cast a line. While veteran fishermen jump continents to get a piece of the action, there are a number of opportunities for the rookie angler, though always dependent on budget and location. Fly-fishing (*pesca con mosca*) is the big story here, but spinning (*lanzamiento*) and trolling (*arrastre*) are also popular in some parts.

There are several hallowed fishing spots in Patagonia. In Argentina, one of the most fought-over is where Lago Huechulafquen spills out to form Rio Chimehuin, sparkling with trout. Famous anglers have been coming here for many years – Winston Churchill to name but one. Junín de los Andes is the official 'trout capital' of Argentina (though towns like Aluminé and Esquel would beg to differ), while the world's shortest river – Rio Correntoso, near Villa La Angostura – is packed with huge trout in November and December. Down in Tierra del Fuego, Rio Grande is world-class. Coihaique is a

fishing nirvana in Chile's Southern Highway section – people come from all over to fish the Rios Simpson, Cochrane and Pollux – as well as the mighty Rio Baker. In Chile alone there are around 5,000 rivers, most of these short, gravel bottomed, ultra-clean, well oxygenated and rich in nutrients.

Choosing where to fish is more than a matter of personal taste – in the northern rivers, you'll have woodlands, towns and services nearby, slightly warmer weather during the fishing season but more rain; south is cooler and windier, but often wilder and more tranquil. If you're planning on a long (three weeks or more) trip or to come to Patagonia more than once, the widest experience is to be gained by spending a week in one of the Lake Districts, a week near Coihaique in Chile and a week in the south of Santa Cruz, Argentina or on Tierra del Fuego.

The fish you're most likely to hear about are the salmoides – trout (*trucha*) and salmon (*salmón*) – introduced to the region from the 1900s onwards. Of the former, you can fish

Arroyo Verde, dubbed the best fishing lodge in the world. *See p105.*

brook, brown and rainbow trout, often challenging fish of five to seven kilogrammes (11 to 15.4 pounds), and even bigger if you're talking steelheads and sea-run trout. A 76-centimetre (30-inch) rainbow trout, while rare elsewhere in the world, is highly possible in Chile, and the big browns compare well with New Zealand – though in Patagonia there's the added bonus of there being a lot more fish per river and far fewer fishermen. With only a few thousand fisher-tourists in either country per year, it's quite likely you'll fish a river unvisited for years by fellow sportsmen.

You can fish for Pacific salmon – chinook and coho varieties – and Atlantic salmon too. While there are not the numbers you might find in migrations in the northern hemisphere, the salmon are big and hooking them a greater challenge than in, say, Alaska. Chinooks range from ten to 25 kilogrammes (22 to 55 pounds), the Atlantics five to 12 kilogrammes (11 to 26.4 pounds) and the cohos between three and seven kilogrammes (6.6 and 15.4 pounds).

Sea fishing is not as well developed as the river and lake scene in Patagonia, though the Pacific Ocean is good for sea bass, corvina and sole (with huaiquil in Chile's saltwater Lago Budi and the Atlantic great for fighting bull sharks, black drum and Brazilian sand perch – Puerto Deseado is popular for the big 'uns.

You won't find huge numbers of freshwater native species, but among them are the perca, comparable to the North American small mouth bass or perch, and the Patagonian pejerrey. The region is also home to puye – native fish that play an important part in the food chain of trout. Other trout meals are the sculpins, which live in fast-water streams. The native species are not as aggressive as trout. In Argentina, there is some fishing for Patagonian silver side and the toothsome trahira.

PRACTICALITIES AND LODGING

Whether you want to book a trip once in the region, or from overseas, sorting out a fishing trip is as easy as shooting trout in a barrel. Most serious sports anglers choose a lodge, where the tackle is good and the advice expert. For between US$1,500 and a hefty US$4,500 a week, you can expect a comfortable cabin or large room, a bilingual guide, equipment if you need it, transfers from the airport and all your food. The standard varies, of course, but in general it's above what a normal fishing fan

The one that didn't get away...

would expect – however, don't assume that every extra US$100 will get you that amount of extra pleasure or service.

Numerous private guides operate in main fishing destinations too – most speak some English – and tourist offices have a list of all recognised, licensed guides in the area. Expect to pay US$100-$200 per day's fishing with such a guide, with transport, equipment and lunch included. Fishing equipment shops also work with a number of experienced local guides.

A lot of Chileans fish without these luxuries and low-budget travellers who fancy a spot of angling should ask at local tourist offices for contacts, rivers and even equipment hire. Independent angling can cost from as little as US$60 a day. Both Argentina and Chile require anglers to obtain licences – provided by the lodge or tour operator for package trips and costing about US$10 in both countries if you are doing it independently. In Chile, the town halls (*municipalidades*) issue licences, and in Argentina you must contact the **Asociación Argentina de Pesca con Mosca** (*see below*).

There's largely a catch-and-release policy in operation in most areas – the limit for catching trout and salmon you might eat or mount is three per day or 15 kilogrammes (33.1 pounds), whichever comes first. The trout/salmon fishing season runs from November to May.

CONTACTS

On the website of Chile's **Servicio Nacional de Pesca** (www.sernapesca.cl) under 'Areas de interés', 'Pesca deportiva', then 'Licensias' are the places you can get a fishing licence and advice. In Buenos Aires consult the **Asociación Argentina de Pesca con Mosca** (Lerma 452, 011 4773 0821, www.aapm.org.ar). For tackle, **Fly Shop** (Avenida Manquehue Norte 1260, Santiago 02 201 8571) or **Buenos Aires Anglers** (Eight Floor, Office 76, MT de Alvear 624, 011 4313 1865) are reputable suppliers in the capitals. For speciality fishing holidays, check the internet – www.argentinachilefly fishing.com, www.flyfishing.com.ar and www.nervouswaters.com are just several of a number of well-organised sites. Local excursion companies, including most named in this book, can organise fishing with experienced guides.

HUNTING

Putting aside the ethical debates around hunting, it's a fact that Patagonia has become one of the ultimate sporting destinations. Whatever you're looking to bag, the southern wilds will satisfy even the most demanding of hunters.

A number of species are strictly off-limits, and those of a trigger-happy disposition can expect to receive a heavy fine for blowing away

Time flies when you're fishing *con mosca*.

an endangered species. However, with an experienced guide and a bit of self-control, such problems are easily avoided.

Most hunting is organised within private *estancias* and ranches, but with the correct papers and a good guide, you can roam the designated areas of a few national parks, most notably Parque Nacional Lanín. Big-game hunting, known here as *caza mayor*, principally targets red deer (*ciervo colorado*), wild boar (*jabalí*), as well as the impressive but problematic guanaco and puma. In some areas hunters are permitted to kill wild bulls.

In Argentinian Patagonia, the wildest hunting takes place in the provinces of La Pampa and Rio Negra, as well as at an array of specialist hunting lodges (*coto de caza*). In Chile, hunting is actively promoted in the Aisén region, with the best opportunities to be found in the vicinity of Pucón.

Hunting seasons vary according to region and prey, but the period between March and October is particularly good. Gun regulations and licensing are complex; there are differences between what is permitted in Chile and in Argentina. Therefore, trips are best organised through specialist travel firms or directly through an *estancia*, though more general guidance is readily available – www.cincorios. com offers tailor-made fishing and hunting trips, while www.enjoy-patagonia.org gives advice on lodging, regions and seasons.

Golf

Head still, hit through the ball – and don't be put off by the volcano.

Forget northern hemisphere pretensions: golfing in Patagonia is refreshingly laid-back, and paisley attire is mercifully kept to a minimum. While there's no shortage of run-of-the-mill nine-holers, there are only a handful of high-quality larger courses. However, bounded as they are by snow-capped mountains and emerald lakes, these are among the most spectacular to be found anywhere in the world. Sure, the odd imperfect green or neglected tee may disappoint the connoisseur, but for most a round beneath the vast Patagonian skies is an unrivalled experience. Strong winds and erratic weather conditions in some areas may test your skills and patience, but it's a small price to pay.

Argentina's first golf clubs were introduced by Henry Smith in 1879. The Scotsman's arrival was met with a mixture of confusion and concern, many mistaking his clubs for lethal weapons. Slowly, however, English railroad workers joined in, and in 1890 the Rivadavia Golf Club was created in Buenos Aires. These days Argentina boasts over 190 clubs and some of the world's top players; Angel Cabrera and his close friend, Eduardo 'El Gato' Romero are regular winners on the PGA tour. And who can forget Roberto 'Spaghetti' de Vicenzo, winner of 230 tournaments but most remembered for mis-scoring his card in the US Masters and losing the tournament by a shot.

In Chile, the scene has developed more sedately but is, nonetheless, on the up. With few past or present golfers of note, hopes rest on the shoulders of Mark Tullo and Francisco Cerda, the top rankers in the country. Some places are much lower key than others. On the island of Chiloé, some locals play golf on the Pacific beaches. They hollow out holes, thrust in sticks and pitch their shots into the winds. It sounds like none of it's taken too seriously, but one of their best players, a Parkinson's sufferer who has only one arm, makes it round the course on a single-figure handicap.

CHOOSING A COURSE

Proportionally speaking, Argentinian Patagonia has fewer golf clubs than the rest of the country but several are absolute musts. Tucked up by the side of the Andes, the palatial **Llao Llao Hotel & Resort Golf Club**

Only the scores are below par at **Llao Llao Hotel & Resort Golf Club**.

(Avenida Bustillo, km 25, Bariloche, 02944 448530) outside Bariloche is a beauty. The 18 holes lie under the hillock on which the hotel was built, with undulating fairways that disappear into backdrops of lakes and rocky forests. Rash players will enjoy the tenth and the do-or-die last: a crunching 200 yard par three, over the jaws of the lake and up on to an elevated green. On a clear day, the glare is as hazardous as the bunkers, so pack a visor.

Once you've conquered Llao Llao, drive your buggy up the road to **Arelauquen Golf & Country Club** (Ruta 82, frente al Lago Gutierrez, 02944 467552, www.arelauquen.com). With an 18-hole course designed by Vicente 'Chino' Fernández and endorsed by, among others, Craig 'The Walrus' Stadler, your only potential headache will be settling on a suitably picturesque nickname.

Close by and in a similar league, the 18-hole **Chapelco Golf and Resort** (Ruta 23, Loma Atravesada de Taylor, San Martin de Los Andes, 02972 421785) is first class. Co-designed by the legendary Jack 'The Golden Bear' Nicklaus and his son, Jack Nicklaus II, it's a beautifully crafted course, well equipped and a strong contender for best in the country.

Meanwhile, in the harsh but gorgeous lands of Tierra de Fuego, **Golf Club Ushuaia** (Valle del Rio Pipo, 02901 430472) is a nine-hole course tailor-made for the squat, punchy player. With relentless winds and tiny greens, it can provide the ultimate test. In mid-summer – companions permitting – you can play from 6am to 11pm.

If the starting point for your travels is the province of Neuquén, the finest of the four courses is 18-hole **El Rincón Club de Campo** (Paraje Rincón de Emilio, 0299 4434066), ten minutes from the capital. At 5,701 yards, it's no Whistling Straits, but set along the borders of the sparkling Río Neuquén, it offers a stiff challenge with holes 13-16 accompanied by five large lagoons. Elsewhere, close to the capital of La Pampa province, is the local **Jockey Club de Santa Rosa** (Dr Mariano Castex 758, 02954 421328). The original nine holes are slightly monotonous and, like the surrounding land, flat. The second nine, however, are a festival of hillocks and rapid greens and include a demanding tenth that requires guile or a daisy-cutter to pass an overhanging caldén tree.

On the whole, the Chileans keep their courses for members only. A few, however, open their fairways to the public. Founded by the English in 1917, the **Club Naval de Campo Río de los Ciervos** in Punta Arenas – commonly known as the Magallanes Golf Club (Camino Sur, 5.5km Sur, 061 266 801) – is a nine-hole course set among ancient lenga trees that peers down on to the Magellan Strait. Although the land and views are spectacular, the conditions can be quite wintery, so after the game, make sure to wrap your fingers around a whisky on the 19th.

Two courses in the Lake District are also worth the trip. **The Bahía Coique Golf Club** (Playa Coique, Futrono, 063 481264) on the banks of a large lagoon is an attractive parkland nine-holer that forms part of a large complex. **Club de Campo Osorno** (Ruta 215, km 2.5, Osorno, 064 237637) is a lively, hilly 18-hole course that the owner claims is the best in Patagonia. Further north, in Valdivia, on the banks of the River Calle Calle is the enjoyable **Club Santa Elvira** (Camino Santa Elvira, Valdivia, 063 216150). However, as with all Patagonian courses, the winds here can whip up, turning a bad day into a club-breaking one. Lessons are on offer at reasonable rates. If not, you can always take solace in the lush beauty of this part of the Pacific coast. In winter the course can get waterlogged, so call up to check if it's open. Snow can cause a problem in winter at all courses and those in Tierra del Fuego open in summer only.

TIPS BEFORE TEEING OFF

Free of the snooty protocol of Anglo-Saxon golf, local clubs are only too pleased to help out visiting golfers. Attitudes towards handicaps and dress codes are equally casual, though golf shoes are often obligatory.

In Chile, expect to pay between US$10 and US$35 per day's play. Green fees and caddies are cheap, especially in Argentina where the cost of a round varies from US$2 to US$15, depending on the course, day and season. Information for courses in both countries is available at **www.interpatagonia.com/golf** – though in Spanish, it's easy to find photos and to get some idea of what to expect. If you just fancy a game on a whim, most of the pro shops hire out clubs – though don't expect spanking new Pings.

Argentina is better geared to specialist golfing holidays, with a number of local and international tour operators catering to those who want to swing their clubs. Check out the packages offered by English-speaking local specialist **Patagonia Golf** (www.patagonia golf.com.ar), which arranges extensions for sightseeing or other activities. United States operator **Golf Destinations** (www.golf destinationsonline.com) organises trips around the world, including ones to courses in Argentina, rated as the 'undiscovered golf destination of the year'. The Argentinian government's website www.turismo.gov.ar also has golf course details (look under 'Attractions', then 'Active tourism'). For general information on golf in Chile, take a look at the Golf Federation's official site, www.chilegolf.cl.

Ranching

Work off those big city blues on one of Patagonia's historic *estancias*.

Fancy your own *estancia* in Patagonia? Unless you're a jetsetter like Ted Turner or Luciano Benetton, two of the region's biggest celebrity ranchers, such indulgences are probably off limits. But even if you can't own your own piece of paradise, it's still possible to play in one, all the while breathing in the fresh prairie air, traditions and down-home hospitality the region's sheep farms are famous for.

The genesis of most *estancias* was the early 20th-century sheep bonanza (further north, *estancias* were dedicated to cattle) that almost overnight transformed empty Patagonia into an wool-providing outpost for the rest of the world. In an effort to expand its authority over the then largely lawless south, the Argentinian, and to a lesser degree Chilean, governments gave away to immigrants mammoth parcels of land on which to graze sheep. In selecting who would benefit from the land grab, the threshold was low. Ex-cons, political agitators, missionaries, gold seekers – homesteading in such a desolate part of the world wasn't yet the exclusive privilege of the filthy rich. Equally diverse were the nationalities and religions represented.

Despite the bright-sounding names the pioneers chose for their farms – El Progreso, La Esperanza, El Porvenir (Progress, Hope and Future) – the dry Patagonian steppe was never really suited for such an abundance of hoofed habitants. Beginning in the late 1950s, the farming lifestyle began to languish, to the point that today in Santa Cruz province, once Patagonia's largest sheep farming district, more than half its 1,200 ranches have been abandoned. In an effort to stem the decline, many ranch owners have woken up to the economic potential of catering to tourists.

An *estancia* makes the ideal hideaway for the globally stressed, and given the surfeit of tourists who've flooded Argentina since its 2002 devaluation, one of the last places to appreciate Patagonia at its Big Sky-best. But when visiting an *estancia*, bear in mind that no two are alike – do your research ahead of time to assure you find a farm that caters to your interests. As Patagonia's tourism industry grows, the lines between family-run farm, kitsch dude ranch and spa-like rural lodge are blurring. Generally, though, given the ruggedness of rural life here,

Watch a sheep get a short back and sides at a working *estancia*.

accommodations tend to be more basic than the French-style châteaux and Spanish-colonial estates that dominate Argentina's vast Pampas plains farther north.

But in such simplicity lies their charm. For the savvy traveller, the opportunity to log off from the internet and plug in to a wild natural setting ends up being the peak experience of their Patagonia holiday. The range of activities on offer is as diverse as the landscapes, but most ranches offer guided horseback riding and trekking; others, particularly in Tierra del Fuego, specialise in fishing. Most will also shepherd tourists to nearby natural attractions. All farms offer full board, which usually includes at least one meal of Patagonian *cordero al asador* – lamb cooked over an open fire.

As a general rule, the farther you get off the main tourist circuit and deeper into the tableland, the more authentic an *estancia* experience you'll have – and at a cheaper price to boot. At such places the biggest attraction is the *estancia* itself and the chance to bask in the natural hospitality that's an ingrained part of the Patagonian way of life. For would-be Bruce Chatwin, nothing gets the adrenaline going like perusing the family heirlooms scattered around the corrugated iron *casco*, or main house, which was the self-reliant settlers' only defence against their hostile environs. One ranch where you'll hear a lot about how things used to be (for better or worse) is the superb **Estancia Telken** (*see p114*).

Among the working ranches still run by the original families, but also offering comfortable lodging, is **Estancia Viamonte** (*see p158*), near Río Grande, which looks almost the same as it did when founded by pioneer Lucas Bridges a century ago. The English ranch's living room, made famous in a photograph Bruce Chatwin took to illustrate the first edition of *In Patagonia*, is untouched.

A more modern alternative is **Estancia Monte Dinero** (*see p156*), along the waters of the Magellan Strait near Río Gallegos, where gauchos tend the farm's 20,000 sheep while riding off-road motorcycles, with GoreTex jackets and walkie-talkies replacing their traditional poncho and extra-long *facón* knives. It's a fascinating dynamic; the pull of tradition against the pull of progress.

RURAL RESERVATIONS
The word is getting out about Patagonia's *estancias*, and since many ranches have only two or three guest rooms, it is recommended you make reservations at least three months in advance. Expect to spend a minimum of US$70 a night; this can rise in ranches close to major destinations or population centres.

The best *Estancias*

For a romantic rendezvous
Alta Vista (*p149*), Peuma Hue (*p103*).

For a horsy hiatus
Huechahue (*p87*), Nibepo Aike (*p149*).

For pretend pioneers
Cabo San Pablo (*p157*), Menelik (*p119*).

For home-grown hospitality
Telken (*p114*), El Pedral (*p125*).

For going gaucho
Monte Dinero (*p156*), Viamonte (*p158*).

For avid anglers
Tipiliuke (*p87*), Arroyo Verde (*p105*).

Most travel agencies recommended in the **Directory** chapter of this guidebook (*see p230*) can make reservations, usually charging a commission, at a select number of the more commercial establishments. There are also a few specialised booking agents; among the best is **Estancias Travel** (011 4748 4440, www.estanciastravel.com).

By far the most helpful and dependable booking agent, covering the gamut of options from barnyard basic to beef baron-only lodges, is **Estancias de Santa Cruz, Patagonia** (In Buenos Aires, Office 3A, Maipú 864, 011 5237 4043, www.estanciasdesantacruz.com), which began as the official representative of the ranches of Santa Cruz province, but now also promotes farms in Chubut and Tierra del Fuego. They work in close liaison with over 40 of the best establishments, never charging commission and offering unbiased and expert advice on everything from an overnight stay to a two-week, guided *estancia* tour. If you're already in El Calafate or El Chaltén, **Lago San Martín** (02902 492858 or 02962 493045), run by Rolando Leserovich, can also organise visits to any *estancia* in Santa Cruz.

Although the welcoming of drop-in guests was the norm for decades at Patagonia's *estancias*, most of them now require advance booking. However, it's a well-kept secret that some ranches accept campers.

Chile doesn't heavily promote holidaying at its *estancias*, but many local tour operators conduct visits to working farms in the Deep South and in the Southern Highway region and horse-riding trips often take in an *estancia* or two. Check out **www.saboresdeaysen.cl** for more holiday ideas.

Outdoor Pursuits

Skiing

There's no business like snow business.

Skier or boarder, novice or veteran, the cold slopes of Patagonia are fast becoming hotspots for snow fiends. Whether carving through alpine forest or exploring the endless back country, there's no shortage of variety and the Andean views are among the best in Latin America.

Introduced to the region in the 1930s, recreational skiing in Argentina was initially confined to Bariloche, but the sport spread quickly south to Punta Arenas in Chile. Ski Club Chile was the first on the map, founded in 1931, while Bariloche's Club Andino was hot on its heels. Despite such history, smaller centres have been relatively slow to mature, but the ever-increasing popularity of the region and its subsequent wealth has enabled the majority of resorts to keep well up to date. Most ski centres now offer a range of alternative activities, including tobogganing, sled-dog rides, 'snowshoe walking' and skiidooing.

SERVICES FOR SNOW HOUNDS

All centres offer equipment for skiers and snowboarders, and most have ski schools – if not, local agencies can organise guides or instructors. More developed resorts have ski and souvenir shops, lockers and childcare. Restaurants are fairly canteen-like, with notable exceptions such as **La Cueva** (*see p102*) or the excellent **Caras Lounge** (Avenida Bustillo km 7966, 02944 525251), both in Bariloche. Resort accommodation is usually pretty straightforward but a number of new and very comfortable lodgings have recently been developed. **Paralelo 41** (02944 460293, www.paralelo41.com) in Bariloche is one of just a few high-end hostels catering to young snowboarders and skiers. Nearby towns have all the services you need. The best resorts are also included in cool, high-end tours such as those offered by **PowderQuest Ski** (www.powderquest.com) or BA-based Andes **Ski Tours** (www.andesskitours.com).

Not many activities in Latin America coincide with the crack of dawn and the slopes are no exception. Locals tend to take a leisurely breakfast (usually following a late night) and rarely hit the pistes before 10am. Skiing against a backdrop of volcanoes, glaciers and even ocean, peering down upon cobalt lakes and rivers, Patagonian snow sports are certainly unbeatable in terms of scenic beauty.

Skiing (here at **Cerro Castor**; *see p162*) and boarding are big in the Andes.

In keeping with world trends, skiing in the Andes also has its high quota of fashion content. Celebrities flock to the slopes of the big resorts, and the season, with all its attendant gossip, is covered slavishly in the national glossies.

RESORT ROUND-UP

Three-quarters of ski resorts in Patagonia are in Argentina. Services, activities and prices change each season; resort websites have current information on conditions, ski hire, passes and special offers. See www.andesweb.com and www.skipatagonia.com for overviews and information. Also worth a look is www.inter patagonia.com, which lists facilities in each centre. Additional descriptions are in this guide.

There are three major resorts in the Argentinian Lake District. **Cerro Catedral** (www.catedralaltapatagonia.com) is the most developed and popular, with 53 slopes, 28 lifts and a snowboard park. International recognition came with its selection as South America's 'Leading Mountain Resorts of the World' representative. Come August, Bariloche plays host to the National Snow Festival, heralding a week of non-stop competitions and firework displays. Near San Martín de los Andes, **Chapelco** (www.chapelco.com.ar) is another well-serviced, large (31 pistes) mountain resort; like Catedral it's a popular choice. It's a great centre for kids, even better for après ski, and one of the best for snowboarders. (For the more advanced, heli-skiing is also available.) The third, **Cerro Bayo** (www.cerrobayoweb.com), close to Villa La Angostura, is popular with young people. It has 17 kilometres (11 miles) of marked runs, principally suitable for intermediate or advanced skiers, and huge expanses of off-piste.

In northern Neuquén, there are two centres. **Caviahue** (www.caviahue-copahue.com.ar/caviahue/centrodeesqui) is a great resort with spectacular back country. The altitude of its base, at 1,650 metres (5,413 feet) above sea level, allows for five months of skiing. Tiny **Batea Mahuida** (just one ski lift) is unique. Created and run by the Puel Mapuche community, it's cheaper and a totally different experience. They have a small amount of gear (and snowshoes) to rent and a couple of snowmobiles.

Another off-the-main-drag centre is little **Perito Moreno**, accessible from El Bolsón. It's just starting to be developed for boarders and skiers but is unlikely to provide much of a challenge for the more proficient. Nearby, close to PN Los Alerces and Esquel, the 24 (and rising) slopes of **La Hoya** (www.camlahoya.com.ar) are ideal for beginners and intermediates, and able snowboarders will be impressed by the off-piste options. Facilities are family-oriented.

Down in Tierra del Fuego, **Cerro Castor**, outside Ushuaia, trades heavily on its 'southernmost' status: these are the most austral slopes in the world. Built in 1999, it's equipped with the latest speedy chair lifts, and climatic conditions produce excellent powder and an extended season from May to October.

Home to the longest run in South America (Las Tres Marías), ski and thermal springs centre **Chillán** is Chile's largest resort, with 28 pistes, all of them in excellent shape. Even closer to Santiago is **Portillo** (www.ski portillo.com), a popular training ground for the world's top ski teams. It may not be the largest resort (17 pistes and 12 lifts), but the quality of skiing and the handsome scenery makes it one of Latin America's top draws.

In the Chilean Lake District, two well-developed, stunningly located resorts cater for all level of skier. **Centro de Ski Pucón** (www.pucon.com) has nine lifts and 22 pistes descending Volcán Villarrica. Views to the lakes from the top of **Antillanca** (www.chilean ski.com/eng/antillanca/info.htm), near the hot-springs resort at Puyehue, on Volcán Casablanca, make it one of the finest for snapping photos. It has 13 pistes, across a 38-kilometre (24-mile) skiable area. Smaller centres also use the face of volcanoes: **Centro de Ski Las Araucarias** has pistes descending Volcán Llaima, and **Centro de Ski Villarrica** (www.villarrica.cl) has nine lifts up the volcano from which it takes its name. Finally, from the one lift up **Cerro Mirador**, near Punta Arenas, there are 20 runs down. It's good for advanced skiers; through the trees lining the slopes you can watch the ocean roll in below.

PISTE PRACTICALITIES

If you find yourself minus the essentials, most gear can be rented or bought locally. Safety standards are high, but make sure you're covered for winter sports on your insurance. Seasons vary from resort to resort; as a rule low season begins mid June and runs to early July. Early July to the end of August is high season, during school winter holidays. From the end of August low-season prices apply and in some areas, skiing is still possible as late as October.

Resorts operate independently – there are no multi-centre passes. The range of prices is broad, but expect to pay US$7-$30 per day's ski pass, with discounts for weekly passes and children. With Argentina still great value for foreigners, Chileans and Brazilians flock across their respective borders, ensuring that top resorts are packed during peak season. If you plan to ski for a week, book well in advance; but if you just fancy a couple of runs, most resorts will be able to accommodate you.

Argentinian Patagonia

IN THE MOST INCREDIBLE PLACES OF PATAGONIA,
THERE IS A LODGE OF BURCO ADVENTURE WAITING FOR YOU.

Burco Adventure is a unique opportunity. A network of exclusive integrated lodges, providing you with maximum comfort and the best services. a variety of activities to live intensely the direct contact with nature: horseback riding, trekking, fly fishing, helifishing, rafting, heliskiing, and adventure. the possibility of enjoying one lodge or several of our lodges. Traveling through the many different and spectacular landscapes between each lodge by boat, land or air in our private vehicles will be a pleasurable part of your experience.
The adventure of traveling begins here, in the last unexplored corners and ends exactly where you wish it.

BURCO
Adventure

Getting Started

Go south – and then go south again.

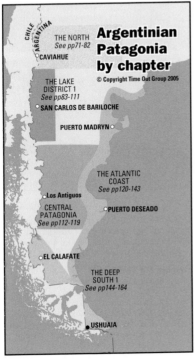

Argentinian Patagonia by chapter

THE NORTH
See pp71-82

CAVIAHUE

THE LAKE DISTRICT 1
See pp83-111

© Copyright Time Out Group 2005

SAN CARLOS DE BARILOCHE

PUERTO MADRYN

THE ATLANTIC COAST
See pp120-143

Los Antiguos

CENTRAL PATAGONIA
See pp112-119

PUERTO DESEADO

EL CALAFATE

THE DEEP SOUTH 1
See pp144-164

USHUAIA

CHILE / ARGENTINA

It will take more than a tourism boom to fill Argentinian Patagonia, one of the world's great empty regions. Normally thought of as the vast triangle measuring over three-quarters of a million square kilometres (over a quarter of a million square miles) south of the Rio Colorado, strictly speaking it comprises the six provinces of La Pampa, Neuquén, Rio Negro, Chubut, Santa Cruz and Tierra del Fuego.

Nowhere is the sense of space more apparent than on the arid, gently undulating deserts of the *meseta* (steppe) that covers the whole central region of Argentinian Patagonia. Here on the plains the 5.5 million sheep way outnumber the humans, the wind snatches your breath away before you can even moan about it, and road journeys (or a slow chug on the **Old Patagonian Express** steam train; *see p109*) take on a Zen quality. If you can adjust your

eyes to the visual monotony, then the subtle palette of the central Patagonian plains can do wonders for your inner calm.

This dry and dusty tableau doesn't just look like the former Wild West; together with several parts of Argentinian Patagonia, it shares some common history with the frontier territory of the United States of old. This was a land that appealed not only to shepherds, farmers and other European settlers, but also to outlaws and gold prospectors, and today you can retrace the steps of Butch and Sundance in **Cholila** (*see p106*). If you take a ride down the Ruta 40 (*see p118* **The long, unwinding road**), you'll get a sense of the original pioneer spirit. The self-reliant attitude and gritty optimism of Patagonia's people – past and present – is a far cry from the lifestyle and outlook of many Argentinian and Chilean urbanites. Indeed, Patagonia has always been, and in many ways still is, another country.

Visiting Rio Negro in the late 19th century, naturalist and writer WH Hudson encouraged infirm urbanites to 'Try Patagonia!' believing it to be a salutary, as well as a mystical, realm. Whatever the final effect, it is a place to shake off city woes and workaday hassles. Though some people, of course, do actually graft here. The hard work is mainly done on wool farms, and visitors can now shack up at isolated *estancias* and share the space with the austral gaucho cowboys – nope, not a rock band, just sublime horsemen – as well as rheas (the local ostrich) and llama-like guanacos.

Yet it's not all barren plains. Where the steppe runs out in the west begins a mountain wonderland: the cold summits and fertile valleys of the southern Andes. Here glacial tongues jutting off the southern ice field shed bergs into turquoise lakes, volcanic peaks pierce the sky and dense forests cling to the mountains of the cordillera in one, great, visual feast.

The lush Andean regions of Argentinian Patagonia are camping and walking idylls, ranking among the world's best destinations for trekkers, nature-lovers, photographers, anglers and skiers. Some just go to chill next to the **Glaciar Perito Moreno** (*see p144*) or float on a lilo in an isolated lake; but if you want to get active and climb into ancient woodlands or stick your crampons into the frozen waves of an ice cap, you can.

Argentinian Patagonia

Argentinian Patagonia: in a realm of such vivid contrasts, only a seal could yawn...

Head east and you'll hit the coastline of the South Atlantic. As you head south, fiercely beautiful seas crash on to the cliffs, carrying whales and seals into the coves and bays. Seeing the southern right whales basking off the **Península Valdés** (*see p128*) is one of the world's supreme marine spectacles, and their companions – elephant seals, killer whales, sea lions – are no less impressive.

Throughout Patagonia, there is abundant bird life, from penguins and cormorants to parrots and giant woodpeckers. Happily, Argentina is increasingly turning its attentions to the protection and conservation of native and visiting species. Across the region, nine national parks (soon to be ten) and three UNESCO World Heritage Sites safeguard many of the finest historical and natural treasures (*see pp48-53* **National Parks**).

The drama continues in the south of the south. Around the city of **Ushuaia** (*see p158*) in Tierra del Fuego where the world, for all practical purposes, ends and the mountains drop into icy seas, the nature experience is still profound and the landscapes wild and wondrous. But here you also get the Magellan sensation – the slightly misplaced pioneering pleasure of being at the 'end of the world', where it still snows in midsummer and Antarctica lies just across the water. Here the toughest of all indigenous American tribes lived and Siberia-style penal colonies were built

to get colonisation moving; now a handful of towns, built by missionaries, ranchers and maritime merchants, ease the journey round the extreme tip of Argentina.

THE LIE OF THE LAND

Argentinian Patagonia is massive, so we have divided it into five navigable regions that pull together places with a common geographical and conceptual theme. The objective is to help visitors either plan a combination of short visits to diverse towns and landscapes or at least to choose one area to explore in depth.

These areas are: **The North**, where you can wander the country's wettest and driest areas (literally) in the footsteps of dinosaurs, soak in volcanic thermals or hit the snowy slopes on a Mapuche winter-sports resort; **The Lake District 1**, in north and central Andean Patagonia, centred around the towns of Bariloche and Esquel but famed more for ancient alerce forests, vast blue lakes and wonderful walks through low passes and over high volcanoes; **Central Patagonia**, one of the continent's least-visited places, and home to petrified forests and abstract hand paintings by prehistoric man; **The Atlantic Coast**, from the Península Valdés by way of Welsh-influenced Gaiman and finally to the waters of the Deseado estuary; and **The Deep South 1**, from Rio Gallegos on the coast to the tip of Tierra del Fuego by way of a stunning zigzag to the Parque Nacional Los Glaciares.

The North

Follow in the footsteps of dinosaurs across the grassy pampas, then head to the Andes for hot thermals and cool skiing.

In the north of Argentinian Patagonia are the provinces of La Pampa, Neuquén and Río Negro. Despite its latitude, La Pampa was officially incorporated into Patagonia in 1996. At La Pampa's southern boundary the plains give way to true steppe: the province of **Neuquén**, where the land begins to rise to form the cordillera, is to all intents and purposes where the Patagonian dream starts.

Many associate Neuquén exclusively with the mountains, but there's more to it than that. The barren eastern region is a loner's lunar utopia, while the area around **El Chocón** has yielded some outstanding dinosaur discoveries. Where the yellow lands of north-western Neuquén melt into the whites and greys of the Andes, the mountains are dotted with welcoming small towns such as **Aluminé** and isolated *estancias*; here too is **Parque Nacional Lanín**. In the south of Neuquén province is the area of outstanding natural beauty known locally as the Distrito de los Lagos (*see pp83-111* **The Lake District 1**).

Santa Rosa & La Pampa

Over the last one and quarter centuries a determined population has made its home in La Pampa. Today just under 300,000 people live in an area roughly the size of Florida or England.

What parts of the land lack in fertility is more than made up for in the *pampeano* imagination. Perhaps it's because, at times, the earth looks like water or the horizon melts into the sky, but the pampas have long inspired poets and dreamers. Nor have the less artistically minded been found wanting in contributing to the collective imaginary output. UFO sightings are commonplace, while other recent phenomena include the intriguing case of the 'Enano Verde' (Green Dwarf), who turned out to be a vertically challenged, green-coated nomad, or the unsolved-at-press-time cases of cattle mutilation. Twilight Zone stuff aside, there are advantages to the terrain. You'd have to go a long way to beat sunset over the pampas, or the wraparound, pincushion night sky.

La Pampa: only 300 kilometres to the next tree.

Parque Nacional Lihué Calel

Driving the two and a half hours to La Pampa's one national park along the almost entirely straight RN35 and RN152 (daily bus services run from Santa Rosa), nothing jars your vision until the red rocks of the Hills of Life – Lihué Calel in the Mapuche tongue, Sierra de la Vida in Spanish – loom in the distance.

These are the principal natural feature of Parque Nacional Lihué Calel, created in 1977. Though small by Andean standards – the highest summit reaches just 590 metres (1,936 feet) – these mountains tower out of the level plains, and though they may be shorter they are much, much older. They were formed around 240 million years ago. A welcome drama in the surrounding landscape, these peaks shelter an abundance of wildlife, as well as some important historical sites.

FLORA AND FAUNA

The park's 99 square kilometres (38 square miles) protect over 40 mountain-dwelling mammals. Spot herds of guanaco peering down from the peaks, or treading quietly you may see a mountain cat, grey fox or puma. The micro-climate around the sierra is wetter than the surrounding dry pampas, enabling 500 types of plants to flourish, including the distinctive yellow margarita. On the higher, drier surfaces, cacti abound. Visit between mid October and late November to see the park in bloom. Birdwatchers are also well served with 160 species to see, including eagles, woodpeckers and hawks.

TREKS AND ACTIVITIES

Self-guided trails wind through the park, for exploring on foot or wheels. Follow the almost too cunningly disguised waymarkers and clamber up the highest peak (Cerro de la Sociedad Científica) for a stunning view. An easy, pretty walk leads to cave paintings left

by indigenous hunter-gatherers around 1,600 years ago. Stick to the trails in summer months if you don't want to meet one of the park's species of poisonous snakes. You can do both circuits in a day, or camp over to really soak up the atmosphere.

FACILITIES

Start by registering at the Intendencia, or park ranger's office, where there are leaflets (in Spanish only) on geology and wildlife. The free campsite has basic facilities that include toilets, showers and *parrillas* (barbecues). You can camp only in this designated area. Bring your own provisions; the nearby ACA service station and one-time motel has very limited supplies, though you can get a basic meal there at lunchtime.

Parque Nacional Lihué Calel

RN152 (02952 436595). **Open** 24hrs daily. **Admission** free.

One third of the province's inhabitants live in the capital. Santa Rosa, a relatively new city, was founded in 1892. City life now, as then, revolves around the **Plaza San Martín**. Many of the buildings around this square – the school, the bank, the Municipalidad and **Casa Gadea**, the house of one of the first families – date from shortly after Santa Rosa's foundation.

The square's strangest building is the **Catedral**, recent additions to which include a representation of the disciples in the form of 12 huge diamond-shaped structures.

All essential shops and services are off the plaza on Avenidas Avellaneda and San Martín. Two blocks away the **Museo Provincial de Historia Natural** is an good introduction to all that flies, swims, runs and crawls in the province. There are some interesting small displays on local geology, and archaeological and palaeontological finds (though information panels are in Spanish only). For cultural diversions, check for musical or theatrical events at the **Teatro Español** on Hilario Lagos, between Avellaneda and Coronel Gil.

At the intersection of Avenida Luro and San Martin, near the bus station and tourist office, is the **Mercado Artesanal**. This is a small retail space where you can buy authenticated leather and woven pieces, weavings and a range of gaucho goodies at fair prices, while supporting local craftspeople and traditions.

For sports activities, ask at the tourist office for details of the 18-hole golf course, riding school and parachuting club, or catch popular local basketball team Estudiantes in action.

EXCURSIONS

An easy and rewarding trip is to the **Reserva Provincial Parque Luro**, 35 kilometres (22 miles) south of Santa Rosa on RN35. It was once the property of Pedro Luro, a bon vivant who at the beginning of the last century built a French-style chateau, imported deer and wild boar from Europe and created what was then the world's largest game reserve. Save its creator, all the elements remain, with the crucial difference that now the idea is to preserve the wildlife. The chateau, a national historical monument, retains many original furnishings. To see around the house join one of the hourly guided tours.

Of the 76 square kilometres (29 square miles) of grounds, one sixth are accessible, with trails leading through three natural environments: caldén forests (emblematic tree of the province), dunes and lagoons – go to the **Centro de Interpretación** just beyond the entrance for information on facilities. Services are organised around **Quincho Parque Luro** (02954 4420071, directions at the entrance) where the ebullient Emilio whips up meals, organises treks or horse rides and offers three cabins to rent (US$10-$12 per person, per night).

Hunting is still big news here. Many of La Pampa's *estancias* organise licensed big- and small-game hunts (*see pp57-59* **Fishing & Hunting**). For those not interested in taking down the local fauna, a wide variety of other activities are available (*see pp62-63* **Ranching**). Standards of accommodation vary greatly; ask the tourist office to explain the different choices and help you make your reservation, or else take a look at www.lapampaestancias.com.ar, a helpful website that features all 16 of La Pampa's ranches that welcome tourists (with some information in English).

Worth the significantly longer 226-kilometre (140-mile) journey from town is La Pampa's one national park, **Lihué Calel**. It's just about manageable as a day trip or, better still, makes an interesting stop en route to the south.

Mercado Artesanal

San Martín 729, entre Luro y Urquiza (02954 430168). **Open** 7am-8pm Mon-Fri; 10am-noon, 5-7pm Sat. **Credit** MC, V.

Museo Provincial de Historia Natural

Pellegrini 180, entre Quintana y Sarmiento (02954 22693). **Open** *Feb-Dec* 8am-noon, 2-6pm Mon-Fri; 6-9pm Sun. Closed Jan. **Admission** free.

Reserva Provincial Parque Luro

Ruta 35 (02954 499000). **Open** *Apr-Oct* 9am-6pm Tue-Sun; *Nov-Mar* 9am-7pm Tue-Sun. **Admission** US$1. *Guided tours* US$2. **No credit cards**.

Where to eat & drink

For a coffee or snack, head to one of the many *confiterías* and pizzerias around Plaza San Martín. Out of the centre, **Restaurant Caldén** (Avenida Eva Perón y Farinatti, 02954 424311, $$), next to its sister motel, is recommended. It's relaxed, has excellent service, and among the many menu choices are five preparations of deer, and good wines. For late-night drinks, try **V8** at 9 de Julio 130. Eighties music, a dancefloor and two bars make this Santa Rosa's hotspot. Alternatively, satisfy all your vices under the neon lights of the **Casino Club** (Arturo Illia 850, 02954 458419, closed lunch, $$).

Where to stay

Santa Rosa's star hotel is **La Campiña Club Hotel** (Ruta 5, km 604, 02954 456800, www.lacampina.com, double US$110). An attractive white-walled villa with large gardens, five minutes out of town, it has 31 tasteful, well-appointed rooms. The airy restaurant has a large stock of reasonably priced Argentinian wines. Facilities are excellent: gym, sauna and a huge swimming pool, plus discounted rates at the adjoining squash court. For short stays, the **Motel Turístico Caldén** (Avenida Eva Perón 2707, 02954 424311, www.hotelescalden.com.ar, double US$25), a classic North American-style motel across from the tiny airport, is a good bet. The ground- and first-floor rooms are simple yet comfortable with good showers, and overlook a large pool in the central patio. In town, the 13-floor **Calfucurá Hotel** (Avenida San Martín 695, 02954 423612, www.calfucurah.com.ar, double room US$20-$26) is a reasonable central choice, with its own restaurant and swimming pool, though rooms are a little gloomy.

Resources

Hospital

Hospital Lucio Molas, Raúl B Díaz y Pilcomayo (02954 455000).

Internet

Locutorio del Paseo, Avenida Luro 364 (02954 432606).

Police station
Pellegrini 587 (02954 422303).

Post office
Hilario Lagos y Rivadavia (02954 433117).

Tourist information
Dirección de Turismo de la Provincia de la Pampa, Avenidas Luro y San Martín (02954 424404/ 425060/www.turismolapampa.gov.ar). **Open** 7am-8pm Mon-Fri; 9am-noon, 4-8pm Sat, Sun.

Getting there

By air
At the time of going to press air services to Santa Rosa had been suspended. Check in Buenos Aires with the domestic airport (*see p234*) or with the **Aeropuerto Santa Rosa** (RN35, km 330, 02954 434490), 5mins/US$2 by taxi from the centre of town.

By road
Santa Rosa is at the intersection of RN5 and RN35 , 611km (380 miles)/7hrs from BA, 535km (332 miles) from Neuquén and 992km (616 miles) from Bariloche. Buses connect with every major destination in the country from the **Terminal de Omnibus** (Avenida Luro y San Martín, 02954 422249).

Neuquén

Lodged on the eastern edge of Neuquén province, the capital, also called Neuquén, sits at the confluences of two rivers some 1,147 kilometres (713 miles) south of Buenos Aires. Largely industrial, it processes and packages the output of the surrounding lands. A popular stopover for tourists heading south, it's also the ideal base from which to make day excursions to the nearby dinosaur destinations of El Chocón and Plaza Huincul.

In 1902, when Ferrocarril del Sud established a railway line linking Neuquén to Buenos Aires, the city breathed a sigh of relief. With the trains came business and businessmen, and finally recognition as capital of the province in 1904. Now obsolete, the old railway tracks bisect the city into distinct areas, *el bajo* (downtown) and *el alto* (uptown). Souvenir shoppers should visit **Paseo de los Artesanos**, next to the old railway station on Vuelta de Obligado, for carefully made local handicrafts; open 10am to 9pm on weekends only. *El alto* is generally the quietest and most relaxed part of the city, where families and shoppers can enjoy a *café con leche*, do a spot of window-shopping or amble into one of the nearby leafy parks, **Plaza Presidente Roca** or **Parque Centenario**. The latter incorporates the **Mirador Balcon del Valle**, a popular viewing point from where the city's suburbs can be seen sprawling out into the river valley.

Culturally, there are several points of interest in Neuquén, but only one that is outstanding. The **Sala de Arte Emilio Saraco** in front of the railway station holds regular art exhibitions while, close by, the **Museo Histórico Cultural Paraje Confluencia**, displays human artefacts from 10,000 years ago, as well as dinosaur fossils. But the real buzz is around the recently opened **Museo Nacional de Bellas Artes**, a landmark in Patagonian cultural activity that is alone expected to bring in thousands of tourists. (*See p77* **Art in the right place**).

Although winters are chilly, when the temperature rises in summer most locals are to be found at one of the *balnearios*, or beach resorts, at the end of Avenida Olascoago. Along this part of the River Limay, the water is tepid and clean and if you're in need of refreshment there are plenty of cafés. Canoeing and kayaking are popular watery pastimes.

Beheaded signposts and strands of old Christmas lights dangling from the trees along Avenida Argentina are symbolic of a city that lacks urban care. But as provincial towns go, this is not a bad one; the city pulse is palpable, the locals friendly and crime (although on the rise) is not the endemic headache that has overwhelmed some Argentinian cities.

Museo Histórico Cultural Paraje Confluencia
Independencia y 25 de Mayo, Parque Central (0299 4429785). **Open** 8.30am-6.30pm Mon-Fri; 5-8pm Sat, Sun. **Admission** free.

Museo Nacional de Bellas Artes de Neuquén
Mitre y Santa Cruz, Parque Central (0299 4436268) **Open** 10am-8pm Tue-Fri; 5-8pm Sat, Sun. **Admission** free.

Sala de Arte Emilio Saraco
Vuelta de Obligado, entre Alberdi y Rivadavia, Complejo Cultural Ferrocarril (0299 4491200 ext 4390). **Open** 8.30am-8pm Mon-Fri; 4-8pm Sat, Sun. **Admission** free.

Where to stay & eat

Neuquén's accommodation, like its eateries, are unpretentious and a tad dull. The most luxurious hotel is **Hotel del Comahue** (Avenida Argentina 377, 0299 4432040, reservas@hoteldelcomahue.com, double US$65). A bevy of butlers hovers around the smart reception area, while upstairs colleagues wait the tables of the smart restaurant. Also worth a look in the *alto* is the inviting **Hotel Amucán** (Tucumán 115, 0299 4425209, www.amucanhotel.com.ar, double US$50), a mid-range hotel with 51 standard rooms and a busy restaurant. If you can't face traipsing

Explore the araucaria forests around **Caviahue**. *See p77.*

uptown, then the modern **Hotel El Prado** (Perito Moreno 484, 0299 4486000, www.hotel-elprado.unlugar.com, double US$100-$130) in *el bajo* comes recommended for its spacious rooms and fair prices. **Residencial Inglés** (Felix San Martin 534, 0299 4422252, double US$45), run by Anglo-Polish Danuta Maria Kugler, has a colourful courtyard to match the 11 rooms.

There are a lot of cheap eating choices downtown; for anything swankier, try the places on and around Avenida Argentina in *el alto*. Formal but excellent **Restaurante 1904** ($$$) in Hotel del Comahue is worth a visit. For a younger, less stuffy vibe, try **La Birra** (Santa Fe 19, 0299 4434344, $$). A local favourite is **El Reencuentro** (Brown 162, 0299 4440835, closed dinner Sun, $$), a no-frills *parrilla* serving huge steaks in a friendly atmosphere.

Resources

Hospital
Hospital Castro Rendón, Buenos Aires 425 (0299 4490800).

Internet
Blue Fish, 25 de Mayo y Alberti (0299 4426046).

Police station
Santiago del Estero 136, entre Carlos H Rodríguez y Juan B Justo (0299 4424192).

Post office
Santa Fe y Rivadavia (0299 4422142).

Tourist information
Dirección Provincial de Turismo – Subsecretaría de Turismo, Felix San Martín 182, entre Río Negro y Corrientes (0299 4424089/3386/www. neuquentur.gov.ar). **Open** 7am-10pm Mon-Sat; 10am-8pm Sun.

Getting there

By air
Aeropuerto Internacional Juan Domingo Perón (Ruta 22 y Goya, 0299 4440244), 7km (4.5 miles) from the centre, has daily flights from BA and regular flights from Comodoro Rivadavia, Rio Gallegos and Ushuaia.

By road
Neuquén is at the junction of RN151 and RN22, 19hrs from BA. Bariloche is 457km (284 miles) south on RN237. The **Terminal de Omnibus** (Mitre 147, entre Avenida Olascoaga y Corrientes) has services heading out in all directions, north and south.

Villa El Chocón

South-west of Neuquén, 79 kilometres (49 miles) down RN237, lies Villa El Chocón (sometimes referred to as the **Valle de los Dinosaurios**), a tiny community that recently put dinosaurs firmly back on the map.

Originally built to house the workers of the nearby dam, **Exequiel Ramos Mexía**, El Chocón roared back into the headlines in 1993 with the discovery of the world's biggest carnivorous dinosaur; the *Gigantosaurus Carolinii* (*see p78* **Fossil fever**). It was unearthed just outside the village by the resident, self-taught palaeontologist and now director of the local museum, Rubén Carolini, after whom it is named. Nowadays, the bones of the long-deceased dinosaur and a spine-tingling replica of its head are on public view in the **Museo Municipal Ernesto Bachmann**.

Just over three kilometres (two miles) south in the **Museo de Sitio**, also known as Parque Cretanario, the huge footprints of the herbivorous Iguanodon lie by the lake. They

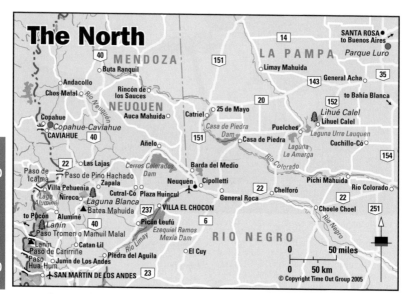

The North

MENDOZA

LA PAMPA

SANTA ROSA
to Buenos Aires

Parque Luro

Argentinian Patagonia

NEUQUÉN

RIO NEGRO

0   50 miles

0   50 km

© Copyright Time Out Group 2005

---

were used unwittingly to build fires in, protected from the wind. It's worth the bumpy ride to marvel at their immaculate condition and sheer size. The site's *guardafauna* (park rangers) offer guided tours for US$4-$5.

To finish off a day out, you can go fishing in **Lake Exequiel Ramos Mexía**, which spreads out for 816 square kilometres (315 square miles) and is easily the biggest artificial lake in the country. If you have your own tackle, spin or fly, you can cast for brown or rainbow trouts and pejerrey.

Coincidentally, the greatest ever herbivore was dug up just 100 kilometres (62 miles) away. Once excavated it was named *Argentinosaurus Huinculensis* and the bones transported to the **Museo Municipal Carmen Funes** in Plaza Huincul, 107 kilometres (66 miles) due west of Neuquén. Although far more populated than El Chocón, Plaza Huincul is essentially a bleak and economically depressed oil town; it was the location for Argentinian director Lucas Demare's celebrated 1960 film about workers' hardships, *Plaza Huincul*. Even now, it remains a hotbed of political protest, with women often at the head of the picket lines.

The easiest way to visit both towns is on day trips from Neuquén – they're just too far to take in both in one day – or you can stop off on your way to destinations further south.

Museo de Sitio – Parque Cretanario

RN237. **Open** 9am-6.30pm daily. **Admission** free.

Museo Municipal Carmen Funes

Avenida Córdoba 55, on RN22, Plaza Huincul (0299 4965486). **Open** 9am-7.30pm Mon-Fri; 1-8pm Sat, Sun. **Admission** US75¢; free under-12s. **No credit cards**.

Museo Municipal Ernesto Bachmann

Centro Comercial, Villa El Chocón (0299 4901223). **Open** *Jan, Feb, July* 8am-9pm daily. *Mar-Dec* 9am-7pm daily. **Admission** US$75¢; free under-6s. **No credit cards**.

Where to stay & eat

If you want to dally over your dinosaur hunting, options in Villa El Chocón are limited. **La Posada del Dinosaurio** (Costa del Lago, Barrio 1, 0299 4901200, www.posadadinosaurio. com.ar, double US$40-$60) is a small hotel comprising six rooms and two suites with beautiful views over the lake.

Resources

Hospital

Centro de Salud, by town entrance (0299 4901252).

Police station

By town entrance (0299 4901222).

Tourist information

Dirección de Turismo y Cultura de la Municipalidad, Unit 1, Centro Comercial (0299 4901230 ext 30/0299 156370908). **Open** 8am-6pm Mon-Fri.

Getting there

By road

Two companies run daily services to El Chocón from Neuquén. The bus station is in front of the Museo Municipal. El Chocón is 79km (49 miles)/2hrs from Neuquén along RN237 in the direction of Bariloche. To reach Plaza Huincul from Neuquén, take RN237 and turn west on to RN22 towards Zapala.

Caviahue & Copahue

Over in the Andes, 360 kilometres (224 miles) west of Neuquén, and just a hop from the Chilean border, tiny Caviahue and Copahue are the centres of a provincial reserve originally set up to protect the araucaria trees.

At 1,600 metres (5,249 feet) above sea level, Caviahue is a delightful village draped between the edge of picturesque **Lago Caviahue** and **Volcán Copahue**. Frequently active, this volcano last cleared its throat in 2000, sending ash and a wave of panic through the village, which was quickly and safely evacuated.

Despite efforts to keep Caviahue low key, its pristine beauty, many activities and hot springs have started to seep into international travel brochures. Caviahue may not yet be a big name compared to other towns in the region but it is increasingly in vogue, so book in advance.

The village set-up includes 650 hotel beds, a brand-new church and distinct zones with tourists sleeping on one side of the village and locals living on the other. The tourist office offers a complete briefing for those looking to relax or exercise their limbs; after all, Caviahue is not just about getting into a hot bath, it's about deserving it as well.

In winter, intermediates and beginners will enjoy **Caviahue Base** ski resort, which gets an average of 2.5 metres (8.2 feet) of snow, and boasts four lifts and 29 kilometres (18 miles) of pistes. The views from the slopes are second to none. Cross-country skiing may not generate the same adrenalin levels, but the trails that cut through the araucaria forests are inspiring. Charismatic ski-instructor Gerard Pied is the ideal guide; contact him via the tourist office.

By late spring the temperatures soar and the activities change. Fishing is just one of the outdoor possibilities at lagunas Escondida, El Rincón and Hualcupén. The main trekking attraction is the stunning trail along the side of the Agrio creek that leads up to the crater

Art in the right place

Argentinian Patagonia is a patchwork of discrete communties stitched together by certain common aims and values, one of which is to never knowingly pass up the chance to get one over on Buenos Aires. So when Neuquén's brand-new Museo Nacional de Bellas Artes (*see p74*) announced in early 2005 that its inaugural exhibition would feature none other than Pablo Picasso (his 'Vollard Suite' etchings), Patagonian art lovers rejoiced; and when it became clear that said show would be bypassing the federal capital, everyone was happy.

With good reason, as it turned out. This rare incursion of modernist art into what most people considered a cultural no-man's land was an unqualified triumph, attracting more than 140,000 visitors over its three-month run. Neuquén city, long regarded by travellers as a place to get through rather than get to, could now boast the most important cultural institution in the region. Proof of how much the museum means to the citizens of Neuquén can be judged from the fact that the costs of transporting the drawings – around US$12,000 – were defrayed by a handful of local businesses.

Another surprise in a country where many construction projects outlive their architects, is that the museum was completed in just nine months. Mario Roberto Alvarez's design is confidently modern, as straight-lined and austere as a shoebox. Get inside and you'll find a permanent collection that includes European art from the Renaissance to the 19th century and Argentinian works from 1800 to the present day. Artists as diverse as Rodin and Toulouse-Lautrec are featured, as well as national heroes such as Quinquela Martín and Antonio Berni.

In fairness, the museum's success owes as much to national co-operation as regional chutzpah. As the first ever branch of BA's Museo de Bellas Artes, the most important state-run museum in the country, it comes under the aegis of the federal rather than the regional government. But to most people in Neuquén this is little more than an administrative detail: the museum, they feel, belongs to them. The hope now is that the success of the enterprise will give impetus to similar projects throughout the region and help trample on the myth that big cultural projects can only flourish in big cities.

Fossil fever

Amazing discoveries in Patagonia in recent years have had dinosaur experts hailing the region as palaeontology's promised land. So what's behind the hype?

To begin with about one hundred tonnes in weight. Recent palaeontological discoveries in south-west Neuquén have brought to light the two greatest contenders known to have inhabited the dinosaur world. In the red corner we have *Giganotosaurus carolinii*, a flesh-rending killing machine weighing in at 10,000 kilograms (22,075 pounds). Big enough to have given its North American cousin T rex a humiliating first round pasting, the world's largest ever meat-eater had a skull larger in size than a man. But the real Patagonian beefcake is a vegetarian. In the green corner, measuring 42 metres (138 feet) in length from head to tail, standing 22 metres (72 feet) high and weighing a whopping 90,000 kilograms (198,675 pounds) is the great, undisputed, heavyweight champion of the prehistoric world, *Argentinosaurus huinculensis*!

OK, not quite undisputed. Scientists in the neighbouring province of Río Negro have recently unearthed a 3.4-metre-wide (11-feet) bones from the neck section of a yet-to-be-named herbivore. Some palaeontologists estimate it came from another giant who would have stretched half a block (48 metres or 160 feet) in length and towered to a mighty five storeys high. With each new find previous records are broken and where the old megalizards used to tear into each other

shreds, now Argentina and foreign fossil hunters are battling it out to dig up the biggest bone on earth.

But, size apart, why is Patagonia such a wonderful fossil cemetery? It appears to be a question of bone quantity as well as quality. Palaentologists have ascertained that during the three periods when dinosaurs walked the earth (Jurassic, Triassic and Cretaceous) thousands of them thundered around Patagonia. Hard though it is to believe, the area was once a lush tropical jungle, a haven for docile plant-eaters who in turn attracted rapacious predators. Both were wiped out mysteriously and then buried for millions of years, and it is only now – due to the force of eroding winds – that these untouched, underpopulated badlands are revealing just how bad they really were.

The evidence is everywhere. Huge footprints by the side of the lake in Villa El Chocón, in south-west Neuquén, point to the existence of plant-eating ornithopods and sauropods. In northern Neuquén, in the late 1990s, a team of dinosaur diggers from the Museo Municipal Carmen Funes (*see p76*) unearthed a cache of thousands of dinosaur eggs. Packed with embryonic bones and tiny teeth, they also contained fragments of fossilised skin, providing the first examples ever discovered of dinosaur tissue. As recently as 2004, Patagonia again grabbed the palaeontological headlines when an enormous, carnivorous bird-like dinosaur, later baptised Talenkauen, was discovered in Santa Cruz. Watch this space...

---

of the volcano, where you can peer into its simmering green lagoon. Along the way you'll pass seven waterfalls. Alternatively, rent a horse in Caviahue from **Patagónica Norte Travesía** (Bungalow 3, Alpino, 02948 495122, December to March only), which does five-day rides or **La Vega** (Casa 8, Volcán Copahue, no phone). A number of other interesting excursions and activities can be arranged through **Caviahue Tours** (Centro Comercial Loc 11, Avenida Bialous, 02948 495138).

Ever since the Mapuche jumped into the mud pools and came out feeling great, the area was destined to become an alternative therapy

resort. The **Hotel Caviahue ISSN** (8 de Abril, 02948 495044) close to the tourist office has thermal baths, open 9am-1pm and 5-9pm daily, with treatments costing from US$5 to $8.

Copahue, being closer to the source, just 18 kilometres (11 miles) up the hill from Caviahue, practically owes its existence to the health industry. Sunk in an old crater with zero vegetation, the village sits atop a brilliantly conceived but practically useless road heating system that fails to keep it open during the long winter months. You can visit Copahue (open November to May) on a day trip from Caviahue or stay in one of its hotels.

The centrepiece of this Soviet-looking resort is **Complejo de Balneaterapia de Copahue**, a complex where massage and mud wraps complement the hot baths. For a mandatory US$9, a local doctor checks you over and prescribes the appropriate 'remedy'.

Alternative muddy attractions include the cool algae-rich **Laguna Verde**, or the popular, splendidly named **Laguna del Chancho** (pigs' lagoon). Wallowing in this open-air pool is undeniably good for you, even if being seen in it is a different matter. Not that anyone seems to care; the punters look happy as, well, a pig in muck, rolling around in it, bantering freely while flicking mud in each other's faces.

Caviahue Base

Service run by Hotel Nevado, 8 de Abril (02948 495042, www.caviahue.com). **Open** *mid June-Sept* 9am-6pm daily. **Rates** *Ski hire* US$12-$15 per day. *Ski pass* US$13-$27 per day; US$70-$140 per wk. *Chair lift* US$6. Children 20% discount. **Credit** AmEx, DC, MC, V.

Complejo de Balneoterapia de Copahue

Cacique Cheuquel (02948 495083 in season/02948 495053 out of season). **Open** *Nov-May* 7am-1pm, 2-8pm daily. Closed June-Oct. **Rates** *Treatments* US$7-$12. **Credit** AmEx, DC, MC, V.

Where to stay & eat

In Caviahue the pick of the bunch is the imposing **Hotel Lago Caviahue** (Costanera Quimey-Có, 02948 495074, www.hotellago caviahue.com.ar, double US$50), run by delightful owners. The service is great and the roaring fire much appreciated by all.

Perched at the foot of the ski resort, two kilometres (1.25 miles) from the village, is **Hotel Farallón** (02948 495085, www.hotel farallon.com.ar, closed Nov, May, double US$40-$60). Ideal for skiers, each of the 60 apartment rooms is well-equipped, and all have views over Lago Caviahue.

In addition to its thermal baths, **Hotel Caviahue ISSN** (8 de Abril, 02948 495044, double US$8-$10) has rooms that are reserved for state workers only, but exceptions are made.

Although there are plenty of restaurants and cafés in Caviahue and Copahue, concessions and owners change rapidly, so ask for advice on arrival. In general, the restaurants within the top hotels are the best bet. One such recommendation is the **Hotel Lago Caviahue** ($$$) where the Mapuche chef faithfully recreates delicious regional specialities.

Most hotels in Copahue were built in the 1960s and have remained in their original state. The best of the bunch are the comfortable,

36-room **Hotel Valle del Volcán** (Herrero Ducloux, 02948 495048, copahueclub@sinectis. com.ar, closed June-Oct, double US$30-$50 full board) and the somewhat more luxurious **Termas Hotel** (Herrero Ducloux, 02948 495057, closed June-Oct, double US$50-$70 full board) which has 60 rooms.

Resources

These contacts are provided for Caviahue, open year round; Copahue closes from June to October.

Hospital

Centro de Salud, Puesta del Sol y Mapuche (02948 495070).

Police station

Mapuche (02948 495068).

Post office

Bungalows 5 & 6, 8 de Abril (02948 495036).

Tourist information

Oficina de Turismo, Bungalows 5 & 6, 8 de Abril, (02948 495036/turismocaviahuecopahue@infovia. com.ar). **Open** 8.30am-9pm Mon-Fri; 10am-1pm, 4-7pm Sat, Sun.

Getting there

By road

There is 1 bus daily from Neuquén. In winter, check to make sure the road from Loncopué (52km/32 miles away) to Caviahue is open. Copahue closed, and usually cut off by snow, June-Oct.

Zapala & PN Laguna Blanca

Windy Zapala, stuck in the middle of the northern sector of Patagonia, is an important crossroads for several popular destinations: Caviahue, Bariloche and San Martín de los Andes. Despite the hubbub around the bus terminal, Zapala is sleepy with a capital S. Most people stop here to hop on or off a bus, but a trip to the **Parque Nacional Laguna Blanca** may see you checking in for the night.

Created in 1940 to protect the black-necked swan, Laguna Blanca National Park – 35 kilometres (22 miles) from Zapala – is a birders' paradise. Although ornithology is the main event in this small park, there's also a cave decorated with primitive etchings.

The swans are accompanied by another 120 bird species, among them flamingos, sandpipers, coots, Andean ruddy duck and waterfowl. Most gather on the lagoon or in the distant sections of the Barda Negra, a steep section of hills that offers protection from the relentless gusts. These more elevated parts are the nesting sites for birds of prey such as the peregrine falcon. For the best birdwatching you should go in August or September. Take your own provisions and windproof clothing. (For more on birdwatching in Patagonia, *see p32* **Catch the condor**).

Parque Nacional Laguna Blanca
*RP46 (02942 431982/www.parquesnacionales. gov.ar). **Open** Oct-Apr 8.30am-9pm daily. May-Sept 8.30am-6pm daily. **Admission** US$2.*

Where to stay & eat

It might need a bit of nip and tuck, but the commodious **Hotel Hue Melén** (Almirante Brown 929, 02942 422414, www.interpatagonia. com/huemelen, double US$30) is still the best in town. Out-of-place pinball machines fill the reception, while the 30 cosy rooms contain all the staple requisites. The restaurant is easily the best in town and serves regional specialities. Closer to the bus terminal, try the modest but clean 23-room **Hotel Pehuén** (Elena de la Vega y Etcheluz, 02942 423135, double US$20).

There's really nothing in Zapala in the way of fine dining, but for a coffee or a snack, look no further than **El Chancho Rengo** (the lame pig) on the corner of San Martin and Etcheluz (02942 422795, $). For grills and pasta try a more fortunate beast, **El Pollo Dorado** (the golden chicken) on Chanetón and Belgrano ($$).

Resources

Hospital
Hospital Regional Zapala, Luis Monti 155, entre Almirante Brown y Mayor Torres (02942 431555).

Internet
Locutorio Telecenter, Etcheluz 527 (02942 430003).

Police station
Italia 233 (02942 421213).

Post office
San Martín 234 (02942 421214).

Tourist information
*Oficina Municipal de Informes Turísticos, San Martín entre Mayor Torres y Almirante Brown (02942 421132/munidesarrollo@yahoo.com.ar). **Open** 7am-8pm Mon-Fri; 8am-1pm, 4-7pm Sat, Sun (hours vary in winter).*

Getting there

By road
Zapala is an obligatory stop for almost all buses heading west. The terminal is on Uriburu between Chanetón and Etcheluz (02942 423191). Zapala is 186km (116 miles) or 2.5hrs from Neuquén along RN22, and 4-5hrs from Bariloche.

Aluminé

At 900 metres (2,953 feet) above sea level, with a population of just over 4,000 and no paved streets, Aluminé is the quintessential Andean town. Sitting high on the banks of Rio Aluminé, looking across the wooded valley of Río Rucachoroi, the town is one of several points from which you can enter Lanin National Park (*see p90*). Despite the surrounding beauty, the area has remained a well-kept secret, attracting nature and fishing enthusiasts and the occasional media mogul. (Ted Turner can often be spotted wielding his rod and tackle.) Geographically pivotal and well organised, Aluminé is the perfect stepping stone to nearby rivers and lakes. It is the area's self-proclaimed rafting capital and the grade two-six runs on Rio Aluminé live up to the boast. Yet not everyone comes for the waters; there is also the attraction of the unspoilt countryside, the comparative lack of crowds and in particular the natural wonder of the araucaria woods.

Born in troubled times, the town was first settled in 1884 after Roca's infamous Conquista del Desierto expelled most of Patagonia's original inhabitants. The area's more peaceful evolution has much to do with Zagreb-born Juan Benigar (1883-1950), a wandering man with a roving eye who fathered 15 children. After his first wife died giving birth to his 11th child, he remarried a Mapuche woman, a coupling that proved the catalyst for his devotion to their community. The local library, **Biblioteca Popular Juan Benigar**, has a room dedicated to his life and works.

Although nothing really happens in Aluminé, nothing really needs to. Being a tourist is simple here. Most of what you need is around the square that lies between the two parallel streets Cristian Joubert and Conrado Villegas. **Mali Viajes** (02942 496310), on the corner of Cristian Joubert and Julio Ayoso, arrange river trips all year round and can fix you up with a horse, a tour of the national park and rafting. Another agency, **Amuyén** (02942 496368), at Conrado Villegas No.348, also organises a range of exciting water excursions.

A strict catch-and-release policy is testament to the fact that in Aluminé, fishing is about sport – although locals restaurants make a notable exception. It also ensures an abundance of trout that attracts fishermen from all over the world. The fishing season starts in mid November and ends in late April. Fishermen Katy (02942 496240, katyfly29@hotmail.com) and Javier, (02942 15 456391) are both local guides with in-depth knowledge about trout movements. Around the town are lakes Hui Hui, Norquinco, Quillén, Moquehue, Aluminé and Rucachoroi. The last of these is home to a settlement of around 700 Mapuche, one of the largest indigenous communities in the country. The most popular spot of all is the magnificent Lago Quillén which is also another entry point into the national park. Bordered by dense flowering vegetation, the view over the lake towards the north face of distant Volcán Lanin is breathtaking.

Biblioteca Popular Juan Benigar

Cristian Joubert 621, y Padre Milanecio (02942 496245/bibliotecabenigar@alumine.com.ar). **Open** 8am-8pm Mon-Fri; 10am-noon Sat. **Admission** free.

Where to stay & eat

He came, he fell in love and he built the **Hotel Pehuenia** (RP23, 02942 496340, pehuenia 2000@yahoo.com.ar, double US$30-$50). Charming Eduardo Nedok's hotel may seem huge in wee Aluminé but sometimes size does count. Packed with wood and rustic touches, family and friends help make your stay a memorable one. They can arrange activities in the area including horse riding, bike excursions and canoeing. The 16 rooms of the **Hostería Aluminé** (Cristian Joubert 312, 02942 496174, hosteriaalumine@hotmail.com, double US$20-$25) may be less swish, but are complemented by a massive fireside reception and bar area, overlooked by a stag's head.

Next door to the Hostería Aluminé is the restaurant **La Posta del Rey** (Cristian Joubert 315, 02942 496248, $$), another oldie but goldie that serves the usual meaty treats expected from the area. Inside Hotel Pehuenia, airy **Restaurante Hotel Pehuenia** (RP23, 02942 496340/496115, $$$) serves up wonderfully flavoursome trout that was probably swimming happily that same morning. For a change from hotel restaurants, the modest **Aonikenk Aluminé** (Avenida Regimiento 4 de Caballería, 02942 496591, $) serves up sizzling steaks at rock-bottom prices. Another budget option is **Parrilla Aoniken** (Avenida 4 de Caballería 139, $), which specialises in the standard Argentinian carbohydrate fixes of thick cheesy pizzas and huge *milanesas*.

Resources

Hospital
Hospital Area Aluminé, 4 de Caballería 549 (02942 496150).

Internet
Centro Tecnológico Quintu-Che, Avenida Rim26 430 (02942 496154).

Police station
Avenida Rim26 347 (02942 496159).

Post office
Conrado Villegas 560 (02942 496187).

Sleigh away at **Batea Mahuida**. *See p82.*

Argentinian Patagonia

Tourist information

Subsecretaría de Turismo de Aluminé, Cristian Joubert 321, entre Torcuato Modarelli y Julio Ayoso (02942 496001/intendencia@fronteradigital.net.ar/ www.alumine.gov.ar). **Open** *May-Sept* 8am-8pm Mon-Fri; 10am-6pm Sat, Sun. *Oct-Apr* 8am-9pm daily.

Getting there

By road

Aluminé is 145km (90 miles) west of Zapala, along RP46. The journey takes up to 3hrs, depending on road conditions. Bus services from Neuquén 400km (249 miles)/6hrs away run 3 times weekly (Mon, Wed, Fri) and from San Martin de los Andes twice weekly (Tue, Fri). The **Terminal de Omnibus** is at Avenida 4 de Caballería 139 (08942 496048).

Villa Pehuenia

Around the rocky loops of the RP23, just north of Aluminé, the beautiful enclave of Villa Pehuenia sits on the banks of Lago Aluminé, close to Lago Moquehue. Purposely conceived for tourism, it has been steadily taking shape since the early '90s. Some modern facilities are lacking, however, and as telephones are a rarity, most people have to use shortwave radios for communication.

Life in Villa Pehuenia revolves around the lakes. It's a real picture postcard setting of little beaches along the water's edge and cows hiding in the dense woods behind.

As is common in these parts, fish are plentiful and guides will happily take you for a gentle spin. **Los Pehuenes** along RP13 in the neighbourhood of Villa Unión (02942 15664827, lospehuenes@hotmail.com) organise guided trips to Rivers Pulmarí and Litrán.

For trekkers, a path curls around the waters of magnificent Moquehue to form a route around the lakes known as Circuito Pehuenia. You can walk it in five days, or admire it through the window of a car in four hours

EXCURSIONS

The tiny community of **Moquehue**, 25 kilometres (16 miles) from Villa Pehuenia is overshadowed by the Batea Mahuida volcano and adjacent mountains. Cloaked in native forests, the slopes offer stunning hikes, including a short jaunt to a lovely waterfall.

The small winter sports centre **Parque Recreativo de Nieve Batea Mahuida** is owned and run by a Mapuche community. The Mapuche-Puel (named after their leader José Miguel Puel) have left behind a life of sheep and goat herding and entered the world of tourism. This hasn't been without some compromises. The intensely nature-oriented culture has found itself guilty of activities such as deforestation

and expects the nearby volcano to explode at any moment and punish the tribe for its crimes.

The good news is that the centre is doing well, employing 18 staff to operate the café and 300-metre-long (186-feet) ski-lift. There is downhill and cross-country skiing on offer from 15 June to 30 September. Although this is no match for the pistes at the far bigger resorts near Bariloche or San Martin, the unbelievable visual panorama, Mapuche culture and low cost is attracting a steady trickle of people from all over the country. In the summer, the centre opens for trekking and horse riding.

Parque Recreativo de Nieve Batea Mahuida

Comunidad Mapuche-Puel. **Open** *mid June-Sept* 9.30am-5.30pm daily. *Dec-Apr* 9.30am-7.30pm daily. **Admission** US$1. *Ski lift* US$3-$6.

Where to stay & eat

Facing the crystalline waters of Lago Aluminé is luxurious 14-room **Posada La Escondida** (02942 691166/570420, www.posadala escondida.com.ar, double US$40-$60). Another good lodging is cabin complex **La Serena** (02942 15 665068, www.complejolaserena. com.ar) which also has a restaurant. As at **Costa Azul** (on the lakeside, 02942 498035, $$), the eaterie gets a thumbs up from locals.

There are several good campsites just outside town, including **Camping Agreste Quechulafquen** (run by Mapuche), **Camping El Puente** and **Las Lagrimitas** (02942 498063). The last two have hot showers, food on sale and charge US$2 per person per night.

In Moquehue, check out the delightful **Hostería Moquehue** (Paraje Moquehue, Circuito Pehuenia, 02942 15 5660301, www. hosteriamoquehue.netfirms.com, double US$35). Each of the 20 rustic bedrooms has spectacular views across the lake.

Resources

Hospital

Centro de Salud Villa Pehuenia (02942 498078).

Tourist information

Secretaría de Turismo de Villa Pehuenia, (02942 498011/498027/compehuenia@zapala.com.ar). **Open** *Oct-Apr* 9am-9pm daily.

Getting there

By road

There are daily buses from Aluminé, 60km (37 miles) away and transport can be arranged from Zapala, 107km (66 miles) away; call tourist office for details.

The Lake District 1

Where Argentinian Patagonia shakes off the dust and bursts into colour.

At the feet of the ice-crowned peaks that form Argentina's western border, where the provinces of Neuquén, Río Negro and Chubut meet Chile, lie billions of gallons of water: the emerald and turquoise lakes that give the region – and a similar one across the Andes – its name. In this, the most developed tourist region of Patagonia, are the bustling towns of **Bariloche** and **San Martín de los Andes**: urban oases for visitors looking for indoor activities and nightlife. Smaller towns like **Villa La Angostura**, perfect for unwinding, hug the shoreline along the tranquil **Ruta de los Siete Lagos** (Seven Lakes Route), and the area hosts two of Patagonia's most impressive national parks: **Nahuel Huapi** and **Lanín**.

Junín de los Andes

Fisherman's mecca and the oldest town in the region, Junín de los Andes (or just Junín) is a sleepy, laid-back town still relatively unspoilt by the tourist frenzy that has led to the kind of population explosions enjoyed – or perhaps suffered – by neighbouring Bariloche and San Martín de los Andes.

The national 'Trout Capital', Junín was founded in 1883 with the construction of a garrison. Still of military importance, it proudly boasts the world's last mule regiment. Heading north of town, you can see the would-be cavalry gently grazing by the side of the river.

Despite the town's apparently sleepy nature, Juninites are clearly party-orientated, with the town boasting a remarkable number of annual festivals. The **Encuentro Internacional de Motoqueros** kicks off the calendar in January with motorcyclists from near and far roaring into town to show off their wheels. In early February the town hosts the **Fiesta del Puestero,** a rural cattle show, gaucho rodeo and general hoedown. The **Encuentro de Escritores**, a writers festival, takes place in April; the **Semana de la Artesanía Aborigen** (Aboriginal Crafts Week) in July; and the **National Trout Festival** wraps things up in December just in time for the festive season. In an attempt to attract visitors in winter, the town is also negotiating the construction of its own ski-slope, which is expected to be underway within two years.

In many other ways too, Junín is a work in progress, its state of flux exemplified by local sculpture project **Via Christi**, which has been under construction since 1999. The hillside project currently consists of 14 statues, with seven more to be added, representing the life of Christ but blending Mapuche symbolism and features into the familiar biblical narrative. Free guided tours are run daily from 9.30am to 12.30pm, and from 5 to 7pm.

Another symbol of the cross-fertilisation of Mapuche and Christian culture and traditions is the splendid white-walled church in the town

Stare into the deep blue yonder at **Lago Nahuel Huapi**.

centre, **Iglesia Nuestra Señora de las Nieves**, on the corner of Don Bosco and Ginés Ponte. Blue stained glass and strong Mapuche symbolism, including a mural narrating the life of tribal Saint Ceferino Namakura, mark out this local place of worship. The other dominant presence is that of Laura Vicuña, who died tragically in 1904 at the age of 13. Vicuña, so the story goes, gave her life to God in exchange for her mother's freedom from the sexual advances of a rich and unscrupulous local landowner. Cited as a youthful ideal for her gentleness and compassion, she was beatified in 1988.

The **Museo Mapuche** is a Mapuche-owned and managed collection of aboriginal art and artefacts from the region. More informative is **Museo Don Moisés**, a perfectly preserved turn-of-the-century general store, with much of the remaining stock on display along with over 400 examples of Mapuche woven fabrics.

No South American town is complete without a central square, and Junín is rightfully proud of **Plaza General San Martín**, whose focal point is a wooden Mapuche carving that relegated the original stone San Martin to a nearby verge some years back.

EXCURSIONS

Junín is a base for exploring the middle of the national park (*see p90* **Parque Nacional Lanín**). Three destinations within the park are musts: Volcán Lanín, Lago Huechulafquen and the Termas de Lahuen-Có.

Volcán Lanín, home of Pillán, the Mapuche god of nature, dominates the skyline. Stunning to look at, this perfectly cone-shaped extinct volcano is also exhilarating to climb. To reach the 3,776-metre (12,400-feet) peak, you need at least two days, a decent pair of lungs and a guide. With the guide you get all equipment and food. Expect to pay around US$40 per person; *refugios* for sleeping in are free. **Bernardo** and **Sebastián Cabezón** (Necochea 227, 02972 491379) are experienced guides who have horses as well. If you're lazier or richer, or both, you can see it from the air with **Aero Club de los Andes** (02972 491379, www.aeroclubde losandes.com.ar; based in Aeropuerto Chapelco, *see p95*) who do half-hour flights over Lanín for US$100, as well as longer glider flights between November and April over the Andes.

Several trails peel around beautifully situated, banana-shaped **Lago Huechulafquen**, 15 kilometres (nine miles) from Junín. Pitch a tent lakeside or cast your rod where the lake spills into Rio Chimehuín. Angel Fontanazza of **Flotadas Chimehuín** (Ginés Ponte 143, 02972 491313) and **Dardo Enrique Tusi** (Avenida Neuquén 291, 02972 491223) organise wade and boat fishing trips. Visit the lake at

Iglesia Nuestra Señora de las Nieves.

dusk when the water's surface reflects a bonanza of woodland colours and whites from the snowy peaks.

If you didn't come via Caviahue, the **Termas de Lahuen-Có** (also known as the Baños de Epulafquen), a pleasant 64-kilometre (40-mile) drive from Junín, may be your first chance for a roll in the mud. Lago Huechulafquen forks out to form two separate lakes, Paimún and Epulafquen, and at the end of the latter are 19 volcanic mud pools (free admission). They are accessible from October to April only, when camping is also an option for US$1 per night.

Museo Don Moisés

Coronel Suárez y San Martín (02972 492322). **Open** *May-Sept* 9.30am-12.30pm, 4-7.30pm Tue-Sat. *Oct-Apr* 9.30am-12.30pm, 4-7.30pm daily. **Admission** free.

Museo Mapuche

Ginés Ponte 550, entre Don Bosco y Nogueira (02972 492322). **Open** *May-June, Aug-Sept* 9am-6pm Mon-Fri. *July, Oct-Apr* 9am-6pm daily. **Admission** free.

Where to eat

For fine food in Junín there's really only regionally famous **Ruca Hueney** (Padre Milanesio y Coronel Suárez, 02972 491113, www.ruca-hueney.com.ar, $$$). It's the place to sample local specialities such as trout, wild

boar and venison, but also boasts some more exotic Middle Eastern dishes, which have to be ordered in advance. For a quick carbohydrate fix, **Preferido de Junín** offers the usual pizza and pasta fare alongside tasty *milanesas* and hamburgers. For the meaty option, try steak house **Parrilla El Fortín** (Juan Manuel de Rosas 36, 02972 491322, $$).

Where to stay

In Junín, hotels are often family affairs from the reception to the restaurant. **Hostería Chimehuín** (Coronel Suárez 750, 02972 491132, www.hosteriachimehuin.com.ar, double US$20-$25) is the oldest in town, on the bank of Río Chimehuín. The rooms lack finesse; the home-made breakfast of scones, buns and tarts and the expansive garden do not. On the RN234, **Hostería Milla Piuke** (Avenida Los Pehuenes, 02972 492378, millapiuke@frontera digital.net.ar, double US$30-$35) offers smart and professional accommodation despite the rather bleak setting. Just next door, the newly opened family-run **Caleufu Travel Lodge** (Julio A. Roca 1323, 02972 492757, double US$25-$30) has a more homely feel, with just eight cosy rooms and breakfasts that include an exquisite *pasta farole* tart. Also slightly out of town, the **Río Dorado Lodge** (Pedro Illera 448, 02972 491548, www.riodorado.com.ar, double US$35-$150) is a classy establishment for anglers, with enormous pine rooms, a fishing shop and a lovely restaurant.

There are numerous *estancias* around. **Estancia Huechahue** (RP234, 02972 491303, jane@satlink.com, closed Apr-Nov, US$200 per person, two-night minimum), 30 kilometres (19 miles) north of town, is a cattle-breeding operation in gorgeous surroundings run by Jane Williams, a British expat. More upmarket still, and straddling kilometres of prime trout-infested river, is **Tipiliuke** (02972 428466, www.tipiliuke.com, closed June but open for groups of four or more July-Sept). Rooms are luxurious, cooking 'home-grown/home-bred', service regal and the hunting and fishing second-to-none. Opulent rural living has its price; US$250-$480 per person (based on two sharing), depending on activities, all-inclusive.

Resources

Hospital
Hospital Rural Junín de los Andes, Ginés Ponte y Padre Milanesio (02972 491162).

Internet
Locutorio Cámara de Comercio, Juan Manuel de Rosas y Coronel Suárez (02972 491319).

Police station
General Lamadrid y O'Higgins (02972 491111).

Post office
Coronel Suárez y Don Bosco (02972 491166).

Tourist information
Dirección Municipal de Turismo, Padre Milanesio y Coronel Suárez (02972 491160/www.junindelos andes.com). **Open** *May-Oct* 8am-9pm daily. *Nov-Apr* 7am-10pm daily.

Getting there

By air
Chapelco airport (*see p95*) is equidistant from San Martín and Junín de los Andes.

By road
Junín is 108km (67 miles) south of Aluminé and 40km (25 miles) north of San Martín de los Andes. Regular daily services with a variety of companies connect these towns. The bus terminal is at Olavarría y Félix San Martín (02972 492038).

San Martín de los Andes

Few towns in Patagonia are aesthetically pleasing in their own right; San Martín de los Andes, its Alpine-style houses and log cabins whittled lovingly from the surrounding forests, is one notable exception to the rule.

That said, the town is nothing but a dull wallflower set against the landscape that blooms all around it. According to Mapuche legend the area owes its natural beauty to an act of divine clumsiness. The story tells how God was roaming the earth, putting the final touches to his creation. While passing through the then-barren Argentinian lake district, he tripped and fell, spilling all of his best work over a single area. Myth was overtaken by expediency in 1898 when the leader of a Mapuche clan gave permission for Argentinians to settle the region, and San Martín de los Andes was born.

During its early years, the town survived off agriculture, cattle raising and logging. When the authorities finally protected the forests, a tourist economy was born instead. Paved roads, pleasure boats and the completion of the airport and Chapelco ski centre sealed San Martín's fate as an international resort.

Nowadays, lovely San Martín is possibly Argentina's most beloved holiday destination. Bariloche may have bigger slopes, bigger clubs and even a bigger lake, but sometimes smaller is more beautiful. Nonetheless, the population has grown fast, reaching around 35,000, and the main artery, Avenida San Martín, hums with activity. Capitalising on the fame and beauty of the lake, many *cabañas* and cheaper hostels lie close to its southern shore.

Argentinian Patagonia

San Martín de los Andes.

Cultural action centres on the **Sala de Teatro de San José** for art exhibitions, plays and the odd musical recital. **Cinema Amankay** screens films and stages plays in the adjoining theatre. Just out of town, the **Paihuen** complex (*see p94*) hosts recitals of chamber music as well as exhibitions by local artists.

To discover more about the region's aboriginal past, visit the **Museo de los Primeros Pobladores** on Plaza San Martín. This tiny three-roomed cabin houses exhibits of pre-Andean fossils, 13,000-year-old primitive tools and Mapuche tapestries and ceramics. Less worthy but more quirky, the **Museo de los Patentes**, housed in local architect Daniel Rubinger's basement on Cortada de los Abedules, displays a collection of some 2,000 Argentinian number plates, some of which are worth up to US$300. To arrange a visit, call him in advance on 02972 427834.

Alternatively, the local **Trampa de Peces** fish conservatory (Teniente General Roca y Avenida Costanera, 02972 422927), open from Tuesday to Sunday all year, offers visitors a guided tour of the project, which is geared towards protecting local fishlife.

For gift shopping, head to **Artesanías Neuquinas** (Avenida San Martín 57, 02972 428396), which sells arts and crafts sourced from local Mapuche communities, or **Lanas Argentinas** (Villegas 830, 02972 423764) for ponchos, scarves, accessories and general woolwear. Chocaholics will find relief at **Mamusia** (Avenida San Martín y Mariano Moreno, 02972 427560) or **Abuela Goye** (Avenida San Martín 807, 02972 429409, www.abuelagoye.com), which doubles as a chocolate shop and café and has become one of the best-known chocolatiers in the country. Local crafts are also on sale year round from stalls in Plaza San Martín.

EXCURSIONS

San Martín is right by Lanín National Park (*see p90* **Parque Nacional Lanín**), and half an hour by car from Nahuel Huapi park (*see p100* **Parque Nacional Nahuel Huapi**), so walks and outdoor adventures are easy options.

It's also just 18 kilometres (11 miles) from Patagonia's second biggest ski centre, **Cerro Chapelco**, with its 29 ski pistes, floodlit skiing and numerous eateries (La Casita del Bosque is particularly good). When the snow melts it transforms itself into an action sports centre offering 4x4 excursions, mountain bikes, horse riding and the increasingly popular ziplining (sliding down a steel cable over a scary, sheer drop, known here as *tirolesa*).

For a view of the town and its breathtaking surroundings, take a trek up the winding track to **Mirador Arrayán**, a viewing point that you can reach in under two hours. It's also the site of a tea shop where you can rest and refuel. If that hasn't tired you out there are further, more isolated spots from which to view the city farther up the track, including one apparently known as the 'mythological viewpoint'.

You can also hire one of the trained Mapuche guides (02972 15411370/15601854/15633071) to take you on a lakeside trail to various viewing points (from US$5) and on to the Mapuche settlement where you can visit the school and buy crafts at the local store.

Other activities around San Martín are dominated by the lake. Four kilometres to the west is the beach resort **Playa Catritre**, and nearby **Quila Quina**, a small shelf of land jutting out into the lake that is home to several Mapuche communities and a few sheltered, sandy beaches. Quila Quina can be reached by boat or road and boasts plenty of attractive walks: trails fan out from the jetty.

Parque Nacional Lanín

Few national parks can compete with the dramatic scenery of Parque Nacional Lanín, created in 1937. It is easily accessible from Aluminé (see p80), Junín (see p83) and, on its eastern border, San Martín (see p87). It's Argentina's third biggest park and boasts 35 lakes, dense alpine forests, the extinct Volcán Lanín and abundant wildlife.

Lanín was the Mapuche heartland: there are more than 50 communities in the park, the biggest being Rucachoroi near Aluminé. These days the Mapuche can live here peacefully, although they are in endless talks with park authorities over the delicate balance between ecosystems and their indigenous lifestyle.

Visit in spring or autumn, on either side of the summer crowds and the icy winds.

FLORA AND FAUNA

Tree-lovers will enjoy Lanín. Amid the rocky expanses you'll find coihues, raulís and oak pellínes, and the middle and northern sections are loomed over by lengas and ñires and the striking araucaria. Most of the park's animals are shy, though you should see Patagonian hares and grey foxes. Endangered deer, the tiny pudú and the larger huemul are trying to make a comeback. Grunting on higher ground are wild boar, while lower down at dusk you'll hear the chorus of red deer.

TREKS AND ACTIVITIES

Lauded as a mecca for fishing, Parque Nacional Lanín is also wonderful for walkers. In summer congested paths may encourage you to explore off the beaten tracks for a bit of adventure; but be careful as the weather and signposting are equally unpredictable.

As well as the climb to the heady heights of Volcán Lanín (see p85) dozens of easier trails cut through the park. Most spectacular are those around lakes Quillén, Lácar, Hermoso and Huechulafquen. Descriptions of treks in English can be found at www.sendasybosques.com.ar. Most campsites rent out horses by the hour, and for a little extra, supply a guide. For other sports, such as rafting and mountain biking, contact travel agencies or the tourist office in nearby towns.

FACILITIES

There are plenty of campsites within the park and one refugio on Volcán Lanín. Serviced campsites offer cooking facilities, hot water, toilets and, in some locations, a mini-market,
while agreste or rustic camping is more basic: cold water and a loo. If you want comfort, stay in hotels or cabins in the nearby towns.

Parque Nacional Lanín

Entrances: 3 within 30-55km (19-34 miles) of Aluminé; 3 within 12-50km (7.5-31 miles) of San Martín; 4 within 45-67km (28-42 miles) of Junín (no phones/laninupublico@smandes.com.ar). **Open** 24hrs daily (recommended entry 8am-8pm). **Admission** Huechulaufquen entrance (access from Junín) Dec-Apr US$2, US$1 under-12s; May-Nov free. Other entrances free. **No credit cards**.

Information offices

Intendencia San Martín: Emilio Frey 749, y San Martín (02972 427233). **Open** 8am-1pm Mon-Fri.
Delegación Junín: Padre Milanesio 596, entre Coronel Suárez y Lamadrid (02972 491160). **Open** Dec-Feb 9am-1pm, 7-10pm Mon-Fri. Mar-Nov 8am-4pm Mon-Wed; 2-7pm Thur, Fri.

Forty-five kilometres (28 miles) down the RP48, at the other end of the lake, begins **Río Hua-Hum**. Rafting trips take you into Chile (where the river is called Rio Pirehueico); if you want to cross the border in a traditional manner, the Hua-Hum Pass is open all year unless the snowfall is particularly heavy. A stunning spot on the way is **Península de Yuco**: through a forest is a lake with sandy beaches and rocky outcrops.

Other trips take in Lago Huechulafquen, and the popular Volcán Lanín (*see p85*).

Guided horse-riding trips around the area are organised by **Anz & Horse** on Rudecindo Roca (02972 42 25 97/02944 15562785), costing US$10 for an hour or US$15 for two. **José Julian** (02972 421038/429539) offers peaceful lake cruises, while those of a more adventurous bent can opt for rafting, either on Rio Hua-Hum or in the whiter waters of the Rio Aluminé. Other activities on offer in the area include kayaking, mountain biking, fishing and canoeing.

San Martín is also one of the start or finish destinations on the **Ruta de los Siete Lagos** (the Seven Lakes Route); *see p104*.

Artesanías Neuquinas

Juan Manuel de Rosas 790, y San Martín (02972 428396/www.artesaniasnequen.com.ar). **Open** *Mar-June, Aug-Dec* 9am-1pm, 4.30-8.30pm Mon-Fri; 9am-1pm Sat. *July, Jan, Feb* 9am-1pm, 4.30-8.30pm Mon-Fri; 9am-1pm, 4.30-8.30pm Sat. **Credit** AmEx, DC, MC, V.

Cerro Chapelco

Via RN234 or RP19 from San Martín (02972 429602/427157/www.chapelco.com.ar). **Open** *Jan, Feb, Easter week, June-Sept.* **Rates** *Ski pass* US$17-$22, US$15-$18 5-11s per day; free under-5s. Summer sports rates vary. **Credit** AmEx, DC, MC, V.

Cinema Amankay

Teniente General Roca 1152, entre Sarmiento y Mascardi (02972 428399/www.cineamankay. com.ar). **Open** 4.30pm-midnight daily. **Tickets** US$1.50. **No credit cards.**

Museo de los Primeros Pobladores

Juan Manuel de Rosas 750, entre San Martín y General Roca. **Open** *June-Sept* noon-9pm daily. *Oct-May* 10am-1pm, 3-7pm Mon-Sat; 3-7pm Sun. **Admission** free.

Sala de Teatro de San José

Capitán Drury 750, entre San Martín y General Roca (02972 428676). **Open** noon-9pm daily.

Where to eat

Fondue Betty

General Villegas 586 (02972 422522). **Open** noon-3pm, 8-11.30pm daily. **Average** $$. **No credit cards.**

Museo de los Primeros Pobladores.

This old favourite retains a warm and welcoming glow. The fondue specialities come in both sweet (chocolate) and savoury (cheese) versions.

El Radal

Perito Moreno 846, entre Capitán Drury y Belgrano (02972 427817). **Open** noon-3pm, 8pm-midnight daily. **Average** $$. **Credit** AmEx, DC, MC, V.

Gloria Ocampo's culinary contribution to San Martín has been on the go for seven years, but the owner, mother of local gastronomy guru Pablo Buzzi, has been in the business for nigh on 35. The focus is on adapting old family recipes to local ingredients, with home-made pastas a speciality.

La Reserva

Belgrano 940, entre Perito Moreno y Rudecindo Roca (02972 428734/www.lareservarestaurant.com.ar). **Open** *Dec-Mar* noon-3pm, 8pm-midnight daily. *July-Dec* noon-3pm, 7pm-midnight daily. **Average** $$$. **Credit** AmEx, DC, MC, V.

Highly recommended by local foodies (always a good sign) this relatively new restaurant boasts smoked meats, trouts and lamb, and a welcoming atmosphere. Some of the most popular dishes are cooked in an *horno de barro* (clay oven).

Restaurante Avataras

Teniente Ramayón 765, entre San Martín y General Roca (02972 427039/www.interpatagonia.com.ar/ avataras). **Open** 8pm-2am daily. **Average** $$. **Credit** AmEx, DC, MC, V.

Avataras breaks the mould with daring Indonesian, Indian, Japanese and Scandinavian dishes. There's also a bar stocked with more than 60 brands of beer and a wide range of cigars, plus live music.

Restaurant Caleuche

Ruta Nacional 234, Km 78 (02972 428154/www. paihuen.com.ar). **Open** 8.30pm-midnight daily. **Average** $$$$. **Credit** AmEx, DC, MC, V.

Lago Lácar. *See p104.*

Caleuche, on top of the Paihuen Resort, remains at the vanguard of new Patagonian cuisine. With spectacular lake views, the stone circular interior makes for an intimate dining experience, with Pablo Buzzi's innovative menu adding imagination and style to local staples like lamb, wild boar and trout, accompanied by an excellent wine list. A live jazz band adds to the ambience.

La Tasca

Mariano Moreno 866, entre Villegas y San Martin (02972 428663). **Open** *Jan-Mar noon-4pm, 7pm-midnight. Apr-Dec 7pm-midnight.* **Average** $$$.
Credit AmEx, DC, MC, V.
One of San Martin's most popular dining options, La Tasca is bright and bustling, offering numerous tapas-style options from an extensive menu. We recommend the wild boar *picada*.

Nightlife

More geared towards eaters than drinkers, San Martin still has its share of watering holes.
Xperience at Elordi No.950 (02972 428318) is the local bar/disco, opening at 10pm every night all year to bring house and electronic music to the masses. The second floor attracts a younger contingent at the weekends. **Casino Magic** at Villegas and Elordi offers just what it says, with slot machines, gaming tables and a room for live bands. Less central, but always buzzing, **Paihuen's** (*see p94*) wine bar is a lively spot,

with handsome young waiters serving up delicious wines and snacks to the strains of local DJs. If the fresh mountain air entices you to further climbing you can drag yourself up to the inevitable 'Irish' bar, **Downtown Matias** at Subida Calderon and Coronel Diaz (02972 421699), where happy hour lasts till 1am.

Where to stay

Cerro Abanico

Ruta 7 Lagos, Km 4.5 (02972 423723/www.inter patagonia.com/cerroabanico). **Rates** US$70-$85 single; US$100-$120 double. **Credit** AmEx.
This small, friendly hotel built into the side of the mountain has only eight rooms, each decorated in a different colour and all with glorious views of the lake below. With a tea-house, a restaurant, a library of old classics and one of the most helpful owners in town, Cerro Abanico has an edge over many of its more impersonal rivals.

La Cheminée

General Roca y Mariano Moreno (02972 427617/ fax 02972 427762/www.hosterialacheminee.com.ar). **Rates** US$80-$145 double; US$130-$250 apartment.
Credit AmEx, MC. V.
Of the countless wooden, Alpine-inspired hotels in town, this is still one of the best. Some rooms even have fireplaces, and there's a pool, jacuzzi, sauna and, best of all, a glorious breakfast. The hotel also has its own shop selling books and art prints.

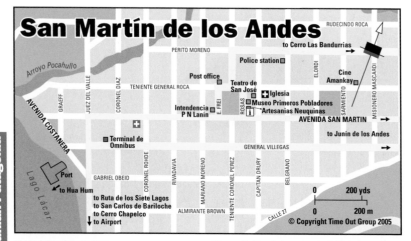

San Martín de los Andes

Hotel Le Chatelet

Villegas 650, entre Mariano Moreno y Coronel Paz (tel & fax 02972 428294/428296/www.hotelle chatelet.com.ar). **Rates** US$70-$130 single; US$80-$150 double; US$110-$210 triple; US$100-$180 suite. **Credit** AmEx, DC, MC, V.

A swish Swiss feel permeates the 32 exquisitely decorated rooms, and there's plenty of extra facilities available, including a gym, pool, kids' area and various business services.

Paihuen

Ruta Nacional 234, km 78 (02972 428154/www. paihuen.com.ar/info@paihuen.com.ar). **Rates** US$70-$150 double. **Credit** AmEx, DC, MC, V.

Just four kilometres (2.5 miles) from town, the Paihuen complex comprises 33 stone cabins on a hill overlooking the lake. The outstanding amenities include sauna, jacuzzi, gym, swimming pool, tennis courts and an in-house tourist agency that organises daily excursions for guests. Take into account the gourmet restaurant and popular wine bar and you'll appreciate why this is regarded as one of the best hotels in Argentinian Patagonia.

Patagonia Plaza Hotel

Avenida San Martín y Rivadavia (02972 422280/ www.patagoniaplazahotel.com.ar). **Rates** US$55-$115 single; US$80-$160 double; US$110-$215 triple; US$140-$260 suite. **Credit** AmEx, DC, MC, V.

Downtown 91-room 'Patagonia' generally gets the nod as the best hotel within the city limits. No 'rustic charm' here; it's plush, slick, bright and modern.

Ten Rivers & Ten Lakes

Circuito Arrayán, Km 4 (Buenos Aires tel & fax 011 4522 7754/www.tenriverstenlakes.com). **Rates** US$180 double; US$250 suite. **Credit** AmEx, DC, MC, V.

The old Arrayán Tea House halfway up the mountain of the same name has turned itself into a gourmet restaurant with the luxury lodge Ten Rivers & Ten Lakes attached. This is a classic romantic getaway; the four spacious rooms each have views to fall in love by. The whole thing is clearly been designed by someone with a passion for the project, down to the oversize beds and bathtubs for two. The service is attentive without being intrusive and the food is top notch.

Le Village

General Roca 816, entre San Martín y Perito Moreno (tel/fax 02972 427698/www.hotelle village.com.ar). **Rates** US$35-$65 single; US$60-$90 double; US$60-$100 triple; US$80-$130 cabin. **Credit** AmEx, DC, MC, V.

A hotel and cabin complex with unfussy Tudor-style decor and great sofas, Le Village is centrally located and has plenty of bonus features, including a sauna and a barbecue area.

Resources

Hospital

Hospital Ramón Carrillo, Avenida San Martín y Coronel Rodhé (02972 427211).

Internet

Locutorio Cooperativa Telefónica, Capitán Drury 761 (02972 428900).

Police station

Belgrano 635 (02972 427300).

Post office

General Roca y Coronel Pérez (02972 427201).

Tourist information

Secretaría Municipal de Turismo de San Martín de los Andes, Avenida San Martín 750, y Juan Manuel de Rosas (02972 427347/www. smandes.gov.ar). **Open** *Apr-June, Aug-Nov 8am-9pm daily. July, Dec-Mar 8am-10pm daily.*

Getting there

By air

Direct flights from Buenos Aires and Neuquén arrive at **Aeropuerto de Chapelco 'Carlos Campos'** (02972 428388), on RN234, 20km (12 miles) from town. Aeroclub de los Andes also operates pleasure flights from this airport.

By road

San Martin is 80km (50 miles) from Bariloche, 40km (25 miles) from Junín and 110km (68 miles) from Villa La Angostura. It is well served by daily bus services to and from local towns as well as BA, though the RP234 (Ruta de los Siete Lagos) to Villa La Angostura is closed in heavy winter snowfall. The **Terminal de Omnibus** (02972 427044) is at Villegas y Juez Del Valle.

Villa La Angostura

Peaceful and sprawling among the trees on the northern shore of Lago Nahuel Huapi and within the boundary of the national park (*see p100* **Parque Nacional Nahuel Huapi**), Villa La Angostura is a serious contender for the title of Argentina's loveliest town. It's a purely touristic haven and was even created as such – the first hotel was built in 1923, 11 years before the foundation of the town itself.

Much of the town's style is the work of architect Alejandro Bustillo (1889-1982). His lasting influence and the neat finish to the wooden shops lends a pleasing Toy Town feel to Avenida Arrayanes, the centre of El Cruce – Villa La Angostura's downtown. While it's hardly a throbbing metropolis – one block from the high street you can listen to birdsong and smell the pine trees – this apparent tranquility hides a population that has quintupled in the last ten years to its current level of around 12,000 habitants. Those with money cling to the water's edge; those without have slipped into the poor quarter hidden from the road. The desire to have a house with a lake view has given rise to several satellite communities, like **Puerto Manzano** (seven kilometres/4.5 miles away), a residential suburb set in among apple trees around the tight enclave of Bahia Manzano.

During winter, the town thrives on tourism to Patagonia's third largest ski resort, **Cerro Bayo**, nine kilometres (5.5 miles) away. Most of the 20 pistes are designed for advanced and intermediate skiers, though with a gentle slope close to the top, beginners can also enjoy the views. In summer the centre opens its doors to trekkers and mountain bikers.

Other warm weather pleasures include bathing in Lago Correntoso, four kilometres (2.5 miles) from El Cruce on the road to San Martin, or indulging in a spot of fishing. Omar 'Banana'

Martínez's professional company **PatagonFly** (Paseo Inacayal, Avenida Arrayanes 282, 02944 494634, www.patagonfly.com.ar) organises fishing trips in the area for up to five days.

Willy Wonka wannabes will enjoy **Danon** (Avenida Arrayanes 188, 02944 495686), where you can see the chocolates being crafted in the small work area behind the store. Handmade local produce can be purchased from stalls that line an alley just off Arrayanes.

The **Museo Histórico Regional** (Nahuel Huapi y El Calafate) helps put the area in its historical context, and displays archeological finds and an 18th-century dug-out canoe.

EXCURSIONS

Villa La Angostura is the start or end point – depending on your direction – on the scenic **Ruta de los Siete Lagos** (*see p104*).

Just a few minutes out of town by car is **El Messidor**, a large castle made of pinkish stone. Designed by Bustillo and completed in 1942, it is now a home for politicians on a junket, sorry, well-earned break. Through the years controversial guests have included Isabel Perón after the 1976 military coup, and more recently Carlos Menem, hiding out until his cosmetic surgery facial swellings – which he roundly denied and blamed on a wasp – had gone down.

One must-see local attraction is the **Parque Nacional los Arrayanes**. It was set up to protect the Bosque de Arrayanes, a unique monoculture of century-old myrtle trees. The

Lighthouse luxury at **El Faro**. *See p97.*

Puerto Manzano. *See p95.*

trees are characterised by the twisted cinnamon-coloured bark that covers their trunks. It was from these gilded woods, some locals say, that Walt Disney drew inspiration for *Bambi*.

To get there, boats leave the pier in the residential part of town known as La Villa, four kilometres (2.5 miles) from El Cruce. Hiking or biking are the most rewarding means of getting there, but only possible in summer. From the park entrance, the 12-kilometre (7.5-mile) one-way walk to the Bosque will take three to four hours. Before setting off you must register with the *guardaparques'* office, close to the jetty.

Close by the base of Cerro Bayo is the access to the **Rio Bonito** waterfall, as well as pretty views for those willing to climb a little. Rafting, horseback riding, kayaking, mountain climbing and ziplining are also available. **Huilen Viajes y Turismo** (Avenida Arrayanes 66, 09244 493844) is a well-established tour operator.

Parque Nacional Los Arrayanes

Within PN Nahuel Huapi, entrance at Seccional Angostura, Puerto 'Modesta Victoria' (02944 494152). **Open** *Apr-Nov* 9am-4pm daily. *Dec-Mar* 9am-6pm. **Admission** free.

Where to eat

Tinto Bistro (Nahuel Huapi 34, 02944 494924, closed Sun, $$$$) is one of the very best dining options in El Cruce, with an adventurous menu that includes deluxe salads, tapas and even some spicy oriental influences. From outside, **Rincón Suizo** (Avenida Arrayanes 44, 02944 494248, $$$) looks a bit theme-parky but the food is an interesting combination of Swiss, Central European and Argentinian cuisines. For a tasty snack, **Vientos Verdes** (Av Arrayanes 126, 02944 494719, $) has garnered a reputation for its home-made empanadas.

Farther out of town but eminently worth the trek, **Las Balsas** (Bahia las Balsas, 02944 494308, $$$$) offers an enticing menu that alongside rabbit and trout offers more than one vegetarian option – almost a collector's item in meat-worshipping Argentina. In the evening a local sommelier glides from table to table offering suggestions of wines to accompany your meal. Another culinary treasure in Villa la Angostura, **Delfina** restaurant (Punta Manzano, 02944 494813, $$$) serves traditional family recipes in the tiny rooms of an ancient house. The *brochette de cordero* (lamb kebab) with two chutneys is not to be missed. Seven kilometres (4.5 miles) from the centre is the exalted **Waldhaus** (Avenida Arrayanes 6431, Puerto Manzano 02944 495123, closed Sept-Oct, $$$). Swiss-mountain style restaurants may seem two-a-peso in these parts, but this gem is definitely worth the taxi ride.

Where to stay

Just two kilometres (1.2 miles) outside town, **El Faro** (Avenida Siete Lagos 2345, 02944 495485, info@hosteriaelfaro.com.ar, double US$45-$65) is one of Villa la Angostura's top lodgings. The lighthouse construction gives this four-star hotel curved edges and stunning lake views. Next door, **La Posada Hosteria and Spa** (Avenida Siete Lagos, 02944 494450, www.hosteriala posada.com, double US$75-$80) has a more traditional feel, with open fires and cosy rooms. Also close by, the recently refurbished **Hotel Correntoso** (Ruta 231, 02944 1561 9728/011 4803 0030, www.correntoso.com, double US$150-$230) blends traditional hospitality (it first opened in 1922) with pure modern decadence. It has a superb restaurant, and comprehensive activity programmes both in summer and winter.

Close to the Cerro Bayo ski centre, the **Ruca Kuyen** complex (Cruz del Sur 203, Bahia Las Balsas, 02944 495099, www.rucakuyen.com.ar, double US$60-$85), complete with a four-room lodge, cabins and a golf course, is built on spectacular grounds in the middle of the mountains. Nearby, **Las Balsas** (Bahia las Balsas, 02944 494308, double US$300-$350) is located right on the lake and has its own private jetty. The gourmet restaurant (*see above*) is one of the best in the area.

Secluded Puerto Manzano is slowly but surely filling up with quality hotels. **Bahía Manzano** (RN231, 02944 494341, www.bahia manzano.com, apartments US$70-$180), is a vast, family-oriented lakeside complex. Down another winding track in the area lies the aptly named **La Escondida** (Puerto Manzano, 02944 494813, www.hosterialaescondida.com.ar, double US$100-$150), with slick, stylish rooms in pleasant lakeside lodgings.

Resources

Hospital

Hospital Rural, Barrio Hospital (02944 494170).

Internet

Ciudad Ikland, Avenida Arrayanes 310 (02944 494084).

Police station

Avenida Arrayanes, entre Cerro Bayo y Cerro Inacayal (02944 494121).

Post office

Avenida Arrayenes 282, local 4 (02944 494177).

Tourist information

Secretaria Municipal de Turismo, Avenida Siete Lagos 93, y Obispo De Nevares (02944 494124/ www.villalaangostura.gov.ar). **Open** *Apr-June, Aug-Dec* 8am-8pm daily. *Jan-Mar, July* 8am-9pm daily.

The fairytale elegance of Bariloche's **Palacio Bustillo**. *See p99.*

Getting there

By road

Villa La Angostura is on RN231, 83km (49 miles) north-west of Bariloche; 6 buses daily connect the two. There is 1 bus daily from San Martin, 110km (68 miles) to the north, and only if the Ruta de los Siete Lagos is open. If snow closes it in winter, you have to take a long circular detour (6hrs) via Junin. The bus station is at Avenida Siete Lagos 35 (02944 494961).

San Carlos de Bariloche

It's brash and bold and unashamedly touristy, with a population that grows by the second (currently standing at 110,000) and suburbs that are spreading out along Lago Nahuel Huapi and up into the mountains beyond. Welcome to San Carlos de Bariloche, Patagonian party capital, tourist mecca and the annual destination for bus loads of high school students who celebrate their graduation in its numerous discos. Bariloche (as it is almost always known) pulses with life in its enclave between the lake to the north, the arid steppe to the east and the Andean peaks to the west. But apart from the urban life that bustles on the cluttered slopes, just outside the city limits you can find plenty pockets of peace, and the city is an excellent jumping-off point for outdoor activities and daytime excursions.

The first whites to come to the area were sniffing around fruitlessly in search of gold. It was only at the end of the 19th century that German immigrants from southern Chile successfully put down roots in the region, establishing commercial links with Puerto Montt in Chilean Patagonia. The first road was paved in honour of a visit by US president Theodore Roosevelt in 1913. In 1921 a plane touched down and another 13 years later the first trains arrived, the same year that saw the creation of the Nahuel Huapi National Park (*see p100*). With transport links established and then hotels built, Bariloche was in business.

Nowadays, the main street, Bartholomé Mitre, is a tourist thoroughfare for most of the year, lined with shops selling tacky souvenirs, excursions, and the ubiquitous chocolate. For the best of the latter, try **Frantom**, (Panozzi y Rosas, 02944 522391), which also offers guided visits where you can watch the chocolate-making process. Other options include **Mamuschka** (Mitre 216, 02944 423294, www.mamuschka.com) and **Abuela Goye** (Mitre 258, 02944 423311, www.abuelagoye.com). It's also a good spot for ice-creams, fondues, quality sweaters and for renting outdoor equipment. For gifts, try the small crafts market, **Feria Artesanal**.

In the heart of the town, the Centro Civico – home to the tourist office and museum – forms a horseshoe that, like everything else, stares out on to the great lake. Making an exception, on the square in front, is the statue of General Roca, head bowed as if in recognition of certain excesses. The **Museo de la Patagonia** is one of the best of its kind in the country, exhibiting old newspaper clippings, information about the area's indigenous tribes, and a highly evocative room that reconstructs 'Perito' Moreno's study, with the original desk and copies of the letters in which he donated the land to create Argentina's first national park.

As in Villa La Angostura, it's difficult to ignore the architectural influence of Alejandro Bustillo. Downtown he conceived the Centro Civico and the neo-gothic Iglesia Catedral, a stone church, inaugurated in 1946, but – owing to a lack of cash – never quite finished. And, in the woods on the outskirts of town, is the graceful country house **Palacio Bustillo**.

On the lake, eight kilometres (five miles) out is secluded beach, **Playa Bonita**, and another 21 kilometres (13 miles) on is **Llao Llao Hotel & Resort** (see p103). Built in 1936, it remains Bustillo's best-known local masterpiece. Its 18-hole golf course is open to non-residents. Boats to Chile leave from the nearby jetty (see p183 **PN Vicente Pérez Rosales**).

Start your visit to Bariloche on the cable car (or on foot if you're feeling energetic) to the revolving tea room and gallery at **Cerro Otto**, a 1,405-metre (3,428-feet) mountain five kilometres (three miles) from the centre. Argentina's most popular ski resort is **Cerro Catedral**, 20 kilometres (12.5 miles) south. Facilities are excellent for mountain skiers, with runs for all levels and a snowboard park. Catedral's apogee is **La Fiesta de la Nieve** (18-26 August), an extravangant gala that snowballs from a torch descent into a non-stop competition to find the best of everything: waiter, sweater, chocolate and, most fiercely coveted of all, Queen of Snow. Cerro Catedral runs year-round; when the snow melts you can trek or rent quad or mountain bikes and horses. Confusingly, two companies – Alta Patagonia and Robles Catedral – run the

resort, though it makes little difference to you. For water-oriented thrills, **Arümco Buceo** (Avenida Bustillo, km 8, Playa Bonita, 02944 523122/15 604306, www.arumcobuceo.com.ar) organises lake dives for both experienced divers (from US$25) and beginners (from US$30).

EXCURSIONS

Day or half-day excursions to **Isla Victoria** in Lago Nahuel Huapi leave from Puerto Pañuelo, 25 kilometres (15 miles) away. The forest-filled land mass is so big you hardly know you're on an island. Apart from rock paintings, believed to be 2,000 years old, the island is famous for its community of pint-sized pudú deer.

Bariloche's most popular excursion is the **Circuito Chico** (Little Circuit), a three-and-a-half-hour bus trip. Heading west along Lago Nahuel Huapi, it passes by several lagoons, Puerto Pañuelo, a tiny chapel and the Llao Llao resort before it loops back via Colonia Suiza, an early Swiss colony.

The **Circuito Grande** (Big Circuit) is a full-day, 247-kilometre (153-mile) trip. It visits, among others, the Valle Encantado (Enchanted Valley) – site of strange natural rock formations such as the Dedo de Dios (God's Finger) – Villa Traful, the stunning Correntoso and Espejo lakes, as well as Villa La Angostura.

For a trip back in time to the halcyon days of Patagonia's once proud rail network, hop on the **Histórico Tren a Vapor** (12 de Octubre 2400, 02944 423858, www.trenhistoricoavapor.com.ar), a Scottish steam train built in 1912 that offers full-day scenic journeys covering 40 kilometres (25 miles) of lakes and mountains. It fires up its remarkably reliable boilers on Tuesdays, Thursdays and Saturdays.

Argentinian Patagonia

Parque Nacional Nahuel Huapi

Nahuel Huapi is the oldest, biggest and most visited of all the national parks in Argentinian Patagonia. Stretching across the lower reaches of Neuquén province into the upper section of Río Negro, it's a whopping 705 square kilometres (272 square miles), incorporating the towns of Bariloche and Villa La Angostura. That it even exists is in great part thanks to naturalist Francisco 'Perito' Moreno, who donated the land in 1919 (it was first designated a National Park in 1934)' (*see p51* **Environmental warrior**). The great lakes are the park's eye-catching feature.

FLORA AND FAUNA

Star among the park's many trees is the alerce, or Patagonian cypress, a magnificent conifer that grows slowly. Other typical specimens are the arrayán and, in humid areas, coihues speckled yellow by the llao llao fungus. The lower sections are covered in green ferns and caña colihue, a reed that flowers every 30 to 40 years and then dies. In autumn the lengas and ñires are a wonderful red and in late spring the orange amancay and pink arvejilla flowers add colour.

Despite the presence of a large number of human visitors, the park remains equally rich in fauna – spot the busy huillín (river otter), herds of guanaco, the Patagonian hare, and condors floating on Andean thermals.

TREKS AND ACTIVITIES

There are numerous excursions that will take you out into the park for nature, for adventure or simply for a different view. Few offer better scenery than the treks around the Lago Traful or are more spectacular than the mountainous walk up the Cerro Tronador. Close to Bariloche you can hop on a boat to visit Isla Victoria or a bus for tours around the Lago Nahuel Huapi (for all, *see p99*). If you just need to stretch your legs, a short trek from the *refugio* Neumeyer cuts through a lovely little forest before reaching the peak of Cerro Chalhuaco.

FACILITIES

There are ten *refugios* and (at last count) 16 serviced campsites in the park. Owing to the proximity of towns such as Bariloche, you will never be too far from provisions.

Parque Nacional Nahuel Huapi

Open 24hrs daily (recommended entry 8am-8pm). **Admission** *Cruce Los Rápidos, Puerto Pañuelo & Villa La Angostura entrances* US$2; US$1 6-12s; free under-6s. *Other entrances free.* **No credit cards.**
Villa La Angostura and Bariloche are within the park's boundaries; it's easily accessible from El Bolsón, too. There are seven points of entry and six areas with rangers' offices.

Intendencia (Bariloche)

Avenida San Martín 24, y Morales, Bariloche (02944 423111/www.parquesnacionales. gov.ar). **Open** 8am-2pm Mon-Fri.

Information office (Angostura)

Boulevard Nahuel Huapi 2193, Bahía La Mansa, Villa La Angostura (02944 494152). **Open** 9am-4pm daily.

Information office (Traful)

RP65, 35km from RN237, Villa Traful (02944 479033). **Open** 24hrs daily.

For some fresh, Andean air take the bus to **Cerro Tronador**, an extinct volcano straddling the Argentinian–Chilean border. A number of glaciers slide off the sides of the mountain, including the famous **Ventisquero Negro** – its dark colour due to sediments in the ice – 3,000 metre-plus (9,800 feet) high and popular with trekkers. If you have time it's a good idea to break up the trip with a night at family-run **Hostería Pampa Linda** (02944

490517, www.tronador.com, double US$30-$45) eight kilometres (five miles) from the mountain; there's also a hostel nearby, costing US$2.50 per person per night, and plenty of interesting and well-organised mountain activities. Detailed maps of Tronador (essential if you're making your own way in the area), and free information and advice about trekking in the vicinity plus help organising excursions, are available from **Club Andino Bariloche**.

Lakeside horse riding at the lovely **Fortín Chacabuco** ranch can be booked for a half day (US$30) or full day (US$40). Contact Alistair on 02944 15 554148 or ask at any travel agency.

Rafting of various levels is also available from **Aguas Blancas** (www.aguasblancas. com.ar), which organises full-day trips on the Manso river that cost from US$40 to US$60.

Luxury sailing trips can be organised with **Velero Gourmet** (02944 15 639387,www. sailingpatagonia.com.ar), which offers half-day (US$250 for two) and full-day (US$350 for two) jaunts, including trips to Victoria Island and various secluded beaches.

Recommended travel agencies in Bariloche are **Turisur** (Mitre 219, 02944 426109, www. bariloche.com/turisur) and **Espacio** (Mitre 139, 02944 431372). For up-to-date English language listings and articles on Bariloche and the rest of Patagonia, look out for the **Traveller's Guru**, a free quarterly newspaper researched and written by long-time Bariloche residents Alan and Ron. Their website is at www.backpackerspatagonia.com and the paper is available in hostels, bars and cafés throughout the region.

Cerro Catedral
Avenida de los Pioneros, km 8 (Alta Patagonia 02944 423776, www.catedralaltapatagonia.com 02944 460062). **Open** 9am-6pm daily. **Rates** *Ski pass* US$10-$15 per day. **Credit** AmEx, DC, MC, V.

Cerro Otto
Avenida de los Pioneros, km 5 (02944 441035/ www.todobariloche.com.ar/cerrootto.htm). **Open** 10am-7pm daily. **No credit cards**.

Club Andino Bariloche
20 de Febrero 30, entre Neumeyer y F Perito Moreno (02944 442226/www.clubandino.com.ar). **Open** 8am-1pm, 3-8pm Mon-Fri.

Feria Artesanal
Villegas y F Perito Moreno. **Open** 9am-9pm daily. **No credit cards**.

El Histórico Tren a Vapor
Terminal de Trenes de Bariloche, RN237, km 1 (02944 423858/historicotrenavapor@infovia. com.ar). **Tickets** US$10 tourist class; US$16 first-class; US$20 sleeper. **Credit** AmEx, DC, MC, V.

Museo de la Patagonia 'Francisco P Moreno'
Centro Cívico (02944 422309/www.bariloche. com.ar/museo). **Open** 10am-1pm Mon; 10am-12.30pm, 2-7pm Tue-Fri; 11am-6pm Sat. **Admission** US$1 discretionary.

Where to eat

El Boliche de Alberto
Villegas 347, entre FP Moreno y Eiflien (02944 431433). **Average** $$. **Credit** AmEx, MC, V.
Of Alberto's three popular Bariloche restaurants, this is the meaty one. There's no music, just respectful silence and the aroma of slowly sizzling steaks. Unusually for late-dining Argentina the queue starts forming at 8pm, a testament to the quality and value of what's served up inside.

Cassis
España 268, y French (02944 431382/www.cassis-patagonia.com.ar). **Open** from 8pm Mon-Sat. **Average** $$$. **No credit cards**.

Cerro Catedral, Bariloche. *See p99.*

This small husband-and-wife-run restaurant – she cooks, he waits – has only ten tables, making for an intimate dining experience. The menu contains a touch of the Germanic – lamb strudel anyone? – but includes some decent vegetarian options.

Chachao Bistro

Avenida Ezequiel Bustillo 3,800, km 3.8 (02944 520574). **Open** *Aug-Mar* from 7pm daily. *Apr-July* from 7pm Mon-Sat. **Average** $$$. **Credit** AmEx, DC, MC, V.

Two sisters run this exquisite, intimate restaurant on the outskirts of town, drawing inspiration from indigenous techniques and ingredients, as well as modern fusion cuisine. The terriyaki trout is a treat.

La Cueva

Cerro Catedral (02944 15 585994). **Open** *mid June-Sept* 7.30pm-midnight daily. **Average** $$$. **Credit** MC.

This stone and glass refuge is accessible by snowbike only. Soft lights and a steam machine to warm the seats add a cosy touch. There are two sittings (7.30 and 10pm) at the five tables, so booking is vital.

Il Gabbiano

Avenida Ezequiel Bustillo, km 24.3 (02944 448346). **Open** 8-11.30pm Wed-Mon. **Average** $$$. **No credit cards.**

Not far from the Llao Llao resort, this quaint cabin offers a simple Italian menu of quality pastas, meat and fish dishes, in a warm ambience.

Kandahar

20 de Febrero 698, y Tiscornia (02944 424702/ www.kandahar.com.ar). **Open** *Dec-Mar, July* 8pm-midnight daily. *Apr-June, Aug-Nov* 8pm-midnight Mon-Sat. **Average** $$$. **Credit** AmEx, MC, V.

This red-hued restaurant named after a ski race is well worth the uphill climb, with a lively ambience, a modern Patagonian menu and excellent service. Offering quality cuisine in a laid-back atmosphere, manager Diego ensures the service is professional without being overly starched-shirt. The stuffed gnocchis are pure pleasure.

Monet

Avenida Ezequiel Bustillo, km 2.5 (Buenos Aires 011 48148700). **Open** from noon-3.30pm, from 7.30pm daily. **Average** $$$$. **Credit** AmEx, MC, V.

The Design Suites hotel's art-themed restaurant is new on the Bariloche scene. The menu echoes the impressionist theme in terms of taste and colour, and includes dishes that Monet himself preferred, like stuffed onions, and leek and potato soup. End the meal with a 'chromatic symphony' – a fresh sorbet extravaganza that leaves your palate tingling.

Nightlife

The base of Cerro Catedral has numerous busy bars and clubs and is where to be during the ski season. In town, this year's most popular spot is the Map Room (Urquiza 248, 02944 456856), a capacious split-level bar-restaurant

with good food (try the Taj Mahal appetiser) and the cheapest beers in town. It's also the only place you can get an authentic American breakfast, which helps make it a favourite with backpackers and is something you'll appreciate if you have a long day ahead of you or a long night behind you. For the slightly surreal experience of an 'Irish' bar in South America, try **Pilgrim** (Palacios 167, 02944 421686). The music is cheesy, but the place is busy and sociable, with a wide choice of beers. For another slice of displaced Emerald Isle blarney, try the **Wilkenny** (San Martin 435, 02944 42444), which fills to the brim on weekend nights with most of Bariloche crammed into its dark interiors – great for meeting fellow travellers or just getting steadily sozzled at the bar. For a more intimate drinking experience, **South Bar** (Pasaje Juramento 30, 02944 522001) offers micro-brewed beers in a cosy locale that fills up late in the evening with a mix of locals and tourists. Everyone keeps drinking until the sun comes up and gregarious barman Pablo calls time. There's a happy hour all night every night, and if you make friends with Pablo (not too difficult) he might deign to play your music requests by delving into his extensive CD collection. Nearby **Cúbico** (Elflein 47, 02944 522260, closed Mon) isn't as square as it sounds, with a slick lounge atmosphere, live DJs and an extensive cocktail lists.

One of the best clubs among many on the lake shore is **Roket** (Juan Manuel de Rosas 424, 02944 431940, www.roket.com.ar, entrance US$8, includes one drink). Everything from deep house to Latin to hip hop swings the three floors of this snazzy venue.

Where to stay

Arelauquen Golf & Country Club

Ruta 82, frente al Lago Gutiérrez (02944 467552/ www.arelauquen.com). **Rates** US$149-$352 double. **Credit** AmEx, DC, MC, V.

This top-of-the-range golf and country club is located on 700 hectares (1,730 acres) of land, 500 of which are part of a protected natural reserve. The five-star lodge boasts enormous rooms with lake views and luxury fittings, and offers all the requisite five-star services. Numerous outdoor activities, including kayaking, horse riding, trekking, climbing and ziplining are organised by the helpful Matias. The complex also boasts a golf course and two polo fields, as well as a mountain-top refuge with excellent views of the lake.

Dazzler

Avenida San Martin 441 (02944 456900/www. dazzlerhotel.com). **Rates** US$108-$130 double; US$142-$165 suite. **Credit** AmEx, DC, MC, V.

Along with slick minimalist rooms and a central location, Dazzler (run by the Argentinian Fen group) offers lake views, first-class amenities, business facilities and advice on excursions.

Design Suites
Avenida Ezequiel Bustillo, km 2.5 (011 425846/50, www.designsuites.com). **Rates** US$100-$170 double; US$150 to $270 suite. **Credit** AmEx, MC, V.

With its sleek design scheme, comfortable spaces and modern furnishings, Design Suites is close to the centre but far from the chaos. A pioneer among Patagonian boutique hotels, and it includes a top restaurant (Monet; *see p102*), heated pool and spa.

Llao Llao Hotel & Resort
Avenida Ezequiel Bustillo, km 25, Parque Nacional Nahuel Huapi (tel & fax 02944 448530/445781/www.llaollao.com). **Rates** US$160-$220 double; US$210-$270 triple; US$497-$690 suite. **Credit** AmEx, DC, MC, V.

This historic 158-room hotel is one of Argentina's best. Set in stunning surroundings, it has its own marina on Lago Moreno, a spa, a plush 18-hole golf course and awesome lake views from the pool.

Peñon del Lago
Avenida Ezequiel Bustillo, km 13 (02944 463000/www.penondellago.com.ar). **Rates** US$53-$58 single; US$63-$70 double; US$92-$103 triple; US$116-$126 suite. **Credit** DC, MC, V.

With just 20 luxurious suites among the trees by the lake, Peñon del Lago offers an exclusive lodging experience. Rooms are plush and spacious, attention is personal and the price includes various activities such as trekking, mountain climbing, ziplining, horse riding and boating, not to mention sauna and massage services. Recommended.

Peuma Hue
Via RN258, 24km (15 miles) from Bariloche (02944 501030, www.peuma-hue.com). **Rates** US$350-$410 double all-inclusive, including transfer from airport. **Credit** AmEx, MC, V.

The name means 'Place of Dreams' in Mapuche, and if you spend too long at this wonderful ranch on the southern shore of Lago Guttieréz you may never want to wake up. All activities are included, and owners Evelyn and Miguel treat guests like family members.

Resources

Hospital
Hospital Zonal Bariloche, Francisco Perito Moreno y Frey (02944 426119).

Internet
Cybercafe, Rolando 217, Local 12 (02944 436814).

Police station
Centro Civico (02944 423434).

Post office
Francisco Perito Moreno 175 (02944 429876).

Tourist information
Secretaria Municipal de Turismo Centro Civico (02944 423022/secturismo@bariloche.com.ar). **Open** 8am-9pm Mon-Fri; 9am-9pm Sat, Sun.

Getting there

By air
Aeropuerto Internacional Bariloche (RP80, 02944 426162) is on RN237, 14km (8.5 miles) outside the city. There are regular direct flights from Buenos Aires and Esquel.

By road
Bariloche is on the RN237/RN258 with regular buses to all the town of the Lake District. The **Terminal de Omnibus** is on RN237, km1 (02944 432860).

By train
The **Tren Patagónico** (www.interpatagonia.com/trenpatagonico) connects Bariloche with Viedma, 16hrs east, arriving at **Estación San Carlos de Bariloche** (RN234, km 1, 02944 431777). **Departures** *Viedma–Bariloche*: Jan, Feb 6pm Mon, Thur; Mar-Jun 6pm Mon, Fri. *Bariloche–Viedma*: Jan, Feb 6pm Mon, Fri; Mar-Jun 6pm Sun, Thur. The train makes 15 stops, including in San Antonio Oeste & Ingeniero Jacobazzi. **Tickets** US$10 tourist class;

Elegant, romantic **Chachao Bistro**. *See p102.*

Argentinian Patagonia

Full steam ahead

After a generation of apathy and neglect, there is a faint light aglow at the end of the tunnel for Argentina's rail network. The impetus for renewal comes from the top: Patagonia-born Argentinian president Néstor Kirchner is a self-confessed train nut who dreams of reviving some of the rail routes that once crisscrossed the entire country.

For now there are only a few ways to do the locomotion in Patagonia. It's not a practical way to travel, but one nonetheless loaded with history and romance. Tourist trains in Ushuaia and Bariloche – El Tren del Fin del Mundo (*see p162*) and El Histórico Tren a Vapor (*see p99*) – offer old-style trips through the wilderness. The former uses narrow-gauge British and German engines from the 1890s. The Histórico, which originally ran on the Buenos Aires–Mendoza line, uses beautiful 1912 Scottish rolling stock, and the old presidential carriage has lavish woodwork.

At six in the evening on Mondays and Fridays the last regular passenger service in Patagonia leaves Viedma on the Atlantic coast, arriving 826 kilometres (513 miles) to the west in Bariloche at around noon the following day. On Sundays and Thursdays it goes the other way. The province of Río Negro keeps this line going when most others have failed, as witnessed by the graveyard of old steam trains and pullman coaches around San Antonio Oeste where the line crosses the old North–South route to Buenos Aires.

For US$40 you can get yourself a clean, comfortable cabin with two bunks, and tickets to the on-board art deco cinema coach thrown in. There's a dining car with kitchen serving freshly cooked food, brought to passengers by attentive waiters in faded tuxedos. You can watch the desolate wild-west landscape of northern Patagonia creep past as the sun sets and you sip your Malbec.

Don't get the wrong idea – this is not a luxury trip. It's charm lies more in its slight absurdity and rarity value; it's a service kept going at least partly through the love of those who run it. On the eastern side you run through flat, endless plains past small groups of bored cattle hiding in the scrub and skittish guanacos. In the west the train winds out of the lakes of Bariloche into the classic Patagonian rolling steppe, connecting tiny halts where a few farmsteads cluster together. In the right frame of mind and in the right company it's an adventure – but don't expect the Orient Express.

Arelauquen Golf & Country Club. *See p102.*

US$20 pullman; US$40 sleeper (credit MC, V). A special service once a week runs in each direction Dec-Mar, with a train with more facilities – check at station for details. *See above* **Full steam ahead**.

Ruta de los Siete Lagos

Sometimes the shortest distance between two points is the most beautiful. This is true of the stunning 110-kilometre (65-mile) 'Seven Lakes Route' along the RN234. Stamped deep into rich forests, it runs from San Martin de los Andes to Villa La Angostura, wiggling its way through the steep mountainsides of two of Argentina's most stunning National Parks: **PN Lanín** (*see p90*) and **PN Nahuel Huapi** (*see p100*).

No one can agree on which seven lakes are the official ones of the route. There are nine contenders in all; from north to south, Lácar, Machónico, Hermoso, Falkner, Villarino, Escondido, Traful, Correntoso and Espejo. In fact the argument is moot – they are all equally blue and beautiful.

To drive from one end to the other takes at least two hours, but it's best to smell the roses and stop overnight along the way. If car rental is out of the budget, several buses run daily between Bariloche and San Martin via Villa La Angostura on this route.

Apart from the obvious lakeside treasures, there are plenty of hidden attractions. The middle section is particularly worth exploring, where **Laguna Pudú Pudú** close to **Lago Escondido** has a little beach with a free campsite and close by is the **Cascada Vulignanco,** a delightful 20-metre (66-feet) waterfall. This is close to where the road runs over a small strip of land that separates Lakes Falkner and Villarino.

Spots to pull over and unwind are plentiful, as well as patches of grass to pitch a tent. In summer, sporting types might be tempted to cycle the 110 kilometres (68 miles). Although hilly, it's manageable and the proximity to nature makes for a wonderful experience. In winter the road – with a small section still unpaved – becomes treacherous and often shuts.

Villa Traful, 63 kilometres (39 miles) north of Villa La Angostura, is a lakeside community of just 300 inhabitants fronting the banks of Lago Traful, cherished for its land-locked salmon. Strictly speaking it's off the main route, 31 kilometres (19 miles) down the RP65, but from here you can explore the surrounding area at leisure. To get a good panorama of the wonderful setting, head five kilometres (three miles) up to the **Mirador Traful,** a lookout point on top of a sheer cliff. From here you can see straight down to the glittering turquoise waters of Lake Traful. Anglers should check out the **Arroyo Verde** *estancia* (011 48017448, www.estanciaarroyoverde.com.ar, all-inclusive packages from US$400), dubbed the best fishing lodge in the world by *Forbes* magazine.

Just up the road from Villa Traful is the office for boat trips to the **Bosque Sumergido** and **Gruta de la Virgen.** The *bosque* is part of the mountain that fell, trees and all, into the lake after an earthquake 30 years ago. If you know how to scuba dive, trips will take you down for a picnic among the trunks that still stand 30 metres (98 feet) under the limpid waters.

For some real exercise, tackle the challenging hike up the **Cerro Negro.** At the summit there's a rewarding view over Lake Traful, the Andes and Volcán Lanín.

Where to stay & eat

The obvious places to bed down or fill up are San Martín or Villa La Angostura; but on the route, Villa Traful is the best bet. It's popular with budget travellers and busy in summer.

Set in huge grounds, **Hostería Villa Traful** (RP65, Villa Traful, 02944 479005, www.7lagos. com/hostvillatraful, double US$12-$28) has

Boutique bliss at **Design Suites**. *See p103.*

snug, carpeted rooms and good-value cabins for up to six people (US$40). Or look out for **Albergue Vulcanche** (RP65, km 35, 02944 494015, www.vulcanche.com, closed May-Sept, US$5-$7 per person). It's simple, sylvan and popular with young travellers for its cheap dorms and large camping space.

Most of the lakes are surrounded with serviced or free capsides; beside Lago Villarino is one of the best places to set up, with a long grassy stretch beside the water; or peg your tent at the rustic (so with limited services) site at Lago Falkner.

If you fancy a quick snack, head to cosy teahouse/restaurant **Ñancu Lahuen** (Centro Civico, 02944 479017, $) in Villa Traful for a slice of Black Forest cake or a DLT (deer, lettuce and tomato) sandwich. Baby goat and Patagonian lamb are on the menu at **La Terraza** (RP65, km 35.5, 02944 479073, $$). The lake is visible through the treetops from the luminous dining room.

Resources

Essential services are in San Martín, Villa La Angostura; information below is for Villa Traful, off the Ruta de los Siete Lagos, between the aforementioned towns.

Hospital
Posta Sanitaria Olga Vivares (02944 479011).

Police station
Villa Traful (02944 479040).

Post office
Villa Traful (02944 479064).

Tourist information & Internet
Comisión de Fomento de Villa Traful, Laffitte (02944 479018/villatraful@ciudad.com.ar). **Open** *Nov-Apr* 8am-2pm, 4-8pm daily.

El Bolsón

This may be Argentina's top hippie retreat but the laid-back atmosphere owes more to pulling weeds than smoking them. The town is neat and tidy and well looked after, testament to the civic pride of its 11,000 habitants. This Mapuche resting place of yesteryear is the refuge of choice for weary urbanites; maybe it's the location, or the weather – temperatures average 4°C (7.2°F) above the rest of the region.

Fruit is major news here. The microclimate and fertile lands contribute to the abundance of red berry fruits that thrive in the fields. After the annual cull, many are jarred and exported. However, a small quantity (the best) is saved for local consumption. At **Cascada de la Virgen**, 20 kilometres (12.5 miles) outside El Bolsón, a cluster of *chacras* (small farms) sell exceptional organic produce to the public.

Beer, another local speciality, is distilled at **Cervecería El Bolsón**, and you can pass by the brewery to sample it. Malt versions have proven popular throughout Argentina; fruitier ones – to put it politely – are an acquired taste. The annual hop harvest culminates in the colourful Fiesta Nacional de Lúpulo (National Hop Festival) in mid February.

Looming over town is **Cerro Piltriquitrón**, almost as much fun to climb as to say. It's a Mapuche name, pronounced 'pill-trick-ee-TRON', meaning 'hanging from the clouds'. If you can't face climbing it, you can fly over it with the **Aero Club El Bolsón** (prices start at US$40 for a half-hour flight), or you can jump off it with your own wings; the thermals are so good you can paraglide up and over the peak and make it back down to earth. The **Club Andino Piltriquitrón** is the information centre for all mountain activities, and anyone climbing or trekking in the area should register here first. They can arrange guides, treks and skiing at the small ski centre, **Cerro Perito Moreno** in winter (one week's skiing including equipment, ski school, passes and transport costs just US$70, no accommodation included). The Club also runs mountain *refugios* where you can bed down for US$2 a night.

An interesting diversion half way up the slopes of Piltriquitrón is the **Bosque Tallado**. In 1998, 13 artists from all over Argentina carved sculptures into wood burnt in forest fire years ago, transforming this small forest into an exhibition of art within nature.

Alternative adventures are the two-hour walk, or 20-minute drive, to the **Cascadas Escondidas** (Hidden Falls) and **Cabeza del Indio** (Indian's Head). Both offer great windows into the local woodland and fantastic panoramic views falling over the valley and

Siete Lagos

Lago Puelo. For fit climbing enthusiasts, pick up a leaflet that details the two-day trip up to the **Refugio Hielo Azul** (Blue Ice Refuge). After six peaceful – and tiring – hours of climbing through forests you'll be within spitting distance of a glacier hidden at the top of the mountain – it's well worth the slog.

EXCURSIONS

Heading south out of El Bolsón on RN258 is **El Hoyo**, known as the 'National Capital of Fine Fruit'. Blessed with an even better microclimate and setting than El Bolsón, it sits close to Lago Epuyén, a renowned fishing lake. Push on a little further and you'll discover **Cholila** (meaning 'beautiful valley'), a delightful little community famous as the one-time home of super-bandits, Señores Butch and Sundance. Between 1901 and 1906 James Ryan and Mr and Mrs Harry Place (aka Butch Cassidy, the Sundance Kid and his wife Etta Place) farmed this ranch in peace and even a semblance of respectability (*see p23* **Butch and the Sundance myth**). The hut, hand-built by the boys 100 years ago and perpetually on the verge of falling down, can be seen from the road. Today, large tranches of land around Cholila are being snapped up by wealthy foreign buyers, keen to own their own slice of Patagonian paradise.

Fifteen kilometres (nine miles) south is the entrance to **Parque Nacional Lago Puelo**, just beyond the village of Villa Lago Puelo on RP16. The park was formed to protect a number of trees otherwise native to Chile and is also home to over 100 bird species. A well-marked wooden walkway leads through the tranquil magic of the **Bosque de las Sombras** (Forest of Shadows) just by the shore of the Lake Puelo. Apart from the campsites offered in the park, Villa Lago Puelo has a fair selection of hostels, cabins, hotels and restaurants.

There's boat, bike and horse hire available by the lakeshore. From the lakeside a fantastic five-to-seven day walk leads to the Pacific coast in Chile. **Patagonia Adventures**, which has an office in El Bolsón at Pablo Hube No.418 (02944 493280, www.argentinachilefly fishing.com) offers fishing trips into Chile (from US$40).

Aero Club El Bolsón
Avenida San Martín y Pueyrredón (02944 492412). **Open** *Dec-Mar* 9am-5pm daily. *Apr-Nov* times vary. **No credit cards**.

Bosque Tallado
1km (0.5 miles) from the base of Cerro Piltriquitrón (no phone). **Open** 24hrs daily (enter in daylight hours). **Admission** *Jan, Feb* US$1. *Mar-Dec* free. **No credit cards**.

Cervezería Artesanal El Bolsón
RN 258, km 124 (02944 492595). **Open** *Dec-Mar* 8am-10pm daily. *Apr-Nov* 10am-6pm daily. **No credit cards**.

Club Andino Piltriquitrón
Avenida Sarmiento y Roca (02944 492600). **Open** *Apr-Oct* 6-8pm Tue, Fri. *Nov-Mar* 9am-10pm daily. **Credit** AmEx, DC, MC, V.

PN Lago Puelo
(Intendencia 02944 499064). **Open** *Park* 24hrs daily. *Intendencia* 8am-1pm Mon-Fri. **Admission** US$1.50; free under-6s. **No credit cards**.

Where to eat

The quality of food in El Bolsón is high, but the best is **Restaurant La Casona de Odile** (closed lunch, $$$). Plucking trout out of the river and bread from her oven, French Odile has fused the very best of Patagonian and Gallic cuisines. Reservations are essential (12 people maximum). **Jauja** (Avenida San Martín 2867, 02944 492448, www.heladosjauja.com, $$) offers one of the finer ways to taste the valley's fruit, meat and fish bounties. To the side is the outlet for the Jauja ice-cream and chocolate factory. Another excellent eaterie is **Valeria** (Avenida San Martín 3261, 02944 493505, www.clic.com. ar/valeria, $$). Sauces, made from five types of local wild mushrooms, are superb. **Cerro Lindo** (Avenida San Martín 2524, 02944 492899, www.cerrolindo.com.ar, $$) has live jazz on a Sunday night. There's a friendly, community feel and those good old Argentinian staples, pizza, pasta and beef. Vegetarians, on the other hand, will be better served at **La Calabaza** (Avenida San Martín 2518, 02944 492910), where the vibe is mellow and the food mostly flesh-free. If you just fancy a beer and a snack, **Il Rizzo** (Azcuenaga 459, 02944 491380) is a buzzing café with good ales on draught.

The jetty-set: backpackers dock at **Lago Puelo**.

Founding the future

In the midst of the vast expanse of dry arid land of the Sancabao valley in Neuquén, a long line of cypress trees leads up to the oasis that is the San Ignacio Education Centre. Here, 190 pupils – 70 per cent of whom are Mapuche – 50 sheep, 20 cows and countless pigs and chickens peacefully coexist on a patch of earth reclaimed from the surrounding desert.

The centre is one of two schools created by the **Fundación Cruzada Patagónica**, a charitable foundation set up 25 years ago to help western Patagonia's rural communities develop skills to help in their survival.

The Foundation began with a school for young Mapuche adolescents who had left the state education system in order to work with their families. The students were encouraged to complete their primary education, or else learn a skill they could bring back to their communities and implement on a daily basis.

'They [the state education authorities] would say that the children couldn't do things, that they weren't able. It's about giving them self-esteem,' explains the Foundation's executive director, Ricardo Rivero.

As word spread, demand grew, and the Foundation now boasts two schools, along with a project that sends teachers out to outlying Mapuche villages to teach adults in their homes, many of whom are illiterate.

The San Ignacio Education Centre is now an agro-technical secondary school, where the students are taught theory in the classrooms and then encouraged to put it into practice on the centre's land. As Rivero explains, if students are not taught how to implement what they learn in the classroom, 'they would be able to calculate the perimeter of a rectangle but not know how much fencing is needed for a patch of land.'

Together, students and teachers have built a working irrigation system and systematically removed rocks to allow them to plant crops and put animals out to graze. The centre sells eggs, chickens, cheese, honey and jams – all produced on the premises.

The children's ambitions have grown at the same pace as the centre's reputation. Since it first opened its doors to kids from the rural outposts, several have gone on to study successfully at university level.

The Foundation is funded through voluntary contributions from individuals and companies, many of which also donate their services.

For more information on the Foundation, and guidance on how you can help out either as a volunteer or contributor, check out their website – which includes an English translation – at www.cruzadapatagonica.org.

Where to stay

Comfortable and central **Hotel Cordillera** (Avenida San Martín 3220, 02944 492235/ cordillerahotel@elbolson.com, double US$30-$40) is the only three-star hotel in town, handily situated on the main street. The relaxing rooms have sizeable balconies and excellent views.
Cabañas La Montaña (Villa Turismo, 02944 492776, www.montana.com.ar, cabin for 2 US$15-$25) is nicely done, a good option for travellers who prefer to look after themselves. Apart from the usual facilities (including a swimming pool), all cabins come with a *parrilla*

for making barbecues, video, and access to a free film library. A little further out, **La Casona de Odile** (Barrio Luján, 6km/3.5 miles from the centre, 02944 4927, www.bolsonturistico.com.ar/odile, closed Easter-mid Nov, US$10 per person, US$18 full board) is an intimate lodge by the side of a lake. In the large gardens, Odile cultivates aromatic herbs which she then uses to scent the rooms and season her cooking (*see p107*). At **Cabañas El Arroyito** (Marquez, Villa Turismo, 02944 492715, www.elarroyito.com.ar, cabin for 2 US$20-$30) cabins have two storeys and the soothing sound of a water feature. The pool is small but there's a big communal space.

Resources

Hospital
Hospital del Bolsón, Perito Moreno y Padre Feliciano (02944 492240).

Internet
Ciber Café La Nuez, San Martín 2175 (02944 455182).

Police station
Perito Moreno y Padre Feliciano (02944 492200).

Post office
Avenida San Martín 1940 (02944 492231).

Tourist information
Secretaria de Turismo de El Bolsón, Avenida San Martín y Roca (02944 492604/www.bolson turistico.com.ar). **Open** *Mar-Dec* 9.30am-8pm Mon-Fri; 10am-8pm Sat, Sun. *Jan-Feb* 9.30am-10pm Mon-Fri; 10am-10pm Sat, Sun.

Getting there

By road
El Bolsón is halfway between Bariloche and Esquel on RN258. Bus services run regularly all year from both towns and stop at company offices. The trip takes around 2 hours and tend to be full in high season.

Esquel

Don't be put off by a name that is Mapuche for 'bog'. Caught in an elbow of the Andean foothills, overlooked by the peak of **Cerro Torres** and at a mere 350 metres (1,150 feet)

above sea level, friendly Esquel is an attractive and fertile relief from the inhospitable scrub of the surrounding steppe.

As the main urban centre for the region, Esquel preserves its cultural and industrial heritage For a quick introduction to Mapuche culture, the photos and artefacts inside the **Museo Indigenista** link the pre-Columbian Mapuche culture to the rituals and activities of the modern tribes. Internationally speaking, modern Esquel gains its reputation from the works of two authors, Bruce Chatwin and Paul Theroux, and the tracks of a famous train, **La Trochita**, known in English as The Old Patagonian Express. The family-orientated ski resort of **La Hoya**, 13 kilometres (eight miles) from town on the slopes of Cerro Torres, stops Esquel closing down to tourists in winter. It has nine pistes, for all standards of snowboarder or skier. In summer, there's a whole range of mountain activities on offer, with treks suitable for everyone. Still on a sporting tip, Esquel is also famous for the quality of its fishing.

EXCURSIONS
La Trochita came into operation in 1945 to take wool from the *estancias* to the markets, 23 years after construction of the 75-centimetre-wide (30 inches) track began. Now only two sectors of the original 402 kilometres (250 miles) of narrow-gauge track remain in service. Trains leave from a perfectly conserved station in Esquel and run via Nahuel Pan en route to **El Maitén**. At the station in El Maitén (Carlos Pellegrini 841, 02945 495190) are the engineer's

La Trochita: part train, part time machine.

workshops. In theory the train runs twice daily in January and February and on Saturdays only during the rest of the year, but this is subject to frequent changes so check the website or with a travel agency. It's a vital part of Argentina's railway heritage and one of the last narrow-gauge railways of its class to still function.

Near El Maitén is one of the country's biggest ranches, Estancia Leleque, owned by the Benetton Group. **Museo Leleque**, a comprehensive exhibit of local indigenous history, was opened in 2000, and, depending on your point of view, exists either for altruistic reasons or to appease the disgruntled groups who claim the land as their own. The entrance fee goes to an independent group investigating the Mapuche culture.

The magnificent **Los Alerces National Park** lies just 40 kilometres (25 miles) away, to the west of Esquel. The massive native alerce trees after which the park is named are often compared to the giant sequoias of California. Some specimens of up to 4,000 years old have been found. The main attraction is the **Bosque de los Alerces**; access to it is by boat on the Safari Lacustre, run by **Esquel Tour** (Avenida Fontana 754, 02945 452704). Full-day excursions provide a dazzling glimpse of **Glaciar Torrecillas**. At the northernmost point of the lake is Puerto Sagrario and the forest itself. In the accessible eastern side of the park is a chain of lakes and rivers, but there are many conservation restrictions in force, so getting a one-on-one feel for nature here is not as easy as it might be. The park's Intendencia at the entrance, just past the tiny town of Villa Futalaufquen, has a small museum.

If you're set on adventure and truly want to disappear into the region's landscape, get in touch with **Fueguito** (011 48159177, www. fueguito.com). It's run by experienced trekkers Alfonso and Horacio, who offer tailor-made seven-day excursions from Esquel to the foot of the Lanin volcano, travelling by 4x4, aeroplane and horseback over 600km (372 miles) of the Andes and through three national parks.

For rafting enthusiasts, to the south of Esquel are the Corcovado and fierce Futaleufú rivers, which take you right into nearby Chile.

La Hoya – Centro de Actividades de Montaña

Cerro Torres (02945 453018/www.camlahoya. com.ar). **Open** *mid June-mid Oct, mid Dec-Mar* 9am-6pm daily. **Rates** *Ski pass* US$10-$25 per day; US$30-$70 per wk. **Credit** AmEx, MC, V.

Museo Indigenista

Belgrano 330, entre Chacabuco y Ameghino (02945 451929). **Open** 9am-1pm, 2-8pm Mon-Fri; 10am-noon, 5-8pm Sat, Sun. **Admission** US75¢; free under-12s.

Museo Leleque

RN 40, km1440 (02945 452600/Buenos Aires 011 43311499/www.benetton.com). **Open** 11am-5pm Mon, Tue, Thur-Sun. **Admission** US$1.

Parque Nacional Los Alerces

Entrances: Portada Norte, RP71 from Cholila; Portada Sur, from Esquel & Trevelin; Portada Centro, RP71 from Esquel (02945 471020/alerces@ ciudad.com.ar). **Open** *Information centre & museum* Dec-Apr 9am-9pm daily; May-Nov 8am-4pm daily. *Park* 24hrs daily. **Admission** *Museum* free. *Park* Dec-Apr US$1.50; free under-12s. May-Nov free to all. **No credit cards.**

La Trochita

Estación del Ferrocarril, Urquiza y Ruggero (02945 453529/www.latrochita.org.ar). **Departures** *Mar-Dec* 10am Sat. *Jan, Feb* 10am, 2pm daily. **Tickets** US$9; free under-6s. **No credit cards.**

Where to eat & drink

Esquel is well served with decent restaurants. **Restaurante Vascongada** (9 de Julio 675, 02945 452229, $$$) is considered a bastion of local dining and deservedly so; the menu is extensive and the service excellent. Ignore the manically waving plastic man outside **Parrilla de María** (Rivadavia 1024, 02945 452503, closed Mon in Apr-June, Sept-Dec, $$); the tastes within are excellent, including the *chivito* (goat). **Pizzería Fitz Roya's** sign says it all: 'It's not expensive because it's pizza. It's not cheap because it's good'. Find it at Rivadavia No.1048 (02945 450512, $$). If you're in search of something to wet your throat, there'll be tea brewing at the **Casa de Té Melys** (Miguens 346, 02945 452677, $).

Where to stay

A relative newcomer to Esquel's hotel scene is **Hostería Cumbres Blancas** (Avenida Ameghino 1683, 02945 455100, www. cpatagonia. com/esq/cblancas, double US$40-$60) with plush decor and good view of the peak. There's a quality restaurant/bar and business services and a sauna add to the package. The name of **Cabañas Rayen-Hue** (Miguens 40, 02945 452185, http://orbita.starmedia.com/rayenhue, cabin for two US$12-$18) means 'place of flowers' and the number of trees set between these Alpine-style cabins gives a definite countryside air (but with all mod cons). The owner, Randall Williams, used to be the local head of tourism and he now runs a small tour company from the same location. **Hostería La Tour D'Argent** (San Martín 1063, 02945 454612, www.latourdargent.com.ar, double US$20) is simple and centrally located, with a family feel. Rooms are compact but comfortable.

Resources

Hospital
*Hospital Esquel, 24 de Mayo 150
(02945 451064/1224).*

Internet
Uniten, 25 de Mayo 528 (02945 451495/93).

Police station
Rivadavia y Mitre (02945 450789/450001).

Post office
Avenida Alvear 1192 (02945 451865).

Tourist information
*Dirección Municipal de Turismo, Avenida Alvear y
Sarmiento (02945 451927/www.esquel.gov.ar).*
Open *Jan-Apr* 8am-10pm daily. *May-Dec* 8am-8pm.

Getting there

By air
Esquel's airport, **Aeropuerto 2001** (RN40, 02945
451354/451676), is 22km (14 miles) from the centre,
accessible by bus. There are 3 flights per week to BA
on Aerolineas Argentinas.

By road
Esquel is 36hrs by road from BA. It lies on RN40
heading south from Bariloche. The bus terminal is at
Avenida P Justo y Avenida Alvear (02945 451566).

Trevelin

Just south of Esquel is the small town of
Trevelin. Now into its sixth generation of
Joneses, Trevelin remains nearly 80 per cent
Welsh in origin and is the most westerly
example of Welsh culture in Argentina.

The town was officially founded in 1918,
although expeditions to the valley from
settlements on the east coast had been taking
place since the 1880s. Scattered throughout
the town and noticeable for their all-brick
construction, are some of the original settlers'
houses. Particularly eye-catching is the recently
restored **Salón Social** right on the edge of the
main square Plaza Coronel Fontana.

If you want to know how Trevelin got its
name ('tre' is Welsh for town and 'velin' means
mill) extend your trip to the **Nant Fach Mill**,
22 kilometres (13.5 miles) away in the village of
Molino. It's a working reconstruction of a water-
powered mill and small museum dedicated to
the first Welsh settlers. For a taste of Wales
there are plenty of teahouses. **Nain Maggie**
(Perito Moreno 179, 02945 480232) offers a full
tea for US$4 and is the truest to tradition.

Many companies offer tours of Trevelin and
its surrounds. Close to the outskirts of the town,
after a gentle trip through local farmlands, are

the **Nant y Fall** waterfalls. There are seven
falls in all, dropping picturesquely down the
mountains; the first three are within a 15-
minute walk of the park rangers' centre.

Nant Fach Mill
*RN259 (02945 15 680836/www.cpatagonia
com.ar/trevelin/molino).* **Open** *Dec-Mar* 9am-noon,
1-9pm daily. *Apr-Nov* 2-7pm daily. Admission US$1;
free under-10s. **No credit cards**.

Where to stay & eat

Recommended in town is the **Hostal Casa
Verde** (Los Alerces, 02945 480091, www.
hostels.org.ar, double US$15), which also has
dormitory accommodation for US$5 per night.
If you prefer cabins try **Complejo Turístico
Oregón** (Avenida San Martin y JM Thomas,
02945 480408, contreraso@ciudad. com.ar,
cabin for 4-5 US$15-$25). **Estancia La Paz**
(South Entrance, PN Los Alerces, 02945 452758,
closed Easter-Nov, cabin for 5 US$70-$100),
located on the bank of Rio Grande, 14 kilometres
(8.5 miles) from Trevelin offers farm lodging
as well as camping facilities.

For filling up, **Patagonia Celta** (25 de Mayo
y Molino Viejo, 02945 480722, $$$) is a fancy
grotto-like steak and pasta house, with the
largest wine cellar around.

Resources

Hospital
*Hospital John Daniel Evans, Avenida San Martín y
John Daniel Evans (02945 438132).*

Internet
*Locutorio Cordillera, Avenida San Martín y Libertad
(02945 480716).*

Police station
*Avenida Patagonia y Almirante Brown
(02945 480101).*

Post office
*Avenida San Martín y Almirante Brown
(02945 480122).*

Tourist information
*Secretaria de Producción, Turismo y Medio
Ambiente, Rotonda 28 de Julio, en la Plaza Coronel
Fontana (02945 480120/www.trevelin.org).* **Open**
Dec-Mar 8am-10.30pm daily. *Apr-Nov* 8am-7pm Mon-
Fri; 9am-7pm Sat, Sun.

Getting there

By road
Trevelin is just 24km (15 miles) south of Esquel on
RN259. You can get there with an excursion, by taxi
or on frequent local bus services from Esquel (hourly
on weekdays, every 2hrs weekends).

Central Patagonia

Are we there yet? Lose yourself in the middle of nowhere.

A thousand miles and more of solitude lies at the rugged heart of Patagonia, an area with just one essential destination, the **Cuevas de las Manos Pintadas** (Cave of the Painted Hands) in northern Santa Cruz. But for travellers weary of tramping from one tourist spot to the next, the centre of Patagonia, dotted with solitary villages and isolated working *estancias*, evokes the Patagonia of yesteryear.

Phone lines and plumbing may be precious luxuries, but offsetting such underdevelopment is the pleasure of discovering an area that has remained so fundamentally unchanged since the early days of immigrants and pioneers. The **Bosques Petrificados** (petrified forests) in the middle of the barren steppe show just how literally time has frozen.

Sarmiento

Sarmiento, in the south of Chubut province, sits smack in the middle of the steppe, halfway between Chile and the Atlantic. Although surrounded by dry flatlands, nearby there is watery relief in the vast Lakes **Musters** and **Colhué Huapi**. The town (population 12,000), nicknamed '*el testigo del tiempo*' (the witness of time), has placed importance on conserving the past and indeed there's an old-time, small-town feel at the core of everything that goes on (which is frankly not a great deal). It's an interesting stop for historians and naturalists who should head to the **Museo Regional Desiderio Torres**, housed in the town's old railway station, and the nearby petrified

Get your kicks... on **Ruta 40**. *See p118.*

forests. The museum's exhibits shed light on the prehistoric social and cultural practices of the indigenous Tehuelche and Mapuche tribes – some artefacts in the extensive collection date back more than 11,000 years.

The petrified forest 30 kilometres (19 miles) out of Sarmiento dates back significantly further – roughly 65 million years. To stop people pilfering the fossilised wood, the area has been turned into a protected park known as the **Monumento Natural Provincial Bosque Petrificado de Sarmiento**. Nothing is as surreal or unforest-like as the lunar terrain, where extraordinary trunks, turned to stone, lie in your path or poke out of the rock faces.

There is another petrified wood, Bosque Petrificado Héctor Szlápelis, nearby. It's on private land and not, strictly speaking, open to the public, though a friendly word with the tourist office may get you a sneak viewing. Closer to the coast is the largest Patagonian petrified forest, a national monument. *See p115* **Trees of the stone age**.

Monumento Natural Provincial Bosque Petrificado de Sarmiento

Follow path 30 km (19 miles) from entrance to Sarmiento (no phone). **Open** *mid Mar-mid Dec* 9am-7pm daily. *Mid Dec-mid Mar* 8am-8pm daily. **Admission** US$2.50; US$1.50 under-12s; free under-6s. **No credit cards**.

Museo Regional Desiderio Torres

20 de Junio 114 (0297 4893401). **Open** *mid Mar-mid Dec* 1.30-7.30pm Mon-Fri; *Mid Dec-mid Mar* 10am-noon, 4-8pm daily. **Admission** free.

Where to stay & eat

You can arrange to stay at a *chacra* (small farm) in the surrounding area via the tourist office. Ask about **Chacra El Labrador** (0297 4893329, double from US$30), a small and hospitable *estancia* that also organises excursions for guests to places of interest in the area. Otherwise, in town, the **Hotel Residencia Los Lagos** (Roca y Alberdi, 0297 4893046, double US$45) has basic ground-floor rooms with en suite bathrooms. Clean and simple double rooms at the **Residencial Ismar** (Patagonia 248, 0297 4893293) cost from US$15 and are arranged around a courtyard.

For food, **Residencia Los Lagos** has a restaurant specialising in fish ($$), or head to **Restaurant Rancho Grande** (Avenida Estrada 419, 0297 4893513, closed Mon, $$) for your fill of meat from the mixed grill and a chance to talk football with the fanatical owner. Alternatively, **Heidy's** (Perito Moreno 600, 0297 4898308, $$) is a well-attended eaterie that dishes up home-made foods.

Resources

Hospital
Hospital Rural Sarmiento, JA Roca y Ingeniero Coronel (0297 4893022).

Internet
Cabinas Sarmiento, Avenida San Martín y Pellegrini (0297 4898335).

Police station
Avenida San Martín 722 (0297 4893005).

Post office
Avenida Ingeniero Coronel y España (0297 4893501).

Tourist information
Dirección de Turismo, Avenida Regimiento de Infantería 25, y Pietrobelli (0297 4898220/ turismo@coopsar.com.ar). **Open** *mid Dec-mid Mar* 8am-11pm daily. *Mid Mar-mid Dec* 9am-2pm, 3-8pm Mon-Fri; 9am-1pm, 2-6pm Sat; 9am-1pm Sun.

Getting there

By road
Sarmiento lies on RN26, 144km (89 miles) or 2.5hrs by road from Comodoro Rivadavia on the coast, from where there are daily buses year round.

Perito Moreno

Perito Moreno (the town, as opposed to the glacier or national park) is the closest bet for a night's rest if travelling to the Cave of Painted Hands. The nondescript town is the final outpost of civilisation before heading into the vast desert farther south along the RN40 (*see p118* **The long, unwinding road**). Although less pleasant as a destination than sister-city Los Antiguos, it is slightly larger and boasts more conveniences for travellers. The town of 4,000 mostly public employees went through three name changes before Congress named it after the revered Argentinian naturalist in 1952. Most hotels and shops are concentrated along a few blocks of Avenida San Martín but the town's tree-covered plaza is three blocks westward on Avenida Rivadavia.

EXCURSIONS
The **Cueva de las Manos Pintadas**, a UNESCO World Heritage Site since 1999, sits tucked away 50 metres (160 feet) above the Rio Pinturas in the high walls of a wide canyon that locals say stretches for 150 kilometres (93 miles). Although it's the painted hands that attract most people this way, the impressive canyon, with its almost tropical microclimate, is a worthwhile diversion from the desert beyond and an ideal swimming hole in summer.

Archaeologists differ on the age of the drawings, but the most common estimate is that the earliest date from 9,350 years ago and were added to until, mysteriously, the painting stopped abruptly around 1,300 years ago. Amid the rock art there are several distinguishable categories. Some are of a higher artistic level, notably the hunting scenes, while others are simpler combination of hand prints, guanacos and abstract figures. The paintings depict the quotidian realities of Tehuelche life: 'With my hands I kill guanaco, therefore I survive.' It's poignant, not to mention ironic, when you consider that the Tehuelche were wiped out earlier last century. There's also at least one guanaco with a horn protruding from its head, proof enough to some dreamers that unicorns once roamed here freely.

Neither easels nor palettes were used – just juice extracted from berries. To protect the paintings, the Tehuelche used a mixture of fats and urine: not a well-known varnish but, given the resplendent intensity of the colours, effective. Against the elements that is – after Argentinian teenagers starting leaving graffitied love messages authorities built a chain-link fence that restricts close access. One of the few men who can get inside the fence is English-speaking guide Juan 'Harry' Nauta, head of **Guanacondor Tours** (Perito Moreno 1089, 02963 432303/0297 154526224, guanacondor@argentina.com). The easiest way to locate him is to call in the evenings or wait for him to come by your hotel scouting for interested tourists.

Nauta can also take you in his Soviet 4x4 van to the less-visited **Arroyo Feo** (Ugly Stream), a narrow and anything-but-unattractive canyon located on a private farm 50 kilometres (31 miles) south of Perito Moreno. Although less impressive than the Cueva de las Manos Pintadas, this canyon also contains numerous paintings that can be explored close-up and in peace. Arroyo Feo also offers excellent hiking opportunities. Both excursions cost US$30 and take a full day, leaving from Perito Moreno.

Where to stay & eat

Estancia Telken (RN40, 02963 432079, www.estanciasdesantacruz.com, closed May-Aug, double US$108) is a real find. Although 25 kilometres (16 miles) south of town, it's conveniently en route to the Cave. Colourful lupins and Lombardy poplars surround the corrugated-iron homestead of this sheep farm, and the owners (of New Zealand descent) give visitors a warm welcome. In the tradition of Patagonian hospitality, meals are served around the family table.

The Cave is within the grounds of **Estancia Los Toldos** (RN 40, 02963 432856, www.estanciasdesantacruz.com, closed May-Oct, double US$75, cabins US$30, hostel US$16 per person), 60 kilometres (37 miles) south of Perito Moreno, though a fair drive from the main house. There's a variety of lodging: the modern hostel sleeps 40 backpackers, while the hostería has more comfortable double rooms. In addition to excursions to the Cave, you can visit the impressive Charcamata cornice (and its cave paintings), by horse or truck.

For a night's stay in Perito Moreno itself, your best bet is one of the clean rooms at **Posada del Caminante** (Rivadavia 937, 02963 432204, double US$15-$20), a modest but cosy two-room B&B, a block from the centre. Bruce Chatwin fans can spend a night at the no-frills **Hotel Belgrano** (Avenida San Martín 463, 02963 432019, double US$15-$20). Owner Munir Mattar may not remember his famous visitor or which of the identical rooms he stayed in, but he will happily share details about another illustrious erstwhile guest – the former Argentinian president Carlos Menem. Mattar can also provide useful tourist information about the local area.

The town's once most prominent lodging is the centrally located **Hotel Austral** (San Martín 1327, 02963 432538, double US$15-$20). These days it's probably a better option for dining than accommodation. There's decent, hearty fare available at the restaurant of the **Hotel Belgrano** ($$). For a quick bite, **Rotisería Chee's I** (25 de Mayo 1896, 02963 432842, $) serves up good empanadas, to eat in or take away. The faded but picturesque bar at the **Hotel Santa Cruz** (Belgrano 1565, 02963 432133) is a great place to observe gaucho types necking whisky on a Sunday morning.

Resources

Hospital

Hospital Distrital Oscar Natale, Colón 1237 (02963 432045).

Internet

Cyber Café Crazy Net, Rivadavia 1078 (02963 432699).

Police station

25 de Mayo 1394 (02963 432012).

Post office

Juan Domingo Perón 1331 (02963 432065).

Tourist information

Oficina de Turismo Perito Moreno, San Martín 1059, y 12 de Octubre (02963 432020/mpmsc@interlap. com.ar). **Open** *Oct-Apr* 8am-7pm Mon-Fri; 10am-noon, 2-7pm Sat, Sun. *May-Sept* 8am-7pm Mon-Fri.

Trees of the stone age

Forget California: the real death valley is in Patagonia. Turning right off the RN3, the already eerie landscape turns hallucinogenic. The 55-kilometre (34-mile) gravel road leading to the entrance of **Monumento Natural Nacional Bosques Petrificados** (administered by PN Los Glaciares; see p150), Patagonia's largest petrified forest, looks straight out of *Star Wars*. If the lifeless grey horizon doesn't convince you you're on the moon then the 400-metre-high (1,312-feet) basalt pyramids will. And for those choosing to spend the night camping here, the howling winds and the glinting, beady eyes of curious foxes and guanacos are downright creepy.

About 120 million years ago this area was covered by a humid forest of araucaria trees. Then the earth moved and gushing volcanoes dumped ash over the entire region. In relatively recent times, the wind lifted the cover off the fallen trees, now rock solid and frozen in time. Today, the 150-square-kilometre (60-square-mile) park, created in 1954, conserves some of the largest petrified logs anywhere in the world, some as long as 30 metres (98 feet). Several examples, some with their stumps still upright, can be visited along an easy, two-kilometre (1.25-mile) walk that starts at the park's small visitor centre.

Although hands-on exploring is encouraged – not even a chainsaw will make these rocks budge – don't even think about taking home a souvenir. Years of neglect led to a major pilfering of many fossils, and what remains is scant compared to decades past.

No public transport to the park currently exists, but several agencies in Puerto Deseado or Comodoro Rivadavia (see pp137-143) can take interested tourists. Camping is allowed at Estancia La Paloma, 25 kilometres (16 miles) from the park entrance along RP49, but park rangers will usually allow you to pitch a tent outside the visitor centre. In either case, bring food and water since this is one of the driest places on earth and no tourist infrastructure to speak of exists. If you arrive here you truly have made it to the middle of nowhere. The closest town is the near-deserted former railway stopover of Jaramillo, some 126 kilometres (78 miles) away. Sarmiento is 240 kilometres (149 miles) away.

Monumento Natural Nacional Bosques Petrificados

RP49 (02977 4851000/www.parques nacionales.gov.ar). **Open** Oct-Mar 9am-8pm. Apr-Sept 10am-5pm. **Admission** free.

Getting there

By road

All buses passing through Perito Moreno start in Los Antiguos, 58 km (36 miles) away (*see below*). Perito Moreno also connects by road to Chile Chico and Coihaique in Chile.

Los Antiguos

Despite the short distance of 58 kilometres (36 miles) separating Los Antiguos from Perito Moreno the change in landscape couldn't be more dramatic. Descending 250 metres (820 feet) from Perito Moreno, the barren plateau gives way to a green oasis (by Patagonian standards) of calafate bushes and fertile prairies. Being closer to the Andes it's also protected from the worst of Patagonia's notorious winds, which may partly explain why the 3,000 inhabitants seem more cheerful and laid-back than their neighbours. Authentic hospitality and picturesque scenery, combined with good hiking and fishing, make this a worthwhile – if somewhat surreal – destination for the curious and open-minded.

Just three kilometres (two miles) from the border with Chile, the town was built on the southern shores of **Lago Buenos Aires** (the Chileans call it Lago General Carrera). It's the deepest and the second biggest – after Bolivia's Lake Titicaca – freshwater lake in South America. According to legend, Los Antiguos derives its name from the Tehuelche saying 'I keu kenk', meaning 'place of my ancestors'. When the elders grew too weak to hunt for guanacos on the run, they came down from the steppe to this retirement home with a view. As proof, local ranch owners still discover occasional burial mounds (called *chenques*).

The town's recent history has been more lively than that of the sedentary days of the senior Tehuelche citizens. When the Hudson Volcano, 150 kilometres (93 miles) away in Chile, unexpectedly erupted in 1991, it dumped 80 centimetres (31 inches) of burning ash on

Raise your hand if you'd like to visit the **Cueva de las Manos Pintadas**. *See p113.*

the town, killing nearly a million farm animals and ruining the livelihood of numerous families. After more than a decade of cleaning up, the town has found its feet again. With a new identity as the 'National Cherry Capital', it has become Argentina's leading producer of cherries, strawberries, blackberries and other fine fruits. The town celebrates its renaissance at the end of the cherry-picking season in early January each year with the **Fiesta Nacional de la Cereza** (*see p45*) The fiesta attracts well-known folk singers from across the country. Other local parties include the Dia del Lago Buenos Aires on October 29 and the town's own feast day, Dia de Los Antiguos, on February 5.

Any traveller to Los Antiguos should definitely pay a visit to one of its attractive fruit farms. More than 20 *chacras* currently welcome tourists, but by far the most popular and successful is the deservedly named **Chacra El Paraíso** (0297 15 6241903, camand@ infovia.com.ar), which also welcomes help from willing fruit-pickers in late December and early January. Another option is **Chacra Don Neno**, which principally grows strawberries. To visit any of the farms in the area, ask for information at the helpful tourist office.

Although Lake Buenos Aires is excellent for rainbow trout and salmon fishing, as well as sailing, there isn't an agency that currently offers organised excursions. However, Juan Carlos Pellón, owner of Hotel Argentino (*see below*), will guide determined anglers.

Heading south out of town the terrain becomes more rugged, opening up numerous off-trail hiking opportunities. The desert landscape that surrounds **Monte Zeballos**, 50 kilometres (31 miles) away, is a place few visitors ever see, but is well worth a visit. Mountain guide Guido Vittone (0297 154130387, guido47sur@hotmail.com) who also doubles as the town's high school English teacher, will take serious trekkers to Zeballos as well as the more remote Monte San Lorenzo. Track him down via the Hostería Antigua Patagonia (*see below*), where his wife works.

Where to stay & eat

The six rooms at **Hostería Antigua Patagonia** (RP43, Acceso Este, Lago Buenos Aires, 02963 491038/055, www.antigua patagonia.com.ar, double US$50), located just out of town, offer a panoramic view of Lake Buenos Aires with the snow-capped Andes behind. **Hostería La Serena** (RP43, 02963 432340/011 1550045474, www.patagonia south.com, closed July-Sept, double US$40-$60), a tourist ranch midway between Los Antiguos and Perito Moreno, on the shores of the lake,

has comfortable lodging for up to 20 guests. They also organise fishing trips and other excursions. More basic lodging and a meal in town can be found at **Hotel Argentino** (Avenida 11 de Julio 850, 02963 491132, double US$25-$30, restaurant $$), whose gregarious owner is an excellent 24-hour substitute for the often hard-to-find-open tourist office. **La Perla del Lago** (Fitzroy y Perito Moreno, no phone, $$) is a cheap and lively *parrilla*. **Heladería y Confitería Populus** (Avenida 11 de Julio, 02963 491166, $) with its antique, 1925 US-made National Cash Register, is a fast-food joint and ice-cream parlour open all year round. If that doesn't satisfy your sugar cravings, head to **Chocolatería y Confitería I Keu Kenk** (11 de Julio 193, 02963 491048, $) for home-made chocolates, cakes and snacks.

Resources

Hospital
Hospital Distrital Los Antiguos, Patagonia Argentina 69, esquina Cruz del Sur (02963 491303).

Internet
Locutorio Los Antiguos, Alameda 572 (02963 491103).

Police station
Avenida 11 de Julio 386 (02963 491250/491312).

Post office
Gobernador Gregores 19 (02963 491355).

Tourist information
Dirección de Cultura y Turismo, Avenida 11 de Julio 446, entre Gobernador Gregores y Perito Moreno (02963 491261/491308/www.losantiguos. gov.ar). **Open** *Dec-Mar* 8am-noon daily. *Apr-Nov* 8am-8pm daily.

Getting there

By road
Los Antiguos is 428km (266 miles), or 5hrs by bus, from Comodoro Rivadavia via RP43 and RN3. Three buses in summer/two in winter run between the two towns and a ticket costs US$9. Perito Moreno is 1hr from Los Antiguos, along the same route. Contact the tourist office or Hotel Santa Cruz in Perito Moreno (*see p114*) for bus timetables. Every two-three days from Dec-Mar Chaltén Travel (San Martín 44, 02963 491140) runs a 24-seater mini-bus between Los Antiguos/Perito Moreno and El Chaltén and on to El Calafate down RN40: it takes 16hrs and costs US$40.

PN Perito Moreno

If you've decided to come as far as the Cueva de las Manos Pintados then getting farther off the beaten path, and visiting **Parque Nacional Perito Moreno**, one of Argentina's

The long, unwinding road

Snaking its way along the eastern edge of the Andes, the fast-becoming-legendary Route 40 ('*ruta cuarenta*' in Spanish) runs for some 5,000 kilometres (3,050 miles) from Rio Gallegos in Patagonia's southernmost province, as far as Jujuy's Abra Pampa. It may lack the pop-culture cachet of Route 66, but it's perfect for the brave roadster who wants to zip through a wide range of climates and landscapes, from the precipitous vistas of Salta to the vineyards of Mendoza and the frozen tablelands of Santa Cruz.

The continuing rise in local tourism has caused many to look closely at Ruta 40's untapped potential: a national monument yet to be fully exploited. The government has been slow in its backing but a number of self-funded schemes are underway, seeking to promote the road so that it emerges as one of Argentina's success stories.

Information geared specifically towards Ruta 40 and the surrounding area is readily available (www.ruta40.net or www.patagonia-argentina.com), and on the southern stretches there are a number of car-rental firms and outfits offering guided tours for anything between one and three weeks (www.ruta-40.com or www.hielos.com.ar).

Most self-respecting Jack Kerouac wannabes will want to snub such luxuries, of course, and do the highway their own way or not at all. But while romance will get you so far, only a set of good tyres and a working suspension will get you the whole way. About one third of Ruta 40 is paved; the rest is gravel (*ripio*). Pragmatic-minded locals regard it as a tyre-thrashing obstacle course.

It's not a road, thus, to be taken lightly; careful preparation is essential to ensure a smooth run. A good toolkit, food, an extra tank of gas and a couple of spare tyres will definitely come in handy, and the more cautious would be advised to include headlight and windscreen protection. Frequent suicide bids by the resident sheep are also common, so beware.

Many choose Perito Moreno as their starting point, but the drive south from Bariloche is well supplied with beautiful scenery and acts as a good warm-up for the tough road ahead. A stop-off at **Parque Nacional Los Alerces** (*see p110*) is also well worth it. The more rough-hewn traveller may opt to camp by the roadside, but there are also a number of 'open-*estancias*' dotted along Ruta 40, though many are closed in winter (www.estanciasdesantacruz.com).

The lonely, 630-kilometre (390-mile) stretch running between Perito Moreno and El Calafate is a lifeline for a few hundred otherwise self-reliant farmers, and, for many, where the real adventure begins. **Estancia Telken** (*see p114*) provides a good stop-off point and offers tours either on horseback or foot to the Cueva de las Manos and along the Río de las Pinturas. Moving south, the first place you reach after 100 kilometres (61 miles) is **Bajo Caracoles**, a small settlement and refuelling station and the crossroads with the even bumpier Ruta 39. Following this road west for 75 kilometres (47 miles) brings you to Hipólito Yrigoyen, a town of 200 hardy souls on the treeless shores of Lakes Posadas and Pueyrredón. This is the base

least-visited national parks, should be no sweat and you won't be disappointed. The difficult access to the park works as an effective filter to prevent hordes of tourists from obstructing its real aim: conservation.

The 1,150-square-kilometre (444-square-mile) preserve, named for the father of Argentina's national park system (*see p51* **Environmental warrior**), protects a delicate transition zone between the desert steppe and old-growth forests of the high Andes. In addition to abundant bird and wildlife – flamingos, upland geese, foxes, guanacos, rheas and condors to name only a few – the park also offers your best chance in Argentina of seeing the endangered – and understandably shy – huemul deer species.

The chain of turquoise lakes also happens to be the preferred habitat for the endangered macá tobiano, a pint-sized, colour-specked coot found only in Santa Cruz.

Activities allowed inside the park are limited to several short, self-guided hikes; the most popular is an eight-kilometre (five-mile) jaunt to the peninsula jutting into Lago Belgrano. Some areas of the park are not accessible to the public due to ongoing archaeological studies. As all visits must be registered with the park rangers, aim to arrive between 8am and 10pm.

Parque Nacional Perito Moreno

Park office, RN40 (02962 491477/ pnmoreno@apn.gov.ar). **Open** 24hrs daily. **Admission** free.

for hardcore climbers attempting to scale the daunting **Monte San Lorenzo**, which at 3,706 metres (12,159 feet) is one of the highest in Argentinian Patagonia. The glacier-covered peak, visible from the road when not draped in clouds, was first reached in 1943 by 60-year-old Padre Alberto De Agostini

Rejoining Ruta 40 at Bajo Caracoles, it's an uninspiring 109-kilometre (68-mile) drive to the eerie township of Paraje Las Horquetas. A brief pause for fuel should be enough to satisfy even the most inquisitive traveller, before either detouring to Parque Nacional Perito Moreno (see p117) or continuing south. If you're in need of a bed for the night, **Estancia La Angostura** (55km west

of Gobernador Gregores, 02962 452010, closed May-Oct, double US$40-$50) offers great local food if modest accommodation.

Trundling through the windswept plains towards El Calafate, signs of civilisation begin to emerge. The famous **Parque Nacional Los Glaciares** (see p150) and Tres Lagos attract hoards of visitors each year and the area benefits from a tourist-friendly infrastructure – a welcome reprieve from the rigours of Ruta 40. For most, arrival in El Calafate marks the end of the road, but those with something to prove can follow their noses for a further 313 kilometres (194 miles) before reaching the end of the road and cracking open the champagne in Rio Gallegos.

Where to stay & eat

There are four campsites within the park (Lago Burmeister, Mirador Lago Belgrano, Cerro de Vasco and Alberto de Agostini) but none of them has facilities and no open campfires are allowed. Otherwise, there are two more luxurious options. **Estancia La Oriental** (PN Perito Moreno, 02962 452196, www.estancias desantacruz.com, closed Apr-Oct, double US$70-$80) offers camping and lodging for up to 25 people and also organises hikes and horse riding around Mount San Lorenzo. At the edge of the park, **Estancia Menelik** (RP37, 011 5371 5555, www.estanciasdesantacruz.com, closed May-Oct, US$70 per person all-inclusive)

also arranges horse riding, and has modern lodgings in the refurbished 1920 homestead. The former shearing shed is now a 19-bed hostel (US$10 per person). Once owned by a German sailor marooned after the World War II battleship *Graf Spee* was scuttled in the Rio de la Plata, the farm owes its name to the physical similarity between its original founder and one-time Ethiopian Emperor Menelik II.

Getting there

There's no public transport to the park; you'll need your own vehicle. Take the turning from the RN40 to the RP37 7km (4.5 miles) north of Paradero Las Orquetas; it's another 90km (56 miles) from there.

The Atlantic Coast

Patagonia's east shoreline is rich in human history and marine marvels.

Where the waters of the Atlantic crash on to the shore, Argentinian Patagonia reaches its eastern limit. A continuous coastal road, RN3, runs its length, linking historical sites like **Carmen de Patagones** and **Puerto San Julián** with the seaside town of **Puerto Madryn**, and connects the Chubut valley, heart of Welsh Patagonia, to the larger cities of the southern shores, such as oil capital **Comodoro Rivadavia**. Interspersed among the human settlements are some of the world's most important marine wildlife reserves – including the UNESCO World Heritage Site **Península Valdés**, breeding ground of the southern right whale and home to a host of other ocean-going species – and kilometre upon kilometre of unspoiled coastal scenery.

Carmen de Patagones & Viedma

Carmen de Patagones is a compelling candidate for Patagonia's best-kept secret; apart from its historical significance as the region's first true population centre, it is also one of the most picturesque small towns in the entire country. Although located in Buenos Aires province, the town is considered by most to be the gateway to Patagonia. Together with sister-city **Viedma**, Carmen de Patagones was founded by Spanish explorer Francisco de Viedma in 1779 as part

of a mission to populate the coast. You can use either town as a base for exploring the other: Carmen has more charm; Viedma a better view and lots more action, relatively speaking, after sundown. To move between the two towns you can use the bridge or hop on a small ferry that leaves every 15 minutes.

The region's first settlers from Maragatería, in northern Spain, lived in caves, remains of which are still found in Carmen. In homage to their roots, the town's 20,000 residents still call themselves *maragatos*. Every 7 March they hold a week-long fiesta to celebrate their 1827 victory over invading Brazilians. Two captured flags are displayed at **Iglesia Nuestra Señora del Carmen** on Plaza 7 de Mayo, but for a complete overview of the region's history, from pre-Columbian times onwards, head to the **Museo Histórico Regional Emma Nozzi**.

Carmen enjoys a remarkably benign climate: summer temperatures reach as high as 40ºC (104ºF), making it one of the few places in Patagonia where residents pray for wind. The clement weather conditions mean that kayaking on the Río Negro is a year-round activity. On sunny days the town's zigzagging, cobblestone streets, colonial architecture and wooden ferries give it an uncannily Mediterranean feel. Indeed, this is the same easy-going environment that once inspired WH Hudson to write his classic *Idle Days in Patagonia*.

Nothing so nice as messin' about on the **Río Negro**.

To get a feel for Carmen's history and architectural heritage head to the huddle of streets between Plaza 7 de Mayo and the port area. The **Torre del Fuerte**, at Dr. Barajas, between Olivera and 7 de Marzo, was built in 1780 and is the last piece standing of the military fort that once occupied the entire block. Rancho Rial and the **Casa de la Cultura**, at Mitre Nos. 94 and 27 respectively, are two fine examples of Carmen's colonial architecture, and La Carlota, at Bynon No.120, is a restored 19th-century home and outpost of the Museo Histórico Regional Emma Nozzi. Contact the museum for visits. At Biagetti No.4, **La Rebusca** is an antiques store-cum-living museum, displaying objects recovered from nearby *estancias*. Located in a brick house dating from 1880, it doubles as the home of artists Arturo and Magdalena Aguirrezabala.

Viedma sits across an antique, German-built iron bridge straddling the Río Negro. Although small enough to be explored on foot, Viedma – capital of Río Negro province – is a lively city.

A few outstanding buildings and one or two museums are worth a look, all on or near Plaza San Martín. On the square, the **Museo Histórico-Antropológico 'Gobernador Eugenio Tello'** houses a sizeable collection of pre-Columbian artefacts, plus educationally minded displays on the peopling of Patagonia. Just off the plaza, several historically important buildings from the 1880s line Avenida Rivadavia, all connected with the Salesians, including the former school, the cathedral, the town's first library and the **Museo Salesiano Cardenal Cagliero**, which retells the story of missionary activity in the area. The **Centro Municipal de Cultura**, in front of the statue to Francisco Viedma, projects movies, stages concerts and exhibits works by local artists. It also houses the Mercado Artesenal, an excellent handicrafts fair that sells authentic Mapuche clothes, rugs and wood carvings.

In mid January, Viedma is the finishing line for the world's longest and most gruelling kayak race, **La Regata del Río Negro**, a 500-kilometre (311-mile), week-long paddlethon that starts in Neuquén.

EXCURSIONS

Just eight kilometres (five miles) from Viedma are a number of small farms, or *chacras*, where organic produce such as fine fruits, cheeses and honeys can be sampled and bought. Take a taxi or contact **Newen Viajes** (Alvaro Barros 420, 02920 429673), which runs excursions to the area. Heading north and further out, 110 kilometres (68 miles) from Carmen de Patagones along the RN3 coastal road, is **La Isla Jabalí**, a rugged, half-moon-shaped island

connected to the mainland by a road bridge. The tiny island's main village, Bahía San Blas, attracts anglers between October and April, the shark fishing season. Anglo-Argentinian **Bruce Trousdell** (02920 15602435) organises a range of nautical excursions, *Jaws* variety and otherwise. Going south, where the Río Negro empties into the Atlantic 30 kilometres (19 miles) outside Viedma, a wild stretch of relatively warm-water beaches begins. The scenic coastal road RP1 runs west from here, along the northern coast of **Golfo San Matías** for 200 kilometres (124 miles) until reaching Las Grutas (*see p123*). Along the way, half an hour from Viedma, is the touristy resort **El Cóndor**, which fills up in summer with local families (buses leave from Plaza Alsina several times a day). Nearby, the **Faro del Río Negro** is Patagonia's oldest functioning lighthouse, dating from 1887. Another half-hour on is the Reserva Faunística Punta Bermeja, or **La Lobería** (RP1, 02920 15 628679, admission US$1), the summer breeding ground for 3,000 cute, noisy and very smelly sea lions and numerous marine bird species. A comfortable walkway along the cliffs offers a bird's-eye view of the sea lion colony below.

For those with a car, it's worth continuing along the coast road to the huge, virgin beaches beyond, many of which are visited only infrequently by fishermen… and, according to myth, Adolf Hitler. In 1996, a local newspaper unearthed a photo showing what appears to be a Nazi submarine beached in a lonely cove along Golfo San Matías. The story meshed well with Argentina's infamous reputation as a haven for Nazis, though a subsequent search by divers revealed nothing.

There are a number of ideal camping spots on **Bahía Rosas** and **Bahía Creek**, where it's also possible to fish for shark. **Caleta de los Loros**, 145 kilometres (90 miles) from Viedma, is a freshwater estuary that looks like a flat lake in the middle of the ocean, teeming with flamingos.

Tritón Turismo (Namuncurá 78, 02920 431131/427041, www.tritonturismo.com.ar) organises seven-day horse rides with stopovers at *estancias* and beach camping (US$635 all-inclusive), as well as city tours, farm visits and trips to La Lobería. For kayaking excursions on the Río Negro, contact **Aqua Ventura** (Alpataco 451, 02920 428229/15605420). Both agencies operate out of Viedma.

Even if you're not taking the train from Viedma to Bariloche, it's worth visiting the station to soak up some of the affection that the train still inspires among the loyal and expert staff whose job it is to keep the 70-year-old wagons in tip-top shape.

Argentinian Patagonia

Carmen de Patagones. *See p120.*

Centro Municipal de Cultura

Avenida Francisco Viedma y Urquiza, Carmen de Patagones (02920 424448). **Open** 8am-midnight daily. **Admission** free.

Museo Histórico-Antropológico Gobernador Eugenio Tello

Avenida San Martín 263, entre 25 de Mayo y Belgrano, Viedma (02920 425900). **Open** 9am-12.30pm, 1-4.30pm Mon-Fri. **Admission** free.

Museo Histórico Regional Emma Nozzi

Avenida Biedma 4, entre Bynon y Comodoro Rivadavia, Carmen de Patagones (02920 462729). **Open** *Apr-Nov* 10am-noon, 2.30-4.30pm Mon-Fri; 5-7pm Sat. *Dec-Mar* 9am-noon, 5-9pm Mon-Fri; 7-9pm Sat, Sun. **Admission** free.

Museo Salesiano Cardenal Cagliero

Avenida Rivadavia 34, entre Alvaro Barros y Colón, Carmen de Patagones (02920 424190). **Open** 8.30am-noon Mon, Wed, Fri; 8.30am-noon, 6-8pm Tue, Thur. **Admission** free.

Where to eat & drink

Sample the Patagonian lamb and seafood specialities at Viedma's riverside **Rigoletto** (JJ Viedma y Bynon, 02920 463687, $$$). Also on the waterfront, **El Orcón** (Emma Nozzi, entre la primera y segunda bajada, no phone, $$) serves up grilled steaks, pastas and picturesque views of the Río Negro.

In Viedma, for more fresh seafood and river views, Spanish-styled **La Balsa** (Avenida Villarino 27, 02920 431974, $$) is popular with both locals and tourists. In warm weather, sit outside. For pizza and beers, **Costa Río** (Avenida Villarino y Saavedra, 02920 421446, $$) is another friendly riverside spot that gets busy. Away from the river, but also popular

with *maragatos*, is **Capriasca** (Alvaro Barros 685, 02920 426754, $$) a traditional Argentinian eaterie offering barbecued cuts and good wines. **Código** (Garrone 245, 02920 428146), a relaxed pub, is also centrally located. On the outskirts, flashy **Crown Casino** (Cardenal Cagliero y Vallese, 02920 425061) has proved a big draw.

Where to stay

Most people come to Carmen during the day and spend nights in Viedma, but if that's too hectic, Carmen's **Hotel Percaz** (Comodoro Rivadavia e Hipólito Yrigoyen, 02920 464104, double US$15-$20) is a good, basic, year-round option. In Viedma, **Hotel Austral** (Avenida Villarino 292, 02920 422615/19, www.hoteles-austral.com.ar, double US$45) was the choice of former president Raúl Alfonsín. The bar overlooking the coast is a great spot for a drink and the '70s decor proves that not everything in the disco decade was in bad taste. For a more pampered stay, try the hotel/spa **Inside Patagónico** (25 de Mayo 174, 02920 430459, spaiturburu@rnonline.com.ar, double US$25), which has a heated pool with masseurs on hand to take out the knots that travelling has put in. As a budget option, some rooms at central **Hotel Peumayén** (Buenos Aires 334, 02920 425222/422580, hotelpeumayen@speedy.com.ar, double US$15-$20) overlook tree-lined Plaza Alsina. Out of the centre, **Nijar Hotel** (Mitre 490, 02920 422833, nijarh@arnet.com.ar, double US$25-$30) is another fine option.

Resources

Hospital

Artémides de Zatti, Rivadavia 391 (02920 425907/422721).

Internet

Arroba Cyber Café, Colón 202 (02920 425526).

Police station

Alen 169 (02920 422111).

Post office

25 de Mayo 457 (02920 424535).

Tourist information

In **Viedma**: *Oficina de Informes Turísticos, Avenida Francisco de Viedma, entre Urquiza y 7 de Marzo (02920 427171/427332).* **Open** *Mar-mid Dec* 8am-8pm Mon-Fri; 9am-8pm Sat, Sun. *Mid Dec-Feb* 8am-10pm Mon-Fri; 9am-10pm Sat, Sun.
In **Carmen**: *Subdirección de Turismo, Bynon 186, entre Marcelino Crespo y Paraguay (02920 461777 ext 253/dirturpatagones@infovia.com.ar),* **Open** *Apr-Oct* 7am-7pm Mon-Fri. *Nov-Mar* 7am-9pm Mon-Fri; 10am-1pm, 6-9pm Sat, Sun.

Getting there

By air

Viedma's airport, **Gobernador Castello** (RP51, 02920 424416/422005), 3km (2 miles) from the centre, is served by flights from Neuquén, Bahía Blanca and San Antonio Oeste. This air service, however, is under threat. Check with travel agents for an update.

By road

BA is 12hrs by road; there are several daily overnight services. Puerto Madryn is 5.5hrs and Rio Gallegos 24hrs away. Buses to Bariloche (14.5hrs) make numerous stops. Viedma and Carmen have separate bus terminals, 2km (1.25 miles) apart. Buses to Carmen arrive at Barbieri (02920 463585); to Viedma at José María Guido 1580 (02920 426850).

By train

Although more expensive, the fastest and most comfortable way to the mountains is on the **Tren Patagónico**. For departure information and ticket prices, *see p103*. The train station is on RP51 in Viedma. The train is run by **SEFEPA** (Servicios Ferroviarios Patagónicos, 02920 422130, www.sefepa.com.ar).

Las Grutas

Called the Caribbean of Patagonia for its transparent waters and white, sandy beach, Las Grutas – though less attractive than Puerto Madryn down the coast – is a popular resort with young Argentinians. It lies in the north-west corner of the Golfo San Matías, 185 kilometres (115 miles) south of Viedma, and 15 kilometres (9.5 miles) from **San Antonio Oeste**, a struggling fishing village. The town proudly lays claim to the warmest waters anywhere along Argentina's coast – in summer, up to 20°C (68°F), a little higher than at Mar del Plata closer to Buenos Aires. As in Mar del Plata the town is invaded every summer by hordes of Argentinian tourists: in Las Grutas 4,000 locals morph into more than 100,000 holidaymakers. The take-off in tourism has led to a construction boom which has eroded much of the town's charm, leaving a Las Grutas that, in peak season at least, is more characterless costa than idyllic Caribbean retreat. Off season, however, it's peaceful – ideal for walking, fishing, surfing or having a picnic. From June to November, whales and dolphins can sometimes be seen from the shore.

Owing to to the high cliffs, access to the beach is via *bajadas* (stairways to the sea). At high tide, it's impossible to swim and the water reaches all the way to the foot. The best way to get around is by quad bike; rent one from **Rocio Trax** (Jacobacci 320, 02934 497708) for US$12 per hour, or **Ocasión** (Galería Antares 11, 02934 497650) for US$11 per hour.

The relatively warm waters and excellent visibility make scuba diving popular. Contact **Cota Cero** (Tercera Bajada, 02934 497278/15 602178, www.cotacerobuceo.com.ar) who can also arrange sea-fishing trips. Every January, the town celebrates the 'Fiesta del Golfo', but the partying is possible all summer long.

EXCURSIONS

If the pace of Las Grutas gets a little too hectic, try the nearby beaches. Heading towards San Antonio Oeste, **La Rinconada** and **Los Alamos** are popular with anglers and birdwatchers. Just over four kilometres (2.5 miles) south, the remote beach of **Playa Piedras Coloradas** contains outlandish rock formations, while, another eight and ten kilometres (five and six miles) on respectively, El Sótano and Cañadón de las Ostras are rugged, fossil-strewn stretches of coastline. Fans of *The Da Vinci Code* should visit **Fuerte Argentino**, 42 kilometres (26 miles) south of Las Grutas. Local legend has it that this bizarre natural phenomenon – a 145-metre (470-feet) high, cross-shaped plateau overlooking Golfo San Matías – was once the site of a pre-Columbian fort established by an order of the Knights Templar in the 13th century as a safe haven for the Holy Grail. Fact or fiction, the jutting plateau does offer stunning views of the gulf. To visit, contact **Desert Tracks** (Viedma 1145, Local 3, 02920 15-577229, www.deserttracks.com.ar) run by ex-war correspondent Fernando Skliarevsky; they employ classic Dodge M60 jeeps to transport visitors on unconventional and adventurous excursions. Skliarevsky also organises tours of the blindingly white expanses of the **Salinas de Gualicho**, the second largest salt mines in South America, situated 60 kilometres (37 miles) inland from Las Grutas, and 72 metres (236 feet) below sea level.

Where to eat & drink

Although choice is not abundant, Las Grutas springs to life in summer. **Malala Restaurant** (Bresciano 209, 02934 497573, $$$) offers modern, fusion cuisine in a candle-lit dining room decorated with African art. **Aladdin** (Avenida Rio Negro 607, 02934 497266, $$) has a loyal following who come for its seafood delicacies. **Aqualung** (Viedma 824, 02934 497221/437221, $$) is a popular restaurant-bar, with a broad, beachfront terrace; best of all, it's open round the clock. For an after-dinner flutter, try your luck at **Crown Casino** (Tercera Bajada, Avenida Costanera, 02934 497378, free admission). For the club set, multi-roomed **Birras** nightclub (Mainque 680, no phone, admission US$2-$4) heaves with an up-for-it-crowd of young Argentinians (it's open during the summer season only).

Where to stay

The summer tourist influx means that there is plenty of accommodation, including over a dozen campsites. **Casablanca Las Grutas** (Viedma 1155, 02934 497151/608, casablanca@canaldig.com.ar, apartment for 2-3 people US$15-$20) has clean apartments overlooking a huge pool that's popular with young people in the summer. It's also party central, especially during Cuban-born manager Armando's thrice-weekly salsa classes.

On the beachfront, **Hotel Mirador del Golfo** (Avenida Costanera y Acceso Norte, Bajado Cero, 02934 497350/497441,www.hotel miradordelgolfo.com, double US$25-$35) has airy, sunny rooms with balconied views of Golfo San Matías, plus internet access. Also on the seafront, **Hotel Riviera** (Avenida Costanera 897, 02934 497357, hotelriviera@canaldig. com.ar, double US$15-$25) is a central, mid-range hotel with internet access. Rooms are clean, spacious and carpeted (a welcome treat in winter) and most have a balcony overlooking the ocean. Though it's a few blocks from the coast, the excellent value **Hotel Patagonia Norte** (Sierra Pailemán 8, 02934 497800, hotelpatagonianorte@canaldig.com.ar, double US$5-$7) still has some rooms with sea views.

Resources

Hospital
Centro de Salud, Pilcaniyeú y Río Negro (02934 497100).

Internet
Escape, Peatonal El Bolsón 600 (no phone).

Police station
Bariloche 555 (02934 497096).

Post office
El Bolsón, y Valcheta (02934 497250).

Tourist information
Subsecretaría de Turismo Municipal, Avenida Río Negro 715 (02934 497463/www.balneario lasgrutas.com). Open Jan-Feb 7am-3pm daily. Mar-Dec 8.30am-8pm Mon-Sat; 10.30am-8pm Sun.

Getting there

By air
The nearest airstrip is 5km (3 miles) away, Schedules for direct flights are very changeable, so check with the airport – **Aeropuerto Saint Exupery** (RP2, 02934 421329) – or directly with airlines.

By road
Las Grutas is 15hrs from BA by road. Daily buses there, and south all the way to Río Gallegos (30hrs) leave from **Terminal Ríos** in San Antonio Oeste (Avenida Antártida Argentina 2556, 02920 421580), though there are 3 smaller terminals too. In summer months buses to San Antonio Oeste from Las Grutas run every 30mins, arriving at **Terminal de Transporte Las Grutas** (San Martín 621, 02920 422573). In winter, the frequency is one per hour.

By train
The train from Viedma to Bariloche (2-3 times weekly, each direction) stops at nearby San Antonio Oeste. For departure and ticket information, *see p103.* The station is at Pasaje Rosato (02934 421314).

Puerto Madryn

Few cities in Argentina can be held up as models of eco-awareness and sustainability; Puerto Madryn, gateway to one of the world's greatest marine-life reserves, gets closer than most. Looking out over the still, blue waters of **Golfo Nuevo**, its centre is built around a beachfront boulevard dotted with bars serving beer and seafood bites, though the rhythm of the place is laid-back and the mood friendly. In the evening, Madryn's numerous – and generally inviting – restaurants fill up with locals and tourists; it's easy to forget that this vibrant place is on the edge of dry, dusty plains.

The key year in the history of Puerto Madryn is 1865, when 153 Welsh folk set sail from Liverpool on the *Mimosa* in search of freedom in Patagonia. The cliffside shelters, where the pioneers first took refuge on reaching terra firma, can be visited five minutes out of town at Punta Cuevas, where the Centro de Interpretación includes displays in English recounting their story. Standing nearby is the **Monumento al Indio**, a work by the celebrated Argentinian sculptor Luis Perlotti, unveiled to mark the centennial anniversary of the Welsh arrival. For more on the Welsh in Patagonia, *see pp12-23.*

In more recent times, Puerto Madryn has built up a deserved international reputation as Argentina's marine showcase. It's a good place from which to organise excursions and to take your first steps towards learning about the nearby seas. The **Museo Provincial de Ciencias Naturales y Oceanográfico** in the elegant, historic Chalet Pujol is well worth visiting. There are exhibits of Patagonia's flora and fauna and you can take in the expanse of the bay from the turreted loft.

Along the seafront is the **Museo de Arte Moderno** with 80 works, including pieces by Argentinian master Benito Quinquela Martín as well as local artists. But if all you have time

If only every coastline were as unspoilt as **Puerto Madryn.**

to do in Puerto Madryn is visit the outstanding **EcoCentro**, your journey will have been worthwhile. Built on the coastal cliffs just on from Punta Cuevas, this shrine to the marine ecosystem fuses environmental education, scientific investigation and artistic statement. The aim is to encourage respect for the environment rather than bamboozle you with facts. Guides answer questions and information panels can be read in both English and Spanish. After exploring the touch-pools, enjoying the exhibits and live events such as orchestral recitals, curl up in the glass tower with a book from the library or enjoy the 360-degree view.

For those who would just as soon sink as swim, Madryn is deservedly regarded as Argentina's scuba-diving capital. With **Scuba Duba** (Boulevard Brown 893, 02965 452699, www.scubaduba.com.ar) novices can dive up to ten metres (33 feet) while their progress is photographed. Advanced scuba fans with the correct paperwork can dive up to 30 metres (98 feet) down to explore shipwrecks (including *The Emma*, a wooden schooner that was chartered by Shackleton in 1916) and marine life. **Lobo Larsen** (Avenida H Irigoyen 144, 02965 15516314, www.lobolarsen.com) even organises aquatic scavenger hunts for sunken German U-boats. During the summer, locals go down to the beach to swim – it's bracing, to put it kindly, but those accustomed to North Atlantic seas should be fine.

EXCURSIONS

The most popular excursions from Puerto Madryn are nature-related trips to Península Valdés (*see p128* **Península Valdés**). Also on offer are visits to Trelew and the charming Welsh villages of Gaiman and Dolavon, along with adventure-sports outings and adrenalin-charged off-road 4x4 excursions. As well as Península Valdés there are other spots for seeing marine life around Madryn. Seventeen kilometres (10.5 miles) from town is the year-round sea lion colony known as **Punta Loma**. Another 61 kilometres (38 miles) further on is the elephant seal colony at **Punta Ninfas**. Here, within grunting distance of the seals, **El Pedral** lodge (011 4331 1919/www.elpedral. com, US$120-$480 all-inclusive packages) offers tailor-made stays in a French period building. The package included transfers to and from Puerto Madryn, guided excursions and great opportunities to spy on signature fauna, including the southern right whale's breeding season between June and December. During the same period, north of Madryn at **Playa El Doradillo**, more southern rights entertain the crowds who stand in awe just metres away.

For a range of excursions, **Argentina Visión** (Avenida Roca 536, 02965 455888, www.argentinavision.com) and **Flamenco Tour** (Avenida Roca 331, 02965 455505, www.flamencotour.com) can supply good, English-speaking guides.

On the green team

It's hard to tell from the flashy mansions and aluminium factory, but Puerto Madryn is stepping forward as Patagonia's green capital. It first came to the attention of environmentalists in the 1970s thanks largely to the study of the area's marine habitat by biologist William Conway for New York's Wildlife Conservation Society (WCS), which made the pages of *National Geographic*. Simultaneously, word about the whales got out due to the pioneering research of another outsider, Roger Payne. Both scientists were later instrumental in creating Patagonia's biggest monument to marine conservation, **EcoCentro** (*see below*).

The area continues to attract attention from international environmental groups, most working in partnership with a growing number of local NGOs. In 2000, the British charity World Land Trust purchased La Esperanza ranch on Peninsula Valdés, remodelling it to include a research centre powered by solar and wind energy. With Madryn-based **Fundación Patagonia Natural** (www.patagonianatural.org) the WLT now promotes sustainable eco-tourism on the peninsula. An environmentally sensitive tourist lodge is to be opened on the ranch.

With international co-operation the current watchword, Payne's Ocean Alliance has joined forces with Argentina's **Instituto de Conservación de Ballenas** (www.icb.org.ar) to promote the protection of Patagonia's endangered southern white whale population. Successful initiatives so far include a whale adoption programme. At the same time, the British environmental group, **Whale and Dolphins Conservation Society** (www.wdcs.org), has teamed up with Argentinian NGO **Cethus** (www.cethus.org) to run awareness-raising campaigns in the Madryn area, which include workshops to enhance the quality of whale-watching tours, and a volunteer programme to aid whale observation and rescue operations.

Smaller-scale, local-only conservation projects have also become more prominent in recent years. Juan Carlos Lopez directs Madryn's **Fundación Orca** (www.fundorca.org.ar), dedicated to preventing the capture for captivity of the region's killer whales and dolphins and the degradation of their natural ocean habitat. In recent times, environmental groups like Lopez's have been compelled to take an increasingly proactive stance in response to perceived threats to their shoreline's fragile ecosystem. In one high-profile act, at El Doradillo, just outside Madryn, local groups pooled resources to protect in perpetuity a beach adjacent to an important breeding area for whales.

In addition to tours of Península Valdés, **Patagonia Southbound** (2nd Floor, Office 204, Mosconi 83, 02965 474402, www.southbound.com.ar) organises unconventional activities: palaeontological and archaeological tours, trips out to *estancias* and private chef-catered picnics with views of the whales. Note that Puerto Madryn can be used as a base for any of the trips that go out of Trelew, and is, frankly, a smaller, more pleasant town.

EcoCentro
Julio Verne 3784 (02965 457470/www.ecocentro.org.ar). **Open** *Jan-mid Mar* 5-9pm daily. *Mid Mar-mid Jul* 3-7pm Thur-Mon. *Mid Jul-Dec* 10am-7pm Wed-Mon. *Oct, Nov* 10am-7pm daily. **Admission** US$6; free under-6s. **Credit** AmEx, DC, MC, V

Museo de Arte Moderno
Avenida Roca 444, entre Sarmiento y 9 de Julio (02965 453204). **Open** 4-9pm Mon-Fri; 10am-1pm, 6pm-9pm Sat. **Admission** suggested contribution US75¢. **No credit cards**.

Museo Provincial de Ciencias Naturales y Oceanográfico
Menéndez y Domecq García (02965 451139). **Open** 9am-noon, 2.30-7pm Mon-Fri; 2.30-7pm Sat. **Admission** US75¢; US50¢ under-12s.

Punta Cuevas Centro de Interpretación
Boulevard Brown s/n (no phone/www.puntacuevas.madryn.com). **Open** *Dec-Apr* 5-9pm Wed-Mon. *May-Nov* 3-7pm Wed-Mon. **Admission** US$1. **No credit cards**.

Where to eat

Cantina El Náutico

Avenida Julio A Roca 790, y Lugones (02965 471404). **Open** noon-2.30pm, 8pm-midnight Mon-Sat; noon-3pm, 7.30-11pm Sun. **Average** $$$. **Credit** AmEx, DC, MC, V.

Formula One legend Juan Manuel Fangio and acclaimed writer Ernesto Sábato are just two of Argentina's A-list celebrities who've sampled the fine traditional fare at El Náutico. Other star diners have their photos framed on the walls – waiters happily point out who's who.

Mariscos del Atlántico

Club Náutico Atlántico Sud, Avenida Rawson 288, entre Gómez y Acosta (02965 15 5552500). **Open** noon-4pm, 7pm-1am daily. **Average** $$. **No credit cards**.

Muster up an image of your perfect fisherman's restaurant and you'd probably be picturing family-run Mariscos, with its ocean view and nets hanging from the rafters. Try the salmon and fresh clams, the latter hand-picked by dad Luis and sons on dawn dives to the depths of Golfo Nuevo.

Mediterraneo

Boulevard Brown 1040, entre Martín Fierro y José Hernández (02965 458145/www.restomediterraneo.com.ar). **Open** 7am-2am daily. **Average** $$$. **Credit** AmEx, MC.

Seconds from the sea, Mediterraneo draws a smart set with its diverse menu of international fine food and locally netted shellfish.

Nativo Sur

Boulevard Brown 2000 (02965 457403/www.nativosurrestaurant.com.ar). **Open** *Jan-Feb* 9am-midnight daily. *Mar-Dec* 8pm-midnight Tue-Fri; noon-3pm, 8pm-midnight Sat, Sun. **Average** $$$. **Credit** AmEx, DC, MC, V.

Life's a beach at **Mediterraneo**.

On the beach out of town, in a candle-lit, wooden lodge, slick Nativo Sur's speciality is Patagonian meat and seafood. The lamb with *cordillera hongos* (mushroom sauce) is superb. Alternatively, try Yoaquina, a more informal seafood restaurant from the same team on the same strip.

Plácido Restaurante

Avenida Roca 508, entre Sarmiento y Gales (02965 455991/www.placido.com.ar). **Open** 11.30am-3pm, 8pm-1am daily. **Average** $$$. **Credit** AmEx, MC, V.

The creative menu and colourful decor at Plácido cater to a fashionable, downtown crowd.

Taska Beltza

9 de Julio 345, entre Marcos A Zar y San Martín (02965 15 668085). **Open** 7.30pm-1am Tue; 11.30am-3pm, 7.30pm-1am Wed-Sun. Closed mid Mar-Jul. **Average** $$$. **No credit cards**.

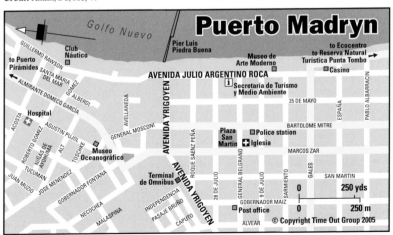

Península Valdés

The waters that surround Patagonia's most spectacular wildlife reserve are so brimming with marine mammal and bird life that to visit Península Valdés is to experience the ocean world's answer to the African savannah. This truly wild, 'Serengeti of the seas' is home to the fearsome killer whale, over two thousand southern right whales, and tens of thousands of elephant seals, sea lions and Magellanic penguins. Presiding over this watery congress are millions of marine birds.

There's also plenty of life on Valdés beyond the shoreline. The parched interior of this 3,625-square-kilometre (1,400 square mile) landmass is home to guanacos, rheas and other dry-land fauna. The reserve, declared a World Heritage Site in 1999, also boasts two salt pans – Salina Chica and Salina Grande near the centre; the latter is the fourth deepest depression on the planet.

Day trips to this eco-spectacle embark from Trelew and Puerto Madryn (US$20-$25) and take visitors to the peninsula's northern or southern areas, depending on the season. The best way, however, to really find the rhythm of this unique place is to stay for a few nights. The reserve's principal attractions, detailed below, are 40 to 100 kilometres (25 to 63 miles) apart.

Before entering the peninsula you must go via the Puerto del Control, on the Isthmus Ameghino, where you pay the admission to the reserve (US$12 adults, US$6 under-12s, free under-3s). Visitors travelling in groups of six or more will have to use the services of a guide, which can be arranged here. A short distance farther along the isthmus is the **Centro de Interpretación**. Displays at the centre's small museum are a good, quick introduction to the peninsula's fauna and flora. North of here, in the still, blue waters of Golfo San José, is **Isla de los Pájaros**. Access to the island is forbidden, but species like cormorants, herons and flamingos may be observed through binoculars via the lookout point at the Centro de Interpretación and various other spots along the coast. The birds are busiest from September to April.

WATCHING THE WHALES

Puerto Pirámides is where the main event takes place: whale watching. A century ago, this port was an important outlet for fish and wool and 3,000 people lived here. Now only 220 remain, seriously outnumbered by the 80,000 sheep. These days the star visitors – southern right whales – turn up every year between June and December.

There are a handful of tour companies at the port. **Whales Argentina** (Primera Bajada, 02965 495015, www.whalesargentina. com.ar, closed Apr, May) is among the best. It's operated by the gregarious Ricardo Pinino who, legend has it, lived in a cave when he first arrived 29 years ago. He runs excursions just before sunset for smaller groups, in which an unspoken code of silence is respected. **Jorge Schmid** (Segunda Bajada, 02965 495012, in Puerto Madryn 02965 451511) and **Peke Sosa** (Segunda Bajada, 02965 495010, www.pekesosa.com.ar) also have years of experience. Trips to observe these beautiful, callosity-covered creatures get you up close and personal. Close enough to be sprayed through their blowholes, winked at, then given a farewell tail-wave. Despite their bulk, southern right whales can lift their huge bodies out of the water in an amazing display of aquatic acrobatics. Boat excursions return via the sea lion colony to cap off an unforgettable experience on the ocean waves. Expect to pay between US$15 and US$20 for a whale-watching trip. There's also horse riding, kayaking, sandboarding and scuba diving (US$40, 2-3hrs) on offer at Puerto Pirámides. Contact **Góos Ballenas** (Segunda Bajada, 02965 495061).

Laid-back Puerto Pirámides is the only village on the peninsula and an ideal overnight destination. The best lodging is the suites at **Hostería The Paradise** (Avenida de las Ballenas, Segunda Bajada, 02965 495003, www.hosteriaparadise. com.ar, double US$40). The Paradise also boasts a log cabin-styled eatery serving up excellent seafood ($$). Another good option is 12-room **Patagonia Franca Hostería** (Primera Bajada, 02965 495006, www. patagoniafranca.com, double US$35-$70). Ask, of course, for a sea view.

OTHER ATTRACTIONS

Punta Delgada, 68 kilometres (42 miles) south-west of Puerto Pirámides via a bumpy, gravel road, is where the lighthouse and the upscale **El Faro Hotel de Campo Punta Delgada** (02965 15 406304, www.punta delgada.com, closed May-July, double US$134-$247) are situated. Knowledgeable guides will answer questions about the fossils scattered around your feet and in the cliffs as you clamber to the beach to wander carefully among the sea lion and elephant seal colonies. A night on the windswept cliffs at the hotel is unique. Activities within the Reserva Delgada with English-speaking guides are included in the room rate; try horse riding, fossil hunts and night walks with coffee and whisky to keep out the chill.

North up the coast is **Caleta Valdés**, a thin spit of land sheltering the bay that draws a variety of marine and bird life, including elephant seals and Magellanic penguins. Killer whales raid the beach in October and November, looking to snack on a baby elephant seal or two. This astonishing, though rarely witnessed, spectacle is more likely to be seen at the elephant seal and sea lion colonies at **Punta Norte**, 45 kilometres (28 miles) north – March and April are the best months. Also at Punta Norte between September and March another huge colony of Magellanic penguins can be observed waddling on to land to nest in burrows beneath the bushes. You need to go with an organised tour to see this colony, which can be arranged through El Faro Hotel, Estancia San Lorenzo or La Ernestina.

For something to eat, **Parador La Elvira** (Punta Cántor, 02965 15 406183, www.laelvira.com.ar, $$) is a scenic spot to stop before exploring Caleta. South-west of Punta Norte is **Estancia San Lorenzo** (02965 15 406304, www.puntanorte.com, closed mid Apr-mid Sept, $$$), a fine place for lunch. Staff at the *estancia* will organise trips in 4x4s out to visit the penguin colony, but you must book in advance.

Inland from Caleta Valdés, **Estancia La Elvira** (02965 474248, www.laelvira.com.ar, double US$110-$203) is a stylishly recycled ranch ideal for outdoor activities or just peaceful repose. Its eight comfortable rooms, each in a different colour, are the epitome of rustic luxury. If you are adamant about witnessing the killer whale attacks at Punta Norte, the four-room **Estancia La Ernestina** (RP3, 02965 458061, www.laernestina.com.ar, closed mid Apr-mid Sept, US$250 all-inclusive) is the most convenient place to rest your head. Ensure that you make your reservation well in advance.

About 18 kilometres (11 miles) outside Puerto Pirámides, the sun-drenched cliffs of **Punta Pardelas** are ideal for camping. Bring water and other goods as no services exist.

Argentinian Patagonia

Taska Beltza offers some of the freshest seafood in town. Ask the delightful Laura about the catch of the day, or watch her husband, 'El Negro', prepare the traditional Basque dishes. It's a popular spot so try to book in advance.

La Vaca y el Pollito

Avenida Storni 49, entre Boulevard Brown y Roca (02965 458486). **Open** noon-3pm, 8pm-midnight daily. **Average** $$. **Credit** AmEx, DC, MC, V.
This is where meat lovers can tuck in, enjoying both the reasonable prices and the irony of eating dead animals in a replica Noah's Ark. The supervised play area makes it ideal for families.

Nightlife

Bars along the beachfront are worth a pit stop for drinks on a summer's evening. For seaside shots try **Vernardino** (Boulevard Brown 860, 02965 474289, www.vernardino clubdemar.com.ar), which also serves good food. Another option is to wash down pizza with cocktails at **La Barra** (Boulevard Brown y Perlotti, 02965 455550). For more liquid delights farther into town, **Margarita** (Roque Sáenz Peña 86, no phone) attracts the biggest crowd for its lively atmosphere and happy hour promotions. **Ambigú** (Roca 97, 02965 472541), housed in a century-old, originally English-owned building, offers a more laid-back alternative. If you want salsa while you sip, have a sing-a-long Cuban style while listening to the terrific house band at **La Oveja Negra** (Hipólito Yrigoyen 144, no phone). The only beachfront nightclub is **Rancho Cu Camonga** (Boulevard Brown y Castelli, no phone, admission US$3). It has a big and attractive outdoor terrace and pulls in a lively crowd of twenty-somethings during high season.

Where to stay

El Gualicho

Marcos A Zar 480, entre Sarmiento y 9 de Julio (02965 454163/www.elgualicho.com.ar). **Rates** US$20-$25 double; US$30 triple. **No credit cards.**
Despite the name (a *gualicho* is a mischievous, sometimes evil, spirit from Araucanian folklore) the vibe in this colourful, well-run hostel couldn't be friendlier. Organised activities include scuba diving and bike tours.

Hostería Hipocampo

Vesta 33, entre Almirante Brown y Morgan (tel & fax 02965 473605/www.hosteriahipocampo.com). **Rates** US$20-$25 single; US$25-$30 double; US$25-$35 triple. **No credit cards.**
Hostería Hipocampo is a fine budget choice with friendly service, cable TV and bar. There are only seven rooms, so it's essential to book in advance. Breakfast is not included.

Hostería Solar de la Costa

Boulevard Brown 2057, entre Humphreys y Apeleg (02956 458822/fax 458823/www.solar delacosta.com). **Rates** US$20-$25 single; US$25-$30 double; US$25-$35 triple. **Credit** AmEx, DC, MC, V.
Friendly, family-run Hostería Solar de la Costa has pleasant, sunny rooms with ocean views. One of the apartments has a kitchenette and jacuzzi and all rooms have private bathrooms. Staff will happily help organise excursions.

Hotel Bahía Nueva

Avenida Roca 67, entre Peña e Hipólito Yrigoyen (tel & fax 02965 451677/www.bahianueva.com.ar). **Rates** US$20-$25 single; US$25-$30 double; US$30-$40 triple. **Credit** AmEx, DC, MC, V.
Hotel Bahía Nueva, overlooking the sea, is a well-attended, brick and wood hotel, built in 1995. In the foyer, a library and video resources help you plan excursions. The tasty home-cooked breakfasts are worth getting up for.

Hotel Península Valdés

Avenida Roca 155, entre 28 de Julio y Peña (02965 471292/fax 452584/www.hotel-peninsula-valdes.com). **Rates** US$92-$112 single; US$102-$125 double; US$150-$160 triple; US$175 suite. **Credit** AmEx, DC, MC, V.
Hotel Península Valdés, with excellent facilities and stunning views, is the cream of the crop, both in terms of price and quality. Its many services include a business centre, gym and spa.

Hotel Tolosa

Avenida Roque Sáenz Peña 253, entre Marcos A Zar y Mitre (02965 471850/fax 02965 451141/www.hoteltolosa.com.ar). **Rates** US$55-$75 single; US$67-$85 double; US$80-$115 triple. **Credit** AmEx, DC, MC, V.
Although a couple of blocks from the ocean, some rooms at Hotel Tolosa have sea views and all are spacious (the superior rooms have full wheelchair access). Internet and use of bicycles are both free.

Resources

Hospital

Hospital Subzonal, R. Gómez 383 (02965 451999/473445).

Internet

Locutorio Telecom, Roque Saenz Peña 153 (02965 471147).

Police station

Mitre 339 (02965 451449).

Post office

Gobernador Maíz 239 (02965 451259/451107).

Tourist information

Secretaría de Turismo, Avenida Roca 223, entre 28 de Julio y Belgrano (02965 456067/www.madryn.gov.ar/turismo). **Open** Dec-Feb 7am-11pm daily; Mar-Nov 8am-9pm daily.

Getting there

By air

Puerto Madryn's airport, **Aeropuerto El Tehuelche** (02965 451909), is 10mins north of the centre. There are flights from BA, Comodoro Rivadavia and Viedma. Trelew airport is another option – it's served by more frequent flights.

By road

There are regular bus services from BA, 20hrs away, and to Peninsula Valdés, plus connections south. The **Terminal de Omnibus** is at Ciudad de Nefyn y Dr Avila (02965 451789).

By sea

Many cruise ships stop at Madryn. The in-town port, **Muelle Piedra Buena** (Hipólito Yrigoyen y Rawson), was originally built in 1910, fell into disuse and was reopened amid much fanfare in 2003. The port authority phone number is 02965 451400.

Trelew

The inland Welsh villages developed after early settlers moved from Puerto Madryn closer to freshwater supplies. **Rawson**, the province's bland capital on the **Río Chubut**, was the first area for Welsh settlement, then Trelew. Located in the valley, Trelew is the ideal spot from which to discover Patagonia's Welsh heritage.

The town's name derives from early settler Lewis Jones. He was the pivotal figure behind the construction of a railway (built between 1886 and 1889) that once linked Chubut Valley to the Golfo Nuevo. 'Tre' means town in Welsh and 'lew' is short for Lewis.

Trelew's population expanded rapidly in the 1980s, mostly due to industrial growth, and today stands at about 106,000. Around tree-lined **Plaza de Independencia** it retains a small-town feel. Waves of immigration have watered down the Welsh influence but not diluted its heritage. Spanish is the common language, but Welsh is still widely spoken. Welsh literary and music festivals (Eisteddfods) take place each spring and there are Welsh chapels to explore in the area. The oldest, **Capilla Moriah**, dates from 1880. Many of the original settlers are buried in its cemetery.

All that remains of Lewis's railway is the old steam engine, and the station, now home to the **Museo Regional Pueblo de Luis**. Exhibits explain how the Welsh survived the early years. Cultural events pertaining to the Welsh community take place at the Centro Cultural Galesa on Avenida Belgrano and San Martín. A prehistoric stone's throw away is first-rate **Museo Paleontológico Egidio Feruglio**. A dinosaur femur stands by the entrance to the collection of fossils, some dating back 550 million years. To authenticate your visit, sound effects breathe life into the full-size models of dinosaur skeletons towering above. The wooded square, Plaza Centenario, next to the museum, was built in honour of Lewis Jones.

Argentinian Patagonia

Bone up on dinosaurs at the **Museo Paleontológico Egidio Feruglio**.

EXCURSIONS

Lagunas del Ornitólogo, just seven
kilometres (4.5 miles) from Trelew, is a natural
bird haven that attracts diehard ornithologists
and amateur twitchers alike. Much of the area's
avifauna, from cacophonous colonies of gulls to
flocks of flamingos and coots, can be observed
here at close quarters. **Playa Unión**, also
accessible by taxi, is worth a look too. In
summer you can sunbathe on the black sand
or surf in Atlantic waves. There are boat trips
from Puerto Rawson, at the southern end of
Playa Unión near the mouth of Río Chubut.
You can take a ride out to see the acrobatics of
the magnificent black-and-white Commerson's
dolphins (toninas). Contact **Toninas
Adventure**, on the pier (02965 15 666542).
Facing the pier, at **Cantina Marcelino**
(Avenida Marcelino González, 02965 496690,
www.cantinamarcelino.com.ar, $$$), you can
eat some of the finest seafood in Patagonia.
Presidents, ambassadors and late, five-time
Formula One champion Juan Manuel Fangio
have all sampled the exquisite *picada de
mariscos* (seafood platter) here.

From September to March an essential
excursion is to the spectacular Magellanic
penguin colony at **Punta Tombo**, nesting
ground for over half a million birds, situated
110 kilometres (68 miles) south. It's not only
larger than the one in Punta Norte but the
largest in South America.

For an altogether more man-made experience,
Dique Florentino Ameghino – a stunning
work of engineering, of dubious benefit to
nature – on RN25 can be marvelled at 120
kilometres (75 miles) from Trelew. You arrive
at the top of this 255-metre-long (738-feet) dam
through a tunnel drilled out of rock, then drop
74 metres (243 feet) into the Alsina valley below.
Camping, horse riding, boat trips, fishing and
guided tours are all available at the dam;
agencies in Trelew can organise trips.

Twice as far, 259 kilometres (161 miles)
away, but serviced by a thrice-weekly bus from
Trelew, and a stop-off for half a dozen cruise
ships each year, is **Camarones** – a ghost town
in which one particular phantom still looms
large. It was in this quaint fishing village that
future Argentinian president Juan Domingo
Perón spent his boyhood summers scavenging
for fossils along the shores. His father owned a
nearby *estancia*. Decades later, while in prison,
Perón wrote to Evita suggesting they chuck
politics and settle here instead.

Although no major attractions exist in
this 1,000-person town, Camarones preserves
Patagonia's distinct architectural heritage
better than most. Modest, corrugated-iron
dwellings splashed with streaks of colour create

an eerie feel of being stuck in time. If you want
to linger, there's the basic hotel and restaurant
El Viejo Torino (Almirante Brown 100, 0297
4963003, double US$10-$15, restaurant $$$).
The helpful tourist office, only open mornings,
is at San Martín No.570 (0297 4963040).

Museo Paleontológico Egidio Feruglio

*Avenida Fontana 140, entre Los Trabajadores y 9 de
Julio (02965 432100/www.mef.org.ar).* **Open** Sept-
mid Mar 9am-8pm daily. Mid Mar-Aug 10am-6pm
Mon-Fri; 10am-8pm Sat, Sun. **Admission** US$5; free
under-6s. **No credit cards.**

Museo Regional Pueblo de Luis

Avenida 9 de Julio y Fontana (02965 424062).
Open 8am-8pm Mon-Fri. **Admission** US$1;
free under-12s. **No credit cards.**

Where to eat & drink

At **Kismarey** (San Martín 1184, 02965 432605,
closed all Sun, Mon lunch, $$) you can sample
fine cuisine, Patagonian-style, from generous
portions of pasta to rabbit, lamb and seafood.
El Viejo Molino (Avenida Gales 250, 02965
428019, $$), located in what was Trelew's
flour mill dating from 1886, offers perfectly
barbecued lamb and pork, seafood starters
and daily specials. Housed in a Gallic-inspired
period building on Plaza de Independencia,
Sugar (25 de Mayo 247, 02965 35978, $$),
boasts a diverse menu embracing everything
from Welsh teas to seafood pastas. Travelling
epicures should try **Chateau Vieux** (25 de
Mayo 497, 02965 421746, $$$), which twins
fine wines with choice Patagonian-style dishes,
including rabbit, lamb and seafood specials.

For a swift half and a few frames of pool
check out **Maria Bonita**, close to the plaza on
San Martín 161 (no phone). It's open 24 hours a
day. Alternatively, art deco-style **Genesis**
(Belgrano 361, 02965 425247, closed Sun) has
live music on weekends and tables outside in
the summer. If you're still awake, head for
cocktails at **Margarita** (Fontana 224, 02965
432126), which has weekend club nights, or
try your luck at the **Casino Club** (9 de Julio y
Pasaje Tucumán 02965 425236, admission US$1
before 10pm, US$2 after). If you like ice-cream
with your pint, **San Javier** (San Martín 57,
02965 423474) is an ice-cream parlour that
doubles as a café, and on weekends, a pub.

Where to stay

Cadena de Hoteles Rayentray (San Martín
101, 02965 434702, www.cadenarayentray.
com.ar, double US$25-$35) was the choice of the
paparazzi who covered Princess Di's 1995 visit.

It's got all the trimmings: pool, spa, bar and a huge restaurant. Famed for its nostalgia and camaraderie in the public bar, the **Hotel Touring Club** (Avenida Fontana 240, 02965 425790/433997, htouring@ar.inter.net, double US$25) has been around for nearly a century. It's part of Trelew's local history – legend has it that Butch Cassidy and the Sundance Kid passed through here, hoping to rob a nearby bank. **Hotel Galicia** (9 de Julio 214, 02965 433802, www.hotelgalicia.com.ar, double US$12-$15) is a fine budget choice. Staff can arrange your excursions. **Hotel Libertador** (Rivadavia 31, 02965 420220, www.hotel libertadortw.com, double US$35-$45) has 70 standard rooms, a bar and a restaurant. Two former Argentinian presidents – Alfonsin and De La Rúa – have stayed in one of the suites (though not at the same time, we should add).

Resources

Hospital

Hospital Zonal Adolfo Margara, 28 de Julio 140 (02965 427543/427560).

Internet

Cyber World, Avenida Fontana 416 (02965 28279).

Police station

San Martín 451 (02965 427587).

Post office

Mitre y 25 de Mayo (02965 421300/420800).

Tourist information

Ente Trelew Turístico ENTRETUR, Mitre 387, y San Martín (02965 420139/www.trelew.gov.ar). **Open** 8am-9pm Mon-Fri; 9am-9pm Sat, Sun.

Getting there

By air

There are daily services from BA to Trelew's **Aeropuerto Internacional Almirante Zar** (02965 433443), located 5km (3 miles) north-east of town on RN3.

By road

Trelew lies 20-22hrs from BA by road. The main **Terminal de Omnibus** (Urquiza, entre Lewis Jones y Abraham Matthews, 02965 420121) has hourly services to and from Puerto Madryn, 65km (40 miles) or 1hr away, running all year round.

Gaiman

West of Trelew, in the fertile Chubut valley, lies the region's most typically Welsh Patagonian village, though it's worth noting that founder David Roberts, who arrived here in 1874, hailed from Pennsylvania in the US. Tiny Gaiman, with a population of 4,500, derives its name from the Tehuelche word meaning 'stony point'. Famous for its teahouses that serve the best cuppa in South America, there is much more to do in this Welsh enclave than just stopping for a brew and a slice of cake.

Start by climbing the hill above the **Túnel del Ferrocarril** (the old railway tunnel) for a view of this picturesque town, protected by its rows of poplar trees. As in Trelew, the old train station is now the site for the excellent **Museo Histórico Regional**. Hung inside are sepia-tinted photos of pioneers, and other Welsh relics. The museum's conscience director, Tegai Roberts, is the proud great-granddaughter of Lewis Jones, founder of Trelew.

Argentinian Patagonia

Ty Te Caerdydd. See p135.

Earl Grey and Princess Di

In November 1995, when the world's most glamorous woman boarded her helicopter and waved farewell to the village of Gaiman, little could she have imagined how deep an impression she had left on its inhabitants.

The visit by Princess Diana (then on an extended tour of Patagonia) to this tiny Welsh settlement in the Chubut valley is still fresh in the memories of local people. Just head to the Ty Te Caerdydd *casa de té*, where Diana dropped in for a quick cuppa.

Today, an immaculate shrine to the late royal stands in the entrance hall to the tea house (*pictured*). A glass display cabinet holds the still unwashed china tea set used by the princess, including her lipstick-stained cup which sits, chalice-like, on the top shelf. On the opposite wall the image of a youthful Diana, head crowned with sparkling tiara, hangs in a framed portrait above a bouquet of freshly picked red roses (Diana had picked one on her visit). The soft, soothing soundtrack of a Welsh choir emanating from the nearby food hall merely adds to the saintly, spiritual flavour of the place.

The tribute, which incidentally stands just yards away from a giant-sized tea pot, is undoubtedly kitsch. But it is, nonetheless, a deeply felt homage to a woman who conquered the hearts of the Patagonian Welsh on a fleeting village tour that also took in Gaiman's Museo Histórico Regional and its Welsh chapels. So strong was the Diana effect on Gaiman that a memorial service is held at Ty Te Caerdydd every 31 August, the anniversary of her death. The ceremony, held in the tea house's beautifully manicured gardens and attended by representatives of local Anglican and Catholic churches along with the general public, includes a floral tribute, a minute's silence and a selection of Welsh hymns sung by a local choir.

Speak to Gaiman's affable locals and you may find, however, that Diana's visit, like most things in her life, didn't pass without its element of intrigue and controversy. Rumour has it that another of the town's *casas de té* – which must remain nameless – was originally chosen as the venue for the royal cuppa, its delighted owner allegedly having been told by the local powers that be to stick the kettle on in preparation for the princess. The owner was delighted to do so – only for the location to be apparently switched just as tea was about to be served.

The Welsh presence is still apparent in the architecture of some houses, churches and chapels. **Primera Casa** (First House), on Juan C Evans, just off the plaza, was built of stone by David Roberts in 1874. Guided visits to the house (in Spanish only) can be arranged at the tourist office. Colegio Camway, on MD Jones, was constructed in 1906 to house Patagonia's first high school, and across the River Chubut, two perfectlym preserved brick chapels, **Capilla Vieja** and **Capilla Bethel**, dating from 1884 and 1914 respectively, were built yards from one another on Roberts. Both chapels can be viewed from the outside only.

You should leave at least an hour to visit **Parque El Desafío** (Challenge Park). Joaquín R Alfonso has spent 24 of his 86 years building this waste work of art in his garden, earning it a place in the *Guinness Book of Records 1988* as the world's biggest recycled rubbish park. Joaquín has also put in some solid work populating Patagonia. When he and his wife arrived there were two of them. Now, with children, grandchildren and great-grandchildren the family stands at 56 (and counting).

Another outdoor attraction is the **Parque Paleontológico Bryn Gwym**, which holds fossil remains of marine life from when the valley was covered by the ocean over 20 million years ago. Exhibits are on show in glass pyramids on a trail as you climb among the mollusc cliffs. Guided visits in English can be organised through the Museo Paleontológico Egidio Feruglio in Trelew (*see p131*). The museum's director also gives historical lectures in English in the Welsh Chapel.

Gaiman is famous for its choirs, who blend traditional songs from Wales with Argentinian folk music. Each October residents celebrate the area's Welsh heritage during the Eisteddfod music and poetry festival; its popularity is even drawing attention back in Wales. At recent festivals, groups of singing bards from the principality have been invited to Gaiman to reconstitute the Gorsedd, a ceremonial order of druids responsible for the pageantry of the Eisteddfod. The choirs are also active each 28 July to commemorate the arrival of the first immigrants from Wales. During the rest of the year you can hear them practise at the musical school, **Escuela de Música** (Avenida Eugenio Tello y 9 de Julio, 02965 491601, open 3-8pm, admission free). Choirs sing at many of Gaiman's teahouses too.

When you're gasping for a brew, a piece of cake or simply a slice of cultural history, go to one of the many *casas de té*, which offer generous helpings of *torta negra* (traditional Welsh fruit cake) and scones. Those listed here generally open between 2 and 3pm and 8pm. One block from the main square is **Ty Gwyn** (9 de Julio 111, 02965 491009). Owner Elena Sánchez Jones – whose late husband was great-grandson to Abraham Matthews, chief pastor on the pioneer ship *Mimosa* – serves an impeccable Teisan Ifan (raisin cake with cream topping). Another teahouse of note is **Ty Nain** (Hipólito Yrigoyen 273, 02965 491126), decked out with grandfather clocks, Welsh artefacts and a Winchester rifle that once belonged to a Texas-born sheriff turned gold prospector. Owner Mirna Jones de Ferrari Doyle is the granddaughter of the first Welsh woman in Gaiman. **Plas Y Coed** (Jones 123, no phone) has attractive gardens and another owner with superb baking skills and impeccable genealogy in Marta Rees. A short ride out of town is **Ty Te Caerdydd** (Finca 202, 02965 491510). The enormous teapot outside may look tacky, but inside everything is authentic. It was the choice of Princess Diana on her visit to the town, and her image still adorns one of the walls (*see p134* **Earl Grey and Princess Di**).

EXCURSIONS

From Gaiman you can head out to smaller, though also typically Welsh, **Dolavon**, 18 kilometres (11 miles) west. Founded in 1919, it can be reached by bus from Trelew or Gaiman. The irrigation canal, still in use, was built by the first pioneers and the flour mill at Maipú No.61, with its working waterwheel, is also a small museum. The little brick chapel outside of town dates from 1917.

Accessible by car another 16 kilometres (ten miles) along a gravel road from Dolavon is the remote Welsh farming village of **28 de Julio**. A number of the small farms, or *chacras*, where fine fruits and marmalades are made, can be visited. Waldo Williams, owner of **Bod Iwan**

A little piece of Wales in Patagonia: **Capilla Bethel** in Gaiman. *See p134.*

Fancy a cuppa? Try **Ty Gwyn**. *See p135.*

Farm (Chacra No.254, 02965 491251/15 661816/ bodwin@terra.com) will prepare hungry travellers an *asado,* as he did when Bruce Chatwin popped in unannounced. Show up between 3 and 8pm if you want to visit.

About two dozen Welsh-built chapels in various states of decay still dot the Chubut valley. Although few are ever used, these architectural gems are the synthesis of Welsh Nonconformist fervour and the reverence the the Welsh held for their natural surroundings. A useful map guiding you to the churches can be obtained at Gaiman's tourist office.

Museo Histórico Regional de Gaiman
Sarmiento y 28 de Julio (02965 491007). **Open** 3-7pm Tue-Sun. **Admission** US$1. **No credit cards.**

Parque El Desafío
Almirante Brown 52 (02965 491340). Open daylight hours daily. **Admission** US$2.50. **No credit cards.**

Parque Paleontológico Bryn Gwym
Follow road signs to the village of Bryn Gwym (02965 432100). **Open** *Apr-mid Sept* 10am-5pm daily. *Mid Sept-Mar* 10am-6pm daily. **Admission** US$3; free under-6s. **No credit cards.**

Where to stay & eat
Slip upstairs for a post-prandial snooze at **Ty Gwyn** (9 de Julio 111, 02965 491009, double US$30, *see also p135*), which has pleasant guest rooms. **Hotel Unelem** (Avenida Eugenio Tello y 9 de Julio, 02965 491663, double US$12), has 13 family rooms, and a bar and restaurant. **Hostería Gwesty Tywi** (Michael D Jones 342,

02965 491292, www.advance.com.ar/usuarios/ gwestywi, double US$25) which couples friendly service with comfortable rooms, while **Hostería Gwesty Plas y Coed** (Irigoyen 314, 02965 15697069, double US$30) is a small B&B known for its cosy, authentic vibe.

If you're in the mood for something stronger than a cup of tea while in Gaiman, **Tavarn Las Pub** (Avenida Eugenio Tello y Michael D Jones, 02965 15661097), offers exactly what its name suggests. It's also the venue for occasional live music and shows. Otherwise, **Nueva Luna** (Belgrano 211, 02965 15579432) has a pleasant terrace for soaking up the sun over beers and fast food. **Gustos** (Avenida Eugenio Tello 156, 02965 491828, $$) is a busy and informal bar/ café serving pizza and sandwiches.

Getting there

By road
Gaiman is on RN25, 17km (102 miles), from Trelew. Local buses run hourly or every 2hrs from Trelew and take 25mins, and there are long-distance buses to/from Esquel, across in the Andes. Buses usually stop in the central plaza, but if you ask the driver you can get dropped off elsewhere.

Resources

Hospital
Hospital Rural John C Evans, Avenida Eugenio Tello 1200 (02965 491002).

Internet
Bar Armonia, Avenida Eugenio Tello 487 (02965 491004).

Police station
Avenida Eugenio Tello 712 (02965 491017).

Post office
John C Evans e Hipólito Yrigoyen (02965 491006).

Tourist information
Oficina Municipal de Informes Turísticos, Belgrano, entre Rivadavia y 28 de Julio (02965 491571/ www.cpatagonia.com.ar/gaiman). **Open** 9am-5pm Mon-Sat; 1-5pm Sun.

Comodoro Rivadavia

The capital of Chubut and of Argentina's oil industry, and the largest city in the province, is a seaside town at the foot of **Cerro Chenque** (*chenque* is Tehuelche for cemetery – they buried their dead on the peak). Like most industrial towns, Comodoro Rivadavia is built for work rather than pleasure, and function here has indisputably triumphed over aesthetics. Still, it's an ideal stepping stone for trips inland to the petrified forests of Sarmiento (*see p115*), and for heading south to Puerto Deseado.

From the lookout point at the top of Cerro Chenque, the city unfurls before your eyes. To the left is the magnificent **Golfo de San Jorge**; to the right the city sprawls along the coast into the distance. Comodoro does have a beach of sorts, the **Playa Costanera**. Here you can rent out windsurfers and kayaks; the blue sea is inviting but icy, so don't fall in.

Most commerce is centered around the main avenues Rivadavia and San Martín downtown. Being Chubut's main city, cultural offerings are varied in Comodoro, although somewhat hidden. In addition to standard Hollywood fare, the 70-year-old **Cine Teatro Español** on Avenida San Martín No.664 (0297 4477700, tickets US$2-$4) shows subtitled art-house films on Monday nights and holds Saturday afternoon debates (in Spanish).

Originally a poor shipping town, Comodoro's fortunes changed in 1907 with the discovery of oil. Amid the ensuing boom, the **Comodoro Hotel** (*see p139*) became the venue for wild and lawless parties, attracting tycoons and chancers in the JR Ewing mould.

These days the scene is more sober, largely due to the oil privatisations of the 1990s, which led to high unemployment in the area. Times, and methods of oil extraction, have changed. If you are here for a day take a wander round the the **Museo Nacional del Petróleo**. Built in 1987, by then national petroleum giants YPF, the museum exhibits a A-Z of the oil industry.

Although the oil is drying up, the town is already eyeing its next energy boom: wind. The 26 windmills on Cerro Chenque and adjacent hills, the largest wind farm in Latin America,

generate 20 per cent of the energy needs of Comodoro's 140,000 residents. To see the wind farm, called **Parque Eólico Antonio Morán**, and located 12 kilometres (7.5 miles) out of town, hire a taxi. A view of a windmill juxtaposed against an oil rig is a metaphor for Comodoro's past, present and future.

Featureless oil outpost **Pico Truncado**, 138 kilometres (86 miles) south-east of Comodoro is also using technology to tame the elements. In 2001 this withered oil town installed two state-of-the-art German windmills that now supply almost half its energy needs. In 2003 the town inaugurated South America's first ever **Parque Sonoro** (Sound Park; check with tourist offices in Santa Cruz for details), an outdoor collection of half a dozen sculptures made from machinery discarded by the oil industry. The kinetic sculptures, which echo with the passage of the wind, are the first of their kind in the world outside a monument in Helsinki to composer Jean Sibelius, made from hollow pipe organs.

EXCURSIONS

The relative prosperity ushered in by the oil industry is visible at **Rada Tilly**, a once-scenic beach resort 12 kilometres (7.5 miles) to the south. Surrounded by cliffs overlooking sandy beaches, the town used to be a quiet holiday spot, but today has been converted into a suburb of Comodoro, inhabited by 3,000 residents, most of them oil execs. South of the town the beaches are equally breathtaking, but deserted; the area is ideal to explore by quad bike. The tourist office (0297 4452423/www.radatilly.gov.ar) is on Almirante Brown in front of the church.

Heading out of Comodoro on RN3, take a quick stop in the gritty oil town of **Caleta Olivia**, 78 kilometres (48 miles) south, to check out the over-the-top homage to a muscular, ten-metre-high (33-feet) oil worker, **Monumento al Obrero Petrolero**. Built in 1958 by sculptor Pablo Daniel Sánchez, it's located on RN3 at the crossroads of Avenida Güemes and Eva Perón.

Museo Nacional del Petróleo
Carlos Calvo y San Lorenzo, Barrio General Moscón, km3 (0297 4559558/www.mipatagonia.com/museo delpetroleo.htm). **Open** *Mar-Nov* 9am-6pm Tue-Fri; 2-6pm Sat, Sun. *Dec-Feb* 8am-1pm, 3-8pm Tue-Fri; 3-8pm Sat, Sun. **Guided tours** (Spanish) *Mar-Nov* 10.30am, 3pm Tue-Fri; 4pm Sat, Sun. *Dec-Feb* 10.30am, 4pm, 6.30pm Tue-Fri; 4pm, 6.30pm Sat, Sun. **Admission** US$1.50; US$1-US$2 concessions. **No credit cards.**

Where to eat

For a cheap and hearty steak dinner, there are plenty of decent *parrillas* to be found among the bric-a-brac on Avenida Rivadavia;

Hermit or hero?

Doug Tompkins hates fences. So the first thing the 62-year-old textile magnate turned conservationist does whenever he and wife Kris McDivitt add a new property to their expanding Patagonian eco-empire is to pull down the barbed wire, and liberate the land from the nefarious impact of man and sheep.

The latest property to be freed is **Estancia Valle Chacabuco** which the Tompkins bought in 2004 for US$11 million through their California-based non-profit Conservación Patagónica (www.conservacionpatagonica. com). The 68,000-hectare (170,000-acre) farm, located outside the Chilean city of Cochrane (see p202), was the biggest in Aisén, settled at great sacrifice in the 1920s by rancher-explorer Lucas Bridges after his adventures in Tierra del Fuego and Rhodesia. The huge land grant was awarded to Bridges' backers in exchange for their promise to export the farm's wool through Chile, a logistical nightmare that required Bridges to dynamite a razor-thin passage through a rocky cliff overhanging the Río Baker.

In literally extirpating Bridges' work, the Tompkins' are laying the foundation for their own future legend. Their story goes back in 1991 when Tompkins, founder of clothing labels the North Face and Esprit, cashed in his corporate holdings, Ferrari and Amish quilt collection, and moved to Chile, where he started buying land through his Conservation Land Trust (www.conservationlandtrust.org). In 1993, he married McDivitt, longtime CEO of Patagonia Inc. The couple then shelled out US$55 million of their own money to build what became **Parque Pumalín** (see p197), the largest private preserve in the world, equal in size to California's Yosemite.

Along the way they earned the enmity of some powerful groups – loggers, energy companies and nationalist politicians – who accused Tompkins of being everything from a CIA spy to a Zionist conspirator (quite a stretch – he's not even Jewish). Tompkins's cause was hurt in part by poor PR and his own quirkiness. A proponent of the Deep Ecology movement, he's happiest living in a shack in Pumalín, connected to the world only by radio and a self-piloted bush plane.

Much of the criticism against Tompkins has subsided as he's learnt to tone down his cavalier approach, and the full extent of his and McDivitt's commitment to the region has become clear. The two now hold more than 810,000 hectares (two million acres) at a dozen projects in Chile and Argentina, the bulk of them in Patagonia. In Argentina's Santa Cruz province, they paid US$1.7 million to buy **Estancia Monte León**, a former farm that has 40 kilometres (25 miles) of virgin coastline. In 2002 they gave the property to the government as part of a deal to create Argentina's first coastal national park (see p143).

With Valle Chacabuco, the Tompkins hope to connect their property with two existing protected areas – Reserva Nacional Tamango and Reserva Nacional Lago Jeminini – to create one, continuous, 247,000-hectare (585,200-acre) national park which, in their own words, will bear comparison to the splendour of Wyoming's Grand Tetons as it was 100 years ago. By giving free rein to the tall grass prairies, and building up the near-extinct Huemul deer population, the Tompkins' ambition is to leave a legacy of wildness for future generations.

---

alternatively, try **Puerto Cangrejo** (Avenida Costanera 1050, 0297 4444590, $$$), a delightful old colonial house, virtually on the seafront, that has been converted into the local specialist for seafood. For exquisitely barbecued lamb and more fresh shellfish, head to the reassuringly named **La Tradición** (Mitre 675, 0297 4465800, $$$$). Late on, **El Sótano Pub** (San Martín 239, 0297 4463768, admission US$2-$3 Fri, Sat) gets crowded out with pool players and Iron Maiden fans. But if Latin rhythms and dance tunes are more your speed try **Punto Com** (Rivadavia 387, no phone, admission US$3-$4), open all year.

Where to stay

The **Lucania Palazzo Hotel** (Moreno 676, 0297 4499300, www.lucania-palazzo.com, double US$70-$90) is the best option at the top end. The huge marble atrium with inviting bar sets the tone for . Rooms are luxurious, and there's a gym and spa. Less swanky, but with friendly and attentive staff, is the **Austral Plaza Hotel** (Moreno 725, 0297 4472200, info@australhotel. com.ar, double US$60-$80), a business hotel with a café and restaurant, close to the seafront.

Its glory days are long gone, but the 104-room **Comodoro Hotel** (9 de Julio 770, 0297 4472300, www.comodorohotel.com.ar, double US$40-$60) is still comfortable, and a pleasant spot for a drink. Like most hotels in town, though, it's geared to business-not-pleasure tourism.

Resources

Hospital

Hospital Regional Dr Sanguinetti, Avenida Hipólito Yrigoyen 950 (0297 4442287).

Internet

Centro Internet Comodoro, San Martín 394 (0297 4460584).

Police station

Rivadavia 101 (0297 4462778).

Post office

San Martín 180 (0297 4472590).

Tourist information

Dirección de Turismo, Rivadavia 430, entre Pellegrini y 25 de Mayo (0297 4462376/www. comodoro.gov.ar). **Open** *Mar-Nov* 8am-3pm Mon-Fri. *Dec-Feb* 8am-7pm. *Oficina de Informes Turísticos, Terminal de Omnibus, Pellegrini 730, y 25 de Mayo (0297 446730/www.comodoro.gov.ar).* **Open** *Mar-Nov* 8am-9pm Mon-Fri; 9am-9pm Sat, Sun. *Dec-Feb* 7am-10pm Mon-Fri; 9am-9pm Sat, Sun.

Getting there

By air

The **Aeropuerto de Comodoro Rivadavia** (RN3, km 11, 0297 4548190) is 17km (10.5 miles) from the city, with daily flights from BA, and direct flights from Rio Gallegos, Rio Grande, Ushuaia and Puerto Madryn.

By road

The city is 26hrs from BA on RN3 and 450km (278 miles) or 6hrs from Puerto Madryn. Good bus connections inland to Sarmiento and beyond and along the coast road from **Terminal de Omnibus** (Pellegrini 730, y 25 de Mayo, 0297 4467305).

Puerto Deseado

South of Comodoro on the north-west coast of Santa Cruz lies Puerto Deseado, a fishing town of 13,000 inhabitants and principal point of access to several wildlife reserves. It took its name from adventurer Thomas Cavendish's boat, *The Desire* (El Deseo), which, in 1586, penetrated the River Deseado. Other great explorers followed, among them Charles Darwin (1833) and Francisco Moreno (1876), before Capitán Oneto established the first settlement on behalf of the Argentinian government in 1884. The town celebrates his arrival each 15 July with a fiesta.

If Patagonia's overlooked Atlantic coastline ever develops into a major tourist attraction, then this picturesque place is bound to become one of the country's most popular destinations, and with good reason. The town lies at the mouth of what must be one of the world's strangest geological formations – the **Ría Deseado**. In a bygone era this waterway was a river with its source in Lago Buenos Aires near the Andes, but eventually the fresh water dried up and glistening turquoise salt water, seeping 42 kilometres (26 miles) inland, took its place.

Seals taking their siesta at the **Ría Deseado**.

The result is an estuary that's a haven for large numbers of marine birds and aquatic mammals, among them cormorants, penguins, ducks, snowy sheathbills, oystercatchers and sea lions. The estuary is also the breeding ground for the Commerson's dolphin, called tonina overa – or eggshell porpoise – which look like miniature killer whales.

Despite the town's abundant natural appeal, the current lifeline for its residents is one that is bound to alienate environmentalists. Around the clock, every day, Spanish fishing vessels of a staggering size put in to dock to refuel at the newly inaugurated **Dique Seco**, before heading back out to sea. Today Puerto Deseado exports 85,000 tons of fish a year and rising, making it the busiest fishing port in Patagonia. A salty smell licks the town, a permanent reminder of its principal business. Walking along the coastal road you can watch the tides ebb and flow – four times a day – a phenomenon that attracts hundreds of gulls that swoop down to snack on crustaceans.

The shifting tides of the waters off this stretch of coast have claimed the lives of many sailors; their memorial is a fine collection of rusting hulks at the mouth of the bay. Inland, the **Museo Provincial Mario Brozoski** exhibits porcelain jars, cannonballs and other objects recovered from HMS *Swift*, which was wrecked in 1770 but only discovered by scuba divers in 1982. Since 1998, diving archaeologists have been studying the wreck and its remains to ascertain the truthfulness of British claims that the well-armed boat, which was docked in the Falklands/Malvinas, was on a scientific – not military – mission.

Before squid was king, the big fish in town was sheep, and Puerto Deseado a major rail centre for the farms of the interior. Left over from that golden age is a historic passenger wagon from 1898, now fully restored and open to the public on the corner of San Martín and Almirante Brown. Residents took to the streets in 1980 to derail attempts by the military government of the time to relocate the wagon, which played a pivotal role in the labour strife of the 1920s, out of town. Equally impressive is the disused mock-Tudor train station along the coast, where relics of the port's railway era can be seen on display each afternoon. The first stop along the coastal line was Jaramillo, 119 kilometres (74 miles) north-west, today a deserted ghost town of 250 residents. A plaque outside the decaying station there remembers the site where labour agitator Facón Grande was gunned down by vengeful Argentinian authorities following the 1920-21 strike, or *guerra* (war) as locals prefer to call it.

EXCURSIONS

The quickest excursion is the 24-kilometre (15-mile) trip to the **Cañadón del Puerto**, for a fine panorama of the estuary and islands. But no trip can be complete without a visit to see the wildlife of the **Reserva Natural Ría Deseado**, as the sunken estuary is known. **Darwin Expediciones** (RP281, Muelle Gipsy, 0297 15 6247554, www.darwin-expeditions.com) and Los Vikingos (Estrada 1275, 0297 4870020, www.losvikingos.com.ar) offers three-hour trips with bilingual guides, from September to April. Most trips include a visit to **Isla Pingüino**, from October to mid March Patagonia's only nesting colony and the only haunt outside the Falkland Islands/Islas Malvinas and Staten Island/Isla de Estados of the colourful rockhopper penguins – the ones with the orange beak and oversized yellow eyelashes. The best time to visit the Ría is during the November breeding season. Darwin Expediciones also goes all the way upstream (an eight-hour round trip) to the Miradores de Darwin – the 100-metre-high (328-feet) red cliffs that the young naturalist considered the most isolated place on earth. Kayaking, diving and windsurfing can all be tried around Puerto Deseado.

Deseado is also relatively close in Patagonian terms to the Monumento Natural Bosques Petrificados, 150 kilometres (93 miles) west of town (*see p115* **Trees of the stone age**), the largest of Argentina's petrified forests. A little further away, 155 kilometres (96 miles) south, is the Reserva Natural Bahía Laura, a secluded bay which is home to a large colony of Magellanic penguins; 95 kilometres (59 miles) back up the coast is a large seal colony.

Estancia La Madrugada (*see p141*), 120 kilometres (75 miles) away, is an ideal base for visiting Puerto Deseado and the surrounding area. The vast farm, founded in 1906 by an Irishman, still has over 5,000 sheep. But the main attraction is its wildlife, in particular the sea lion colony, which is the largest in Santa Cruz province. The *estancia* also serves as the laboratory for environmentalists exploring ways to shear the soft, high-quality fur of the guanaco as an alternative to lower-priced wool.

The Ría Deseada and the Atlantic coast teem with fish. Avid anglers can tussle with sharks, *pez elefante* (elephant fish), pejerrey, sea bass, rays and other denizens of the deep.

Museo Provincial Mario Brozoski

Colón y Belgrano (0297 4870673, mariobrozoski@ yahoo.com.ar). **Open** *Apr-Nov* 10am-5pm Mon-Fri; 5-8pm Sat, Sun. *Dec-Mar* phone for details. **Admission** free.

Where to stay & eat

Los Acantilados (España 1611, 0297 4872167, acantour@pdeseado.com.ar, double room AR$66-$105) is a 38-room hotel with majestic ocean views and a comfy glass-panelled café. In the centre, try smaller **Hotel Isla Chaffers** (San Martin y Mariano Moreno, 0297 4872246/ 4870476, islachaffers@yahoo.com.ar, double room AR$95). Cheaper, but still decent lodging is available at **Hotel Colón** (Almirante Brown 430, 0297 4870082, hotelcolon@pdeseado. com.ar, double room AR$50). For a comfortable stay in a well-equipped cabin, try **Las Nubes: Cabañas y Quincho** (Florentino Ameghino 1351, 0297 156210278, lasnubes@viadeseado. com.ar, cabin for two from US$75 all-inclusive). **Estancia La Madrugada** (011 53715500/ 0297 15 6242263, 0297 4461136, rates US$75 all inclusive) has snug, stylish rustic accommodation in a recycled stable block of locally quarried granite.

For a bite check out **Puerto Cristal** (España 1698, 0297 4870387, closed Wed lunch, mains AR$16-$25) or the seafood specialties at **El Viejo Marino** (First Floor, Pueyrredón 224, 0297 4872765, set menu AR$13). **El Pingüino** (Piedra Buena 958, 0297 4872105, closed Sun, mains AR$15-$30) specialises in lamb and steak. For nightlife, **Quinto Elemento** (12 de Octubre y Don Bosco, no phone, admission AR$5) is a pub/club popular with young locals on Friday nights. The local disco, **Jackaroe** (Moreno 633, no phone, admission AR$7) is open for a boogie on Saturdays only. For slots and roulette the **Casino Club** (12 de Octubre 720, 0297 4870566, admission $1) opens till late.

Resources

Tourist information

Dirección Municipal de Turismo, San Martín 1525, entre Pueyrredón y Sarmiento (0297 4870220). **Open** *Apr-Nov* 9am-6pm Mon-Fri. *Dec-Mar* 9am-10pm daily.

Hospital

Hospital Distrital de Puerto Deseado, Avenida Lotufo y Almirante Brown (0297 4870210/4870941).

Net access

La Galería, San Martín y Alte Zar (0297 4872243).

Police station

Ameghino 1080 (0297 4872777).

Post office

San Martín 1075 (0297 4870362).

Radio taxi

0297 4870645.

Getting there

By air

The Aeropuerto de Puerto Deseado (Ruta 281, 0297 4872333) is located 4km (2.5 miles) out of town. Flights to Puerto Deseado, via Comodoro Rivadavia, leave Buenos Aires twice a week (Mon, Fri). Return flights leave once a week (Fri).

By road

Puerto Deseado is 4.5hrs south of Comodoro Rivadavia along RN3 and RP281. Buses from Comodoro, Río Gallegos, Caleta Olivia arrive at the bus station on Sargento Cabral (no phone).

Puerto San Julián

Charles Darwin spent eight days in Puerto San Julián – for most modern-day voyagers 24 hours will suffice. Yet from a historical perspective, you'd be hard pressed to find a more alluring destination. As its 6,500 residents like to point out, San Julián is the genesis of the Patagonian myth. It boasts a roll call of firsts, all with a common ancestry: Portuguese explorer Ferdinand Magellan first made landfall here in 1520, soon to be remembered in San Julián with the construction of a life-size replica of the explorer's *Nao Victoria* vessel. It's also here where the word Patagonia was first uttered (*see p21* **The name game**). Then there's the first-ever Mass on Argentine soil he celebrated, marked by the **Monumento a la Primera Misa** (on Roca and Almirante Brown); the first dead Europeans on Argentine soil; the first Argentine city mentioned on a European map. The list continues. The most important Magellan haunt is the Banco Justicia, the name of the small island chosen to banish two mutinous officers.

Later visitors included Francis Drake and, in 1780, 78 Spaniards sent by their king to colonise the coast. Archaeologists are surveying the original settlement, 13 kilometres (eight miles) out of town, which lasted just three years, with the hope of creating a replica. Darwin's visit was marked by the death of one of the *Beagle*'s officers, Robert Sholl, whose tomb lies on a scenic bluff overlooking the bay. Once a major wool-exporting port, at last count only 30 of an original 250 ranches still operate in the area. Among them is the vast San Julián Sheep Farming Company, another ranch owned by Italy's Benetton clothing family. Don't even think about sneaking a look – the gates are permanently padlocked. Local lore has it that, when the president of Italian car-maker Fiat came a few years ago, he was made to wait outside for half an hour while the caretaker confirmed his visit. Today, San Julián scrapes by thanks to business generated by the Cerro Vanguardia gold mine, Argentina's largest.

Argentinian Patagonia

Parque Nacional Monte León.

EXCURSIONS

Bahía San Julián, stretching 15 by five kilometres (9.5 by three miles) at its widest point, is home to a huge range of bird and wildlife species. Between November and April, **Excursiones Pinocho** (Elcano 653, 02962 454333/15 620743, nonoy@sanjulian.com.ar) runs two-hour tours of the bay, taking in Banco Justicia, penguin, sea lion and grey cormorant colonies, and a chance to observe Commerson's dolphins. Magellanic penguins that nest one kilometre (0.5 miles) away sometimes waddle fearlessly into town.

About 48 kilometres (30 miles) south starts the Gran Bajo de San Julián. At 105 metres (344 feet) below sea level in some places, this natural depression is the one of the lowest spots in the Americas. Access to the trough is limited to dirt roads used mostly by oil companies. Only those with a lot of time on their hands will bother testing whether the force of gravity will speed up your watch by 24 seconds for every full day you spend here.

Located on the north bank of the Río Santa Cruz, 120 kilometres (75 miles) south of Puerto San Julián, **Comandante Luis Piedra Buena** lacks major attractions but is a useful stopover. The gritty town (population 6,000) is named after Argentine naval captain Luis Piedra Buena, guardian of marooned sailors, who settled on Isla Pavón in 1859, where there is a reconstructed model of his home. Anglers should come for the National Trout Festival in late March, when steelhead season is in full swing. Guide **Mario Zwetzig** (02962 497688) can help fishermen in the summer.

Thirty-four kilometres (21 miles) south of Piedra Buena is the red-roofed, former shearing shed marking the entrance to **Parque Nacional Monte León**. Bought in 2001 by American businessman turned environmentalist Douglas Tompkins, the 630-square-kilometre (243-square-mile) preserve has been transformed into Argentina's first national park on the Atlantic coast, protecting 48 kilometres (30 miles) of shoreline. From RN3, in summer only – it's too icy in winter – a 24-kilometre (15-mile) winding, gravel road descends to a desolate beach, where you can camp and where most natural attractions are located. No organised excursions exist yet and campers should pack all necessary supplies, including water. Monte León derives its name from a thin 400-metre (1,312-feet) bluff that extends out into the sea in the shape of a puma. Beneath these cliffs, out of human reach but still visible, is one of Argentina's largest sea lion colonies. The park is also home to pumas, foxes, 50 bird species and one of Patagonia's largest Magellan penguin rookeries. When the tide is low, you can walk across the beach to what

locals call La Olla – 'The Saucepan' – an astonishing half-dome cavity supported by a 30-metre-high (98-feet) natural arch.

Where to stay & eat

Just one kilometre (0.5 miles) from the coastal road RN3, and eight kilometres (five miles) from the entrance to Monte León Nacional Park, is the upscale **Estancia Monte León** (02966 15629274, msoler@infovia.com.ar, closed Apr-Oct, all inclusive US$290). Its grounds include 24 kilometres of pristine coastline. Back in San Julián, **Hotel Bahía** (Avenida San Martín 1075, 02962 454028, nico@sanjulian.com.ar double room AR$65-80) is a comfortable, modern business hotel, with a snack bar. Cheaper still is the **Hostería Municipal de Turismo** (Avenida 25 de Mayo 917, 02962 452300, centur@videodata.com.ar, double room AR$48). **Nao's** is a typical cantina overlooking the bay that serves up fresh seafood (9 de Julio y Mitre, 02962 453009, mains AR$15-$25). In addition to camping possibilities on Isla Pavón, there is the friendly and clean **Hostería El Alamo** (Lavalle y España, 02962 454092, double room AR$36).

Resources

Tourist information

CENTUR Centro de Informes al Turísticos, San Martín 500, entre Moreno y Rivadavia (02962 454396, www.sanjulian.gov.ar/www.santacruz. gov.ar). **Open** *Apr-Nov* 7am-9pm Mon-Fri; 3-9pm Sat, Sun. *Dec-Mar* 8am-10pm daily.

Hospital

Dr Miguel Lombardich, El Cano y 9 de Julio (02962 452020).

Net access

Portal Patagonia, Avenida San Martín y Rivadavia (02962 454619).

Police station

Avenida San Martín 864 (02962 452202).

Post office

Avenida San Martín 155 (02962 452016).

Radio taxi

02962 454441.

Getting there

By road

Puerto San Julián is situated on RN3. It's roughly equidistant between Río Gallegos to the south and Caleta Olivia to the north – about 350km (217 miles) away from either place. Several buses daily, all year round, from Río Gallegos, arrive at the Terminal de Omnibus (Avenida San Martín y Pellegrini, no phone).

The Deep South 1

It's the end of the world as we know it – and you'll feel fine. Take in Argentina's trekking capital, stunning glaciers and the world's most southern city.

Argentina's far south is all about frozen water, sculpted by the elements and set against wild and dramatic backdrops that were themselves carved by glacial activity. Those in search of an antidote to central Patagonia's endless monochrome plains will find it in southern Santa Cruz, a land of staggering contrasts and photogenic natural wonders.

Santa Cruz, Argentina's second largest province, is the size of the United Kingdom, but home to just 160,000 people and more than ten times as many sheep. It sweeps unvaryingly from east to west until climbing dramatically on reaching the Andes. Its highlight is the World Heritage Site of **Parque Nacional Los Glaciares**, with its headline-hogging attraction **Glaciar Perito Moreno**. The easiest access point is the town of El Calafate. Also within the park are the dazzlingly beautiful peaks of the Fitz Roy massif, close to Argentina's trekking capital **El Chaltén**, and a magnet for photographers. South of glacier country is the small mining town of Río Turbio through which you may pass if heading across the border towards Chile (*see pp210-220* **The Deep South 2**), while to the east is the province's coastal capital, **Río Gallegos**.

The largest island of southern Patagonia's archipelago is called just that: Isla Grande, but it's more commonly known by the name given to the whole province, Tierra del Fuego. Synonymous with isolation and beauty, it is the point where the Andes taper out to form '*el fin del mundo*' (the end of the world). The island is part-Chilean, part-Argentinian; in the area belonging to Argentina is angler's destination **Río Grande**, the small, but colourful town of Tolhuin, wild Peninsula Mitre with its shipwreck-littered coastline and Argentina's ultimate austral destination, **Ushuaia**.

El Calafate

Calafate is Tehuelche for a native purple berry – according to local folklore, if you eat it you'll return to Patagonia one day. If the current rate of expansion continues, you may not recognise the town if you do. Founded in the 1930s as a stopover for wagons transporting wool from *estancias*, El Calafate is today a town defined by tourism, an industry that gathered pace

here in the 1980s. Most people came, and still come, to gawp at Perito Moreno glacier, 80 kilometres (50 miles) away. Few come to visit the town itself: despite the unrelenting drive to expand the place (the 'high season population' has doubled over the past few years) it stubbornly retains a parochial street-pulse. Most visitors stay only a night or two, using the town as a base from which to see some of the country's most spectacular scenery.

As a result, the place has something of a conveyer-belt feel, as groups of tourists are bused in and out. The construction of more and more hotels and businesses to cope with the increasing demand is worrying some residents, who anticipate negative effects on the sensitive local environment. The pre-boomtown days are recounted in the **Museo Regional Municipal El Calafate**.

Avenida Libertador, the main commercial and gastronomic drag, runs through the town's centre; above it, near the residential district, is the bus station and tourist information office, reached by a flight of steps. Most of the accommodation options are on the other side of Libertador, on lower ground. At the town's outskirts is **Lago Argentino**'s 1,466 square kilometres (566 square miles) of freezing water, with its dramatically changing hues. The lake attracts a rich collection of birdlife, including black-necked swans and flamingos, and can still be enjoyed in relative peace despite the construction of a new road along its shores. The **Laguna Nimez** reserve nearby is an even greater draw for ornithologists, with around 80 different species of bird (US$1 entrance fee).

El Calafate is served by direct flights from Buenos Aires. The majority of tourists come in January and February, when the average temperature is 18.6°C (65°F), and warmer weather incites the countryside into a kaleidoscope of colours. Prices also tend to bloom at this time of year, partly a result of the local labour shortage.

EXCURSIONS

Glaciar Perito Moreno, the most famous of the glaciers in the national park (*see p150* **Parque Nacional Los Glaciares**) is for many the *raison d'être* of any visit to the area. An awesome 30 kilometres (19 miles) long and

Around **El Calafate** See p144

Planet Earth, the way it used to be.

Perito Moreno Glacier, Santa Cruz

four- and-a-half kilometres (three miles) wide, the glacier sweeps down from the mountains, a mass of serrated spikes chafing the valley walls. Who knows what words came out of Chilean explorer Juan Tomás Rogers' mouth when he came upon this great glacial tongue in 1879? The blue-and-white creaking, disintegrating mass is undeniably one of the world's great natural spectacles. (It's also the perfect photo opportunity; Argentinian president Néstor Kirchner, born and bred in Santa Cruz, has made a habit of bringing foreign dignitaries here.)

From El Calafate, a two-hour dusty journey by road takes you to **Península de Magallanes**, the facing strip of land 150 metres (490 feet) away, where spectators gasp from the boardwalks as a sharp crack heralds the birth of another *serac* (huge chunk of ice), which tumbles down the glacier face into the water below, in a process called calving. According to earlier data, the glacier once lay 750 metres (2,460 feet) from the peninsula. This distance gradually narrowed until the water channel was completely blocked by the 'advancing' glacier in 1917, and again in 1935. In 1939, the adjacent fjord rose and flooded nearby territories, forcing the military to bombard the glacier – to no avail. It then entered into a four-year self-rectifying cycle, advancing several metres a day until ruptured by pressure from the adjacent waters – an uproarious performance sending massive icebergs spiralling down the channels. Following a 16-year break the last major rupture, witnessed by over 10,000 cooing spectators and broadcast live on national television, occurred in March 2004. Experts now prefer to describe the glacier as neither advancing nor retreating, but rather in a state of equilibrium, in contrast to the 'retreating' status of most other glaciers.

Among the many local tour operators, both **Interlagos Turismo** (Booth 5, Terminal de Omnibus, 02902 491179, interlagos@cotecal.com.ar) and **Taqsa** (Booth 3, Terminal de Omnibus, 02902 492531, espitur@cotecal.com.ar) offer a return day trip for around US$40 between October and March (the park entrance of US$10 is extra). Alternatively, take your own transport or go by taxi, but make sure you leave yourself around four to five hours at the ice itself. Boat trips (there are one-hour rides from the lookout point near the glacier, or longer trips with the tour operators listed below) get you up close. But for a real close-up, book a mini-trek (from September to April only) on top of the glacier with **Hielo y Aventura** (Avenida del Libertador 935, 02902 491053). US$250 (plus

park entrance) buys you two hours on the ice; for a more challenging six- to seven-hour trek, pay an additional US$17 for the 'Big Ice' option.

Perito Moreno is by no means the only glacier worth seeing. **Glaciar Upsala** is reckoned to be the biggest in all of South America: five kilometres (three miles) wide, 60 kilometres (37 miles) long, 60 metres (197 feet) high. **Sunny Tours** (Avenida del Libertador 1315, 02902 492561) and **Upsala Explorer** (9 de Julio 69, 02902 491034) offer a variety of excursions and boat trips.

Farther south, the Spegazzini glacier boasts the biggest snout, reaching 130 metres (426 feet) in parts; the Onelli and the Agassiz glaciers, both on the Laguna Onelli, are the antithesis of Perito Moreno: few tourists, no boardwalks, just a precious zen-like silence in which to ogle the pristine beauty. Most excursions to these other glaciers depart from Punta Bandera, 50 kilometres (31 miles) from El Calafate, with the majority sailing under the flagship of kingpin **René Fernández Campbell** (First Floor, Avenida del Libertador 867, 02902 491428, www.glaciaressur.com.ar). Upsala (*see above*) offers a one-day boat tour of all the glaciers for US$60, and also the options of a boat trip and horse riding at the otherwise inaccessible, but historic, **Estancia Cristina** (www.estancia cristina.com) between September and June.

Most non-glacial excursions are based around *estancias*, and normally include *cabalgatas* (treks on horseback), Patagonian cooking (barbecued lamb if you're lucky) and sheep-shearing demonstrations. Close to Lago Roca and 56 kilometres (35 miles) from El Calafate is **Estancia Nibepo Aike** (*see p149*), a family-run farm whose founders hail from the Balkans. You can visit as part of a day tour or stay the night. Nearer to El Calafate is Patagonia's most infamous *estancia*, **La Anita**, site of a 1921 workers uprising that resulted in the massacre of dozens of farm hands. There are believed to be mass graves hidden on the extensive farmlands. Next to Rio Santa Cruz is **Estancia Rincón** (02902 491965, www.estanciarincon.com.ar), offering day visits for US$30 per person. **Estancia Alice**, aka El Galpón del Glaciar, on the road Glaciar Perito Moreno, is a good base for birdwatching and provides overnight lodging (02902 491793, www.estanciaaalice.com.ar).

For those with less time, **Cerro Frias** (02902 492808, www.cerrofrias.com) organises *cabalgatas* from Estancia Alice. On a clear day, you'll be gifted spectacular views of the Torres del Paine and the Fitzroy massif. For US$35 you'll get three hours on horseback and some of the best cooking to be found in the area. Other horse-trekking options are available through **Cabalgata en Patagonia** (02902 493278, www.cabalgataenpatagonia.com), which offers tours of the birdlife-rich Bahía Redonda or trips to the **Walichu Caves** (which can also be visited independently) eight kilometres (five miles) out of town, with their 4,000-year-old rock paintings. US$20 buys you a two-hour trek.

Museo Regional Municipal El Calafate

Avenida del Libertador 575 (02902 491081). **Open** *Oct-Apr* 9am-1pm, 2-8pm Mon-Fri; 2-8pm Sat, Sun. *May-Sept* 9am-5pm Mon-Fri. **Admission** free.

Where to eat & drink

Casimiro Biguá, Parrilla & Asador

Avenida del Libertador 963 (02902 492590/www. interpatagonia.com/casimiro). **Open** 9am-3am daily. **Average** $$$. **Credit** AmEx, MC.
This upmarket modern *parrilla* has all the cuts and offal you need and plenty you probably don't. For a more comprehensive range of pasta and fish dishes, try the adjoining restaurant and wine bar.

Punto de Encuentro

Los Pioneros 251 (02902 491243/www.glaciar. com). **Open** noon-3pm, 7.30pm-midnight daily. **Average** $$. **No credit cards.**
The busy restaurant of popular Hostal del Glaciar serves up hearty and authentic Patagonian cuisine; it's way above typical hostel fare.

Pura Vida

Avenida del Libertador 1876 (02902 493356). **Open** from 8.30am daily. **Average** $$. **No credit cards.**
Don't let the lurid purple-and-green exterior put you off. Fresh and comforting home cooking, with particularly good vegetarian options, as well as lake views, good music and personable service make this one of the best options in town.

El Rancho Pizza Bar

Gobernador Moyano y 9 de Julio (02902 496164). **Open** *Nov-Mar* 6.30pm-midnight daily. *Apr-Oct* 6.30pm-midnight Tue-Sun. **Average** $$. **Credit** AmEx, DC, MC, V.
El Rancho is a classic pizzeria that also serves up those other traditional Argentinian specialities, pasta and meat. The tasty and tender *bife de chorizo* (rump steak) is as good as any in town. The place iteself is small and cosy, with a young vibe.

Rick's Café

Avenida del Libertador 1105, y 9 de Julio (02902 492148). **Open** *Nov-Mar* 10am-1am daily. *Apr-Oct* 11am-3pm, 6pm-midnight daily. **Average** $$. **Credit** MC, V.
Of all the steak joints, in all the towns, in all the world, you could do a lot worse than walk into this one. Rick's Café is a bright and cheery, set-menu *parrilla*, serving up limitless portions of various cuts of meat from the local farms.

Shackleton Lounge

Avenida del Libertador 3287 (02902 493516/ www.shackletonlounge.com). **Open** 5pm-3am daily. **Average** $$. **Credit** AmEx, MC, V.
A long walk or a short taxi ride up Libertador brings you to the Shackleton Lounge and Bar, with its Brazilian and electronic beats, contemporary art and marvellous lake views. Serving cocktails and bar snacks to a young and laid-back crowd, it's a little too trendy for its surroundings but nonetheless a daring initiative. Afternoon tea is served from 5pm and happy hour runs from 7-9pm.

La Tablita

Coronel Rosales 24, y Libertador (02902 491065). **Open** noon-3pm, 7pm-midnight daily. **Average** $$. **Credit** AmEx, DC, MC, V.
If eating alone is your idea of hell, then welcome to gastro heaven. Full to brimming lunch and supper with a lively mix of locals and tourists, La Tablita is a classic, no-frills *parrilla* where what you see is what you get. Tender portions of meat and excellent service make for a winning formula.

Where to stay

Albergue & Hostal del Glaciar Libertador

Avenida del Libertador (tel & fax 02902 491792/ www.glaciar.com). **Rates** US$50-$65 double; US$90-$100 apartment for 4. **No credit cards.**
A second Hostal del Glaciar opened in 2004, offering the same quality facilities as the Pioneros version (*see below*). The forest-green wooden building is the smartest in town, and rooms are correspondingly well designed (all en suite), albeit with prices to match. Those on a budget should note that shared rooms for four are significantly cheaper.

Albergue & Hostal del Glaciar Pioneros

Calle Los Pioneros 251 (tel & fax 02902 491243/ www.glaciar.com). **Rates** *Hostel* US$30-$35 single/double. *Hotels* US$55-$60 single/double. **No credit cards.**
Completely refurbished in 2002, this eco-friendly mini-complex may be pricier than others and a little out the way, but with 17 years' experience, plus a good restaurant (Punto de Encuentro; *see above*) and a travel agency running well-organised excursions, it's deservedly popular.

Apart Hotel Libertador

Avenida Del Libertador 1150, entre 25 de Mayo y 9 de Julio (tel & fax 02902 491511/492079/www. aparthotellibertador.com.ar). **Rates** US$30-$45 single/double; US$38-$55 triple. **Credit** MC,V.
Inconspicuously tucked away off the town's main street, Hotel Libertador consists of eight apartments and 17 rooms set around a surprisingly pleasant and quiet courtyard. Cosy, compact and well equipped, it's a wee bit chintzy, but clean and very central. Ideal for a couple or family.

In case you were wondering, **Glaciar Perito Moreno** is in Argentina.

Hostería Alta Vista

33km (21 miles) from El Calafate (02902 491247/
altavista@cotecal.com.ar). Closed Apr-Sept. **Rates**
US$220 double; US$360 full board & excursions.
Credit AmEx, DC, MC, V.
Attached to Estancia La Anita, the luxurious Alta
Vista is set up for high-roller guests. In the vast
grounds it offers horse riding, fishing and other
ranch activities for city slickers taking a break.

Hotel Bahía Redonda

Padre Agostini 148 (tel & fax 02902 491743/
hotelbahiaredonda@cotecal.com.ar). **Rates** US$25-
$32 single; US$35-$40 double; US$40 triple. **Credit**
AmEx, DC, MC, V.
A spacious self-contained complex located towards
the outskirts of town, Bahía Redonda has a large
range of bright and well-maintained rooms, all with
views of Lago Argentina.

Hotel de Campo Kau Yatún

Estancia 25 de Mayo (02902 4091059/www.
kauyatun.com). **Rates** US$60-$75 single; US$80-$90
double. **Credit** AmEx, DC, MC, V.
Housed in the plush main building of a working
estancia, this four-star hotel combines rustic charm
with attentive personal service. Overlooked by the
vulgar building that houses the new Kempinski,
KauYatún is a more relaxing experience, with
spacious, wildlife-filled grounds.

Nibepo Aike

55km (34 miles) southwest of El Calafate (02966
422626/420180/nibepo@internet.siscotel.com.ar).
Closed Apr-Sept (can open by prearrangement).
Rates from US$400 per person for 2 nights all-
inclusive. **Credit** AmEx, DC, MC, V.

This *estancia* offers quaint, rustic accommodation
in the century-old main house, from which you can
just about glimpse Perito Moreno glacier.

Los Notros

82km (51 miles) from El Calafate (tel & fax 02902
491144/491186/www.losnotros.com). Closed June-
Aug. **Rates** from US$930 per person for 2 nights all-
inclusive; US$1,550 per person for 4 nights.
Credit AmEx, DC, MC, V.
If it's a room with a view you're after, it has to be
Los Notros, in the National Park – it's the only hotel
facing Perito Moreno head-on. Rooms are well
equipped with jacuzzis and a lounge area, but it's
the views of the glacier that will take your breath
away (along with your life savings). Predictably
popular, so book months in advance.

Posada Los Alamos

Gobernador Moyano y Bustillo (tel & fax 02902
491144/491149/www.posadalosalamos.com).
Closed Aug. **Rates** US$80-$100 single; US$140-
$195 double; US$180-$230 triple; US$250-$290 suite.
Credit AmEx, MC, V.
If you think big is better, Los Alamos is by far the
most impressive of El Calafate's hotels; it's really an
entire complex. In 1984 it had just 11 rooms. Today
there are 144 (plus four suites), all tastefully
decorated. Facilities include a tennis court, library,
horse riding and a restaurant with adjacent putting
green. A brand new and much-hyped swimming
pool complex is due to be unveiled in late 2005.

Posada Patagónica Nakel Menú

Puerto San Julián 244 (02902 49371/www.argentina
hostels.com). **Rates** US$8 per person dorm; US$27
double. **No credit cards**.

Parque Nacional Los Glaciares

Parque Nacional Los Glaciares extends 170 kilometres (106 miles) along the Chilean border. Established in 1937, Argentina's second largest national park was declared a World Heritage Site in 1981. El Chaltén in the north, within the park's boundaries, is the gateway to the panoramic Fitz Roy massif. El Calafate in the south is base camp for discovering the Perito Moreno glacier. Of the stunning 6,600 square kilometres (2,548 square miles), almost half are cloaked in continental ice fields and 15 per cent covered by lakes. In addition to the Glaciar Perito Moreno and its understudies, the Upsala, Onelli and Spegazinni glaciers, there are more than 50 other important glaciers in the park. Currently an entrance fee is only charged at the El Calafate entrance.

FLORA AND FAUNA

An impressive array of flora and fauna exists within the park including lenga and ñire forests and shrub vegetation dappled with the red notro flower. Around 100 bird species live there or visit, including Andean condors, Magellanic woodpeckers, austral parakeets, black-necked swans, red-backed hawks and torrent ducks. There are 14 species of mammal, including guanacos, grey foxes, skunks, rheas and the elusive huemul deer.

TREKS AND ACTIVITIES

There are around 30 easy walks that do not require a guide. For the experts, there's more serious trekking and climbing; the less experienced wanting to tackle bigger walks or climbs should make plans to go with an excursion company or professional guide. For activities around the glaciers, *see p154*; for trekking around El Chaltén, *see p152*.

FACILITIES

Near Perito Moreno glacier there are two restaurants, a snack bar and a paying campsite. Los Glaciares is one of the few parks where you don't need to bring all your provisions; there are restaurants and snack bars within the park. There are also lots of designated camping areas, including free and paying sites about 20 minutes' walk from the glacier. The two best *estancias* in the park are Nibeko Aike (*see p149*) and **Helsingfors** (Lago Viedma, 02966 420719, www.helsingfors. com.ar, double from US$150).

Parque Nacional Los Glaciares

El Chaltén entrance: *RP23, km 98 (02962 493004).* **Open** 24hrs daily (recommended entry 8am-8pm). **Admission** free.
El Chaltén Information centre: *Avenida San Martín, before bridge into town (02962 493004).* **Open** *Dec-Feb* 8am-10pm daily. *Mar-Nov* 9am-4pm daily.
El Calafate entrance: *Camping Mitre, RP11 (no phone).* **Open** 24hrs daily. **Admission** US$2; free under-12s.
El Calafate administration: *Avenida Del Libertador 1302 (02902 491005).* **Open** *May-Sept* 8am-4pm Mon-Fri. *Oct-Apr* 8am-4pm Mon-Fri; 1-4pm Sat, Sun.

Part of the excellent Argentina Hostels chain, Nakel Menú offers clean and spacious rooms and a great opportunity to meet fellow travellers. Expert excursion advice and a warm welcome guaranteed.

Resources

Hospital
Hospital José Formenti, Avenida Julio A Roca 1487 (02902 491173/491001).

Internet
Cooperativa Telefónica, Comandante Espora 194 (02902 491011).

Police station
Avenida del Libertador 835 (02902 491077).

Post office
Avenida del Libertador 1033 (02902 491012).

Tourist information
Secretaria de Turismo – Centro de Informes, Teminal de Omnibus, Avenida Julio A Roca 1004 (02902 491090/www.calafate.com). **Open** *May-Sept* 8am-9pm daily. *Nov-Apr* 8am-10pm daily.

Getting there

By air
Aeropuerto Internacional El Calafate (RP11, 02902 491220) is 23km (14 miles) from the centre of town and is open all year, with daily flights from BA in summer; otherwise the schedule is improvised according to the vagaries of the weather. There are international flights (45 mins) to/from Puerto Natales in Chile, Oct-Apr only; tickets are available from Turismo Rumbosur (02902 492155/491854).

By road
El Calafate lies 320km (199 miles) or 4hrs from Rio Gallegos by road, and 222km (138 miles) south of El Chaltén. From the bus station, **Terminal de Omnibus** (Avenida JA Roca 1000, no phone) there are daily buses Nov-Apr to El Chaltén (4.5hrs), plus daily service all year to Rio Gallego (4hrs). From May-Oct 3 buses per wk go to El Chaltén

El Chaltén

With its valley location, dusty roads and random smattering of A-frame houses (often without street numbers), El Chaltén retains a frontier outpost feel that El Calafate has long since lost. It's ironic, then, that this is in fact Argentina's newest town, founded in 1985 in a geo-political manoeuvre to counter Chilean claims to the area of Lago del Desierto

Like El Calafate, El Chaltén is in the tourism business; the town is now firmly established as the trekking and climbing capital of Argentina. In summer, the permanent population of the town doubles to a still-tiny 700 residents who cater for

Pizza at **Patagonicus**. *See p154.*

the several thousands of visitors who come to tackle the peaks of the Fitz Roy massif, some of the most difficult in the world to climb.

Although located in the northern section of Los Glaciares National Park, 222 kilometres (138 miles) north of El Calafate, El Chaltén is most easily accessed from the south. The granite spires of the massif that includes Mounts **Fitz Roy** (3,405 metres/11,171 feet), Torre (3,102 metres/10,177 feet), Poincenot (3,002 metres/9,850 feet) and Egger (2,900 metres/9,514 feet) are clearly visible en route from El Calafate, and from El Chaltén itself, enticing climbers and trekkers to get their boots on. Chaltén means 'smoking mountain', a name given by the native Tehuelche who mistook Cerro Fitz Roy (often scarfed in clouds) for a smouldering volcano.

Just before arriving in town, visitors must stop off at the national park information centre for advice on how to preserve the unspoilt natural surroundings (and to protect the endangered Huemul deer), and for climbers to register their details. The town has ambitious urban plans, with evidence of large-scale, uncontrolled construction taking place – there's talk of a civic centre and even an airport. Many of the residents feel ambivalent about this growth; despite pressing for structural improvements – there is still no proper sewage system or street paving – they are fearful that continued growth will alter the unique character of the place, with additional consequences for the natural environment. For the moment, though, the town still becomes near to inhospitable in the winter, and as good as closes down from the end of May to early October.

Downtown El Chaltén is located near the entrance to the town, and amounts to a police station and a few businesses dotted around Avenida Güemes – the town's main drag – and Avenida Lago del Desierto, which intersects it. A small monument to Padre Alberto de Agostini, early explorer of the area, sits on the

Argentinian Patagonia

intersection. Most buses from El Calafate stop on Avenida San Martín a bit further on, where there are more lodging and eating options.

If you need to rent camping, hiking or climbing equipment, try **Patagonia Mágica** (Hensen 56, 02962 493066/www.patagonia magica.com), **Viento Oeste** (Avenida San Martín, 02962 493200) or **Eolia** (Avenida San Martín, 02962 493066). In addition to equipment hire and traditional souvenirs, **Supermercado El Súper** (Avenida Lago del Desierto, 02962 493039) also has a surprisingly large selection of books about the region, many of them out of print and impossible to find elsewhere. In terms of facilities, El Chaltén is no Chamonix, but in its limitations you find its charm.

TREKKING AND CLIMBING

Most visitors arrive with adventure in mind. From the town several trails snake their way up to the base of the massif. Paths vary in length and gradient and, although most are well marked, you are advised to buy a map. At these altitudes, mountain sickness will not pose a problem, but the weather is temperamental and savage winds periodically blow up. Even in summer you should pack cold-weather gear for the occasional snow squall.

Among the most beaten paths is the one to **Laguna Torre** (with great views of Cerro and Glaciar Torre if the weather is good), a winding, tree-studded 15-kilometre (nine-mile) return hike that can be extended into a two-day trek with a night spent at Campamento D'Agostini (previously called Bridwell). The longer and more exciting 25-kilometre (15-mile) trek to **Laguna de los Tres** can be done in one day – if you are happy to be up at the crack of dawn – or combined with an overnight stay in Campamento Poincenot (or, for climbers, at Campamento Rio Blanco, ten-minutes further up). The setting combines woodlands, bogs, streams and crystal clear lakes and, if the weather cooperates, the final uphill stretch offers mind-blowing views of Fitz Roy (although be prepared to suffer a little for the privilege). A two- to three-hour trail linking Poincenot and D'Agostini campsites, for longer stays on the mountain range, can be done in either direction, and passes the *lagunas* Hija and Madre en-route.

Professional mountain guides are available from several agencies, such as Patagonia Mágica (*see above*) and **Mountaineering Patagonia** (E. Brenner 88, 02962 493194, info@mountaineeringpatagonia.com); they will organise all aspects of the treks, and also run overnight expeditions. In summer there are also horse-riding trips costing around US$30 for a two-hour ride with a guide; longtime resident gaucho Rodolfo Guerra is recommended (to locate him, ask in town), or try **El Relincho** (Avenida San Martín, 02962 493007).

For an easy initiation to trekking on ice, **Fitz Roy Expediciones** (Lionel Terray 212, 02962 493017,fitzroy@infovia.com.ar) runs day excursions to Glaciar Torre for US$50 (Oct to Apr). For a more testing five- to nine-day ice-trek, strap on your crampons and join its expeditions to the Southern Patagonian ice field (US$500-US$950 plus tax). A number of other companies now run similar excursions, including **NYCA** (Avenida Güemes, 02962 493185, www. nyca.com.ar) and **Viedma Discovery** (Avenida Güemes s/n, 02962 493103/viedmadiscovery@ cotecal.com.ar), which organises trekking on Glaciar Viedma near Puerto de Bahía Túnel, 15 kilometres (nine miles) north.

Although far from the highest mountains in the world, **Mount Fitz Roy** and **Cerro Torre** are among the most challenging for climbers: two colossal snow-capped incisors that perforate the skyline. Bombarded by violent winds, these snowy peaks are particularly risky as they are in constant danger of disintegration. The **Capilla Egger**, or Capilla Austríaco (next to the Puente Colgante) – a chapel dedicated to deceased Austrian climber Toni Egger and others – is a sobering reminder of the perils; the memorial list is already a few dozen long and every year a handful more are added. Attempts on the summits are only for pros.

When strong gusts haven't carried away the Puente Colgante, in under an hour you can walk along a well-marked path to the homestead of Danish pioneer Andreas Madsen, recently converted into a museum. Madsen came to Patagonia at age 15 as an orphaned stowaway. Overcoming numerous initial hardships he eventually became a source of invaluable support to the first generation of climbers to descend on the area in the 1930s. Madsen died in Bariloche in 1964, but his remains were later transferred to the family cemetery next to his home in the shadow of Mount Fitz Roy. Madsen's story is recounted by Don Alejandro, who runs guided tours to the house through **Lago San Martin EVT** (02902 493045, lagosanmartin@cotecal.com.ar).

For a really remote walk, several agencies, including Viedma Discovery (*see above*) can take you the 37 kilometres (23 miles) to Lago del Desierto, a thin, emerald-coloured crevice that slices through the surrounding forested Andes. Where the gravel road ends at Punta Sur, it's possible to hike four and a half hours to **Punta Norte**, where there's a pleasant camping spot and National Guard outpost. For more experienced trekkers, it's now possible to continue on to **Lago O'Higgins** in Chile, via

Fitz Roy massif.
See p150.

Argentinian Patagonia

a newly opened border crossing only for trekkers, from where there are once-weekly boats to Villa O'Higgins (*see p205*). Less daunting is the 45-minute gentle ascent to the steadily melting **Glaciar Huemul**, offering stupendous views of the Fitz Roy massif. Longtime hermit Tito Ramírez, a local legend, owns a wooded campground at Punta Sur for those wishing to spend the night.

Where to eat & drink

Many restaurants are open from November to April only, but a reliable year-round bet is **Restaurant Las Lengas** (Avenida Güemes, 02962 493044, $$) at the town's entrance, a family-run restaurant in the truest sense, offering an honest range of good-value meat and pasta dishes. For more sophisticated dining, with a good range of Patagonian dishes, try **Ruca Mahuida** (Lionnel Terray 104, 02962 493018, $$$) off Avenida San Martín or its neighbour, **Restaurant Fuegia** (Avenida San Martín 493, 02962 493019, $$$). **Malbec** (Antonio Rojo, y Cabo Garcia, 02962 493195, $$$) manages to be simultaneously rustic and cool and does a mean *bife de lomo*.

Patagonicus (Avenida Güemes, 02962 493025, $$) is a popular pizza joint, decked out with interesting black-and-white photos of pioneer climber Cesarino Favre (the place is owned by his daughter). For home-made chocolate and cakes try laid-back **La Chocolatería Josh Aike** (Lago del Desier to 104, 02962 493008, *chocolatería*, closed May-Oct, $). Similarly atmospheric is cosy **Cervecería El Bodegón** (Avenida San Martín s/n, 02962 493109, $$) where home-brewed Czech-style pilsner is on tap. It's very friendly and proceedings are occasionally livened up with impromptu guitar jams. Or for a younger, backpacker vibe, try restaurant-bar **Zafarrancho** behind Albergue Rancho Grande (Lionel Terray, 02962 493005, $$) which projects twice-weekly film screenings and has an internet café upstairs.

On your way in or out of town, go to **Parador La Leona**, halfway between El Calafate and El Chaltén on RN40 (no phone): all buses between the two towns stop there. Locals playing *sortija*, an old gaucho drinking game, give this eaterie the feel of a real *pulpería*, as such bygone hangouts were known.

Where to stay

If travelling to El Chaltén in high season, book accommodation well in advance. For an up-close (and warm) view of Fitz Roy, the secluded **Hostería El Pilar** (RP23, km 17, 02962 493002, www.hosteriaelpilar.com.ar, closed Apr-Sept, double US$90-$130), situated some 17 kilometres (11 miles) past El Chaltén, is highly recommended. Climber/owner Marcelo Pagani, who has attempted Fitz Roy several times, built this cosy lodge in the style of the corrugated-iron *estancias* of old, but with all mod cons. In town, **Hostería El Puma** (Lionel Terray 212, 02962 493095, www.elchalten.com/elpuma, closed Apr-Sept, double US$45-$50) has rustic furniture, thick beams and an all-important fireplace. The eight bedrooms have views across the valley. Climber/owner Alberto del Castillo (of Fitz Roy Expediciones) is one of the town's oldest residents and an unbeatable repository of local lore.

There are numerous rudimentary budget options. **Albergue Rancho Grande** (Avenida San Martín, 02962 493092, rancho@cotecal. com.ar, closed May-Oct, US$6 per person dorm) is a lively, impeccably run youth hostel, popular with Argentinian and foreign tourists alike. On rainy days its large restaurant is the place to hang out. **Albergue Patagonia** (Avenida San Martín 493, 02962 493019, www.elchalten.com/patagonia, closed mid Mar-Oct, US$7 per person dorm) offers similar quality service but in a more intimate setting. **Albergue Cóndor de los Andes** (Avenida Rio de las Vueltas y Halvorsen, 02962 493101, www.condordelos andes.com, closed Apr-Sept, US$8 per person dorm) is a stylish and perfectly located option with knowledgeable and helpful staff, while the welcoming and good-value **Posada Poincenot** (Avenida San Martín 615, 02962 493022, www. calafate.com/chalten/Alojamiento, double US$18-$25), has pleasant rooms, a convivial communal living room and a small bar. The excellent **B&B Nothofagus** (Hensen s/n, 02962 493087, double US$20) is part of the well-reputed Argentina Hostels (AHC) chain.

If you want to get closer to nature, or just save some cash, consider pitching a tent. As well as the free campsites that link the trails in the mountains, there are several free options on the edge of town – Campamento Madsen being the most popular. Good paying sites include **Ruca Mahuida** (02962 493018) and **El Refugio** (02962 493221).

Resources

Hospital

Puesto Sanitario, De Agostini, entre Güemes y Costanera Sur (02962 493073).

Internet

As well as resto-bar Zafarrancho, there is a *locutorio* with internet access on the corner of Avenida Güemes and Avenida Lago del Desierto.

Police station
*Río de las Vueltas y Güemes (02962 493003/
493074).*

Post office
Avenida Güemes 21 (02962 493011).

Tourist information
*Comisión de Fomento del Chaltén, Avenida Güemes
21, entre De Agostini y Costanera Sur (02962
493011).* **Open** *Nov-Mar* 8am-7pm daily. *Apr-June*
8am-7pm Mon-Fri. *July-Oct* 9am-7pm Mon-Fri.

Getting there

By road
El Chaltén is 222km (138 miles) or 4.5hrs from El
Calafate. There are daily buses in summer, and 3
buses per week in winter. **Chaltén Travel** (02902
491833) does the trip and also has buses in summer
to Perito Moreno.

Río Gallegos

Once the gateway to southern Patagonia, Río
Gallegos (population 88,000), the administrative
and commercial capital of Santa Cruz, has
witnessed a decline in visitors since the opening
of El Calafate airport in December 2000.
Although most historians pinpoint its birth
to the late 19th century, Río Gallegos really
came into its own between 1912 and 1920, when
a policy of preferential farming conditions
enticed migrant workers from the Falkland
Islands/Islas Malvinas and southern Chile.

On the back of the sheep-rearing industry,
Río Gallegos became the most important port
in Patagonia, shipping livestock to distant
markets. The port remains a key commercial
facility, exporting a variety of ovine products,
locally extracted crude oil and coal mined in
nearby Río Turbio. Although the heady days
of the boom have long gone, there is a certain
bustle around the main strip, Avenida JA Roca,
which has plenty of neon-bathed shopfronts
and workaday restaurants (whose heyday
was in the 1970s and '80s).

If you have a few hours to kill visit the
Museo de los Pioneros, an immaculately-
maintained old Patagonian house that offers
a compelling insight into the city's past. The
other museum worthy of a visit, the **Museo
Regional Padre Manuel Jesús Molina**,
exhibits a bizarre mix of prehistoric fossils
and contemporary art and sculpture, as well
as one or two artefacts from the region's more
recent past, including a kneading bowl
belonging to the city's first baker.

Located in the city's **Centro Cultural**, (José
Ingenieros 60, 02966429479), you'll come across
a government-run crafts fair selling some of the
finest hand-made wool products in Patagonia –
all made from wool donated by local farms – at
affordable prices. Get your gifts here.

Museo de los Pioneros
Juan Bautista Alberdi y Elcano (02966 437763).
Open 10am-8pm daily. **Admission** free.

Museo Regional Padre Manuel Jesús Molina
*Ramón y Cajal 51, y Avenida San Martín (02966
423290/fax 426427/cultura@spse.gov.ar).* **Open**
8am-8pm Mon-Fri; 3-8pm Sat. **Admission** free.

EXCURSIONS
Although most people use Río Gallegos as
a quick stopover, if you fancy a nature trip,
it's 134 kilometres (83 miles) down the coast
to the tip of mainland South America, **Cabo
Vírgenes** – formerly Cabo de las Once Mil
Vírgenes (Cape of 11,000 Virgins), christened
by Magellan no less, in 1520. It's something
of a misnomer for a place where you can see

Estancia Cóndor, Patagonia's largest sheep farm. *See p156.*

80,000 couples of Magellanic penguins come ashore to breed between October and March. Take plenty of provisions as the reserve has no infrastructure, let alone virgins.

Along the way you'll pass **Estancia Cóndor**, Patagonia's largest sheep farm, owned by a company linked to Italian clothing magnate Luciano Benetton.

Climb the 91 steps up the lighthouse located at Cabo Virgenes for spectacular views of the entrance to the Magellan Strait, dotted with offshore oil rigs. If the weather turns rough – and it often does – you can take refuge in **Al Fin y Al Cabo**, a teahouse above the cliffs overlooking the strait.

About ten kilometres (six miles) before Cabo Virgenes is **Estancia Monte Dinero**, a working ranch with a fascinating small family museum. The farm is one of the most modern in Patagonia; gauchos here herd sheep on mopeds: *A Fistful of Dollars* meets *Quadrophenia*.

Anglers should check in at **Trucha Aike** lodge, 30 kilometres (19 miles) outside Río Gallegos for some of the best trout fishing in the region. For horse lovers, **Hill Station**, also called Estancia Los Pozos, 64 kilometres (40 miles) from Río Gallegos, is a stud farm run by the great-grandchild of its original owner. All the above *estancias* have day activities and lodging; call for details (for all, *see below*).

Where to stay & eat

The **Costa Río Apart Hotel** (Avenida San Martín 673, 02966 423412, www.advance.com.ar /usuarios/fjmontes, double US$45-$55) is the swankiest inn in town with 54 spacious rooms. More modest is the well-equipped **Hotel Santa Cruz** (Avenida JA Roca 701, 02966 420601, www.advance.com.ar/usuarios/htlscruz, double US$25-$32). Excellent value **Hotel Seheun** (Rawson 160, 02966 425683, hotelsehuen@ hotmail.com, double US$20-$25) looks like a converted church. Inside it's chirpy and spotless. **Estancia Monte Dinero** (RP1, 02966 426900, www.montedinero.com.ar,closed Mar-mid Sept, double US$80-$95) has superb accommodation in the century-old main house. Overnight stays at **Trucha Aike Lodge** (RN3, 02966 436127/011 4394 3513, www.estanciasdesantacruz.com/ Truchaike/truchaike.htm, closed mid Apr-mid Nov) costs US$450 per person per night, all-inclusive, with bilingual fishing guide. A stay at **Hill Station** (02966 15 621783, www.estancias desantacruz.com) costs US$65-$80 per person.

Most restaurants are located on Avenida JA Roca. For a taste of days gone by check out **Club Británico** (Avenida JA Roca 935, 02966 427320, $$), where according to Bruce Chatwin, you're unlikely to find anyone who speaks

English, though there is a full-sized snooker table. The club was founded by a Scot, George MacGeorge, as a meeting place for himself and his farm workers so they could forget about sheep and women. Ninety years on, that macho recipe still works, helped along by good food and reasonable prices. Also popular with the locals is **El Horreo** (Avenida JA Roca 862, 02966 426462, $$), notable for its hip decor and food as Spanish as a tortilla.

Resources

Hospital
Hospital Regional Río Gallegos, José Ingenieros 98 (02966 420025).

Internet
Locutorio X-Press, Avenida JA Roca 1084 (02966 427183).

Post office
Avenida JA Roca y San Martín (02966 420046).

Police station
Avenida JA Roca 534 (02966 420016).

Tourist information
Subsecretaría de Turismo de la Provincia de Santa Cruz, Avenida JA Roca 863, entre Alcorta y Bosco (02966 438725/www.scruz.gov.ar). **Open** Oct-Mar 9am-10pm Mon-Fri; 10am-8pm Sat, Sun. Apr-Sept 8am-8pm Mon-Fri; 10am-1pm Sat; 3-8pm Sun.
Also see the municipal government's website (www.mrg.gov.ar) for a wealth of info on the city.

Getting there

By air
Daily flights from BA, Ushuaia, Río Grande and Comodoro Rivadavia arrive at **Aeropuerto Internacional de Río Gallegos** (RN3, km 8, 02966 442344), 5km (3 miles) from the centre. There are also twice-weekly flights to/from El Calafate.

By road
Río Gallegos lies on RN3, a huge 36hrs by bus from BA to the **Terminal de Omnibus** (Avenida Eva Perón, 02966 442159), 3km (2 miles) from town. It's 4hrs from El Calafate, 12hrs from Comodoro Rivadavia and 16hrs from Río Grande by road.

Río Grande

Few places on earth can conjure up the paradox of extremes like Tierra del Fuego. This 'land of fire', as it directly translates, is the coldest, southernmost part of Argentina, separated by water from the rest of the country. If you wish to visit this tip of the South American continent then you have to cross the Magellan Strait, named after the explorer who discovered this body of water, Ferdinand Magellan. And the first major settlement you come to on the other side is Rio Grande, the so-called 'garden city'.

Flat and sprawling, Rio Grande is flanked by the river it was named after to the south and the Atlantic Ocean to the east. The city developed thanks to the sheep above ground and the oil below it. The town is picturesque in places, with colourful houses, but a constant sea gale stirs up so much dust it's difficult to keep your eyes open to enjoy it. But do keep them peeled for the sunrises – they're like slow-motion firework displays.

The main streets for visitors are Avenidas San Martin and Elcano. The small **Museo Municipal de la Ciudad de Río Grande** contains a wealth of great historical information on the area's pioneers, including gold coins and relics belonging to gold kingpin Julio Popper. It's also where anyone not going to Puerto Natales in Chile can see a life-size model of a giant, ice-age ground sloth (*see p212* **Bruce and the giant sloth**).

Eleven kilometres (seven miles) north you can visit **Misión Salesiana 'La Candelaria'**, once a mission and now an agricultural college. It was founded in 1893 by missionary José Fagnano in an attempt to protect the indigenous Ona population from sheep farmers and gold prospectors. Worth the trek out for the interesting chapel architecture, and the museum, which has some rarely exhibited photos, and explains the customs of Tierra del Fuego's native tribes. Breakfasts and lunches are also available, along with horse-riding excursions and lessons.

Little wonder, what with the ocean, the myriad lakes and rivers, that, from November to April, fishing is the main reason why many rod-reeling folk head for this town. It's a record-breaking trout- and salmon-fishing destination, and one of the key angling spots in Patagonia. For all information regarding fishing trips,

contact the tourist office, or agencies such as **Mariani Travel** (Rosales 281, 02964 426010, www.tierradelfuego.org.ar/agencias/riogrande) who can provide bilingual fishing guides.

Museo Municipal de la Ciudad de Río Grande

JB Alberdi 555, entre Avenida Belgrano y Rivadavia (02964 430647/http://www.nuevamuseologia.com.ar /museo_de_la_ciudad.htm). **Open** 9am-noon, 2pm-8pm Mon-Fri; 3-8pm Sat, Sun. **Admission** free.

Misión Salesiana 'La Candelaria'

RN3, km 2800 (02964 421642/www.misionrg. com.ar). **Open** 8.30am-12.30pm, 2-5pm Mon-Fri; 9am-12.30pm, 3-7pm Sat, Sun. **Admission** US$1.50.

EXCURSIONS

If donning waders for some hooking and releasing doesn't appeal, there are a number of attractive *estancias* to discover in the area. Highly recommended is historic **Estancia María Behety** (Rio Grande, 02964 430345/011 43315061, www.maribety.com.ar, closed Apr-Nov), 15 kilometres (11 miles) south-west, which boasts the world's largest sheep-shearing shed. With its own church, school and plaza, it resembles a small town. The *estancia* also has a tourist restaurant with a *parrilla*, which also organises tours of the ranch. As this is a working farm you'll need to phone ahead to arrange visits. From December to March anglers can fish on the *estancia*'s land by prearrangement with The Fly Shop (see the *estancia*'s website for links), and the complex boasts a fishing lodge with eight rooms.

If you crave wilderness, use Río Grande as a base to explore Peninsula Mitre, the eastern extremity of Isla Grande. **Mariani Travel** (*see above*) organises trips to the 'real end of the world' with accommodation at **Estancia Cabo San Pablo** and extended horse rides along the shipwreck-ridden shores. For trips to Tolhuin, halfway between Ushuaia and Rio Grande, in the heart of the Fuegian forest, *see p162*.

If the wind doesn't take your breath away at **Estancia Harberton**, the view will. *See p163*.

Faro Les Eclaireurs. *See p161.*

Where to stay & eat

One of the best overnight options is 45km (28 miles) from Río Grande along the coast. Homely and comfortable, **Estancia Viamonte** (RN3, 02964 430861, www.estanciaviamonte.com, double US$165 including dinner) is a working farm founded in 1902 by Lucas Bridges and his brothers at the request of the local Ona people, and where Bruce Chatwin took tea with owner Adrian Goodall. In town, right by the bus station, but with views of the ocean and a shore alive with seabirds, **Hotel Isla Del Mar** (Güemes 963, y Costanera, 02964 422883, isladelmar@arnet.com.ar, double US$35) offers comfortable rooms with private bathrooms, and serves a good breakfast.

Hotel Posada de los Sauces (Elcano 839, 02964 430868, www.posadadelossauces. com.ar) has double rooms for US$55-$70 and its pub/restaurant serves up Río Grande's best seafood. **Parrilla el Rincón de Julio** (Elcano 805, entre Avenida Belgrano y Laserre, 02964 15604261, $$) is recommended for meat, while the best local pasta is served at **La Nueva Colonial** (Fagnano 669, 02964 425353, $$). There's not much in terms of nightlife in Río Grande besides the **Casino Club** (Monseñor Fagnano 633, 02964 431600), a few *confiterías* and a couple of discos for locals. **Liverpool Pub** at Elcano No.433 has regular live music events, though no record contracts have been signed there as yet.

Resources

Hospital
Hospital Regional Río Grande, Ameghino 755 (02964 422086).

Internet
Telecom, Avenida Belgrano 580 (02964 427327).

Police station
Monseñor Fagnano 1167 (02964 422988).

Post office
Rivadavia 968 (02964 420987).

Tourist information
Dirección de Turismo de la Municipalidad de la Ciudad de Río Grande, Rosales 350, entre Monseñor Fagnano y Espora (02964 431324). **Open** 9am-8pm Mon-Fri; 10am-5pm Sat.

Getting there

By air
There are daily flights connecting Río Grande with BA from **Aeropuerto Internacional Hermes Quijada** (RN3, Acceso Aeropuerto, 02964 420699/421612), and direct services to Río Gallegos, El Calafate, Ushuaia and Comodoro Rivadavia.

By road
Río Grande is on RN3, 218 km (135 miles) or 4hrs from Ushuaia, serviced by daily buses. Travel by road north to Río Gallegos involves going via Chile, taking a boat across the Magellan Strait and 2 border crossings. In short, it's best to fly. The **Terminal de Omnibus** is at Belgrano y Güemes (02964 420003/431700).

Ushuaia

People have always been drawn to geographical and physical extremes; this explains, in part, the attraction of the southernmost city in the world, Ushuaia (pronounced oo-SWY-ya).

The city lies at the bottom of Isla Grande, clustered between the snowy peaks of **Cerro Martial** and majestic **Monte Olivia** and the icy waters of the Beagle Channel. Arriving by air is the best way to savour that end-of-the-world feeling as the plane descends over the rugged coast, sheer mountains and desolate scattered islands. Once in town, the thrill subsides somewhat; in the last few decades, modern civilisation and marketing have caught up with Ushuaia, making it feel less like a remote pioneer outpost of yore.

Ushuaia is the provincial capital of the Argentinian part of Tierra del Fuego, with a population of just over 50,000 (four-fifths of whom arrived in the last 20 years, drawn by industries created on the back of its duty-free status). The majority of tourists visit during summer when milder temperatures average 12°C (54°F), though visually speaking the best time to visit is in late April, when the winds drop and the countryside is in full autumnal red.

The city's name comes from Yamana, and means 'the bay that faces the west'. The area was originally populated by the Selk-nam, Alakalufe, Haush and Yamana people.

The first outsiders to settle in Ushuaia were Anglican missionaries in the 1870s, and the town was officially established in 1884. To establish a permanent Argentinian settlement, the government's original idea was to convert Ushuaia into a penal colony. In 1896 the first 14 convicts arrived on a naval ship and were holed up in huts. Though the idea of a penal colony was subsequently downsized, construction of a prison on the same site began in 1902, and nine years later opened its padlocked doors to offenders. Throughout its inglorious history, the jail housed some of Argentina's most notorious criminals (*see right* **Stir crazies**).

Although closed to convicts for more than half a century, today two wings of the former prison have been converted into the **Museo Marítimo y Presidio de Ushuaia**. Partly devoted to maritime exhibits, the big attraction here is the prison building itself and its reconstruction of prison life.

In its 'heyday' it contained 600 inmates in 380 cells, who were put to work locally as bakers, electricians, carpenters, firemen and printers. Although the chances of escape were plentiful – parts of the perimeter were totally void of fences – chances of survival outside were slim. Infamous for its grim austerity, the prison was shut down by president Juan Domingo Perón in 1947. Now each cell of this quirky, fascinating museum depicts a tale of prison hardship or a poignant historical event.

Ushuaia is a city built on slopes, with steep roads leading away from the water, but much of the action is focused on the main thoroughfare, Avenida San Martín. Here you'll find an odd mélange of retail and commercial activity, chocolate shops and a disproportionate number of 4x4 vehicles. From the main drag, the town morphs into a chaotic streetscape that slopes from south to north. In the barrios at the top, the architecture is a mix of neat wooden cabins and A-frame chalets, but there are also entire houses built from packaging materials pilfered from local factories. Considering the obvious lack of urban planning, the town's natural appeal comes as a pleasant surprise. It's the reason why a huge contingent of foreign sailing fanatics – among them Jean Paul Bassaget, the retired captain of Cousteau's *Calypso* – have settled here permanently.

At the bottom, arched around **Bahía Ushuaia**, the waterfront is a focus for seafood restaurants, hotels and colourful housing projects. East along Maipú, the docks are sprawling and messy, although the passenger port, **Puerto de Ushuaia**, where cargo ships and behemoth-sized cruisers dock, is orderly. Icebreakers pull in bound for Antarctica, a mere 1,000 kilometres (620 miles) south and sailboats

Stir crazies

During its history, Ushuaia's far-flung federal jail housed numerous colourful and sometimes very violent inmates. Among them were 'The Big-eared Short Guy', 'The Mystic' and 'The Handsaw'.

Big ears, 'El Petiso Orejudo', was the most notorious. Cayetano Santos Godino was imprisoned in 1915 at the age of 16. This pint-sized, jobless serial killer specialised in strangling, drowning or beating to death young children in Buenos Aires. However, prison justice ended El Petiso Orejudo's life: he was killed by his fellow inmates in 1944.

Mateo Banks, aka 'The Mystic', was convicted in 1924. His disturbing case was Argentina's first multiple homicide. Burdened by debt, Mateo schemed to inherit his family's ranches. However, his cunning plan to poison the family and blame the farm workers went awry when the family realised the food tasted strange and Mateo had to finish off them and two labourers with a shotgun. He was granted parole in 1944, though he died in a bathtub in Buenos Aires a few days later.

The man they called simply Herns or 'El Serruchito' (The Handsaw) became the prison butcher while serving his sentence, demonstrating that the authorities knew how to use inmates' unusual abilities to their advantage. Herns was committed for butchering his business partner and throwing his chopped remains into Palermo lake in Buenos Aires.

Argentinian Patagonia

Parque Nacional Tierra del Fuego

The Parque Nacional Tierra del Fuego, founded in 1960, stretches north from the Beagle Channel, its western limits defined by the Chilean frontier. Up until the opening of Monte León (*see p143*) it was Argentina's only coastal park, 15 kilometres (9.5 miles) west of Ushuaia. Stretches of the vast lakes Fagnano and Roca are within the park, and the scenery is dramatic: mountains, waterfalls, glaciers, forests. You can arrive at the park by road or on the **Tren del Fin del Mundo** (*see p163*).

FLORA AND FAUNA

Within the 63 square kilometres (24 square miles) are a wide variety of trees, among them lenga, ñire and coíhue. Terrestrial wildlife is rare though there are 20 mammal species, including guanaco, timid grey foxes who only surface when hungry, and battalions of pesky (and non-indigenous) beavers that have single-handedly devoured large chunks of the forest. Ninety species of birds are found here: steamer ducks, woodpeckers, oystercatchers, condors and the austral parakeet (the world's most southerly parrot) being just a few that waddle and flap their way around the park.

TREKS AND ACTIVITIES

Large areas of the park are closed to tourists to protect the environment. Most treks are short and easy with the exception of the trek to Guanaco Mountain, 971 metres (3,186

feet) above sea level. The Senda Costera offers thrilling views over the Bahía Ensenada and Islas Estorbo and Redonda. Many of the more ambitious treks can be combined with kayaking to these islands in the Beagle Channel. Highly recommended, non-conventional guided tours using 4x4s and kayaks, cooking up delicious improvised barbecues along the way, are on offer from local tour company **Canal Fun and Nature** (Avenida Rivadavia 82, Ushuaia, 02901 437395, www.canalfun.com).

FACILITIES

There are five places to camp; Bahía Ensenada and Río Pipo are among the four free sites, but only have very rudimentary facilities. A better option is to pay the US$2 a night at the attractive lakeside site at Lago Roca, which has showers and a well-stocked snack bar.

Intendencia PN Tierra del Fuego

San Martín 1395, entre Patagonia y Sarmiento (02901 421315/www.parques nacionales.gov.ar). **Open** 8am-4pm Mon-Fri. Buy your entrance ticket at this office in town if you are intending to arrive at the park any time outside 8am to 8pm, November to April.

Parque Nacional Tierra del Fuego

RN3, km 3047 (no phone). **Open** 24hrs daily. **Admission** Nov-Apr US$1.50; free under-12s. *May-Oct* free to all.

also depart from here for trips to Cape Horn and beyond. For information on travel to Antarctica or the islands of the South Atlantic, *see pp221-228* **Antarctica & the Islands**.

Although many come to use the town as a base for forays into the surrounding wilderness, there's also plenty to see for the culturally curious in Ushuaia, which was nominated as one of the World Capitals of the Millennium (Argentinian ballet superstar Julio Bocca danced to celebrate it). Every June, the city organises the **Bajada de los Antorchas**, a torchlight skiing event down Cerro Martial to mark the opening of the ski season on the

southernmost pistes in the world. In November, the town hosts the popular **Ushuaia Jazz Festival** (*see pp44-46* **Festivals & Events**).

Downtown, visit the **Museo del Fin del Mundo**. Established in 1979, the museum is split into four sections, tracing the history of the region's indigenous peoples, the settlers, the old grocery shops that were once the town's commercial life line, bird life (feathered and jail variety) and maritime history. The latter section features the figurehead from the prow of the *Duchess of Albany*, which ran aground off Tierra del Fuego in 1893. The remains of the ship can still be seen on the shore. A little bookshop at the back stocks literature relating to Tierra del Fuego, while anyone who wishes to send a postcard from 'the end of the world' may do so from the post office. A detailed exploration of the life of the Yamana (known also as Yahgan) is on view at the **Museo Mundo Yámana**.

For a bird's-eye view of Ushuaia, head up to the **Glaciar Martial** above Cerro Martial. Apart from simply being a wonder of nature, this massive chunk of ice also supplies Ushuaia with the best part of its drinking water. If you're feeling energetic you can try walking the seven kilometres (4.5 miles) from town, though the easier route is to take a taxi to the **Centro Recreativo Glaciar Martial**'s chairlift, take a ride part of the way up and clamber the rest of the way up to the base of the glacier. Don't put it off until your retirement, though; experts predict that the receding glacier will disappear entirely over the next 50 years. On the way back down you can stop off at the base for a rejuvenating pot of tea and cakes at **La Cabaña**.

Golfers can tee off at the nine-hole golf course just out of town, next to the Rio Pipo. The course is generally considered to be tricky and the last two holes, called, in the native tongue, Hasha (wind) and Akaui (to be cold), sum up the blustery conditions.

EXCURSIONS

If weather permits, take a scenic boat trip into the Beagle Channel. Tickets can be purchased on the **Muelle Turístico** (tourist pier) from **Rumbo Sur** (San Martin 350, 02901 421139/ 422275, www.rumbosur.com.ar, US$30 for a two-and-a-half-hour trip) or from **Motonave Barracuda** (Gobernador Godoy 62, 02901 433488, barracuda@tierradelfuego.org.ar). Boats head out via the hillsides studded with lenga trees to the **Les Eclaireurs** lighthouse, stopping off at the Isla de los Lobos (sea lion colony) and the Isla de los Pájaros (bird colony) on the return journey. Longer excursions go to **Estancia Harberton** (estanciaharberton@ tierradelfuego.org.ar; *see p163*).

The best way to visit Estancia Harberton is by boat, though you can go overland – an 85-kilometre (53-mile) trip due east from Ushuaia. The *estancia*, the oldest in Tierra del Fuego, is an isolated farm with a stunning backdrop perched on the very edge of the continent. It was built by the English missionary Thomas Bridges, and is still lived in and worked by his direct descendants. Nowadays, guided tours in English and Spanish take you via the family cemetery, gardens and sheep-shearing sheds. Displayed in the small but informative **Museo Acatushun**, within the *estancia*, is material related to Tierra del Fuego's marine life, including huge fossils from beached whales found by Natalie Goodall, the American-born wife of farm owner Tommy Goodall.

After decades of neglect, the Lucas Bridges Heritage Trail was reopened in 2001 by Simon Goodall, a descendant of Lucas (the son of Thomas Bridges) whose family runs Estancia Viamonte (*see p158*) near Rio Grande. The trail was first opened in 1900, envisioned by the adventurous Lucas as a means of transporting sheep between Viamonte and the family's other farm, Estancia Harberton.

Puff and pant your way up **Glaciar Martial** for a postcard-perfect view of Ushuaia.

Although the farms are only 50 kilometres (31 miles) apart as the crow flies, the trail is an obstacle course of fallen trunks, peat bogs and fast-moving rivers. The biggest impediment, however, is the dams left by the rapidly multiplying beaver population.

Those completing the trail are rewarded with a warm dip in the thermal baths of the Río Valdés. That plus the sense of discovery that comes from following in the footsteps of such an unheralded legend. The three-day hike can only be done with a guide from **Compañía de Guías de la Patagonia** (*see below*).

An extremely popular excursion is to the national park (*see p160* **Parque Nacional Tierra del Fuego**). Most people go via the gravel RN3, but other possible means of entry are by catamaran from Ushuaia or aboard the **Tren del Fin del Mundo**. The original tracks of this train were laid in 1896 by prisoners, to link the jail under construction to the nearby forests. The railway fell into disuse when the prison closed down in 1947 but reopened in 1994 as a tourist attraction. This latest version is pulled by a locomotive imported from England in 1995. Passengers can travel in tourist or first class, or rent the President's Wagon, which seats eight for a king crab and and champagne dinner. The five-kilometre (three-mile) trip takes 45 minutes and stops off at a reconstruction of a Yámana settlement. Departures are daily, with extra trips made during summer. Commentary is in English and Spanish.

While the skiing at Cerro Martial is perfect for novices, the more serious option is **Cerro Castor** (www.cerrocastor.com), 26 kilometres (16 miles) from town. This resort ranks with

those in the French Pyrenees, with 19 pistes, three ski lifts, two teleskis and one bambi lift, and is, naturally, the southernmost ski resort in the world. The various ski resorts around Ushuaia are also known for the best nordic skiing on the continent. The ski season climaxes on 17 August, with the annual Marcha Blanca (White March), a re-enactment of independence hero José de San Martín's crossing of the Andes.

For trekking on glaciers, over mountains or hiking in snowshoes, contact Compañía de Guías de la Patagonia. (Gobernador Campos 795, 02901 437753, www.companiadeguias. com.ar). The company also organises various skiing trips, including heliskiing. **Témpanos Viajes** (San Martín 626, 02901 436020) specialises in both standard excursions and unconventional offerings, like sailing trips to Cape Horn or hiking on uninhabited islands off the Beagle Channel.

If you fancy braving the icy waters of the Beagle Channel, diving is another option, and is particularly recommended between March and October although a drysuit is essential. Dives include those to the Bridges islands, and the Monte Cervantes shipwreck. **Ushuaia Divers** (L.N. Alem 4509, 02901 444701/ 15619782, www.tierradelfuego.org.ar/divers) organises dives and snorkelling all year round, running from US$60 in low season to US$80 in high season.

For some zen tranquility, the still, mirrored waters of Lago Fagnano sit in the hollow of a glacier 104 kilometres (65 miles) from Ushuaia. The sixth largest lake in South America, its icy waters teem with trout and salmon. Nestled beside the lake, the little village of Tolhuin

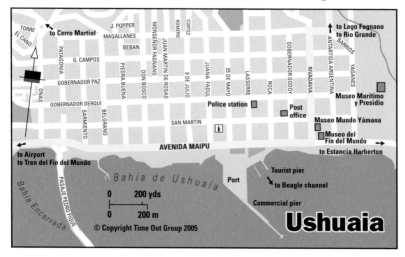

(population 1,487) offers a great day's fishing, horse riding, walks, mountain biking and other outdoor activities. There are various lodging options in among the trees for overnight stays. Try the cute cabins of **Cabañas Khami** (Cabecera Lago Fagnano, 3km from Tolhuin, www.cabaniaskhami.com.ar, 02964 15 611243). They cost from US$40 per person per night.

The town's social hall is its bakery, **Panadería La Union** (Cerro Jeujepén 450, 02901 492107), which owner Emilio Saez keeps open 365 days a year and has decorated with pin-ups of Argentinian celebrity Graciela Alfano, his unrequited love. Less titillating is a snapshot of former Paraguayan dictator General Lino Oviedo, who visited the bakery while living in exile nearby in 1998. The coup leader was not thrilled with his new home. In requesting a transfer, his lawyers used the argument that Tierra del Fuego's intense wind was incompatible with a recent hair transplant.

Centro Recreativo Glaciar Martial
(02901 15568587/www.tierradelfuego.org.ar). **Open** *May-Sept* 10am-5.30pm daily. *Oct-Apr* 10am-7pm. **Rates** *Chairlift* US$2.50; US$1 4-8s; free under-3s. *Ski pass per day* US$6; US$3.50 under-18s; free under-5s. **Credit** MC, V.

Cerro Castor
RN3, km 26.5 (02901 15 605595/www.cerro castor.com). **Open** Mid Jun-mid Oct. **Rates** *Ski pass per day* US$18-$25; $15-$20 5-11s; US$100-$150, $70-$110 5-11s per wk. *Ski/snowboard hire* US$10-$16 per day; free under-5s. **Credit** AmEx, DC, MC, V.

Estancia Harberton
85km (53 miles) east of Ushuaia (02901 422742/ www.estanciaviamonte.com/Harberton). **Rates** US$80-$110. *Set menu* $$$. **No credit cards**.

Museo Acatushun
Estancia Harberton (www.acatushun.com). **Open** *Oct-Apr* 10am-7pm. **Admission** US$10 (includes tour).

Museo del Fin del Mundo
Avenida Maipú 173, y Rivadavia (02901 421863/www.tierradelfuego.org.ar/museo). **Open** *May-Sept* 3-7pm Mon-Sat. *Oct-Apr* 10am-1pm, 3-7pm daily. **Admission** US$2.50; free under-14s.

Museo Marítimo y Presidio de Ushuaia
Yaganes y Gobernador Paz (tel & fax 02901 436321/437481/www.tierradelfuego.org.ar/museo). **Open** *May-mid Oct* 10am-8pm daily. *Mid Oct-Apr* 9am-8pm daily. *Guided tours* (Spanish) 6pm. **Admission** US$5.

Museo Mundo Yámana
Rivadavia 56, entre Maipú y San Martín (02901 422874/www.tierradelfuego.org.ar/mundoyamana). **Open** *May-Sept* 10am-7pm daily. *Oct-Apr* 10am-8pm daily. **Admission** US$2; free under-13s.

Tren del Fin del Mundo
RN3, km 3042, 8km (5 miles) from Ushuaia (02901 431600/www.trendelfindelmundo.com.ar). **Rates** US$20 return tourist class. **Credit** V.

Where to eat

Chez Manú
Avenida Luis Fernando Martial 2135 (02901 432253). **Open** 11am-3pm, 8pm-midnight daily. **Average** $$$. **Credit** MC, V.
Opposite Hotel del Glaciar, Chez Manú is home to the best French food in town. Spaciously laid out, with stunning views through the bay windows, it's the ideal spot to treat yourself to a fine wine, good service and tasty home-made bread.

Kaupé
Avenida Roca 470 (02901 422704). **Open** 12.30-3.30pm, 7.30-11.30pm daily. **Average** $$$. **Credit** AmEx, V.
Regional ingredients like trout, sea bass and the ubiquitous king crab are transformed into gourmet delights by chef Ernesto Vivian in this family-run restaurant. There's a nice wine bar too.

Marcopolo
Avenida San Martín 748, entre Juana Fadul y 9 de Julio (02901 430001). **Open** noon-4pm, from 8pm daily. **Average** $$$. **Credit** AmEx, MC, V.
This slick and popular new addition to the Ushuaian culinary scene offers a varied menu in a pleasant atmosphere, with the additional plus of a café menu serving lunch and snacks throughout the day.

Le Martial
Las Hayas Resort Hotel, Avenida Luis Fernando Martial 1650 (02901 430710). **Open** noon-3.30pm, 7.30pm-midnight daily. **Average** $$$$. **Credit** AmEx, DC, MC, V.
In terms of sheer luxurious elegance, Le Martial has no rival in Ushuaia. A five-star restaurant in a five-star hotel (Las Hayas Resort Hotel, *see p164*), its perfectly executed dishes are almost as good as the view. The wine list is the best in town.

Rancho Argentino
Avenida San Martín 237, entre Rivadavia y Gobernador Godoy (02901 430100). **Open** noon-3.30pm, 7.30pm-1.30am daily. **Average** $$. **Credit** AmEx, DC, MC. V.
Rancho Argentino serves up traditional Argentinian dishes, but beyond the sacred *bife* are options like barbecued lamb that will have you ordering seconds.

Tía Elvira
Avenida Maipú 349 (02901 424725). **Open** *Oct-Apr* noon-3pm, 6.30pm-midnight daily. *May-Sept* noon-3pm, 6.30pm-midnight Mon-Sat. **Average** $$. **Credit** AmEx, MC, V.
Facing the Beagle Channel, Tía Elvira is renowned for seafood. Amid photos of prisoners and the Pope, charts on the walls help you make your selection from the complex menu.

Argentinian Patagonia

Volver
Avenida Maipú 37, entre Yaganes y Antártida Argentina (02901 423977). **Open** Oct-Apr 7.30am-midnight Mon; noon-3pm, 7.30pm-midnight Tue-Sun. *May-Sept* 7.30pm-midnight daily. **Average** $$$. **Credit** AmEx, DC, MC, V.

Volver means 'go back', and this place is a genuine blast from the pioneer past: hanging pots and pans, old newspapers, wooden beams and a capacious fireplace by which to toast your toes. The fish of the day is invariably excellent, not to mention the plethora of king crab dishes.

Where to stay

Hotel Albatros
Avenida Maipú 505, entre Lasserre y 25 de Mayo (tel & fax 02901 423206/422658/reservas@albatros hotel.com.ar). **Rates** US$40-$50 single/double; US$50-$62 triple. **Credit** AmEx, MC, V.

Once the top lodging in Ushuaia, 70-room Hotel Albatros has lost a little of the polish, not to mention quite a lot of the paint, that once garnered it this reputation. That said, its central location, views, and top food justify its four-star rating.

Hotel Cabo de Hornos
San Martín y Juan Manuel de Rosas (tel & fax 02901 422187/www.hotelcabodehornos.com.ar). **Rates** US$22-$28 single; US$25-$35 double; US$38-$45triple; US$45-$56 apartment. **Credit** AmEx, MC, V.

Convenient Cabo de Hornos has comfortable rooms, excellent service, and a warm, homely atmosphere radiating over morning coffee and croissants. They also run a small local-history museum.

Hotel Cap Polonio
San Martín 746, entre 9 de Julio y Juana Fadul (02901 422140/fax 422131/www.hotelcappolonio. com.ar). **Rates** US$25-$72 single; US$30-$85 double; US$42-$110triple/suite. **Credit** AmEx, DC, MC, V.

Hotel Cap Polonio is reasonably priced, more modern than most hotels in the area, and about as central as it gets. Book in advance to get a room with a view on the top floor.

Hotel del Glaciar
Avenida Luis Fernando Martial 2355, 4km (2.5 miles) from Ushuaia (02901 430640/ www.hoteldelglaciar.com). **Rates** US$180-$230 double; US$245 $270 triple; US$300-$380 suite. **Credit** AmEx, DC, MC, V.

The 123 rooms of the Hotel del Glaciar are yet another Ushuaia option with stunning views across the bay. All new guests are served welcoming drinks around the fireplace. Restaurant Temaukel serves a slap-up Sunday brunch as well as all other meals.

Las Hayas Resort Hotel
Avenida Luis Fernando Martial 1650, (02901 430710/fax 430719/www.lashayashotel.com). »**Rates** US$210-$240 single/double; US$260-$425 suite. **Credit** AmEx, DC, MC, V.

At the foot of Cerro Martial, the five-star, 92-room Las Hayas boasts stunning views of the city and excellent facilities. Prices reflect its reputation as one of Ushuaia's most luxurious hotels, but rates are justified by the standards of views, service, and the addition of gym pool and spa.

Hotel Tolkeyen
Del Tolkeyen 2145, nr Río Pipo (02901 44-5315/ fax 445318/www.tolkeyenhotel.com.ar). **Rates** US$65-$90 single/double; US$110-$160 suite. **Credit** AmEx, DC, MC, V.

Four kilometres (2.5 miles) out of town on the road to the national park, this hotel in the forest by the water has 34 rooms on its own swath of unspoiled land. A tranquil, rustic retreat.

Resources

Hospital
Hospital Regional de Ushuaia, Maipú y 12 de Octubre (02901 421439/421278).

Internet
Café.net, San Martín 565 (02901 434592).

Police station
Gobernador Derqui 492 (02901 421773).

Post office
San Martín 301 (02901 432500/421347).

Tourist information
Secretaría de Turismo Municipal, San Martín 674, y Juana Fadul (02901 432000/www.tierradel fuego.org.ar). **Open** 8am-10pm Mon-Fri; 9am-8pm Sat, Sun.

Getting there

By air
Arriving by air is definitely the best option. Ushuaia's airport, **Aeropuerto Internacional Malvinas Argentinas** (Península de Ushuaia, 02901 431232) is 7km (4.5 miles) from the town centre, and is served daily by flights to/from Buenos Aires, Río Gallegos, El Calafate, Trelew and Comodoro Rivadavia.

By road
Getting there from the north by road on the RN3 involves Argentinian and Chilean customs points, a ferry crossing and a lot of time on the road. Buses from BA, 3,496km (2,172 miles) away, go via Río Gallegos, 19hrs on top of the 36 to Río Gallegos, and connect with services to Río Grande: 2 daily in winter, 4 in summer, via Tolhuin. Buses to/ from Punta Arenas go daily in summer, 4 per week in winter. There is no central bus terminal – buses stop at company offices.

By sea
Some cruises from BA and Punta Arenas in Chile make stops in Ushuaia, but there is no regular passenger transport by sea.

Chilean Patagonia

Getting Started

Width isn't everything: the thin end of the Patagonian wedge boasts every scenic, seasonal and sporting variation imaginable.

Like the rest of the country, Chilean Patagonia is a skinny affair. Its widest point is at the northern limit, around Temuco, where it is over 250 kilometres (155 miles) wide. South of Puerto Montt it tapers off to just 30 kilometres (19 miles) across near Hornopirén, becoming a mere squiggle hugging the western flank of the Andes, till even those lands dissolve into an archipelago south of Cochrane. Where Chilean Patagonia begins depends on who you ask; this guide – following local trends, especially in the travel business – takes both sides of Patagonia from roughly the same latitude southwards. In Chile this includes the lakes south of the Río Biobío, the island of Chiloé and all lands down to the southernmost points. Officially this area divides – north to south – into Regions IX, X, XI and XII, also called Araucania, Los Lagos, Aisén and Magallanes.

This slender sliver of the planet is a real stunner. Chile is sometimes described as a mirror-image of California with some of British Columbia added in. This useful comparison is based on the landscape of wild woods, glaciers, coastline and, outside Patagonia, the wine country and the desert. It fails, however,

to take into account the fact that Chile has no Hollywood, Los Angeles, nothing as flash or trashy as Disneyland and far, far fewer multi-millionaires – though Douglas Tompkins in **Parque Pumalín** (*see p197*) is a notable exception. Considered frontier country for much of the past 500 years, there is still something wonderfully unspoilt about the Chilean south.

The sheer diversity along the length of Chilean Patagonia – the mountainous terrain, its proximity to the ocean, its weather systems and its rich and complex human history – means zero boredom for travellers. Follow a straight line south either on terra firma or combining overland travel with sea journeys, and you'll see the full spectrum. In the more populated north, an excellent infrastructure combines with luxury services and modern communications, but gradually, heading south, nature in the form of ice, water and wild countryside comes to dominate.

The Lake District was once ruled by the Mapuche, but eventually colonised by European – mainly German – settlers. A drive down the Pan-American Highway, with detours to unmissable sights like the **Volcán Villarrica**

Lakes and rivers, mountains and mysteries: find it all in **Chilean Patagonia.**

(*see p172*) and **Parque Nacional Vicente Pérez Rosales** (*see p183*), is a chance to explore the Valdivian rainforests, camping out or staying in impressive lakeside hotels. The snow-capped peaks of other volcanoes rise away from the verdure, their slopes steaming with sulphuric hot springs.

Chile's south is a haven for trekkers, skiers, birdwatchers and idle romantics, and the chain of national parks makes exploring easy. An undisputed highpoint for hikers and aesthetes alike is **Parque Nacional Torres del Paine** (*see p214*), where the natural drama of granite, ice and glacial lake compete for your attention.

Stretches of the Pacific coast are wild and nigh-on inaccessible, the great exception being **Valdivia** (*see p176*), the cultural hub and a bright, airy, waterlocked city steeped in colonial history. A necessary detour for anyone who wants to see more seaside is **Isla Grande de Chiloé** (*see pp188-193*). Most buildings on this dreamy, misty island are made of wood, from the most ordinary plank ranch to the tiled UNESCO-protected churches, and people are always taking to the water – to fish or dive, to visit families, even to move house.

From Puerto Montt down there's the sea or the lonely lanes of the one road to choose from. Around the Southern Highway avid drivers can discover the remoter corners of Chile's unpopulated hinterland. This area is also an angler's paradise, whether you want to rough it independently or luxuriate in a five-star lodge. Even well-travelled Chileans consider the southern reaches of this road, where Lago General Carrera and Chile's longest river, the Río Baker, push out to sea, uniquely stirring. By boat, the parallel route down to **Glaciar San Rafael** (*see p207*), or beyond through the fjords to Puerto Natales is a faster and easier passage with its own, icy highlights.

Chileans, perhaps inspired by their indigenous predecessors, manage to live anywhere: tiny populations inhabit the archipelago, through Tierra del Fuego, where usually north–south Chile has an easterly kink, and beyond as far as Isla Navarino and the island specks around Cape Horn. At the austral extreme of the continent is the once grand, still fascinating, city of **Punta Arenas** (*see p216*). To travel the whole length of western Patagonia might appear something of a logistical challenge, but down a glass of pisco, slurp a fresh oyster and think: when in Chile…

THE LIE OF THE LAND

As with Argentina, we have divided Chilean Patagonia into five conceptual and physical regions. These are: **The Lake District 2**, a region of watery expanses nestled between

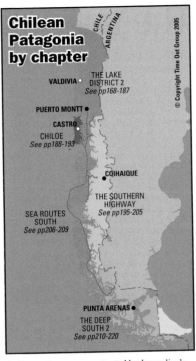

Chilean Patagonia by chapter

VALDIVIA — THE LAKE DISTRICT 2 *See pp168-187*

PUERTO MONTT ●

CASTRO — CHILOE *See pp188-193*

COIHAIQUE ●

THE SOUTHERN HIGHWAY *See pp195-205*

SEA ROUTES SOUTH *See pp206-209*

PUNTA ARENAS ● — THE DEEP SOUTH 2 *See pp210-220*

© Copyright Time Out Group 2005

Andean volcanoes, punctuated by large, lively towns like Temuco and Puerto Montt and thermal bath complexes where you can soak up the hot minerals and shake off symptoms of urban stress; the island of **Chiloé**, where fishermen and farmers keep up old traditions and where there are as many ox-carts as 4x4s; **The Southern Highway**, the land route south, driving from Puerto Montt down the Carreterra Austral to Chaitén and Coihaique, by way of ancient alerce trees, rafting rivers and plummeting cascades; **Sea Routes South**, for those who want to head for the fjords or far south by boat and enjoy glacial views of the Southern Ice Field; and **The Deep South 2**, where local life centres round historic Punta Arenas, but visitors more usually flock to the trekking paradise and wildernesses of Torres del Paine National Park.

The route followed through Chilean Patagonia, roughly a straight line, runs north to south. The text details road connections via mountain passes, as well as lake and sea crossings to the Argentinian side of the Andes. To help you explore whole regions, cross references to destinations in Argentina are given throughout. *See also p237* **Passing over**.

The Lake District 2

From hot springs to brooding volcanoes, Chile's lakeland soothes and inspires.

The Chilean Lake District is, by Patagonian standards, a positively hectic region, with several fair-sized cities – **Temuco**, **Valdivia**, **Osorno** and **Puerto Montt**. Each conurbation jostles for position as 'heart' or 'doorway' of the Chilean south, but much of the prettiest stuff is in the smaller towns and in parks; the cities are less attractive, but are useful hubs for eating, resting, sightseeing and changing buses.

The Lake District incorporates a large section of two northern regions of Chilean Patagonia – Araucanía and Los Lagos. Ruta 5, the Pan-American Highway, runs through a valley between low coastal mountains and the lakes in the Andean foothills, from busy Villarrica down to big Llanquihue. Navigation is easy; it's never more than a one-hour drive from the motorway to one of the lakeside towns. All year, mountainside resorts boast fishing, watersports, rafting and trekking facilities and, in winter, ski centres, such as **Antillanca**, operate on the slopes of conical volcanoes.

Immigration from Germany has left its stamp. Streets are dotted with the steeples of Bavarian churches, people eat *kuchen* with their afternoon tea and you'll even see the odd descendant of an old *colono* wearing a Tyrolean hat. This area is also the original home of the largest concentration of Mapuches. If you ride out to the more remote corners of Araucanía you'll come across indigenous families living off the land as they did of yore. From 1640 right through to 1892, the river where Araucanía begins, the **Río Biobío**, was known as the *frontera* – the official frontier between Spanish (and later Chilean) territory and the lands of the Mapuche. The indigenous descendants of those who resisted assimilation are rightly proud of their history in this beautiful region.

Temuco

There is something culturally schizophrenic about Temuco, the capital of Araucanía (or Region IX) and home to over 240,000 people – with some 50,000 more commuting in every day, for work and for the shops and markets. It's Chile's fastest growing city, with a booming service industry, but at the same time it can sometimes feel like an overgrown village. Araucanía remains one of the poorest regions in the country, and the Mapuche living in outlying rural districts and on the coast still use Temuco as a market town. Fast food outlets and US telecommunications offices are sprouting up and Temuco is struggling to decide exactly what it will be in the future.

As a doorway to Patagonia, it's slightly corny, its **Mercado Municipal** crammed with backpackers rummaging for pseudo-authentic ponchos and woolly hats before moving on to prettier places. The frame of the market building – British-style cast iron – is more culturally edifying than much of what's on sale. But you can eat well here – seafood, local *pastel de choclo* (sweet corn pie) or a regional sweet made from fine fruits – at prices as humble as the setting. This city is also a kind of regional, even world, capital for the Mapuche civilisation and a symbol of indigenous resistance. Anyone expecting a Bolivian-style encounter with ethnically clad natives, however, will be disappointed. Temuco is a modern, fairly westernised city. There is a degree of rusticity evident down at the Feria Libre food market, a vibrant nexus of feverish trading, stimulating smells and mad-looking seafood.

The German legacy, meanwhile, lives on in the names of hotels, street names and in the **Bar Restaurant Club Alemán** where descendants of the first ex-pats still socialise (*see p171*).

The Mapuche are sometimes also called Auracanos but as the friendly staff will tell you, the **Museo Regional de la Araucanía** is not a 'Mapuche museum'. Rather, it is dedicated to the complex history of Temuco and its environs. The museum is small but concise and there is a life-size reconstruction of a Mapuche *ruca* (grass hut) that you can go inside – unless you're a gang of primary schoolkids. Outside is a pleasant garden, planted with Canary palms.

With so many peaks and forests nearby you might think a trek up Temuco's diminutive local hill **Cerro Nielol** not worth the trouble, but believe the Temucanos when they tell you it's special. Aside from the political-ecological importance of preserving a 'Monumento Natural' bang in the middle of a major town, the lush forests and picnic areas are truly lovely. Compared to the national parks, it's only a smallish mound but packs in wild vegetation, a good information centre and a restaurant (045 214336, closed dinner Sun, $$) and huge views (though misty in winter).

EXCURSIONS

If you want something bigger and wilder still, there's no shortage of options. The closest park is **Parque Nacional Conguillío** (pronounced 'cong-ee-YEE-yo'), about 80 kilometres (50 miles) east of the city. One fair-sized lake, the park's namesake, and three others – Verde, Arco Iris and Captrén – are at the heart of dense woodlands of native trees, with sculptures of recently spilt, jagged lava and waterfalls in exposed areas. There are three entry points to the park, one of which leads to the foot of the twin-cratered **Volcán Llaima** – 3,050 metres high (10,007 feet); one of the craters was shot to bits by an eruption in 1984 and reawoke in 1996. Near the volcano is a sector called Los Paraguas (The Umbrellas), in reference to the shape of the very old monkey-puzzle trees growing here – they lose their lower branches over the centuries. The BBC filmed *Walking With Dinosaurs* here, proof that their researchers found the greenery wild enough to look authentically a few million years old. Half a dozen campsites and the same number of marked trails, as well as picnic areas make the park a popular weekend break with Temucanos. Skiing on the volcano is possible in winter at **Las Araucarias**, and while small-scale and not heavily marketed, the resort is scenically attractive. Conguillío, which gets up to a thousand visitors a day in the fair seasons, is perhaps the most developed park in the region, in terms of infrastructure; in the heart of the park is 'kilometre zero', the official start-point for the country's projected Sendero de Chile (*see p176* **Walk this way**).

Two other national parks, **PN Nahuelbuta** and **PN Tolhuaca**, are close to Temuco, the former of particular importance as it is located in a mountain range near the Pacific coast. Climb the 1,380-metre (4,528-feet) **Piedra del Aguila** to see, in the distance, the ocean and the Andes; trails get you close to the araucaria trees swathed in lichen. Tolhuaca, near Victoria, has great trekking and birdwatching and hot springs, including a steamy pool inside a cave.

Centro de Ski Las Araucarias
Volcán Llaima, PN Conguillío, Sector Los Paraguas (information 045 562313/www.skia raucarias.cl). **Open** *June-Oct* daylight hrs. **Rates** *Ski pass* US$22-$30 per day; US$15-$22 under-10s. **No credit cards.**

Feria Libre
Avenida Pinto, y Balmaceda. **Open** 7am-2pm Mon-Fri; 7am-4pm Sat; 7am-5pm Sun. **Admission** free.

Mercado Municipal
Diego Portales 980, entre Bulnes y Aldunate. **Open** *Jun-Nov* 8am-7pm Mon-Sat; 8.30am-4pm Sun. *Dec-May* 8am-8pm Mon-Sat; 8.30am-4pm Sun. **Admission** free.

Monumento Natural Cerro Nielol
Avenida Prat (045 298222). **Open** *Park* 8.30am-8.30pm daily. *Information centre* (inside park) 8.45am-12.45pm, 2.15-6pm daily. **Admission** US$2; US70¢ under-12s. **No credit cards.**

Don't come to the **Chilean Lake District** without your hat and poncho.

Museo Regional de la Araucanía

Avenida Alemania 084, entre Pasaje del Bosque y Thiers (045 730062). **Open** 9am-5pm Mon-Fri; 11am-5pm Sat; 11am-1pm Sun. **Admission** US$1; US70¢ concession; US40¢ under-12s. Free to all Sun. **No credit cards.**

PN Conguillio

Entrances Sector Norte, Caprén; Sector Sur, Truful Truful; Sector Oeste, de los Paraguas (045 298201). **Open** 8.30am-6pm daily. *Apr-Sept* Sector Oeste only. **Admission** Sector Norte & Sur US$6; US$2 under-12s. *Sector Oeste* free. **No credit cards.**

Where to eat & drink

Bar Restaurant Club Alemán

Senador Estebanez 772, entre Holandesa y Alemania (045 240034). **Open** 11am-midnight daily. **Average** $$$. **No credit cards.**
Dark, oaky and non-private, the Club Alemán serves the best of the wurst in town. The big menu offers hearty mains like Kassler cutlets and sauerkraut or Frankfurt steak, washed down with Kunstmann ales from Valdivia and Chilean wines.

Madonna Pizza

Avenida Alemania 0660, entre Senador Estebanez y Hostterter (045 329393). **Open** noon-4pm, 7pm-midnight daily. **Average** $$. **Credit** AmEx, DC, MC, V.
Probably the town's most reliable place for pizza, Madonna's has heaps of varieties from margharita to seafood. Popular with young Temucanos.

Marítimo Jairo's

Avenida Alemania 0830 (045 248849). **Open** noon-3pm, 7pm-midnight daily. **Average** $$$. **Credit** AmEx, DC, MC, V.
Jairo's is formal and a bit crusty but serves fine fish – the salmon is succulent – seafood and pasta. Live music is from an organist and his Casio – groovy!

Pub Restaurant Brumby

Calle Thiers 504 (045 406484). **Open** 8pm-4am Mon-Sat. **Average** $$. **Credit** AmEx, DC, MC, V.
Lively young eaterie-cum-tavern for beer, flirtation, seafood and grilled steaks; the staff are as welcoming as the atmosphere.

Restaurante El Criollito

Local 38, Mercado Municipal, Diego Portales 980, entre Bulnes y Aldunate (045 212583). **Open** 9am-7pm daily. **Average** $$$. **No credit cards.**
Turkey casserole, seafood, oven-cooked suckling pig and empanadas are just some of the scrumptious dishes offered by this stalwart of the old market.

Tien Xiang

Avenida Prat 295, y Rodríguez (045 214485). **Open** 11.30am-5pm, 6.30pm-1am Mon-Thur; 11.30am-1am Fri-Sun. **Average** $$$. **Credit** AmEx, DC, MC, V.
The usual noodles, rice and assorted sauces, using local fish and seafood as the base for many dishes, are available at Temuco's best, biggest Chinese.

Where to stay

Frontera Hotel y Centro de Convenciones

Bulnes 733, entre Antonio Varas y Bello (045 200400/www.hotelfrontera.cl). **Rates** US$80 single/double; US$95 suite. **Credit** AmEx, DC, MC, V.
The Frontera offers business accommodation, with international corporate services and lavish buffets in the restaurant. For travellers the piano bar is the spot for a late cocktail after a hard day's commuting to virgin forests and lakes.

Hostal Austria

Hochstetter 599, entre Alemania y Holandesa (045 247169/www.hostalaustria.cl). **Rates** US$25 single; US$435 double. **No credit cards.**
Big breakfasts in what looks like grandma's best parlour, warmly decorated rooms (with cable TV) and easy access to the centre of town are the high points at this popular backpacker hotel.

Hotel Continental

Varas 708, y Vicuña Mackenna (045 238973/www.turismochile.cl/continental). **Rates** US$37-$40 single; US$46-$50 double. **Credit** AmEx, DC, MC, V.
Old-fashioned and family-run, the once grand Hotel Continental may now be a little creaky, but it's full of history. Salvador Allende and Pablo Neruda have graced these highly-polished interiors.

Hotel Don Eduardo

Andrés Bello 755, entre Vicuña Mackenna y Prat (045 214133/www.chilecontact.com/es_chile/Hotel DonEduardo_376.html). **Rates** US$75-$90 single/double; US$100-$110 suite. **Credit** AmEx, DC, MC, V.
Nine-storey Don Eduardo is a modern tower block apart-hotel with comfy – if slightly fusty – big rooms; great views and friendly service too.

Hotel Terraverde

Avenida Arturo Prat 0220, y Cerro Nielol (045 239999/www.panamericanahoteles.cl). **Rates** US$105 single; US$115 double; US$130 suite. **Credit** AmEx, DC, MC, V.
The Hotel Terraverde is the city's most luxurious, a smart, imposing block at the foot of Cerro Nielol, with a good restaurant and pool. Rooms are lavish and there's every additional service imaginable.

Resources

Hospital

Hospital Regional, Montt 115 (045 296100).

Internet

Cibercity, Avenida Prat 350 (045 270500).

Police station

Luis Claro Solar 1284 (045 211604).

Post office

Diego Portales 801 (045 295100).

Chilean Patagonia

Tourist information

Sernatur, Bulnes 586, y Luis Claro Solar (045 211969/www.sernatur.cl). **Open** *Mar-mid Dec* 9am-1pm, 3-5.30pm Mon-Fri. *Mid Dec-Feb* 8.30am-8pm daily.

Getting there

By air

Regular direct flights from Santiago (1hr15mins) arrive at Temuco's **Aeropuerto Maquehue** (045 337782), 7km (4.5 miles) from the city on Ruta 5. From the airport a taxi to Temuco costs US$5, to Villarrica US$45 and to Pucón US$48. Buses run regularly to Temuco and Pucón from the airport. The city is also a stopover point for flights to Osorno and Puerto Montt.

By road

Temuco is on Ruta 5, the Pan-American Highway, 677km (421 miles) from Santiago and 339km (211 miles) from Puerto Montt; several buses every hour in either direction plus onwards connections from the bus station **Terminal Rural**, at Pinto and Balmaceda, to Villarrica, Pucón and parks and lakes.

By train

Temuco is the end of the only railway line south. Daily trains run to/from Santiago, via Curico, Talca and Chillán, in 13hrs. Tickets cost US$10 for a seat, US$27 for a bed, US$75 for a private compartment one-way. The station (045 233416) is at Barros Arana and Lautaro Navarro and there's a ticket office (045 233522) at Bulnes 582, just off the plaza.

Pucón

Almost everyone loves Pucón. It could be because this pretty village-cum-town on the shore of **Lago Villarrica** presents lots of trekking possibilities in nearby parks. Or it could be the skiing, the climate, the hot springs or a whole load of easily enjoyable activities on offer – but the thrill, more than anything else, is the stunning proximity of **Volcán Villarrica**. Like a strange magnet, the conic, snow-clad summit draws the eyes skywards wherever you wander. Sooner or later – though probably immediately – you'll want to abandon the coffee bars and lake gawping for an encounter with the steep slopes or the caves that bore into them. Pucón is the departure point for the volcano, for **PN Huerquehue** and **PN Villarica** and also for visiting Argentina's Lanin volcano and national park (*see p90*).

Unless you want to ignore all this and stay in **Hotel del Lago**'s casino (*see p175*), Pucón's main functions will be as a bed, a meal and a booking office. Not that it's ugly: green, clean and compact, Pucón is a bucolic little town for a daytime stroll and in the evenings, a wander along Avenida O'Higgins or Fresia street shows up the buzzing eating and drinking scene. On

the edge of town are two black-sand beaches – one, **Playa Grande**, to the north on the open lake and another west in the protected inlet called **La Poza**. At both you can swim and do watersports, and from La Poza, tourist launches depart across Lake Villarrica in summer.

There's an easy walk along the side of the lake; turn right at the northern end of Ansorena down Costanera Gudenschwager and just walk. You can also get mountain bikes and horses to explore near the town, play golf, go whitewater rafting, get climbing guides or anything else you fancy. As well as numerous tour operators, Pucón is also a handicrafts and food centre.

There are lots of hotels in Pucón, from the friendly and familiar to newer architectural affronts to the scenery. Only one is worth a visit for its setting alone – **Antumalal** (*see p174*), a Bauhaus-style building on a steep cliff just minutes by taxi or half an hour's walk on the road towards the town of Villarrica.

EXCURSIONS

Volcán Villarrica is eight kilometres (five miles) from town at the north-eastern extreme of the 610-square-kilometre (236-square-mile) **Parque Nacional Villarrica**. Along with Llaima, the 2,840-metre-high (9,318-feet) Villarrica is one of Chile's most active volcanoes, spewing forth its molten entrails ten times during the 20th century. Part of a chain of five active volcanoes forming the Chilean front row of the Pacific Fire Rim, Villarrica can be seen smoking by day or glowing by night and a climb to the top is rewarded with a slightly disturbing view of the bubbling fires of magma rising up from the earth's core. You can walk up the volcano and back down in about four hours but you must go with a guide as crampons are needed and the moody weather and crevasses can make the climb tricky. There's a CONAF information hut in Sector Rucapillán. In winter the **Centro de Ski Villarrica** is a busy skiing centre, still informal but increasingly catching the attention of Chilean and international skiers.

Another volcano, **Quetrupillán**, lies within the park boundaries, and stands out for not standing out – its low-slung crater last blew off during a phreatic (steam-driven) eruption in 1872. A trek round the cone takes three or four days; the park's campsites are by the volcano.

To get to the other nearby park, **PN Huerquehue**, take a north-east road for 35 kilometres (22 miles) towards Lago Caburga, where there are several campsites, hotels and white-sanded beaches. Within the park, there is a good four-hour return walk – the Tres Lagos – past Lago Tinquilco, in the heart of the lake, and up to the araucaria forests at the top of a hill. The sometimes steep trail cuts through a

Guanacos grazing near **Pucón**. *See p172.*

dark, dense forest of trees and ferns, with views back to Lake Tinquilco. Up here, about three kilometres (two miles) in, is **Refugio Tinquilco** (09 5392728, www.tinquilco.cl, double US$40-$50), a fairly luxurious refuge which allows you to bed down in the silent forests. The trail continues up to a waterfall, the Nido de Aguila (pretty in summer, dramatic in winter) and three lovely lakes – Lagunas Chica, El Toro and Verde – where you can camp and, if you dare, swim. At the very top are perhaps Chile's most impressive araucaria trees, ranked up on the ridges like an army of native warriors.

Lago Caburga and PN Huerquehue can be visited independently or with tours, some of which combine visits with rafting on nearby Trancura and Liucura rivers. Check with **Enjoy Tour** (Ansorena 123, 045 442213, www.enjoytour.cl) at the Hotel del Lago for a whole range of excursions. The roads become tricky in winter, but you can still explore Huerquehue on foot, and snow and ice add something to the scenery. There's a good park rangers' office and visitor centre inside the park. If you want information on both parks before heading out of Pucón, go to the CONAF office in town (1st floor, Lincoyán 336, 045 443781, closed 1-2.30pm, all Sat, Sun).

The hot springs of **Termas de Huife** – a hotel and health complex – are a short ride from Huerquehue or Pucón and are a welcome rest from climbing, with food and beer as well as massages and treatments to melt the muscles. There are lots of different styles of cabins to stay in, ranging in price from US$130 to $300 per night, some right by the river. Guests have included top Chilean football-player Marcelo Salas and ex-Miss Chile Cecilia Bolocco. For a less-organised dip, there are *pozones* (holes) up the same hill where you can just jump in, whatever the season.

Centro de Ski Volcán Villarrica

Volcán Villarrica (045 441901/www.skipucon.cl). **Open** *Jul-Oct* 9am-5pm daily. **Rates** *Ski hire* US$15 per day. *Ski pass* US$20-$32; US$14-$24 under-12s. **Credit** AmEx, DC, MC, V.

Parque Nacional Huerquehue

Entrance via Camino a Caburgua from Pucón. Open 8.30am-6pm daily. **Admission** US$4; US$2 under-12s. **Credit** AmEx, DC, MC, V.

Parque Nacional Villarrica

Camino Pucón-Villarrica, km 25. **Open** 8.30am-6pm daily. **Admission** US$2.50; US$1 under-12s. **No credit cards.**

Termas de Huife

33km (21 miles) from Pucón (045 441222/www. termashuife.cl). **Open** 9am-8pm daily. **Rates** US$12-$15; US$6-$8 under-10s. **Credit** AmEx, DC, MC, V.

Where to eat & drink

Bar Mamas & Tapas

O'Higgins 597, y Arauco (045 449002). **Open** 5pm-3am Mon-Sat. **Average** $$. **Credit** AmEx, DC, MC, V.
This lively little joint buzzes in summer and winter, serving up good small bites and lots of beer. A classic pre-dancing place and very sociable.

Buonatesta

Fresia 243, interior, entre Urrutia y Jerónimo Alderete (045 444627/www.interpatagonia.com /buonatesta). **Open** *Nov-May* noon-3am daily. *June-Oct* noon-4pm, 6-11.30pm daily. **Average** $$. **Credit** AmEx, DC, MC, V.
Buonatesta is ideal for pizza, pastas or just grabbing an early evening beer. The cabin-style decor and friendly waitresses make it warm and welcoming.

Restaurant Ecole

General Urrutia 592, y Arauco (045 443201/www. ecole.cl). **Open** *Dec-Mar* 8am-midnight daily. *Apr-Nov* 8am-10pm daily. **Average** US$2-$6.50. **Credit** AmEx, DC, MC; V.
This is a vegetarian nirvana – quiches and crêpes are mouthwatering, as are hot soups or cool salads, cookies, grainy bread, and even that good old faithful, vegetarian lasagne.

Restaurante Marmonhi

Ecuador 175, entre Lincoyán y Caupolicán (045 441972). **Open** *Dec-Mar* 9am-midnight daily. *Apr-Nov* 10am-10pm daily. **Average** $$. **No credit cards.**
Marmonhi is a lovely-looking, lakeside wooden restaurant, with a menu of Chilean standards – fish and meat to the fore – but a notch above other traditional places in town.

Restaurante Milla Rahue

O'Higgins 460, y Palguín (045 441610). **Open** *Apr-Nov* 10am-midnight daily. *Dec-Mar* 9am-2am daily. **Average** $$$. **Credit** AmEx, DC, MC, V.
This is the place that locals recommend for fine grilled fish steaks and seafood. Outdoor tables are ideal for soaking up the lunchtime rays.

Where to stay

Altos del Lago

10km (6 miles) from Pucón (045 450022/www.altos dellago.com). **Rates** US$39-$107 cabin for 2; US$43-$107 cabin for 4; US$83-$143 cabin for 8. **Credit** AmEx, DC, MC, V.
Altos del Lago has classy cabins by the lake with volcanic views and stylish rooms. It's an ideal base from which to launch for rafting, trekking, horse riding or skiing excursions.

Antumalal

Casilla 84 (045 441011/www.antumalal.com). **Rates** US$90-$135 single; US$115-$170 double; US$260-$500 chalet. **Credit** AmEx, DC, MC, V.

Built in 1950 by Czech immigrants, Antumalal is tasteful, minimalist and luxurious – Queen Elizabeth II and Neil Armstrong have been guests – and has a great restaurant and views to die for.

Cabañas Hueney

10km (6 miles) from Pucón (045 450933/www.inter patagonia.com/hueney). **Rates** US$60-$135 cabins for 2-6; US$85-$200 cabins for 8-10. **Credit** DC, MC, V.
Competition for 'best cabin on Lake Villarrica' is fierce, and the Hueney, set in attractive woodlands, with pleasant verandas and a fine pool, is a strong contender for the title.

Ecole

General Urrutia 592, y Arauco (045 443201/ www.ecole.cl). **Rates** US$14-$17 single; US$30 double; US$6-$8 per person dorm. **Credit** AmEx, DC, MC, V.
Pucón prides itself on being the youthful hiking hub of the lakes – in contrast to Puerto Varas' middle-aged bourgeois appeal – and this trendy hostel for the international backpacking brigade is the It-place.

Hotel del Lago

Miguel Ansorena 23, y Pedro de Valdivia (045 291000/www.hoteldellago.cl). **Rates** US$180-$300 double; US$400-$400 suite; US$1,500 presidential suite. **Credit** AmEx, DC, MC, V.
This latest addition to Pucón's booming hotel scene, is five-star city-style luxury: a cavernous, modern lobby, room service, floor shows and a casino.

Resources

Hospital

Hospital San Francisco, Uruguay 325 (045 441177).

Internet

Brinck House Cyber Café, Miguel Ansorena 243 (045 443357).

Police station

Avenida Libertador Bernardo O'Higgins 135 (045 441196).

Post office

Fresia 483 (045 441164).

Tourist information

Información Turística, O' Higgins 483, y Palguín (045 293002). **Open** Apr-Nov 8.30am-7pm daily. Dec-Mar 8.30am-10pm daily.

Getting there

By air

Aeródromo de Pucón on Ruta 199 towards Caburga, km 4, is 15mins from town. In summer LanChile flies four times a week from Santiago.

By road

Pucón is 109km (68 miles) from Temuco, 26km (16 miles) from Villarrica. Regular daily bus services connect all three towns.

Villarrica

Coming from Temuco or leaving Pucón you'll pass through Villarrica. The lake shore along the Camino Villarrrica–Pucón road joining the two is one of Chile's most important tourist centres – lots of facilities as well as traffic in summer and, sadly, too much construction on the lakeside. How far the builders can go remains to be seen – Chilean law protects the coasts of lakes from private initiatives bent on acquiring exclusive lakeside tracts – but some visual damage is already done.

Somewhat less quaint than its touristy neighbour, the lake's namesake is nonetheless worth a stopover. Like an old cowboy town it has a slightly more urbane feel about it and you'll pay less for a decent snack than in Pucón. Villarrica was actually founded in 1552 but the Mapuches laid siege to it and kicked out or killed the Spanish settlers. By 1600, the region was theirs again – the town was only refounded in 1882. In the third week of February there is a week-long celebration of Mapuche culture.

EXCURSIONS

Many people go from Villarrica to Valdivia via the Pan-American Highway, but if you've got a car, motorbike or bicycle – and are good at reading maps – you can take a detour on the long, winding **Circuito de los Siete Lagos** (Seven Lakes Circuit). Taking you past Lakes Calafquén, Pellaifa, Neltume, Pirehueico, Lácar (in Argentina but draining into the Pirihueico), Panguipulli and Riñihue – all linked by short rivers – the road also visits **Lican Ray**, a lovely small town at the heart of the lake region and a good place to spend a night or two. The glacial moraines here are responsible for the dramatic countryside – and difficult roads. Five of these lakes drain into **Panguipulli**, which in turn flows into Riñihue where, at the western end, there is a river that flows to the Pacific.

Where to eat & drink

A pleasant, modern place with good coffee, fresh fruit juices and filling steak sandwiches is **Café Bar 2001** (Camilo Henríquez 379, 045 411470, $). The walls are a museum-cum-tribute to keyrings, with fobs from everywhere you can imagine. Part of three-star Hotel Monte Bianco, serving international food with an Italian bias, **Bella Cuccina** (Pedro de Valdivia 1011, 045 411798, $$$) does a good thin-base *pizza a la piedra*; seafood and fish are also specialities. The cosy wooden bar room is ideal for beers and cocktails. The cook at **Restaurante Yachtingkiel** (General Körner 145, 045 411631, $$$) has been turning out the house

Walk this way

Most countries and even continents have their own official trails. There's England's cute 505-kilometre (314-mile) Pennine Way, or the 1,930-kilometre (1,200-mile) Pacific Northwest trail in the United States. But Chile is 4,270 kilometres (2,653 miles) long and a matter of time before it came up with the hill walk to beat all hill walks.

The Sendero de Chile will connect Visviri on the Peruvian border to the extreme south of Tierra del Fuego, and will be suitable for walking, cycling or horse riding. Challenges will include the deserts of Chile's north and the southern icefields, but, perhaps even more ambitiously, the government's environmental commission, CONAMA, hopes to have the Chilean Way up and running by 2010, in time for the bicentennial of the first declaration of independence.

Progress is slow but steady. CONAMA is hoping that 1,000 kilometres (620 miles) of the trail will be usable by early 2006. The sections of the trail are not yet contiguous; rather than start at the north and grind their way south, CONAMA has opted to develop shorter stretches in regions with contrasting environments (desert, lakes, cordillera, and so on) on a piecemeal basis. Only later will the sections be joined up, giving trekkers the opportunity to walk from A to B without having to take a side trip through Z.

So, just 3,000 kilometres (1,863 miles) and five years to go. Workers are already asking themselves what generations of mad backpackers will be wondering for centuries to come: when will I get there?

The website www.senderodechile.cl has up-to-date news, press releases and maps.

speciality – trout – for two decades now. Superb views of the lake and the volcano add yet more to its appeal.

Where to stay

Cheaper than Pucón, Villarrica has *hosterías* and cabin complexes. Plush **Hotel El Ciervo** (General Körner 241, 045 411215, www.el ciervo.cl, double US$57-$77) is set in lovely gardens by the beach and serves up a fine German breakfast. Out-of-town **Hotel El Parque** (Camino Villarrica-Pucón, km 2.5, 045 411120, www.hotelelparque.cl, double US$40-$65) has a hotel and cabins. It's a bit cheaper and just as grand, with an English-style lawn, tennis courts and lake views.

Resources

Hospital
Hospital Villarrica, San Martín 460 (045 411169).

Internet
Graficom, Valentín Letelier 754 (045 416360).

Police station
Manuel Antonio Matta 230 (045 411433).

Post office
Anfión Muñoz 315 (045 412860).

Tourist information
Oficina de Informaciones Turísticas, Pedro de Valdivia 1070, entre Zeger y Acevedo (045 206618/ www.villarrica.co.cl). **Open** *Apr-Nov* 9am-1pm, 2.30-6.30pm Mon-Fri. *Dec-Mar* 8.30am-11pm daily.

Getting there

By road
Villarrica is 83km (52 miles) south of Temuco and 26km (16 miles) west of Pucón (either airport is convenient). Lots of buses run regularly along the Temuco–Pucón road. There's a terminal for Buses Jac at Francisco Bilbao 610 (045 411447) and for Tur Bus at Anfión Muñoz 657 (045 413652).

Valdivia

The history books will tell you Valdivia is about 'The Germans', but unless you are on a Teutonic Tour of the Chilean lakes, your first impression will be rather more elemental: water. Not quite on the coast, Valdivia is bounded by **Ríos Valdivia**, **Calle Calle** and **Cruces**.

Unlike the other large towns in this region, which only came into existence in the late 19th century, Valdivia was founded way back in 1552 before being besieged and sacked by the local Mapuche tribespeople. Nothing if not persistent, the Spanish founded it again in 1640

– and since they valued strategic coastal towns far more than inland settlements it was eventually fortified in 1671.

The town is pleasant but unremarkable. Some old buildings have survived seismic and manmade incursions, but the general impression is of flux and encroaching modernity – for which read cement. The best place is down on the waterfront Feria Fluvial where seals bark at busy, tough-looking guys gutting and filleting the day's catch of hake, corvina and conger eel, among other seafood and vegetable stalls. Cross **Avenida Prat** and you can try some of these things freshly cooked, usually for a bargain price at the numerous roadside cafés. The eateries are much of a muchness but you can't go wrong just slipping into the nearest one when hunger beckons. Across the Pedro de Valdivia bridge at the end of Carampangue Street, is **Isla Teja**, a tranquil suburb of the main town.

Valdivia as it is a university town and an important regional centre for the arts, with a major film festival every October (*see p46*). Among the cultural highlights are the eclectic **Museo de Arte Contemporáneo** and the **Museo Histórico Antropológico Maurice Van de Maele**, with a sizeable collection of colonial, Germanic and archaeological items.

EXCURSIONS

Fuerte Niebla – full name Fuerte de la Pura y Limpia Concepción de Monfort de Lemus, or the Fort of the Pure and Clean Conception – is located out at Niebla, a beach resort some 18 kilometres (11 miles) from Valdivia. Recognised as a National Monument, the 18th-century site boasts 18 guns, a wall built of local cancahua stone to prevent access from the sea and a furnace for heating the cannonballs. Three other fortresses – at Isla Mancera, **Castillo de San Pedro de Alcántara**, at Corral, **Castillo de San Sebastián** (the most impressive of all) and at Amargos, **Castillo de San Luis de Amargos** (for all – 063 471816, closed noon-1.30pm Dec-Mar, admission Castillo de San Sebastián US$1, others free). They are also National Monuments and are part of the same excursion that takes in Niebla. In 1820, these battlements were used against the Chileans as the last dregs of Spanish imperialism struggled to maintain a stronghold – Chile's foremost naval hero, Cochrane, would have none of it and stormed the garrisons in a nocturnal assault.

Lots of companies do cruises to the forts, leaving from the jetty at Prat and Arauco. **Catamarán Extasis** (063 212464) and **Motonave Neptuno** (063 218952) seem to be among the most efficient. They work all year round, closing around lunch for an hour.

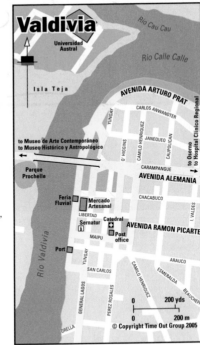

A less bellicose approach to Valdivia's waters is to go birdwatching. Around 70 species can be spotted on and around the city's main river. Among more common birds, specialists will enjoy seeing the slender-billed parakeet, the Chilean tinamou and the black-throated huet-huet. **Lodge Santa María** (*see p178*) is a lovely country house, catering for serious birdwatchers who want to concentrate on their passion in peace and comfort.

Feria Fluvial
Avenida Prat. **Open** 8am-3pm daily.

Fuerte Niebla
Niebla (063 282084). **Open** *Apr-Nov* 10am-5.30pm Tue-Sun. *Dec-Mar* 10am-7pm Tue-Sun. **Admission** US$1; US40¢ concessions; free under-8s.

Museo de Arte Contemporáneo
Los Laureles, Isla Teja (063 221968/www.mac valdivia.uach.cl). **Open** *Oct-Apr* 9am-1pm, 2.30-6.30pm daily. **Admission** US$1.50; US70¢ concessions.

Museo Histórico y Antropológico Maurice Van de Maele
Los Laureles (063 212872/www.uach.cl). **Open** *Dec-Mar* 10am-1pm, 2-8pm daily. *Apr-Nov* 10am-1pm, 2-6pm Thur-Sun. **Admission** US$2; US45¢ concessions.

Chilean Patagonia

Valdivia's **Isla Teja**. *See p177.*

Where to eat & drink

Approach

Avenida Los Robles 150, y Los Laureles, Isla Teja
(063 234810). **Open** 11am-1am daily. **Average** $$
Credit AmEx, DC, MC, V.

Over the bridge on Isla Teja, trendy, friendly and
cosy Argentinian-owned Approach is the best place
in town for pizzas and pastas.

Cervecería Kunstmann

Ruta T350 No.950, Niebla (063 292969/www.
cerveza-kunstmann.cl). **Open** *Apr-Nov* noon-midnight
Mon-Sat; noon-7pm Sun. *Dec-Mar* noon-1am daily.
Average $$$. **Credit** AmEx, DC, MC, V.

If you've done the guided tour, try the bock and the
pale ale with a few Germanic or Chilean bites –
cooked meats, cheeses, wurst and mains like smoked
pork and ribs cooked in beer.

Restaurant Don Pedro

Carampangue 190, entre O'Higgins y AvenidaPrat
(063 290535). **Open** 8am-midnight daily. **Average**
$$$. **Credit** DC, MC, V.

Working hard to raise town standards, this hotel
restaurant serves good-looking, creative seafood –
the clams in parmesan are exquisite – as well as
pasta and meat dishes.

Restaurant La Perla del Sur

Avenida Prat 500, y Libertad (063 245531). **Open**
June-Nov 8.30am-8pm daily. *Dec-May* 8.30am-1am
daily. **Average** $$. **Credit** AmEx, DC, MC, V.

This cantina-style seafood place is unfussy, unflashy
and ideal for trying the produce of the port. Fish and
molluscs dominate, with good *pailas* (runny soups).

Where to stay

Germania Hostelling International

Avenida Picarte 873, y Alemania (063 212405).
Rates US$12 per person dorm. **No credit cards.**

This great wooden house turned hostel has 30-odd
beds, common rooms and a café. No frills, no
luxuries and nothing to complain about.

Hotel Naguilán

General Lagos 1927 (063 212851/fax 063 219130/
www.hotelnaguilan.com). **Rates** US$50-$78 single;
US$62-$89 double; US$120 suite. **Credit** AmEx,
DC, MC, V.

This grand-looking out of town place is part of the
Best Western chain. A river setting and the gardens
are its strengths and the big bungalow architecture
is a clever pastiche of local German style.

Hotel Pedro de Valdivia

Carampangue 190, y O'Higgins (063 212931).
Rates US$50-$95 single; US$60-$120 double; US$90-
$185 suite. **Credit** AmEx, DC, MC, V.

The façade looks plain, but everything inside is old-
style smart with a popular and lively bar and a good
restaurant, Don Pedro (*see above*). For sunny days,
there's a pool in the big garden.

Hotel Puerta del Sur

Los Lingues 950, Isla Teja (063 224500/www.hotel
puertadelsur.com). **Rates** US$100-$130 single;
US$125-$140 double; US$185-$207 suite. **Credit**
AmEx, DC, MC, V.

This bulwark of a building has great views over the
Río Cruces and is a tranquil place to bed down.
Guests have free use of bikes, and there's a pool,
sauna, gym, open-air jacuzzi and even canoes.

Lodge Santa María

Information and bookings, General Lagos 1868
(09 6423279/www.hualamo.com). **Closed** Apr-Aug.
Rates US$105-$115 per person, all inclusive.
Credit AmEx, DC, MC, V.

To get in the spirit of things, you have to catch a
boat to get here. With water everywhere, lots of land,
absolute silence, great grub and friendly hosts, it's
hard to find finer lodging. This is a birder's place,
though, so don't expect lots of TV and techno nights.

Resources

Hospital
Clínico Regional Valdivia, Simpson 850 (063 297000).

Internet
Café Phonet, Libertad 127 (063 341054).

Police station
Beauchef 1025 (063 213000).

Post office
O'Higgins 575 (063 212167).

Tourist information
Sernatur, Avenida Prat 555, entre Libertad y Maipú (063 342300/serna13a@entelchile.net). **Open** *Apr-Nov* 8.30am-5.30pm Mon-Fri. *Dec-Mar* 8.30am-8pm Mon-Fri; 10am-8pm Sat, Sun.

Getting there

By air
Aeropuerto Pichoy (063 272295) is 32km (20 miles) from Valdivia on Ruta 5 Norte. Flights from Santiago arrive via Concepción and Temuco.

By road
Valdivia is 3hrs from Villarrica and a short drive from the Pan-American Highway. There's a bus terminal at Anfión Muñoz 360 and **Buses Jac** (063 212212) and **Tur Bus** (063 226010) offer regular connections to the lakes, Temuco and Puerto Montt via Osorno.

Osorno

Passing through here researching his book *Lost Cowboys*, Hank Wangford called Osorno a 'German cattle town' and stayed at the Riga Guesthouse. There are indeed significant groups of Lithuanians, Latvians and Germans and these, melded into a Hispanic *huaso* (cowboy) culture, give the otherwise drab-looking town a bit of colour and life.

The best place to see some architectural colour is on Mackenna Street, where six houses are listed as Monumentos Nacionales. These fine wooden buildings have tiled roofs supported by columns that jut out to create pretty rain-free verandas. All have German names and date to the 1870-90 immigration period. O'Higgins, Matta and Cochrane are also dotted with fine residences; in this same neighbourhood, at the **Museo Histórico Municipal**, you can catch up on Osorno's earlier history, from the first founding, through Mapuche rebellion – when the city was abandoned in some haste by the Spanish – to the 'repopulation' of Osorno begun at the end of the 18th century. On the banks of the Río Rahue are the ruins of the Fuerte Reina Luisa (1793),

built to honour the wife of King Carlos IV of Spain – at the order of local governor Ambrosio O'Higgins. He lived there while coordinating the repopulation programme.

Cheese and, especially, meat are good in Osorno and you can visit the biggest cattle market in Chile – the **Feria Ganadera de Osorno** (on Inés de Suárez) – a picture-book amphitheatre of mooing, bidding and bustle.

EXCURSIONS
Two lakes lie west of Osorno. Lago Puyehue, named after the puye – a sprat of a fish considered a delicacy here – is on Ruta 215, the main link road for the Argentinian border, and there are several hostels on the southern lake shore. Visiting the latter allows you to take in a great little private museum, the **Auto Museo Moncopulli**, with wonderful Studebakers and lots of car-related desirable objects, and the small town of Entrelagos, where there's a turning south to long **Lago Rupanco**, a popular fishing area. Camping is possible at both lakes. The unmetalled Rupanco road continues, slowly, to Puerto Octay and Ensenada on Lago Llanquihue, taking you through Chile's dairy country – 80 per cent of the country's milk is produced here. North-west of Osorno are Lagos Ranco and Maihue. These are off the beaten – or rather, muddy – track, and the woods, landscape and lifestyle are native and basic. Fishing and camping are possible and you can do watersports on Ranco's western river outlet, the Río Bueno.

Auto Museo Moncopulli
Ruta 215, Km 25 (064 210744/www.moncopulli.cl). **Open** *Apr-Nov* 10am-6pm daily. *Dec-Mar* 10am-8pm daily. **Admission** US$3; US$2 concessions; US$1 under 10s.

Feria Ganadera de Osorno
Sector Ovejería, Recinto de Remates, Cochrane 460 (064 269100/www.fegosa.cl). **Open** from 2pm Mon. **Admission** free.

Museo Histórico Municipal de Osorno
Manuel Antonio Mata 809, entre Bilbao y Manuel Rodríguez (064 238615/www.interpatagonia.com/paseos/museo_osorno). **Open** *Apr-Nov* 9.30am-5.30pm Mon-Fri; 2-6.30pm Sat. *Dec-Mar* 9.30am-6pm daily. **Admission** free.

Where to eat & drink

Go to **Café Central** (O'Higgins 610, 064 257711, $) for snacks – ideal for lunching on steak sandwiches, pizzas or empanadas. For a more meaty moment, **Restaurante las Brasas** (Ruta 5 Norte, Sector Barro Blanco,

064 236589, $$) is one of the best beef holes, serving the full cow of fillets, rumps and offal, with good salads and many red wines. **Club Alemán** (O'Higgins 563, 064 232784, $$$) offers German standards in a Teutonic setting. If you're all steaked out, try **Restaurant Fogón Rehuenche** (Concepción 258, 064 237261, $$) – it's another good grill house but has a tasty *cazuela de aves* (chicken stew) alternative.

Where to stay

The closest thing to lodging luxury to be found in Osorno is at **Hotel García Hurtado de Mendoza** (Mackenna 1040, 064 237111, www.hotelgarciahurtado.cl, double US$120), although this modern hotel lacks character. Nearer to the plaza and the commercial area, **Hotel Waeger** (Cochrane 816, 064 233721, double US$70-$80) is dull but reliable and has an accidentally cool retro reception area. The rooms are more motel than hotel. A good budget alternative is **Cabañas Aldea Juvenil** (G Argomedo 753, 064 233008, aldea@telsur.cl, US$10-$25 per person) – 23 cabins in a green and pleasant setting. Take note that it's run by an Osorno-based Young Christians' Association.

Resources

Hospital

Hospital Base, Avenida Dr Guillermo Buhler 1765, (064 235571).

Internet

Cyberk@fe, Patricio Lynch 1334 (064 240455).

Police station

Justo Geisse 846 (064 263502).

Post office

O'Higgins 645 (064 235176).

Tourist information

Sernatur, Edificio Gobernación Provincial, First Floor, Bernardo O'Higgins 667, entre Ramírez y Mackenna (064 234104/infosorno@sernatur.cl). **Open** *Apr-Nov* 8.30am-5.30pm Mon-Fri. *Dec-Mar* 8.30am-6.30pm Mon-Fri.

Getting there

By air

Osorno is served by the small **Aeródromo Carlos Hott Siebert** (064 318857) on Ruta 215, 7km (4.5 miles) from town. Flights to Santiago via Temuco.

By road

Almost all north–south bus services pass through Osorno, stopping at the **Terminal de Buses Interprovincial** (Errázuriz 1400, 064 234149). For routes to Argentina see Puyehue below.

Parque Nacional Puyehue

One of Chile's most popular parks, Puyehue (pronounced 'poo-YAY-way') is better known for its high-end attractions – hot springs and skiing – and for the fact that it's on one of the best roads to Argentina, for its woods and wilderness. Protecting evergreen Valdivian rainforest – dominated by thick ulmo trees – and, higher up, cooler, transitional forests of lenga and coihue and scrub, the park is home to puma, foxes, skunks, monitos del monte and huemul. While there are some challenging hikes, there's also a lot of easy walking on trails and round the foothills. Both the national parks' administration CONAF and nearby hotels can organise guides who will explain the birdlife and the different trees found here.

The main peak is **Volcán Casablanca**, which can be tackled in a three-day walk round the plateau at the bottom – known as Pampa Frutilla (Strawberry Fields) because of the strawberry-like fruit that grows there – or as a day climb to the crater and back. **Volcán Puyehue** can also be explored, with its geysers, bubbling springs and fumaroles – steaming vents that deposit sulphur on the rocks. Anticura is the starting point for this trek.

If you're heading for Puyehue, chances are it's to take a dip in hot water. All over Chile, the area is famed for its termas (hot springs) – the pleasant, tourist-friendly side to the country's seismic supervolence. The main draw is the grand resort **Hotel Termas de Puyehue** (*see p182*). The Termas company also make their own cold mineral water – proving you can drink from the pools, if you like. Kids are very welcome as the place has its own gleeful kindergarten. There is a slightly wilder patch of hot water – the **Termas Aguas Calientes** cabin-and-springs resort actually inside the national park – here you can use outdoor pools or go down to the river: move the rocks and channel the water till the temperature is just right. In winter, PN Puyehue boasts one of Chile's most visually stunning ski resorts on the slopes of Volcán Casablanca – **Centro Turístico y Deportivo Antillanca** (meaning 'sun jewel') – with views across to other conic volcanoes and of Cerro Tronador in Argentina. In summer Antillanca offers trekking trails, horse riding and mountain biking, as well as fishing and canoeing nearby.

Centro Turístico y Deportivo Antillanca

Volcán Casablanca, PN Puyehue (064 235114). **Open** *June-Oct* 8am-5.30pm daily. **Rates** *Ski hire* US$23 per day. *Ski pass* US$25 per day; US$15 per day under-12s. **Credit** AmEx, DC, MC, V.

Volcán Osorno. *See p182.*

PN Puyehue

Aguas Calientes, 4km (2.5 miles) from Ruta 215 (064 1974572/73). **Open** *Park* 24hrs daily. *Visitor centre* 9am-1pm, 2-6pm daily. *Administration* 8.30am-1pm, 2-6.20pm daily. **Admission** *Park* free. *Sector Anticura (waterfalls)* Nov-Feb US$2; free under-12s. Mar-Oct free to all. **No credit cards.**

Termas Aguas Calientes

PN Puyehue Ruta 215, km80 (064 197 4533/www. termasaguascalientes.com). **Open** 8.30am-8pm daily. **Rates** US$3-$10; US$2-$6 under-10s. **Credit** AmEx, DC, MC, V.

Where to eat & drink

Restaurant Aguas Calientes (Ruta 215, km 80, 064 236988, $) is a basic canteen serving steaks, sandwiches, snacks and typical Chilean food. **Restaurant El Quincho** (Ruta 215, km 80, 064 236988, $$) is a barbecue restaurant in the heart of the park, with fish and meat dishes and healthy options for those recently emerged from the hot springs. Both close at 9.30pm. At the ski resort, open only between June and September, try **Restaurant Rayhuén** (064 202001/02, $$), which has buffet fare, including salads, basic pasta dishes, vegetarian meals and good desserts. In the evenings **Pub Patagonia** (Antillanca, 064 202001/02, closed lunch daily) is the in-place for young snow lovers; great music and beer on tap.

Where to stay

Cabañas Aguas Calientes (Ruta 215, km 80, 064 236988, www.termasaguascalientes.com, cabin for 2 US$80-$100) has simple A-frame cabins, set in lovely woodlands. **Hotel Antillanca** (Ruta 215, km 100, 064 235114, double US$75) offers comfortable lodging on the slopes of Casablanca volcano for anyone using the region strictly for skiing. Staying at **Hotel Termas de Puyehue** (Ruta 215, km 76, 064 371382, www.puyehue.cl, double US$84-$104) is a cross between residing in a vast castle and going to a holiday camp: everything is provided, from horse rides to trekking with guides. There are also restaurants, shops and a hairdresser.

Getting there

By road

PN Puyehue is 2.5hrs from Osorno on Ruta 215. The road continues to Paso Cardenal Samoré on the border with Argentina – the main pass heading to the Lake District towns of Villa La Angostura and Bariloche. Antillanca is 18km (11 miles) from Aguas Calientes. From Osorno there is a reliable daily bus service in summer; check the winter schedules with the tourist office. Most of the larger hotels can arrange transport to the park.

Puerto Varas & around Lago Llanquihue

According to local legend, a Mapuche called Pichi Juan led the Spaniards to the Lago Llanquihue – 'the secret place'. It must have been a shocking secret to uncover, since this the third biggest lake in the Americas (after Titicaca on the Peru–Bolivia border and Lago Buenos Aires/General Carrera on the Argentina–Chile border).

No longer a secret, having been settled by German *colonos* in the 19th century, Lago Llanquihue, with its pretty lakeside towns of Puerto Varas, Puerto Octay, Frutillar and Ensenada is one of Chile's most popular destinations. **Puerto Varas** competes with Pucón as the trekking mecca, mainly because of its proximity to an important national park *(see p183)*, but also because Llanquihue's overlord – **Volcán Osorno** – is a great climb and the pride of all locals. It is, they say, like Mount Fuji, perfectly symmetrical, daubed with snow and ice all year round in a perfect cone.

Heading towards Osorno on the Pan-American Highway the first town you hit is Frutillar on the western limit of the lake. From here you can either go clockwise to Puerto Octay, Ensenada and Parque Nacional Vicente Pérez Rosales or anticlockwise towards the tiny town of Llanquihue and Puerto Varas, the lake's premier resort. If you are driving around the lake, look out for the German-style churches in the towns and at Los Bajos and Playa Maitén.

While popular for its own rhythms and atmosphere, Puerto Varas's main role is as the hedonistic hub for people visiting Parque Nacional Vicente Pérez Rosales – the huge **Casino Puerto Varas** on the lake shore speaks volumes. Puerto Varas has lots of plus points – not least the abundance of eating and drinking options for such a small place. The generally high standard of cooking was recognised when the government hosted a culinary festival here. Used to foreigners, Puerto Varas is also an easy place to meet people, make arrangements for forward travel and, at nightfall, go for a drink and even a dance. In summer, folk music and national dances like the *cueca* are performed.

Today, some 15 per cent of Varas residents are descended from original German settlers. Several of the town's older houses are nice examples of austere country elegance, a few recognised as national monuments, and visiting them makes a good city tour on foot – look out for **Casa Kuschel** with its Bavarian onion-shaped tower, **Casa Yunge, Casa Opitz** and **Casona Alemana**. Most are beside the long

PN Vicente Pérez Rosales

Opened in 1926, Vicente Pérez Rosales was Chile's first national park, named after the explorer and naturalist who roamed and mapped these regions in the 1850s. As the park came after the area had been settled, it still plays host to some farming. Inside the park, the springs, rivers and ravines give you the feeling that this is the beginning of archipelagic Chile. The Petrohué and Negro rivers and a delta of feeder streams on the north side of the lake slice into the greenery and most treks require a boat trip across **Lago Todos los Santos**.

FLORA AND FAUNA

There are some 30 mammals in the park, including pudús, pumas, mountain cats, nutrias in the rivers and native marsupials like the rat possum (Comadrejita trompuda) and the monito del monte. Grebes dominate the lakes, while kingfishers, upland geese and hummingbirds inhabit the forests – these vary from lakeside olvillo woods to important evergreen coigüe and alerce reserves. Ulmo trees are also notable, and look out for the white copihue or Chilean bell-flower, Chile's national flower, which turns red in autumn.

TREKS AND ACTIVITIES

Many people come to the park either to see the **Salto Petrohué** waterfalls on a day trip or to use Todos los Santos as a waterway to or from Argentina. The boat that makes the lake crossing, operated by **Andina del Sud** (Antonio Varas 437, Puerto Montt, 065 257797), leaves from Petrohué, usually linked to tours from Puerto Varas that take in the falls on the way. Originally a Jesuit route, the full journey – involving land crossings at Peulla and Puerto Alegre and boats across Lakes Todos Los Santos, Frías (on the border) and Nahuel Huapi – takes about four hours. If you want to have a go at one of the park's trails ask the rangers for advice, as some involve traversing lakes or difficult river terrain. Volcán Puntiagudo, standing 2,490 metres high (8,169 feet), is a popular park climb.

FACILITIES

There are two paying campsites in the park: Camping Petrohué by Lago Todos Los Santos (no electricity but hot water), and Puerto Oscuro in Sector Ensenada (very basic). There are private refugios around Volcán Osorno, or for something smarter, go to **Cabañas Petrohué** (Petrohué, 065 212025, www.petrohue.com, cabin for 4 US$120-$140). By the border is stunning **Hotel Puella** (02 196 4182, double US$144).

Parque Nacional Vicente Pérez Rosales

Entrances from Puerto Vara via Ruta 215, signs to Volcán Osorno; from Osorno via Balneario Cascada (065 212036). **Open** *Park* 24hrs daily. *Saltos de Petrohué* 10am-6pm. **Admission** *Park* free. *Saltos de Petrohué* US$2.50. **No credit cards.**

CONAF – Puerto Montt

Amunategui 500 (065 486701). **Open** 9am-1pm, 2.30-5.30pm Mon-Fri.

curve of the railway line. The Catholic church, the **Iglesia del Sagrado Corazón de Jesús**, proudly erected at the centre of the town, was built in 1918 by German Jesuits and is a copy of the Marienkirche in the Black Forest.

For open-air activities, there are pleasant walks along the lake shore (towards Ensenada), with beaches a few miles up the coast. For an overview, go up to **Parque Philippi** behind the town – walk to the end of Klenner and turn left across the railway lines. Osorno volcano and the lake look stunning from this angle.

Prettier than Puerto Montt, Varas is a key centre for organising trips, not only for the boat service across to Argentina and Pérez Rosales, but also for trips to Cochamo, Chiloé and down the Southern Highway. Lots of companies are bidding for custom: **Al Sur Expediciones** (Klenner 299, 065 233132, www.alsurexpeditions. com) and **Protours Chile** (Imperial 0655, 065 234910, www.protourschile.com, closed Sun) offer group excursions, specialists tours, watersports and hikes. Al Sur also runs kayak trips around Parque Pumalin.

AROUND LAGO LLANQUIHUE

Frutillar (full name Frutillar Bajo) was founded in 1866 as a shipping port for the Germans – naturally there's a **Museo Colonial Alemán**, which recounts their early history. The lovely view of the volcano, the Chilean palms (the most southerly palms in the world), the pretty promenade, the flowers and the beach have made the town popular with tourists. Its classical musical festivals during February are a sophisticated extra.

The small town of Puerto Octay is set against rolling hills and farmhouses. It was once a hub for steamers crossing the lake, though Puerto

Varas has long since replaced it as the chief resort. The former convent and the church are reminders of the German period and the Museo del Colono gives an insight into the agro-boom of the late 19th century, with machinery for making the local (and lethal) apple-based alcohol, *chicha*, on display.

Near the entrance to the park is the hamlet of Ensenada, the lake's most easterly point and the best place from which to take day trips into the park. Between Ensenada and Puerto Varas, stop at the old water mill **Die Wassermühle** and, further on, at the **Capilla del Río Pescado**, on the river of the same name.

Casino Puerto Varas

Del Salvador 21 y Costanera, Puerto Varas (065 346600/www.casino.cl/puerto_varas). **Open** noon-1am daily. **Admission** free.

Museo Colonial Alemán

Vicente Pérez Rosales (s/n), Frutillar (065 421142). **Open** 10am-2pm, 3-6pm Tue-Sun. **Admission** US$2; US$1 under-10s.

Museo del Colono

Esperanza 555, Puerto Octay (064 391490/www. puertooctay.cl/museos.htm). **Open** *Dec-Mar* 9am-1.30pm, 6-7pm daily. **Admission** US$1.

Where to eat & drink

In Puerto Varas there's a wide choice of quality restaurants and bars, most dishing up a range of seafood specials. **Donde el Gordito** (Unit 7/8, Mercado Municipal, San Bernardo 560, 065 233425, closed June, $$) is the place for market grub – no fancy decoration but it's quick and cheap; the crab and eel dishes are great. Although it's popular with tours, you still get honest, uncringing service. **Ibis** (Avenida

Breaking the journey at **Lago Llanquihue**.

Vicente Pérez Rosales 1117, Costanera, 065 235533, $$$) is a classic, not aimed at the young. **Restaurant La Olla** (Avenida Vicente Pérez Rosales 1071, 065 233540, $$) gets packed at lunchtimes. Try the *salmón a la manteca* or the chicken and meat platters. The haute cuisine choice is prize-winning **Restaurant Merlín** (Imperial 0605, 065 233105, $$$$), a lovely tiled wooden house turning out modern, high-class food and great cocktails. The produce used comes from their organic gardens, the nearby woods and the sea.

In Frutillar, a good fast-food restaurant is **Selva Negra** (Antonio Varas 24, 065 421164, $$). In Ensenada there's excellent modern European-Chilean dining at Yankee Way Lodge's (*see below*) **Latitude 42** restaurant, which has the south's longest wine list ($$$$).

Where to stay

Puerto Varas is packed with places to stay. **Hotel Colonos del Sur** (Del Salvador 24, 065 233039, www.colonosdelsur.cl, double US$76-$85) is the grand place on the prom, popular with conference delegates and wealthy Santiagueños. Fine views, the big café and restaurant, and tastefully decked out rooms are the draws. There are luxury cabins at **Cabañas del Lago** (Klenner 195, 065 232291, www.cabanasdellago.cl, double US$110-$125) in a woodland setting just five blocks from the main plaza. Big wide beds, big wide views and a massage in case it all gets too much, and one of the best breakfasts in town. More upmarket still is **Ruca Chalhuafe Lodge** (Casilla 625, 02 222 2222, www.rucachalhuafe.cl, from US$150 per night all inclusive), a fishing lodge with all the extras. The highly rated restaurant, great service and expert guides make this one a top spot. **Hostería Outsider** (San Bernardo 318, 065 232910, www.turout.com, double US$35-$54) is Varas's young, low-budget choice, equipped to sort out excursions and day trips.

In Frutillar there are several hotels along the front; one of the best is good-value **Hotel Ayacará** (Avenida Phillipi 1215, 065 421550, double US$40-$60). At Ensenada there are two interesting hotels. On the lake side is **Yankee Way Lodge** (Ruta 225, km 42 towards Ensenada, 065 212032, www.southernchile xp.com, bungalow for two US$280) a five-star *cabaña* complex specialising in fishing trips for wealthy US visitors. **Hotel Ensenada** (Ruta 225, km 45, 065 212028, www.hotelensenada.cl, double US$60-$90) is a slightly run-down bastion of nostalgia and faded romance. The original 1930s reception area and lounge are packed with antiques and sepia-hued junk, and rooms come with raised tin baths.

Resources

These contacts are for Puerto Varas, although essential services are also in Puerto Octay.

Hospital

Hospital San José, Dr Otto Baber 810 (065 346337).

Internet

Internet Call Center, San Francisco 430 (065 338114/338115).

Police station

San Francisco 333 (065 237441).

Post office

San José 242 (065 232396).

Tourist information

Oficina de Turismo, Piedraplen (065 237956/www. puertovaras.org). **Open** *June-Nov* 9am-1.30pm, 3pm-7pm Mon-Fri; 10am-1.30pm, 3pm-7pm Sat, Sun. *Dec-May* 9am-11pm daily.

Getting there

By road

Puerto Varas is 85km (53 miles) from Osorno and 20km (12.5 miles) north of Puerto Montt. Regular minibuses from the latter, many of which continue to the other towns on the lake.

Puerto Montt

For travellers who come south, not via Chile's central region but from Argentina, Puerto Montt is often their first experience of this country and its Patagonian sliver. After the chocolate and mock Alpinesque architecture of Bariloche, Puerto Montt, capital of Los Lagos region, can feel like a smack in the face. The entry into gritty reality is usually helped by drizzle and a generally greyer climate than on the eastern flank of the Andes.

In many ways it is the end of the Lake District and a reminder that you need an active economy to sustain a country as well as plenty of postcard scenery. The lucrative salmon-farming trade is the driving force behind Puerto Montt and down at the port there is frenetic activity from dawn to dusk. The salmon industry generates jobs and Puerto Montt is visibly expanding from a small port town into an spreading industrialised blot.

Life is dominated by the **Seno de Reloncaví**, the sound that gives Puerto Montt its bracing climate and clean air. Puerto Montt is the virtual end of continental Chile. It's the starting point of the Carretera Austral (the Southern Highway), and the terminus for boat connections towards Chaitén and Magallanes province in the Deep South. The bus and ferry terminals are on the coast road. About 60 kilometres (37 miles) south, at Pargua, is the port for ferries to Chiloé.

Two kilometres (1.25 miles) from the main square – Plaza de Armas – is the area of **Caleta Angelmó**. Angelmó (which takes its name from a slurred pronunciation of 19th-century townsman Angel Montt) is where artisans from nearby islands come daily to flog their handiwork on the main avenue. It's the most rustic-looking part of Puerto Montt's sprawl and it is here that generations of backpackers have picked up unwearable waistcoats and rucksack-overwhelming wool blankets. Baskets, leather goods and woodwork ships – some made from protected trees – are for sale too. You can also get seafood at the market – though many locals say it's not always fresh (especially in winter). Favourite dishes include *tortilla de erizo* (sea urchin omelette), *choro zapato* (big clams) as well as salty stews and soups. Along Avenida Diego Portales is an area called the **Pueblito de Artesanos Melipulli** (065 435316, closed from 1pm Dec-Mar), a kind of quaint shanty district where you can eat from an *olla común* – a big, communal bowl of fishy grub – while live folk music is strummed.

For aesthetic, contemporary stimulation check out the arts and culture scene at **Casa de Arte Diego Rivera**, a block from the Plaza de Armas. It's a small multi-purpose venue for plays, concerts and exhibitions. Puerto Montt is a major service centre. It has scores of hotels and restaurants, half a dozen campsites, car-hire companies (useful if you aim to drive the Southern Highway), cybercafés and more tour operators than it needs.

Casa de Arte Diego Rivera

Third Floor, Quillota 126, y Antonio Varas (065 261817). **Open** 9am-1.30pm, 3-7pm daily. **Admission** free.

Where to eat & drink

The Argentinian chef at **Country Pub** (Avenida Diego Portales 736, 065 253162, closed dinner Sun, $$$) turns out the town's best sandwiches and tapas. Check out the posters of tango legend Carlos Gardel. There's pork and beef on the grill at large **Los Tocones de Pelluco** (Avenida Juan Soler Manfredini, 065 319000, closed dinner Sun, $$), or if you want some action with your meat, at **Rodeo Chile Restaurant** (Balneario Pelluco, Media Luna, 065 257878, closed Apr-Aug, $$$) you can watch a rodeo show while you tuck in. Puerto Montt's smartest café, **Sherlock** (Antonio Varas 452, 065 288888, $$), is inspired by a Conan Doyle story in which the famous detective comes to this town to have a cup of tea and buy tobacco. Nowadays this is the best place for non-Nescafé coffee and fine pastries; excellent shots and cocktails too.

Where to stay

Hotel Don Luis (Quillota 146, 065 259001, www.hoteldonluis.cl, double US$98) is a decent metropolitan hotel, popular with salmon traders, with a fine breakfast and nice first floor bar. Rooms are airport hotelish, with big beds and satellite TV. **Hotel La Península Marina Resort** (Camino Chinquihué, km 8.5, 065 260800, www.hotellapeninsula.cl, double US$120-$140) has fabulous views across the water to Isla Mallén, and the tranquility has made this a boom hotel for visiting business people. Taxis to town take ten minutes and it's a great spot for coastal walks. The bar is small but efficient and staff very helpful.

Resources

Hospital
Hospital Base, Seminario (065 261100).

Internet
Mundo Sur, San Martín 232 (065 344773).

Police station
Río Yely (065 431375).

Post office
Rancagua 126 (065 252719).

Tourist information
Sernatur, Seminario 480, entre Ejército y O'Higgins (065 254580/sernatur@telsur.cl/www.sernatur.cl). **Open** 8.30am-5.30pm Mon-Thur; 8.30am-4.30pm Fri.

Getting there

By air
Aeropuerto de Puerto Montt 'Tepual' (065 294161) is 11km (7 miles) west of the centre.Flights go to/from Santiago, Balmaceda and Punta Arenas, and from the latter on to the Falklands/Malvinas.

By road
Puerto Montt has a major bus terminal on the front (Avenida Portales at Lota, 065 253143). Scores of mini buses into the Lake District and regular mid- and long-distance services to Chiloé, Temuco, Santiago and intermediate points. Also has buses for Coihaique and the Southern highway and Punta Arenas via Argentina. There are hourly services to Bariloche in Argentina.

By sea
Puerto Montt is the major boat terminus for services by sea heading south, including Navimag services to Puerto Natales. *See pp206-209* **Sea Routes South**.

Idle days in Patagonia

Long beloved of the budget backpacker and thunder-thighed walker, Patagonia has always benefited the lean of wallet, since the best thing about it – its stunning landscape – is available free of charge. Add to that a favourable exchange rate, good camping facilities and cheap entrance fees to national parks and the result is all sorts of skinflint youngsters roaming the plains and peaks. So long as trekkers are willing to eat powdered soup and drink Tetra-pak wine, they can hang loose in the region for months on end.

But, today, a new and more demanding species of tourist has emerged. Sophisticated and spendthrift, they still want awesome views, wild weather and an extreme experience, but with all the home comforts thrown in and then some. A 'posh Patagonia' is emerging, where the name of the game is luxury; and even if you don't want to trek, climb or hike, you can make the most of this breathtaking part of the world in a variety of different, less demanding and infinitely more expensive ways.

The first to tap this high-end market were the hot spring resorts that opened in the '30s – among the classiest complexes are **Hotel Termas de Puyehue** (*see p182*) and the newer **Puyuhuapi Lodge & Spa** (*see p199*).

Modern day versions of the Roman spa, they offer massages, hydrotherapy, seaweed and mud treatments, plus a whole range of healthy outdoor activities that make relaxing a serious occupation. You can go horse riding if you want – but you can also buy chocolates, choose wines and lounge about in bubbling hot water until you begin to feel faint.

In 1950 a swanky hotel in Pucón upped the ante on southern style. **Antumalal** (*see p174*) on a steep cliff overlooking Lago Villarrica, was – and still is – the ultimate in Designer Patagonia. As the owner says, 'We wanted every window in every room to be like a frame for an artwork.' People, many of them celebrities (Queen Elizabeth II for example), go to look, luxuriate and eat well. Five-star hotels such as **Llao Llao Hotel & Resort** (*see p103*), **Explora's Hotel Salto Chico** (*see p215*) in Torres del Paine and the more exclusive estancias are latter-day attempts to recapture this pre-packaged aestheticism, at the same time giving punters the chance to blow from US$400 to US$800 a day.

The other big-buck bracket is occupied by fishing lodges. If those two words conjure up images of gangs of tough men impaling worms on the steps of some remote log cabin, you wouldn't be far wrong – it's just that the anglers in this target market carry money as well as maggots. Modern lodges like **Yankee Way** (*see p185*) and **Arelauquen** (*see p102*) are likely to drive you in intimate groups of two by 4x4 to select streams for your day's fishing and then serve up fusion cuisine and fine wines in the evenings.

Expect to spend from US$600 a day for such fancy fishing, and if you've still got some readies left, Antarctic cruises have long been the travel industry's preferred method of turning rich clients upside down and shaking hard. A summer circumnavigation of the big ice can cost up to US$70,000 per head. Breakfast is usually included.

Chiloé

Misty, mellow and magical: don't miss Chile's *isla bonita*.

Chiloé evolved along similar lines to the rest of Chile, but, as islands are wont, deviated from the modes and manners of the mainland. During the 17th and 18th centuries Chiloé's Spanish and indigenous inhabitants coexisted in relative harmony – in contrast to the tensions in the Lake District – and it was the last island to embrace Republicanism, shrugging off the Spanish yoke only in 1826 (eight years after Chile announced its independence).

Chilean historian Rodolfo Urbina has called Chiloé '*la frontera cerrada*' (the closed frontier) in reference to its separateness and unique way of life. This individuality is as evident in the solidarity of the Chilotes who live there as in the distinctive churches (16 of which are UNESCO World Heritage Sites) the brightly coloured cemeteries and the houses on stilts – called *palafitos* – that dot this gentle, green island.

One way or another Chiloé is an enigma. After the scenic joys of the lakes or southern Patagonia you might wonder why you are visiting this rainy, misty place. But talk to the islanders themselves and they'll tell you it's a special, even enchanted place. 'Wood, wool and water,' say the Chilotes, are the elements of life here. Some would add 'witches', as there is also a strong, and extant, tradition of magic.

The archipelago of Chiloé is a group of 40-odd islets around the 180-kilometre-long (112-mile) main island of **Isla Grande de Chiloé**. Its landscape is lush temperate rainforest – large and virgin in some sections – and rolling grazing land. The main hubs of Chiloé Grande – **Ancud**, **Castro**, **Chonchi** and, solely for its port, **Quellón** – and a few other small towns occupy its eastern edges. The rest is a sparsely populated wilderness, mostly low-lying but with a coastal range on the western flank that rises to 900 metres (2,952 feet). The island is narrow – 30-70 kilometres (19-43 miles) wide – but due to a limited intrastructure it is difficult

The untroubled waters of **Ancud**. *See p189.*

to visit the west and most visitors only manage to do so at Cucao, the entry-way to **Parque Nacional Chiloé** (*see p190*). Here, you can scramble through humid forests to find the Pacific lashing onto long stretches of sandy beach or up onto the rocky promontories.

Ancud

You'll probably come to Ancud after crossing the Canal de Chacao on a ferry from Pargua, 87 kilometres (54 miles) from Puerto Montt and landing at Chacao. The 30-minute trip is a high point in itself. When the skies are clear, the air is lung-excavatingly pure and porpoises are often seen dancing in the boat's wake. If you're hungry and not in a hurry – by far the best way to approach Chiloé – start at homey German-run **Die Räucherkate** (*see p190*) restaurant down the road from Chacao.

Pretty Ancud, founded in 1767, is to the west. The population is around 50,000 and though it feels more like a spread-out village these days, it was once a key seaport and a strategic vantage point for Spanish and, later, Chilean naval forces. The **Fuerte San Antonio** fort near the town was built in 1770 to guard shipping routes – it was also where the Spanish eventually surrendered to Chilean troops.

Make a point of popping into lovely **Museo Regional Aurelio Borques Canobra**. You can play with an interactive display dedicated to the *Golera Ancud* – the schooner that the Chileans had built on the island and sent to Punta Arenas in 1843 to assert dominion over the Magellan Strait. There are also mythological figures and craftwork relating to the Huilliche (a subgroup of the Mapuche), the main Chilote indigenous group. The original indigenous peoples of the island, the Chono, were largely absorbed by the Mapuche; those that were not were forced to find a home in the Aisén archipelago south of Chiloé.

A nice town to spend a day or two, Ancud has one major drawback – it receives the full force of the Pacific coast climate – sodden winds and awesome amounts of rain, even in summer. This can be very dramatic when the clouds shroud the uplands; it can also be very annoying if camping, trekking or trying to take that photo of an ox-cart or Chilote farmer.

EXCURSIONS

Another museum worth a look is 15 kilometres (9.5 miles) outside town at the home of local character Don Serafin. The Quilo 'museum' – **Museo Punta Quilo** – is an institutional expression of Chiloé at its most vivid. The old guy, when not fishing, simply gathers anything he finds and displays it in a ramshackle shed or

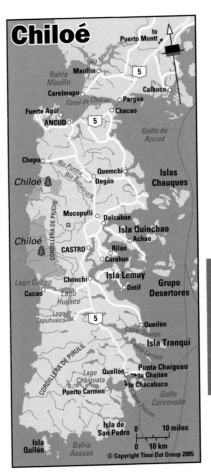

even in the garden. Penguins and seals, stuffed with newspapers, hang from the roof and overlook fossils, old rocks, shells, petrified wood, skeletons and even bits of rusty fittings from the house. When you leave, give Don Serafin a tip – US$1.50 seems to be plenty. Oh, and if all this seems amateurish, note that lots of experts come along to see these assorted items and even study them.

To dip into Chiloé's maritime history, take a bus or taxi out to **Fuerte Agüi** on Península Lacuy. This 1779 fort was built by the Spanish as a lookout and to block entry into Chiloé. Dutch and French pirates had made moves in the south and the budding imperial forces were alert to the vulnerability and strategic importance of Chiloé. The views from the fort ruins are stunning, whether you look out to open sea or back towards Chiloé, with groups of cormorants skimming the waters and fishermen buzzing around oyster traps down below.

Museo Punta Quilo
Puente Filo, 20km (12.5 miles) from Ancud (09 245 0490). **Open** 8am-9pm daily. **Admission** US45¢; US15¢ concessions. **No credit cards.**

Museo Regional Aurelio Borques Canobra
Libertad 370, Plaza de Armas (065 622413). **Open** *Apr-Nov* 10am-5.30pm Mon-Fri; 10am-2pm Sat, Sun. *Dec-Mar* 10am-7.30pm daily. **Admission** US85¢; US45¢ concessions. **No credit cards.**

Where to eat

Restaurant Die Räucherkate
Ruta 5, km 1082 (09 444 5912). **Open** 10am-6pm daily. **Average** $$$. **No credit cards.**

Just down the road from Chacao you can go salmon tasting (this place has its own *ahumadería* or smoker, in reality a converted fridge) and try Chilean wines.

Restaurant Ostras Caulín
Caulín Alto (09 643 7005/www.ostrascaulin.cl). **Open** *Dec-Mar* 10am-9pm daily. *Apr-Nov* 10am-7pm daily. **Average** $$. **Credit** AmEx, DC, MC, V.
Run by a colourful old local, this is the place to try the island's freshest oysters right on the beach. Figures from Chilote mythology fill the garden.

Restaurant La Pincoya
Avenida Arturo Prat 61, y Costanera (065 622613). **Open** *Apr-Dec* 11am-8pm Mon-Fri; 10am-8pm Sat, Sun. *Jan, Mar* 10am-11pm daily. **Average** $$$. **No credit cards.**
One of the most reliable restaurants to try *curanto en olla*. The two floors are cosily decorated, and the place is staffed by helpful waiters, who dish out great seafood *cazuelas* (stews).

Parque Nacional Chiloé

If you think temperate rainforest sounds gentle and humid, the great tract of land on the north-west coast of Chiloé might just change your mind. When it rains here, it does so with a vengeance. Even the road from Castro to the park can be problematic after long downpours, so be warned.

There are Huilliche villages situated within the park and though (thankfully) there's no trip to see 'the natives', you might bump into them all the same. They have, by and large, opted out of the increasingly modern temper of Chiloé and prefer to live in old *rucas* (huts), with a central fire – for heating, drying, cooking and smoking – and few furnishings.

There are two mountain ranges on Chiloé's west coast, the Cordillera de Pirulil in the south and, running the length of the Parque Nacional, the Cordillera de Piuche. With so few coastal areas protected, this environment of evergreen forest is of particular importance. The park also includes a small island, Metalqui, off the northern coast; as it's a reserve, any trips there have to be arranged with CONAF.

FLORA AND FAUNA
When it's dry, the place is quite special. The dense woods of arrayanes, ciprés de las guaitecas, canelos and other trees are fun to walk in even if you can't see much – you'll hear all the birds though, especially the common chucao (happily chirping 'chucao!'

all day). You may see a Chilean fox or a pudú scuttering at knee-level. When the trees fall away at the coast, you come out to face the always pounding, sometimes raging Pacific. Beach birds include red knots, Hudsonian godwits, whimbrels and Baird's sandpiper.

TREKKING AND ACTIVITIES
There are nine marked trails in the park, most of them in the southern sector. There are also lots of raised wooden paths to walk on, but the going is difficult when wet: it can be pretty slippery and the branches are tricky. The most popular walk is the day-long hike to Cole Cole. Before going into the park for any extended stay, stock up on essential provisions in the village of Cucao.

FACILITIES
The main entrance is at Cucao. If to want to explore the northern section of the park, it's a long, circuitous trip to Chepu, near Ancud. There's a *refugio* at Cole Cole, and camping in Sector Chanquín Cucao.

Parque Nacional Chiloé
Sector Chanquín, Cucao (no phone). **Open** 8.45am-6pm daily. **Admission** US$1.50; free under 12s. **No credit cards.**

Administration – Castro
CONAF, Gamboa 424 (065 532507). **Open** 8.45am-1pm, 2-5.45pm Mon-Fri.

For a tomb with a view, visit Castro's **Cementario Católico**. *See p192.*

Where to stay

Galeón Azul

Libertad 751, y Costanera (065 622567/galeonazul @sudnet.cl). **Rates** US$46-$55 single; US$55-$68 double; US$68-$79 triple. **No credit cards.**
The Galeón Azul is a brightly painted, welcoming hostelry close to all the town's amenities.

Hostería Ancud

San Antonio 30, y Baqueano (065 322340). **Rates** US$49-$74 single; US$65-$83 double; US$80-$92 triple. **Credit** AmEx, DC, MC, V.
This is the smartest hotel in Ancud and possibly the island, with a spacious, stone-clad reception, good fish restaurant, pleasant gardens and green views. (At time of going to press the hotel was about to switch ownership; check with them in advance.)

Hotel Lacuy

Pudeto 219 (065 623019/jyk@entelchile.net). **Rates** US$22-$30 single; US$28-$34 double; US$34-$37 triple. **Credit** AmEx, DC, MC, V.
The Lacuy is a reasonably priced, quiet, clean hotel. All rooms come with TV and private bathroom.

Resources

Hospital

Hospital Ancud, Almirante La Torre 301 (065 622355).

Internet

ENTEL, Pudeto 219 (065 623839).

Police station

Plaza Centenario (065 628650).

Post office

Pérez Blanco, y Pudeto (no phone).

Tourist information

Sernatur, Libertad 665 (065 622665). **Open** *Apr-Nov* 8am-5.30pm Mon-Fri. *Dec-Mar* 8am-8pm daily.

Getting there

By road

Ancud is 33km (21 miles) from Chacao, where the transporters from the mainland dock. Several buses run every hr from Puerto Montt, many continue to Castro. Tickets include the boat crossing in the fare.

By sea

Boats run every 5-10mins from Pargua on the mainland to Chacao, near Ancud on Chiloé. The crossing costs US$11 per car or US$1.50 per person.

Castro

Chiloé's capital looks modern but is one of the three oldest cities in Chile, along with Santiago and La Serena. Founded in 1557 by Martín Ruiz de Gamboa, the town is on a hill overlooking the **Fiordo Castro** (Castro Fjord). Old stilt houses, called *palafitos*, shipyards, a **Mercado de Artesanías** craft market on Lillo between Encalada and Thompson streets and restaurants are down by the sea with the main square, the **Plaza de Armas**, and amenities at the top of a steep rise.

Castro was provincial capital till 1788, when Ancud was given that status, but increasing importance during and after a timber boom in

Seafood special

Curanto is the Chilote meal *par excellence*, though it may first have been cooked up on Easter Island and travelled here with ocean-going immigrants. Preparing *curanto* is quite a ceremony: the ingredients are cooked with the heat from round stones and maqui leaves and placed in a hole in the ground. Over the stones, they put layers of fish, seasonal shellfish, potatoes (said by some to have originated in Chiloé), meat and, in some cases, vegetables. There are also dumpling-like stodge-bombs either white-coloured (called *chapaleles*) and made from boiled potatoes and flour, or black (*milcaos*), a mixture of fried raw spud, butter and crackling.

The strange – but tasty – combination of fresh shellfish with more durable stomach-fillers is probably due to the old habits of fishermen: they'd take long-lasting victuals with them in case the weather turned and they were forced to stay away. To add life to the older foodstuff they mixed in fresh fish or seafood from their catch. It is still possible to get *curanto* cooked in the ground (*en el hoyo*) but most restaurants now cook it in a pan (*a la olla*). It is always a massive meal and *curanto* virgins should share on the first sitting. Seaweed is also big business in Chiloé, much of it sold to Japan as a pharamaceutical gel, but you may also find it in *cochayuyo* soup.

the late 19th century led to growth and the town was made capital again in 1982. Less tidy and more urban than Ancud, Castro and its waterways look nicest from up at the *mirador* (viewpoint) on the hill behind the **Cementerio Católico** on Calle Freire.

Castro's church, the seat of the Jesuit and Franciscan missions that evangelised Chiloé, is on the north-west corner of the plaza and a focal point for the town. Unlike the dark wooden tiled churches that dominate elsewhere, the Castro building is a 1912 brick edifice which combines local design traditions with neo-gothic elements. It was designed by Italian architect Eduardo Provasoli to replace the former church, destroyed in a fire in 1902.

Though the past 50 years have seen considerable assimilation of mainland culture, it is still possible to find remnants of a 16th-century way of life on the island. Old traditions like the *minga de tiradura*, when a person moves house by simply moving the house

(using oxen to pull it on a sled and then a raft on the sea), impossible in the forward-looking Chile of the north, are part of everyday life on Chiloé. Castro's **Museo Municipal de Castro** has some interesting photos of the *minga* and of carts and items from the old way of life.

EXCURSIONS

Between eastern Chiloé and the continent is an inland sea where the Pacific has rolled in to flood the sunken central valley. Numerous island groups huddle round the waters off Castro, most of them green and rolling with low hills.

Just 23 kilometres (14 miles) south of Castro is **Chonchi**, a place the Spaniards called 'the end of Christianity'. The road from Castro to Chonchi takes you past the 18th- and 19th-century churches of **Nercón**, **Vilupulli** and **Chonchi**, all Chilean National Monuments and UNESCO sites. From Chonchi a launch leaves for Ichuac on Isla Lemuy. On the island you'll find the churches of **San Carlos**, a fine wooden building with arches and a squat tower, and **Ichuac**, **Detif** and **Aldachildo**, three more World Heritage Sites.

Having sampled the laid-back rhythms of Isla Grande, you might feel the need to visit more of the islets. Each of the small islands is, according to locals, entirely unique, but most foreigners will find these distinctions subtle. The biggest and closest is **Isla Quinchao**, reached on a small ro-ro transporter. The boat crosses the narrow gap (in just ten minutes) between Dalcahue, where there's another UNESCO church, and the island. The trip is nicknamed the 'wool route' in recognition of the core, local economic activity.

There are three places to visit on the island. At **Curaco de Vélez** you can catch great views over the surrounding islands and see a wide range of lovely, decaying old buildings (Las Animas and Galverino Riveros are two streets crammed with shack-like houses and mansions). **Achao**, the only town of any description, 25 kilometres (16 miles) across on the far side of the island, is home to the 1740 **Iglesia de Achao**, the oldest of all churches on Chiloé. Finally, **Quinchao** is where the biggest Chilote church sits. Finished in 1890, the current building was preceded by several others in earlier centuries.

Between all this worthy ecclesiastical sightseeing, you can feast on a *curanto* or pile of shellfish at one of the many cheap eateries on the coast. Several firms in Castro offer trips to the islands, one of the best being **Pehuén Expediciones** (Blanco 299, 065 632361), whose office is near the plaza.

A 90-minute bus journey takes you the 34 kilometres (21 miles) from Castro to the village

Chilean Patagonia

of **Cucao** (population 1,000), passing through the pretty village of Huillinco and skirting the southern edge of long, thin Lago Huillinco. There's not a lot to do at Cucao, where only a 20-kilometre (12.5-mile) white-sand beach survived a tidal wave in 1960. But this is the way into the **Parque Nacional Chiloé** (*see p190*) and you can buy some supplies here before entering the wilds.

From the Castro area, you can take trips to the mainland. Although physically separated from Chiloé, the unpopulated lands across the waters of the Ancud and Corcovado Gulfs are often referred to by islanders as 'Chiloé Continental'. **Altué Sea Kayaking** have extensive experience on Chile's waterways and offer a range of adventurous rowing trips from their green cabin near Dalcahue – they go to several islands off Chiloé as well as the fjords near Parque Pumalin. To arrange an excursion with Altué, contact their Santiago office (2nd Floor, Encomenderos 83, Las Condes, Santiago, 02 232 1103, www.seakayakchile.com).

One way to go to the mainland is via tiny port town **Quellón**, 99 kilometres (62 miles) south of Castro, from where boat services head for Chaitén on the mainland. There are a few small hostels and a campsite at **Punta Lapa**. During summer, Transmarchilay (*see p209*) runs twice-weekly five-hour services for cars and passengers across the inland sea, an ideal option for those who want to visit the Southern Highway section of Patagonia without retracing their steps through Puerto Montt.

Museo Municipal de Castro
Esmeralda (065 635967). **Open** *Apr-Nov* 9.30am-1pm, 3-6.30pm Mon-Fri; 9am-1pm Sat. *Dec-Mar* 9.30am-8pm Mon-Sat; 10am-1pm Sun. **Admission** US$1 suggested contribution. **No credit cards.**

Where to eat & drink

Años Luz
San Martín 309 (065 532700). **Open** 9am-midnight Mon-Fri; 11am-midnight Sat, Sun. **Average** $$. **Credit** AmEx, DC, MC, V.
Años Luz is a hip – by Chiloé standards – and lively bar-restaurant with a mixed clientele of bohos, twentysomethings and ordinary townfolk. Try the lovely *tablas* (platter of bites) and tasty *choritos* (mussels).

Octavio
Avenida Pedro Montt 261, y Gobernación Marítima (065 632855). **Open** 11am-midnight daily. **Average** $$. **No credit cards.**
Octavio, an established favourite, does a very good *curanto en olla* – also called *pulmay* – with all the trimmings. Walls are used to promote local painters.

Sacho
Thompson 213 (065 632079). **Open** *Dec-Mar* noon-midnight daily. *Apr-Nov* noon-4pm, 8pm-midnight daily. **Average** $$. **No credit cards.**
Usual seafood and soups with great views of the sea from the first floor, and regular local clients – keeping the food fresh and good. Try the stuffed fish and the crab carpaccio.

Where to stay

Hostería de Castro
Chacabuco 202, y Thompson (065 632301/www. hosteriadecastro.cl). **Rates** US$46-$61 single; US$56-$69 double. **Credit** DC, MC, V.
This A-frame hotel looks like a church and has its own nightclub (Public). In-house restaurant Las Araucarias serves good salmon and shellfish dishes.

Hotel Chilhué
Blanco Encalada 278, entre San Martín y Thompson (065 632596/hotelchilhue@hotmail.com). **Rates** US$24-$32 single; US$30-$46 double; US$39-$56 triple. **Credit** AmEx, DC, MC, V.
The 26 rooms of Hotel Chilhué, all with TV and heating, are arranged over three floors. A good option for those on a low budget.

Hotel Unicornio Azul
Avenida Pedro Montt 228, y Blanco Encalada (065 632359). **Rates** US$35.50-$45.50 single; US$42-$56.50 double; US$50-$66.50 triple. **No credit cards.**
The 'blue unicorn', sister hotel to Ancud's Galeón Azul, has cosy, simple rooms, friendly staff and a small bar and restaurant.

Resources

Hospital
Hospital de Castro, Freire 852 (065 632444).

Internet
La Brújula, O'Higgins 308 (065 633229).

Police station
Diego Portales 440 (065 631811).

Post office
Firenze 338 (065 634384).

Tourist information
Casilla de Informes Turísticos, Plaza de Armas (no phone). **Open** *Dec-Mar* 9am-9pm daily. *Apr-Nov* 11am-4pm Mon-Sat. Information also available at Hostal y Turismo Quelcún (San Martín 581, 065 632396).

Getting there

By road
Castro is 77km (48 miles) or 40mins, south of Ancud on the Pan-American Highway; regular buses run from Ancud, Puerto Montt and Santiago.

Chilean Patagonia

The Southern Highway

If you love the open road, the Carretera Austral is your highway to heaven.

If you were ever in doubt about the vast cultural chasm between Argentina and Chile, look no farther than their approach to road building in Patagonia. Whereas bickering politicians in Argentina have traditionally been loathe to pave – or even routinely grade – its heavily travelled Ruta 40, across the border, giant earthmovers heroically forge their way through the wilderness on the Chilean side to build two-lane roads only a trickle of vehicles will ever traverse.

Nowhere is this truer than along the 1,240-kilometre (770-mile) Camino Longitudinal Augusto Pinochet, or Ruta 7, which unites Puerto Montt with Villa O'Higgins in Región XI (Aisén). This Pharaonic undertaking was started in 1976 by then president Pinochet. While the road is acknowledged as being an 'achievement' of the dictatorship, Chileans quickly scuttled the official name in favour of the curt and apolitical **Carretera Austral**.

Officials rightly brag that the highway is a key component of national unity, linking otherwise isolated rural communities. But the road's economic – not to mention environmental – justification is less convincing. Only 100,000 people live in Aisén, nearly half in the capital Coihaique, and traffic is so thin that in places you're more likely to run into a deer than a fellow motorist. The next planned stage of construction is just as startling: a 953-kilometre (592-mile) extension to Puerto Natales, in Region XII. It will take something like 30 years and nine water crossings to complete.

Tourists, however, wouldn't have it any other way. South of Puerto Montt, Chile collapses into an archipelagic riot and the Carretera passes through all the scenic ups, downs and arounds on this straggling stretch of volcanoes, icecaps and fjords. Some of the continent's biggest lakes, Chile's strongest

Heading south on the **Carretera Austral**.

flowing river (Río Baker) and Southern Patagonia's tallest peak (Monte San Valentin) are so close you can almost touch them.

But don't expect an easy-going road trip: the same erosional forces that carved the stunning landscapes are still at work. Frigid winds blowing in from Antarctica and monsoon-like downpours of up to 3,000 millimeters (116 inches) a year are common in several places. The highway is covered in *ripio* (gravel), and only is occasionally flattened by rollers.

The section from Puerto Montt to Chaitén, involves two short and one substantial boat journey. To skip these, or in winter when there is no boat between Hornopirén and Caleta Gonzalo, put your car on to a transporter and go directly to Chaitén. For information on boat services *see pp206-209* **Sea Routes South**. If you don't want to drive the whole highway, Chaitén and Coihaique are useful hubs, linked by bus and air services (*see p196*).

Puerto Montt to Chaitén

Onwards from Puerto Montt

Opposite the Plaza de Armas in Puerto Montt (*see p185*) is the official zero kilometre point of the Carretera Austral – from here to Chaitén it's 242 kilometres (150 miles). The first place you'll pass, four kilometres (2.5 miles) on, is **Pelluco**, a seaside resort of sorts with beaches lapped by freezing water and places to eat. Further along, the bays of **Coihuín** and **Piedra Azul** are attractive viewpoints with places to grab a snack; in summer you can unwind on the white beaches by the seaside cabins. At **Lenca** – 33 kilometres (20 miles) from Puerto Montt – is a left turn and seven kilometre (four mile) drive for **Parque Nacional Alerce Andino**.

The park is a 393-square-kilometre (151-square-mile) reserve named for the majestic alerce trees at its centre. For its mammoth size and millennial lifespan – examples commonly reach heights of 50 metres (165 feet) and 3,000 years – the alerce is sometimes called the redwood of South America. A few muddy trails past isolated *lagunas* to hidden groves make this an ideal but challenging trekking destination. To stay in the area, the best option is the isolated but lavish **Alerce Mountain Lodge** (Carretera Austral, km 36, 065 286969, www.mountainlodge.cl, US$450-$560 all-inclusive), which organises horse rides to the 3,800-year old Tata (daddy) tree as well as visits to rodeo shows at nearby farms and trips

into the forest. You'll need to call ahead since the lodge is only accessible by 4x4 (they'll happily pick you up if necessary).

From Lenca, the highway continues 21 kilometres (13 miles) on to La Arena, from where, in 90 minutes, you can take a tour of a salmon farm (Surmarino Tours, 065 4310660, www.surmarino.cl) to see where your maki roll comes from. In recent years Chile has surpassed Scandinavia as the world's biggest salmon supplier and many of its most productive hatcheries are located in Patagonia.

To plod ahead from Caleta La Arena, you must board the Transmarchilay's *Tehuelche* for the crossing of the Estuario Reloncaví. The crossing to Caleta Puelche takes 30 minutes, and runs upon demand, all year. Once off the boat, you'll drive on to a *caleta* (cove) named Puelche, Mapuche for 'people from the east' – access to this region was historically from the other side of the Andes. About 60 kilometres (37 miles) south you'll come to **Hornopirén**. The CONAF office in Puerto Montt at Amunategui 500 (065 486701) has information on PN Alerce Andino and PN Hornopirén (*see below*).

PN Alerce Andino
Entrances from Sector Correntoso from Puerto Montt via Ruta UV65, Camino al Lago Chato; Sector Chaica from Carretera Austral. **Open** 9am-6pm daily. **Admission** US$2; free under-12s. **No credit cards.**

Hornopirén

The tiny town of Hornopirén gets its name, meaning oven of snow, from its location at the base of the volcano of the same name. For lodging there's a few cabins and budget hotels, though for a few extra bucks you can get ferried from town to the Isla de Llancahué, home to a fair hotel with thermal springs called **Termas de Llancahuée** (09 6424857, US$35 all inclusive). The volcano itself is located east of town in the **Parque Nacional Hornopirén**, which also boasts a number of alerces. The volcano is a popular climb, though many people are drawn to the park for the fishing on the Blanco and Negro rivers.

PN Hornopirén
From Hornopirén, 16km (10 miles) along the Carretera Austral. **Open** 24hrs daily (recommended entry 9am-noon). **Admission** free.

Caleta Gonzalo

Bid adieu to the puddle jumping – you are now joining a road that runs continuously for the next 860 kilometres (534 miles). A sign on the road shows distances from Caleta Gonzalo southwards. Chaitén-based bus firm **Chaitur** (*see below*) picks up bus travellers from the town, which has comfy lodges and a café-restaurant near where you disembark. The town is the northern gateway to the private **Parque Pumalín** (*see p197*), deservedly one of the region's biggest attractions. The 60-kilometre (37-mile) drive through the park from Caleta Gonzalo to Chaitén takes you past stunning cliffs topped with mists and hung with dense vegetation. Take care while driving the steeper sections, and go slowly to catch views of Lago Blanco and Lago Negro.

Chaitén

Chaitén would be an utterly forgettable pit stop along the Carretera Austral were it not for its proximity to Pumalín. Indeed, until the 1940s the town was too small even to be called a hamlet and its outlet to the world was via a once-monthly boat. A military outpost gives the town a martial air, but bar watching the buzzards wait around for the next dead dog, there's little to do in the town itself.

Nonetheless, the 4,000 Chaiténses have managed to make a good living from the tourist trade spurred by its privileged location. There are plenty of cheap hotels and a dozen basic restaurants. From the *costanera* (coast road), cafés and a market look out on the **Volcán Corcovado**. It's worth sticking around a day or two to hike among the many nature trails or to explore the rivers – the Yelcho, the Futaleufú and the Palena – and nearby lakes.

The best source for tours is Chaitur (bus terminal, Diego Portales 350, 065 731429), which in addition to operating buses to Caleta Gonzalo and south to Coihaique can also organise treks, horse riding, kayaking, and canyoning on the Río Futaleufú.

Where to stay & eat

The nicest place to lodge in town is also one of the oldest: **Mi Casa** (Avenida Norte 206, 065 731285, hmicasa@telsur.cl, double US$40-$50). Like most places in town the decor is drab, but there's a great bar and kitchen, plus lofty views over the town and, in the distance, the Michinmahuida volcano. A fine alternative, albeit one that costs more than the name suggests, is **Schilling** (Avenida Corcovado 320, 065 731295, double US$45-$60), whose rooms afford good views over the bay. Pumalín's concession, right above the park's information centre, is the wood-shingled **Hostal Puma Verde** (O'Higgins 54, 065 731184, www.parque pumalin.cl, double US$50-$68), which is by far the smartest place in town. The friendly,

Argentinian-owned **Los Coihues** (Pedro Aguirre Cerda 398, 065 731461, closed June-Oct, double US$45-$50) is built from a log cabin and is good if you want to sort out fishing, ice-treks and excursions to Pumalín.

El Quijote (O'Higgins 42, 065 731293, $) is a great little grotto of a place for beer and bluster with locals, and the friendly barman-owner knocks out good sandwiches. For more sophisticated fare, check out **Corcovado** (Corcovado 448, 065 731221, $$) and **Café-Restaurant Flamengo** (Avenida Corcovado 218, 065 731448, $$), both of which have fresh fish when the catch comes in and well-stocked cellars of Chilean wine. **Las Brisas del Mar** (Corcovado 278) is another eaterie noted for its daily seafood specials.

Resources

Hospital
Hospital de Chaitén, Avenida I Carrera Pinto 153 (065 731244).

Internet
Oficina ENTEL, Libertad 408 (065 731603).

Police station
I Carrera Pinto 435 (065 731962).

Post office
O'Higgins 285 (065 731481).

Tourist information
Sernatur, Gobernación Provincial de Palena, O'Higgins 254 (065 731082). **Open** 8.30am-1.30pm, 2.30-5.30pm Mon-Fri.

Getting there

By road
It's 203km (126 miles) by road from Puerto Montt (not counting the several sea crossings) and 420km (261 miles) south to Coihaique. Both routes are covered at least once a day during the high season by both **Chaitur** (Diego Portales 350, 065 731429) and **B&V Tours** (Libertad 442, 065 731390). There is a road to the Argentinian town of Trevelin via the Santa Lucia junction.

By sea
Throughout the summer, but more frequently in summer, there are boats connecting Chaitén with Puerto Montt and Quellon, Chiloé (see *pp206-209* **Sea Routes South**).

By air
There are flights from Puerto Montt to the tiny aerodrome (065 731579) at Chaitén, 2km (1.25 miles) from the centre down the Southern Highway – popular with anglers who don't want to take the slow road/boat. **Aerosur** (065 731228) and **Aeromet** (065 731275) have at least one flight per day. It takes around 30 minutes.

Parque Pumalín

Parque Pumalín is only one of 32 national parks in Chile, but it probably generates more publicity than all of the others put together. Why? Because Pumalín does not belong to the state and to the people but to one man: Douglas Tompkins, billionaire ex-owner of the North Face and Esprit clothing labels turned deep ecology campaigner and rural recluse (*see p138* **Hermit or hero?**).

It's ironic that a human being should get all the attention in this untouched paradise of coastal cliffs and woodlands. The park is a stunner. Even those uneasy with the presence of Tompkins accept that he made no mistake when he chose these 3,000 square kilometres (1,158 square miles) of virgin forests, lakes and mountains. There's even a volcano – 2400-metre (7,874-feet) Michinmahuida – inside the park.

FLORA AND FAUNA
The outstanding species is the slow-growing alerce (the second longest living tree in the world after the bristlecone pine), with some giants just off the road near Caleta Gonzalo. The umbrella-leaved nalca, an edible plant sometimes compared to rhubarb and typical of the south lakes/Aisén regions, lines the roads. As well as woodland animals and birds – pumas, pudús, foxes, woodpeckers – the edges of Pumalín are visited by sea lions, dolphins and Magellanic penguins.

TREKKING AND ACTIVITIES
There are two sections to the park, *norte* and *sur*. The middle bit is owned by an electricity company to whom the government granted this land at least partly to prevent Tompkins owning a continuous mini-country. There are some 15 well-marked trails, some challenging, others mere strolls. You'll find information centres at Chaitén, Caleta Gonzalo (which issues fishing licences) and Hornopirén, where you can enquire about horse riding. In the Cahueló Fjord, there are lovely *termas* – call the Hotel Hornopirén for entry and to camp (the springs are privately owned). The park allows kayak companies from surrounding areas to sail into otherwise inaccessible inlets. A few farms make organic honey and the like – you can visit the *fundo* (farm) and hives at Reñihue, Vodudahue and Pillán. All the information you need is on the excellent website www.parquepumalin.cl.

Chilean Patagonia

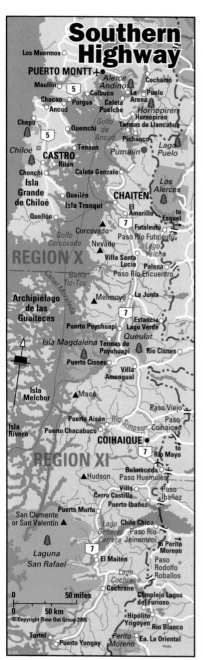

Southern Highway

Los Muermos ○

PUERTO MONTT ✈
Maullín ○   Alerce   Cochamó
    5   Andino ⛰
Chacao ○ Pargua Calbuco ○ La ○ Puelo
    ○ Ancud Puelche Caleta Arena ○
Chepu   ○ Quemchi de Hornopirén
⛰   5   Ancud Termas de Llancahue
Chiloé □   ○ Tenaún Pichanco
    CASTRO   Pumalín   Lago
⛰   ○ Rilán   Puelo
Chonchi ○   Caleta Gonzalo ○
Isla   Los
Grande   ○ Queilén   Alerces
de Chiloé   CHAITEN ●
Isla Tranqui   El
Quellón ○   ○ Amarillo   to
    7   Esquel
Corcovado ⛰   Futaleufú ○
Golfo   Nevado   Paso Río Futaleufú
Corcovado   ⛰   Lago
    Villa Santa   Yelcho
    Lucía   Palena ○
REGION X   Paso Río Encuentro
    Bahía
    Tic-Toc
Archipiélago   ○ Melimoyú   La Junta
de las
Guaitecas   7   Estancia
    Puerto Puyuhuapi ○ Lago Verde
    Queulat
Isla Magdalena Termas de
    Puyuhuapi ⛰ Río Cisnes ○
    Puerto Cisnes ○
    Villa
    Amengual
Isla   ⛰ Macá
Melchor
    Paso Viejo
    Puerto Aisén ○ Río   Paso
Isla   Simpson   Coihaique
Rivero   Puerto Chacabuco ○
    COIHAIQUE ●
REGION XI   7   to
    Río Mayo
    Balmaceda ○
    ⛰ Hudson Paso Huemules
    Villa ○   Paso
    Cerro Castillo   Ibáñez
    Puerto Ibáñez ○
Puerto Murta ○
San Clemente
or San Valentín ⛰   Lago Chile Chico ○
    General   Paso Río
    Carrera Jeinemeni
    7   ○ Perito
Laguna   ○ El Maitén   Moreno
San Rafael   Paso
    Lago   Rodolfo
    Cochrane   Roballos
    ○ Cochrane
0   50 miles   Complejo Lagos
    del Furioso
0   50 km
© Copyright Time Out Group 2005   ○ Hipólito
    Yrigoyen
    Río Blanco
Tortel ○   Perito   Ea. La Oriental
    ○ Puerto Yungay Moreno

Chaitén to Coihaique

Onwards from Chaitén

From Chaitén, most people race through the
long, 420-kilometre (261-mile) stretch, by hot
springs and a fine national park, to **Coihaique**.
But along the way there are plenty of good
detours, none more impressive than the bucolic
hamlet of **Futaleufú**, 78 kilometres (48 miles)
west of the fork at Villa Santa Lucía.

The town derives its name from the azure
Futaleufú River, and is affectionately known as
the 'Fu' by the hundreds of kayakers who come
every summer to test their skills on the river's
unforgiving Class V rapids. Although one of the
planet's toughest rivers, there are gentler runs
for novices as well as rafters, and there's plenty
of hiking and fishing options in the nearby
Reserva Nacional Futaleufú. Ironically,
the Fu's raging whitewater could soon be
reduced to a mere trickle if energy conglomerate
ENDESA goes ahead with plans to build a
dam. To fight for this mythic river's permanent
protection, local residents have joined with
their rapids-shooting friends abroad under the
banner of FutaFriends (www.futafriends.org).

Futaleufú has a number of hotels and
services catering to tourists. For everything
from kayak instruction to guided rafting trips,
consult **Expediciones Chile** (Hostería Río
Grande, O'Higgins 397, 065 721320, www.
exchile.com), run by US resident Chris Spelius,
a former Olympic kayaker. A fine-looking hotel,
modelled on old-style wooden-tiled houses, is
El Barranco (O'Higgins 172, 065 721314,
www.elbarrancochile.cl, double US$60-$80).
A similar but cheaper option is **La Antigua
Casona** (Manuel Rodriguez 215, 065 721311,
double US$30-$45), which doubles as a good
restaurant. Outside of town, **Futa Lodge**
(www.futalodge.com, in Buenos Aires 011
4331 0444, from US$350 all inclusive) is one
of Patagonia's premier fishing lodges, an
exclusive, three-bedroom ranch done up in
rustic elegance where you'll feast on the 16-inch
rainbow and brown trout you hopefully hooked
earlier. Futaleufú is a mere 65 kilometres
(40 miles) from Esquel, in Argentina, but the
road is poor and it's easier to reach the town
taking a van from Chaitur in Chaitén.

The long section from the T-junction at Villa
Santa Lucia to the junction for Puerto Cisnes
passes through the cool (in both senses) jungles
of **Parque Nacional Queulat**. The camera-
clicking attraction here is the **Ventisquero**

Colgante (Hanging Glacier), from whence tumble impressive cascades, some as high as 70 metres (230 feet). From the park's campground it's a three- to four-hour hike to a panoramic outlook at the glacier's base.

At Puerto Puyuhuapi a private boat service goes to the luxurious **Puyuhuapi Lodge & Spa** (Bahía Dorita, Aisén, 02 225 6489, www. patagonia-connection.com, three-night package from US$1,150 all inclusive), an exclusive hot-springs complex located across the Ventisquero Sound. An interesting and convenient place to stay at Puyuhuapi itself is **Casa Ludwig** (Carretera Austral Norte, km 220, 067 325220, www.contactchile.cl/casaludwig, double US$22-$35). This house is the one-time home of four young Germans who arrived here in 1935 from the Sudetenland. The Ludwig hotel's owner can help set up excursions to the national park, as well as fishing expeditions. He's also more than happy to show visitors the town's carpet factory and German coffee shop.

Puerto Cisnes itself is a slight detour from the highway, a compulsory one if you want to see what a handful of Italian immigrants – led by the town's ex-mayor and heroine Eugenia Pircio Biroli – managed to build in the 1960s in nowhere land: a quaint, well-ordered village with an agricultural school, smart buildings and a growing number of hotels and eateries. Between Puerto Cisnes and Coihaique you'll pass Piedra del Gato (Stone of the Cat), a spot where the difficulty of blasting the road caused a number of fatal accidents.

CONAF

Ignacio Serrano 190, Coihaique (067 212125). **Open** 8.30am-6pm Mon-Fri.

Parque Nacional Queulat

Entrances from Chaitén or Coihaique via Carretera Austral. **Open** *Dec-Mar* 8.30am-9pm daily. *Apr-Nov* 8.30am-5.30pm. **Admission** US$2; US$1 under-12s. **No credit cards**.

Coihaique

A growing provincial capital of 45,000 inhabitants and capital of Aisén province, Coihaique has long ceased being the quaint alpine town depicted by the tourist authorities. Luckily it's only a few clicks in any direction until you're surrounded by dramatic, rolling hills and rustic homesteads that looks straight out of *The Sound of Music*. Moreover, in its burgeoning, overpriced urbanity, you'll find pretty much everything you need to fix a driving derby southward: banks, car rental agencies, reliable internet, even an airport – the only place until faraway Punta Arenas to catch a flight back north to Santiago.

Chill out at **Mincho's Lodge**. *See p201.*

Coihaique is also a major angling center, thanks to its proximity to the Simpson and the 370-kilometre-long (230-mile) Río Baker, the Río Pollux, and vast Lago General Carrera. The other main attraction is the San Rafael Glacier, which can be reached by boat from **Puerto Chacabuco**, 82 kilometres (51 miles) away. Drier than Puerto Montt, Coihaique has pleasant summers, though the plains get cold at night.

At the **Museo Regional de la Patagonia** you can gen up on the area's natural history and story of its settlement as a livestock centre. There's also an interesting exhibit about the building of the Carretera Austral.

EXCURSIONS

There are enough destinations easily reached from Coihaique to keep you sated for several days, if not weeks. The best way to tour is in your own vehicle – be sure to reserve in advance. **Budget** (Errazuriz 454, 067 255174) has a good inventory of 4x4s with full insurance. Otherwise, there's a plethora of travel agencies – **Andes Patagónicos** (067 216712, www.ap.cl) inside **Café Restaurant Histórico Ricer** (*see p201*) gets good reviews – that can arrange leisurely half-day tours. Among the top destinations are Seis Lagunas and Lago Elizalde. Travel agency **Aisén Bridges** (Casilla 5, 067 233302, www.aisen.cl) customises road trips along the southern highway, arranging everything from car rental to hotel reservations. They can also take you on a crest-line hike for a rare, up-close view of an Andean condor nesting site.

Compared to destinations farther north and south, Aisén has been unfairly neglected as a major trekking destination. But it's not due to a lack of options. For rugged trekkers and novice mountaineers, **Patagonia Adventure Expeditions** (Riquelme 372, 067 219894, www.adventurepatagonia.com) offers top-notch guided hikes through Aisén's

Chilean Patagonia

How to take the high road

Some might say that driving in Patagonia is craziness. The roads are bone-rattlingly bad, the drivers palm-sweatingly mad and bus travel is speedy, comfy and cheap.

All this is true – extreme caution and steely nerves will contribute far more to a smooth road trip than will many of the roads. But if you still feel the pull of the open road, there can be few places in the world as perfect as the vast, empty and achingly beautiful Patagonia in which to indulge yourself.

However, there are certain precautions you should take to ensure that your abiding memories of the trip are not of being crouched at the side of the road, blinded by dust and cursing the day you didn't pack the right tools to change a flat.

Only the over-cautious insist Patagonia should only be tackled in a 4x4 with miles of clearance and several fat inches of truck-tyre tread; but strong suspension, good tyres and a bit of clearance will help over the worst of the *ripio* (gravel roads).

When it comes to spares, take not only a wheel with good tread (some drivers recommend two) but a carjack and tools for changing it. Carry spare air, oil and fuel filters as well as wiperblades, bulbs, fuses, spark plugs, fan belt and oil. Carry antifreeze if going south in winter. Have your oil changed and your brakes, battery and wheel alignment checked before the off.

To protect your car from flying stones you could cover the radiator in chicken wire secured with plastic sliplocks, both available cheaply from ironmongers (*ferreterias*). Help prevent your windscreen shattering by pressing a thumb to the glass when passing other vehicles. No, really.

To get south you have two options – Ruta 3 traces the great Atlantic Ocean and Ruta 40 follows the Andean foothills. Ruta 3 is paved, flat and featureless, giving an awesome sense of Patagonia's vastness. Ruta 40 is difficult, mainly *ripio* and legendarily beautiful. At the time of writing, the most taxing parts from north to south were: from Perito Moreno town to the junction with Ruta 37; from the north of Lago Cardiel as far as Tres Lagos; and from El Cerrito to the Ruta 7 junction.

Straying from Ruta 40, Ruta 23 to El Chaltén is also arduous. Always ask locals about road conditions. If your Spanish isn't too hot, point at the car and then the road. If they laugh, consider an alternative route. If they cry, consider an alternative route.

The southern stretches are also where fuel is at its most scarce. Always carry some spare. The Automóvil Club Argentina, with offices in most cities, publishes an excellent route map, the *Guía Turística* (US$8), complete with town plans and most gas stations clearly marked. Petrol in Patagonia is subsidised and will tax only the most frugal of budgets.

Of the cross-country routes, one of the least sung and most beautiful is paved Ruta 25 from Trevelin to Trelew. The road is almost empty and traverses some stunning landscapes. Stop for coffee at the gas station 50 kilometres (31 miles) east of Paso de Indios to really see what it is like to live and work in an empty, empty land.

Whatever your route, spare no caution. Argentinians appear to discard careful driving in favour of putting their faith in ubiquitous roadside shrines. (Chilean drivers, on the whole, tend to be more safety aware.) Do not be surprised to round a corner and find yourself faced with a juggernaut overtaking a coach on a blind bend while another juggernaut attempts to drive up your behind. Be patient, stop for regular breaks, pick a good soundtrack, tear up your bus tickets, flick on the engine and try to enjoy the ride. *Suerte*!

back country, including hikes into the rarely visited and hence astoundingly unspoilt Northern Patagonia ice cap. Another top trip is to drive out to Puerto Ibañez and cross over Lago General Carrera (on the transporter) to Chile Chico. The nearby pass, Paso Río Jeinemeni, connects with the small town of Los Antiguos in Argentina, and beyond that, Perito Moreno. A road runs south from Chile Chico and eventually reconnects with the Southern Highway at Cruce El Maitén.

Aisén's biggest attraction is the giant-sized San Rafael glacier, inside the largely inaccessible Laguna San Rafael national park. Although receding rapidly, at 4km (1.5 miles) long and rising 70 metres (230 feet) from the water, this icy behemoth is still an awesome sight to behold. **Transportes Don Carlos** (Subteniente Cruz 63, 067 231981, www. doncarlos.cl) and **Aerohein** (067 232772, www.aerohein.cl) both offer charter flights over the northern Patagonia icefield from Coihaique, including a landing at the glacier's base, quick approach via a dinghy, and the obligatory *whisky con hielo milenario* (whisky with millennial ice). But most tourists opt for the more economical option of going by sea from Puerto Chacabuco, a trip that can easily be booked in town. (*See pp206-209* **Sea Routes South** for more information.)

Two national reserves, RN Coihaique and RN Río Simpson, can be easily explored from Coihaique – the latter is good for fly fishing and both have campsites. If you continue down the west-bound RN Río Simpson road (opened in 1901 and the first trail in the region) you'll come to **Puerto Aisén**, the main port before Puerto Chacabuco was developed, and a lively little town packed with amenities. CONAF has a tree nursery just outside Puerto Aisén. Their office is at Ignacio Serrano No.190 (067 212125).

One good way of exploring the Carretera is by visiting the small family farms that keep alive many of the region's traditions. **Sabores de Aysén** (Arturo Prat 350, 067 237208, www.inter patagonia.com/paseos/sabores_del_aysen) is a self-guided agro-tourism route that takes in ten of these farms, many of which offer tastings of homegrown produce as well as lodging.

Most people do the Carretera Austral in summer; but if you happen to be a cold-blooded loner down here in the long-night season, you can hit the five powder pistes of **El Fraile** ski centre east of Coihaique on Ruta 245. You need a 4x4 and perhaps some chains too; check in town before leaving. It's easier to go with **Transfer Aventura Turismo** (General Parra 22, 067 234748), which operates a service leaving Coihaique at 8.30am and coming back before the sun sets at 3pm.

El Fraile

40km (25 miles) from Coihaique via Camino a Balmaceda (067 210210). **Open** May-Sept 10am-5pm Tue-Sun. **Rates** *Ski pass* US$15; US$8 under-12s. *Equipment hire* US$10. **No credit cards**.

Museo Regional de la Patagonia Central

Lillo 23 (067 213174). **Open** *Jan-Mar* 8.30am-8pm daily. *Apr-Dec* 8.30am-5.30pm Mon-Fri; 9am-2pm Sat. **Admission** US$1.50; free under-12s. **No credit cards**.

RN Coihaique

Open 8.30am-6.30pm daily. **Admission** US$1.50; US75¢ under-12s. **No credit cards**.

RN Río Simpson

Entrances from Visitor centre, Camino Aisén–Coihaique, km 32; Sector San Sebastián, km 28. Open 8.30-6pm daily. **Admission** *Visitor centre* US$1. *Sector San Sebastián* US$12 per tent. **No credit cards**.

Where to stay & eat

Inexpensive *residencias* catering to backpackers are a dime a dozen here, but the best low-budget choice is out of town. **Las Salamandras** (067 211865, www.salamandras.cl, US$7 per person dorm, double from US$15), two kilometres out of town towards the airport has shared and private rooms and an excellent atmosphere with jacuzzi, massages and open kitchen, all set in a pine forest.They also organise treks and winter sports. In town, try the **Hostal Belisario Jara** (Francisco Balbao 662, 067 234150, double from US$60), a charming wood-built lodge with nine odd-shaped rooms, or the larger but very efficient **Hostería Coihaique** (Magallanes 131, 067 231137, www.hotelsa.cl, double US$70-$85). Just south of town, **Mincho's Lodge** (Camino del Bosque 1170, 067 233273, www. minchoslodge.com, double US$140-$175) is Coihaique's cosiest and most popular B&B – each room has panoramic views of the forested Simpson Valley, and the owner, a qualified geologist, is a walking wealth of information on the region. A few blocks from the plaza, the Araucauria-flanked **El Reloj** (Baqueadano 828, 067 231108, double US$45-$60) is another recommended inn. It has a good restaurant and most rooms come with a view.

When you're hungry, the slightly dodgy **Litos** (Lautaro 147, near the bus terminal, $$) serves up big steaks that are popular with locals. For seafood and good service, try the elegant **La Casona** (Obispo Vielmo 77, $$). The most obvious and popular spot in town, with terrace dining on the Horn *peatonal*, is **Café Restaurant Histórico Ricer** (Horn 48, 067 216712, $$$), which serves up pricey but

Chilean Patagonia

authentic Patagonian specialties; check out the museum curios and old photos upstairs. Vegetarians will appreciate the varied menu at **Café Alemana** (Condell 119, no phone, $).

Resources

Hospital
Hospital Regional Coihaique, Jorge Ibar (067 233172).

Internet
Visual Com, 12 de Octubre (067 236300).

Police station
Baquedano 534 (067 215105).

Post office
Cochrane 202 (067 231410).

Tourist information
Sernatur, Bulnes 35 (067 231752). **Open** *Apr-Nov* 8.30am-5.30pm Mon-Fri. *Dec-Mar* 8.30am-9pm Mon-Fri; 10am-7pm Sat, Sun.

Getting there

By road
Coihaique is linked to Argentina via the Huemules, Coihaique and Ibañez passes. Buses run to Los Antiguos, Perito Moreno and on to Comodoro Rivadavia in Argentina. Daily service southward along the Carretera goes as far as Cochrane.

By air
There are flights from Santiago/Puerto Montt to **Aeropuerto Balmaceda** (067 272146), 60km (37 miles) from town. There are transfers into Coihaique (1hr) with every flight, US$4.50 per person. **Transportes Don Carlos** has 2-3 flights weekly to Cochrane and Villa O'Higgins.

By sea
The nearest port is **Puerto Chacabuco**, with regular services to Puerto Montt. *See pp206-209* **Sea Routes South**.

South of Coihaique

South of Coihaique is Chilean Patagonia's last great, unexplored frontier – a region of curious wildlife, furious rivers and postcard-perfect peaks. The paucity of visitors to this remote stretch of Aisén makes the task of describing its attractions almost futile. Moreover, those who get lost here, either deliberately or by mistake (we advise the former), are usually hesitant to let out the secrets of its pristine beauty.

Before leaving Coihaique, load up on cash since bartering is likely to get you farther than a credit card and ATMs are non-existent. After about two hours you'll notice lording over the pampa like a turreted castle the 2,675-metre

(8,777-feet) Cerro Castillo, part of the RN Cerro Castillo. There's a superb four-day trekking circuit around the mastiff, but even if you don't lace up, check out the bucolic settlement of Villa Cerro Castillo, population 300.

From here, it's a scenic 275 kilometres (171 miles) to **Cochrane**, the only settlement south of Coihaique that qualifies as a township. But if you've made it this far you're probably not on a rushed itinerary and should consider breaking up the trip over several days and exploring some of the detours along the way. The Carretera itself mostly climbs and winds around isolated branches of **Lago General Carrera** (called Lago Buenos Aires over the frontier), the deepest and third biggest lake on the continent. Dark blue at its centre, turquoise in the bays, Carrera empties into the Pacific via the Rio Baker, the greatest volume of flowing river water in all Chile.

The first logical overnight destination is **Puerto Tranquilo**, 228 kilometres (142 miles) from Coihaique, where you can take a hour-long boat ride to see the strange Capillas del Mármol – 'marble chapels' carved over millennia by the lake waters. If you're feeling more adventurous you can drive the new road westward to Bahia Exploradores, where after about 52 kilometres (32 miles) there's a somewhat hidden trailhead that leads you, after an easy 15-minute ascent, to a 360-degree lookout point over **Glaciar Exploradores** and the majestic **Cerro San Valentín** – at 4,058 metres (13,314 feet) the highest peak in southern Patagonia. The trail cuts through land owned by Santiago Croxatto, a Santiago-born photographer and mountain guide who is also the owner of **El Puesto** (Pedro Lagos 258, 02 1964555, double US$55-$60), a smart B&B in the town centre that feels like the inside of a tree house; it's one of the friendliest lodges in this part of the world, which is saying something.

Back on the Carretera, it's 71 kilometres (44 miles) to the picturesque hamlet of **Puerto Bertrand**, which hangs over the lake of the same name. It's where the mighty Rio Baker begins its winding, 200-kilometre (124-mile) flow to the Pacific. The town owes its existence to the Sociedad Explotadora del Baker, a once colossal farming enterprise that was administered by restless pioneer Lucas Bridges after he got bored of befriending Ona Indians in Tierra del Fuego. In 2004, the last vestige of that failed enterprise, the Estancia Valle Chacabuco, was bought by two modern-day Patagonian legends, North American conservationists Doug Tompkins and Kris McDivitt (*see p138* **Hermit or hero?**). The ranch's modern and unattractive administrative centre is a small detour from the Carretera as you head south to Cochrane along the east-heading road to Paso Roballos and Argentina. If you follow the barely travelled, guanaco-infested road all the way, you'll ram against Cerro Lucas Bridges and the abandoned, Victorian-styled home he built for himself just before the border crossing. Because of its idyllic beauty and the wide-open, high-walled valley that straddles the border, Bruce Chatwin was moved to speculate that it was the source, if not in fact then in spirit, of the Ciudad de los Césares myth that so captivated Patagonia's early explorers.

Several high-end resorts and fishing lodges that are getaway destinations in themselves surround Puerto Bertrand and the grimier city

Beautiful, isolated **Caleta Tortel**. *See p204.*

of Puerto Guadal, 30 kilometres (19 miles) north-east. Among the best, the French-owned **Terra Luna Lodge**, located outside Puerto Guadal (067 431263, www.terra-luna.cl, double US$50-$70) has two-floor bungalows with a view of General Carerra lake and amenities that include rustic, wood-burning hot tubs. The professional staff can arrange anything from flyovers of the northern Patagonian icecap to guided mountaineering expeditions. Farther south along the lake, anglers will want to check out the Argentinian-run **Río Baker Lodge** (in Buenos Aires through Estancias de Santa Cruz, 011 4863 9373, www.estanciasdesantacruz.com), whose dining room hangs so precipitously over the crystalline waters you might fall in looking at yourself after a few pisco sours.

Cochrane

Fifty kilometres (31 miles) south of Puerto Bertrand you'll reach **Cochrane**, the biggest township south of Coihaique, with a population of 2,500. The town is surrounded by acres of planted pine trees that sit like matches waiting to spark in the arid summer heat.

Adjacent to town is **RN Tamango**, a 7,000-hectare (17,000-acre) preserve that's the protected home to 52 of the last 2,000 or so remaining huemul deers, the animal whose robust silhouette emblazons Chile's national coat of arms. Before the arrival of European settlers, the huemul population was plentiful and its range stretched almost to the Atlantic coast. Although the indigenous Telhueche and Mapuche tribes treated the animal with respect, today more than a century of reckless hunting, deforestation and – most drastically – sheep grazing, has severely depleted the majestic deer's numbers to under an estimated 2,000. As a result the once curious and human-friendly species has been forced to isolate itself in the protective cover of the high and rugged Andean forests. The good news, for curious humans at least, is that canny local guides from Cochrane can take travellers on a dinghy to chase the furtive animal up and down the Río Cochrane. They will all but guarantee you a sighting for US$20-$25. For more information and lots of photographs, see www.huemul.net.

Munro-baggers will want to check out the isolated alpine lake that's the apex of a two-day loop through the reserve; with under 1,000 visitors a year to Tamango, you're likely to get this killer camping spot all to yourself. More intrepid hikers will want to check out the glaciated valleys below the 3,706-metre (12,159-feet) Monte San Lorenzo – considered one of Patagonia's wildest and most beautiful ranges; ask around town for information about reaching the mountain *refugio* run by horseman Señor Soto de la Cruz and his wife. Soto de la Cruz also runs 11-day horse rides along an abandoned gaucho trail to Villa O'Higgins.

Cochrane residents are incredibly friendly and anyone staying more than a night will have no trouble adjusting to the town's lazy pace. For lodging, your best bet is **Hostal Latitud 47** (Lago Brown 564, 067 522280, turislat47sur @hotmail.com, double US$30-$45), which is made of little more than clapboard but run by a friendly retired bank manager who delights in getting sloshed on whisky with his guests. Another hotel, with many more amenities but at a higher cost, is **Hotel Wellman** (Las Golondrinas 36, 067 522171, double US$60-$75). Those on a tighter budget should consider **Residencial Cero a Cero** (Lago Brown 464, 067 522 158, ceroacero@ze.cl, double US$15-$20).

Wherever you stay, take your meals at **El Fogón** (San Valentin 653) which serves up an excellent *bife a lo pobre*, or the more modern **Café Nirrañtal** at the bottom of O'Higgins, with the red-flashing 'Coffe' sign on the front.

CONAF
Río Neff 417, Cochrane (067 522164). **Open** 8.30am-6pm Mon-Fri.

Reserva Nacional Lago Cochrane
Follow signs from Cochrane along dirt road for 4km (2.5 miles). **Open** 8.30am-6pm daily. **Admission** US$3; US$1 under-12s. **No credit cards**.

RN Tamango
From Cochrane, 4km (1.5 miles) along gravel road leading northeast. **Open** *Dec-Mar* 8.30am-9pm daily. *Apr-Nov* 8.30am-6.30pm daily. **Admission** US$3.

Caleta Tortel

Certain to become a huge attraction in coming years, **Caleta Tortel** is one of those places that simply has to be seen to be believed. If the name sounds vaguely familiar to you, it's probably thanks to the UK's Prince William: he spent three months working here in 2000 as part of his gap year.

Located 128 kilometres (80 miles) south-west of Cochrane, this picturesque and hauntingly isolated town cleaves to the side of a rocky promontory overlooking a rain-soaked cove and is surrounded on all sides by rugged, jungled islets and intersecting fjords that form a landscape not unlike the South China Sea. Every home is built on stilts, and seven kilometres (three miles) of cypress-built stairs and walkways fulfil the function of roads.

Despite Tortel's location on the coast, its 500 resilient inhabitants don't depend on fish. Instead, they make their livelihood harvesting wood from the native coihue, tepu and cypress forests that cover the outlying islets. Until a 25-kilometre (16-mile) road was built in 2003, linking the town to the Carretera, virtually the

The Carretera Austral meets a watery end at **Villa O'Higgins**. *See p205.*

only connection to the outside world was a passing ship (less than a decade ago cashless locals still bartered wood for alcohol) or an uncertain, day-long journey up the Baker. These days, during summer, **Buses Acuario 13** in Cochrane (Rio Baker 349, 067 522143) runs a mini-van service here six days a week.

The road was built, following a divisive community debate, to encourage tourism, and the town's humble residents, converted almost overnight into hoteliers and restaurateurs, are well organised. Although outside influences are apparent, at least for now, the town's charm and traditional way of life has barely changed. Lumberjacks still strut nonchalantly around town with huge trunks hoisted on their shoulders, and of the handful of vehicles parked at the town's entrance, most belong to outsiders.

Most tourists will be amply entertained just observing Tortel's quirky, *Northern Exposure*-like daily life, but you can also hire local boats for a tour around the bay. All tours stop at the dilapidated cemetery on the **Isla de los Muertos**, the burial ground for 120 labourers who, depending on who you believe, either succumbed to scurvy or were poisoned for protesting work conditions at the Sociedad Explotadora del Baker in the 1920s.

Despite the fact that Tortel has no hotels, several enterprising residents have opened their homes to guests, or else built basic but pleasant B&Bs to lodge tourists. One worth recommending is former *hachero* (lumberjack) Javier Pinilla's **El Estilo**, surrounded by hummingbird-infested chilco shrub in the 'Sector Centro'. Another option is **Hospedaje Costanera** (067 234815), which has an attractive garden and clean rooms.

Thankfully, for purists at least, there are as yet no private telephones in Tortel; instead residents rely on an ingenious system of public intercoms, one every 100 metres, that connect with the municipality's outside line (067 211876). This is also the best means of obtaining tourist information.

Villa O'Higgins

Returning to the Carretera from Tortel, it's one last, exasperating push to the end of the road – at least for now – in **Villa O'Higgins**. At Puerto Yungay, alongside a monument to the man who built it all, ex-dictator Pinochet, you board a ferry for a 45-minute crossing of the Mitchell Fjord before the final, slow crawl into Villa O'Higgins.

As you tread along perilous scree slopes past precariously hanging glaciers, gushing waterfalls and jungled hillsides, you can't help but marvel at – or perhaps pity – the stubbornness of the Chilean engineers. This final section of the Carretera Austral, opened in 1999, is notorious for toppling cars, and more than a few motorists have perished in accidents on this particular stretch.

From Cochrane, **Buses Los Nadis** (067 522196) makes the entire 131-kilometre (81- mile) journey during summer once weekly, but along the way they are willing to pick up passengers from outside Caleta Tortel, on the condition that they have reservations.

In O'Higgins you can camp, rest, eat, try to unbuckle your crippled backbone… but you can't drive on. The dusty town's end-of-the-road feel is poignant, but except for some isolated trails up to **Río Mosco** glacier, there's little to do here – not even a restaurant in which to chill out. But herein lies its allure – although less scenic, it's probably as close as latecomer tourists will ever get to experiencing what Argentina's El Chaltén felt like 20 years ago when mass tourism to Patagonia was only a dream. It's a certainty that the next two decades won't be so unobtrusive.

For years, the few tourists that came here had only one choice: return the long way they came, by road or wait for one of the very irregular flights. But now it's possible to sail, hike and sail some more onward to El Chaltén. In 2005, the refurbished catamaran Quetrú, operated by **Hielo Sur** (067 670313, www.villaohiggins. com), made its maiden voyage across the shimmering blue Lago O'Higgins (known as Lago San Martin on the Argentinian side). The navigation takes three hours and costs from US$30, but you won't feel ripped off as you cruise around the giant icebergs and 60-metre (197-foot) wall of O'Higgins glacier, one of the largest in Patagonia.

However you choose to get there, you'll be dropped off at **Estancia Candelaria Mansilla**, where, after getting your passport stamped, you can hike or ride the seven kilometres (three miles) upward to the border crossing with Argentina. From the Eiffel-looking steel *hito* (border marking) you descend a forested trail for another two hours, taking in incredible views of the Fitz Roy mountain range. You'll then reach the northern tip of Lago del Desierto, where wisecracking Argentinian *gendarmes* (border police) might solicit you for 'donations' to keep the trail clean – don't expect a receipt. Here you can camp, traverse the length of the lake (which takes around five hours) or take a boat to the southern end and then a regular shuttle the remaining 37 kilometres (23 miles) into El Chaltén. But once you've reached the increasingly ugly epicentre of Patagonia's tourist boom, you may begin to miss the sleepy, unspoilt charms of Villa O'Higgins.

Chilean Patagonia

Sea Routes South

Reached the end of the road? Then take to the water.

For travellers of a youthful and independent disposition, averse to any proscribed, style-cramping mode of transport, the mere idea of sailing on a cruise ship will be enough to induce a squirm of bohemian revulsion – you might just as well ask them to voyage with a personal valet. In Chilean Patagonia, however, travelling by boat is as practical and proletarian as a ride on the No.10 bus – and a good deal more fun.

Some people will head south on the Southern Highway, itself dependent on fjord crossings at two points, and use the bus or a car to cross into Argentina and back over the frontier at Torres del Paine. This is fine if you like the open road. But following in the wake of the native Chonos and Alacaluf and taking to the water is also a highly pleasurable and revealing way into Patagonia – and arguably the only way to get to know archipelagic Chile. Serene as it is, the sea route south is dramatic – in the fjords, the Andes are submerged and you are actually within their glacially eroded valleys. Once in Magallanes province, you eventually sail to the west of the mountain range.

Out of the port at **Puerto Montt** (Avenida Angelmó 1763, 065 252247), two Chilean firms – **Navimag** and state-owned **Transmarchilay** – run large roll-on/roll-off type cruisers to docks at **Puerto de Chaitén** (Sector Piedra Blanca, 065 731267), **Puerto Chacabuco** (Bernardo O'Higgins, 067 351444) and **Puerto Natales** (Pedro Montt 380, 061 411290). These boats were originally designed to transport container-carrying lorries and a few cars (useful if you've hired a vehicle) but have been modified to seat or sleep foot passengers. Accommodation and amenities are at best humble and at worst painful – the slow night boat in winter from, say, Chaitén to Puerto Montt is a cramped, insomniacal affair and there's neither a restaurant nor views to help you while away the hours. (If you regard cruising as irredeemably bourgeois, this is the trip for you.) The upside is that these services – commuter lines between central and southern Chile – are not going to cost you a lifetime's savings. Navimag is currently the only company connecting Puerto Montt to Puerto Natales in the Deep South.

The icy peaks of the **Glaciar San Rafael**.
See p207.

No doubt in response to the lack of tourist-friendly luxury, several firms offer rather more lavish cruises from Puerto Chacabuco – about 1,200 kilometres (746 miles) south of Puerto Montt – while **Catamaranes del Sur** sails tourist services out of Puerto Chacabuco. Of the posh cruisers, **Skorpios'** boats, for instance, kitted out for week-long luxury cruises from Chacabuco into the fjords, are bound for obvious attractions like the San Rafael glacier and compete with smaller catamarans that sail from within the Southern Highway section. These companies, which of course charge more for comfort and catering, are interested in leisure travellers so operate mainly in summer. Contact information for operators is listed alphabetically on *p209*. The duration of a voyage on longer, luxury trips often has less to do with the distance covered or hours of actual navigation, than with the amount of time different boat operators allow in each stop off point. Company websites are very helpful and show clear maps of routes and up-to-date timetables; most have good English versions.

Puerto Montt & Chiloé to Chaitén

Chaitén is the entry-point for the **Parque Pumalín** (*see p197*), just a few miles to the north, or for taking a bus or driving south to Coihaique and beyond.

Pleasant breezes and the generally calm waters of the inland sea are all you get on this journey, with the odd dolphin thrown in if you're lucky. Chiloé and its islands are on the right and Pumalin on the left, though all you see from the deck is hazy woods, the occasional house or farm and some fishing boats bobbing back and forth. Doing this trip non-stop is a useful alternative to driving the early, messy parts of the Southern Highway.

At time of going to press only one firm was operating the direct sea route from Puerto Montt to Chaitén: Transmarchilay. Navimag had previously run this route in January and February only, on the cargo transporter (in Spanish, *transbordadore*) *Alejandrina,* but the future of this service is uncertain so you should call their office or check their website (*see p209*) for up-to-date information. Transmarchilay's *La Pincoya* covers the approximately 150-kilometre (90-mile) trip in a generous ten hours. The chug at nine knots per hour is great for slowing down after your trek through the lakes, but the seating areas are small and the on-board food is in no danger of winning any Michelin stars. Take a picnic and a flask if you've got one – and a good, thick book.

Transmarchilay also runs a thrice-weekly service between Chaitén and the port of Castro on the island of Chiloé, also using *La Pincoya.* The trip takes around seven hours.

Transmarchilay

Vessel *La Pincoya* (64 passengers). **Route** Puerto Montt–Chaitén (9hrs). **Rates** US$32; US$120 cars. **Departs** *Puerto Montt–Chaitén* noon Mon; 8pm Tue; 10pm Thur, Fri. *Chaitén–Puerto Montt* 11.59pm Mon; 11.59pm Wed; 9am Fri; 8pm Sun. **Route** Chaitén–Castro (7hrs). **Rates** US$32; US$120 cars. **Departs** *Chaitén–Castro* 8.30am Mon; 9am Sat; 9am Sun. *Castro–Chaitén* 4pm Wed; 4.30pm Sat; 4.30pm Sun.

Puerto Montt to Chacabuco & Laguna San Rafael

This tourist service is regarded by Patagonian travellers as a high point. As well as the peace and beauty of the fjords, you get a look at one of the region's most remote glaciers – **Glaciar San Rafael** (also called San Valentín) – at the southern end of a saltwater lagoon of the same name. This tidewater glacier, at the northern end of the Northern Ice Field (Campo de Hielo Norte), the closest of its kind to the Equator, is just the tip of the ice-filled **Parque Nacional Laguna San Rafael**, a vast reserve of wooded mountains. The park is home to giant ferns, chilco fuchsias, canelos and lengas – and labyrinthine channels.

You can do the photo-friendly cruise to San Rafael with Navimag. Alternatively, there are smaller, semi-luxury ('semi' because a bit claustrophobic) cruisers like those owned by Skorpios, Catamaranes del Sur (*Catamarán Iceberg Expedition*) and Patagonia Connection. Trips take three, four or seven days, depending on your schedule, and while the ferries have reclining seats and bunks, the smaller cruisers have several classes of cabin. You can also charter a smaller cruiser (which can incorporate landings and visits to narrower channels) from Puerto Montt or Puerto Chacabuco. If you want a cheap, local deal, talk to the men who run *goletas* (small boats) from **Puerto Palos** and **Puerto Aguas Muertas** in Puerto Aisén, just 14 kilometres (8.5 miles) from Puerto Chacabuco, since they go into the fjords regularly to deliver goods and pick up people.

Navimag's *Puerto Edén* and *Magallanes* goes to Chacabuco and San Rafael. *Patagonia Express* and *Skorpios I, II* and *III* offer a variety of trips including the San Rafael glacier. (Note that *Skorpios III* operates out of Puerto Natales). There are also a few smaller firms operating out of Puerto Chacabuco. Check with the tourist offices in Puerto Montt or in Coihaique.

Chilean Patagonia

Laguna San Rafael. *See p207.*

Catamaranes del Sur

Vessel *Catamarán Iceberg Expedition* (70
passengers). **Route** Puerto Chacabuco–Glaciar San
Rafael (5hrs). **Rates** US$310 full-day excursion.
Departs *Apr-Nov* every 2nd Sat. *Dec-Mar* Sat, Tue.

Navimag

Vessels *Puerto Edén* (170 passengers) & *Magallanes*
(210 passengers). **Route** Puerto Montt–Laguna San
Rafael–Puerto Montt (5 days). **Rates** US$370-$600.
Route Puerto Montt–Laguna San Rafael–Puerto
Chacabuco (4 days). **Rates** US$320-$500.
Route Puerto Chacabuco–Laguna San Rafael–
Puerto Chacabuco (2 days). **Rates** US$280-$450.
Route Puerto Montt–Puerto Chacabuco (1 day).
Rates US$65-$90.
One departure per week, all year round. Check dates
at any of their offices or at www.navimag.cl.

Patagonia Connection

Vessel *Patagonia Express* (70 passengers). **Route**
Termas de Puyuhuapi–Laguna San Rafael–Puerto
Chacabuco (6 days). **Departs** *mid Oct-Apr* Mon, Tue,
Thur, Sat. **Rates** US$1,000-$2,100.

Skorpios

Vessel *Skorpios I* (70 passengers). **Route** Puerto
Chacabuco–Glaciar San Rafael–Puerto Chacabuco
(4 or 5 days). **Departs** *Sept-May* Fri, Mon. **Rates**
US$630-$1,000.
Vessel *Skorpios II* (110 passengers). **Route** Puerto
Montt–Glaciar San Rafael–Puerto Montt (7 days).
Departs *Sept-May* Sat. **Rates** US$1,000-$1,800.
Vessel *Skorpios III* (92 passengers). **Route** Puerto
Natales–Glaciar XI–Puerto Natales (6 days).
Departs *Sept-May* Sat. **Rates** US$1,750-$2,950.
Check departures dates with Skorpios.

Puerto Montt to Puerto Natales

This is the big one. Navimag, who operate this
service exclusively, are sailing a route of some
political significance. In 1978, Argentina, then
under the jackboot of the Videla dictatorship,
closed the southern border crossings with Chile,
so those Chileans – also led by an unelected
general, Pinochet – who needed to get to Tierra
del Fuego had need of a maritime passage.

Regarded by I'd-never-go-on-a-cruise-man
backpackers as a cheap and hip, er, cruise, this
trip combines touristy visions of fjords and
ultra-remote forests on island mountains with a
practical way of getting from A to B. The 1,460-
kilometre (907-mile) journey takes three nights
and four days, so those who like quick thrills
may get a bit bored – otherwise there's lots of
time for expert Chile talk on deck with all the
World Travellers who use this service.

The canals are alive with steamer ducks,
porpoises and seals, and gulls and skuas will
often follow the boat for hours in the hope of
a scrap of bread. A sublime pause is the short
visit to **Puerto Edén**, on Isla Wellington near
the immense PN Bernardo O'Higgins. About
200 people live here, including a few dozen
mixed-race Alacaluf. As well as the relief at
seeing real people rather than backpackers
– people who have roots here – the simple
presence of a village in such glorious isolation
is a reminder of what Patagonia once was: a
scattered wilderness of self-sufficient people at
one with nature in its fiercest expression.

The other main event on the trip is when the
boat sails parallel to the **Southern Ice Field**
(Campo de Hielo Sur) – the 13,000-square-
kilometre (5,019-square-mile) glacier left behind
by the ice age. It appears in the distance like a
flat white line behind peaks and at sunset glows
pink and orange – a surreal high point.

Because the canals are protected from
gales and swollen seas by the low mountains,
there's little in the way of vomit-inducing
swells and yaws – those throwing up overboard
are far more likely to be afflicted with alcohol
poisoning than with seasickness. The only
place where character-building weather is likely
is during the last 24 hours when the boat pulls
out into the **Golfo de Penas** and takes on the
Pacific for half a day. Afterwards comes the
Canal Messier, where you are crossing the
Andes – the narrow channel, which can only
be used at high tide, is effectively a pass in
the cordillera. As this is also the watershed, it
might well rain here – it usually does: up to
4,000 millimetres (157 inches) fall annually.

Aboard Navimag's long-established megatug
Puerto Edén – a converted transporter ship
– the accommodation and dining falls short
of VIP lounges and lobster thermidore. There
are, rather, a range of bunks and cabins and
way down in the hull, communal *literas* – where
most fun of the raucous kind) is to be had.
Navimag introduced the *Magallanes* in 2002,
a refurbished cargo ship with classier service,
which replaces the *Edén* for part of the year.

Navimag

Vessels *Puerto Edén* (170 passengers) and
Magallanes (210 passengers). **Route** Puerto
Montt–Puerto Natales (4 days) **Departs** 4pm Mon.
Route Puerto Natales–Puerto Montt. **Departs** 6am
Fri. **Rates** *May-Sept* US$210-$720. *Oct, Apr* US$275-
$1,180. *Nov-Mar* US$325-$1,690.

Boat operators

In addition to the principal boat operators
listed below, the following run useful services:
in Punta Arenas, **Transbordadora Austral
Broom** (Avenida Bulnes 05075, 061 218100,
www.tabsa.cl) connect Tres Puentes Punta
Arenas with Porvenir all year round; **Ferry
Chelenco** (067 233 466) and **Pilchero** (067
234240) in Coihaique run services between
Puerto Ibáñez and Chile Chico all year round;
Cruceros Australis (02 442 3110, www.
australis.com) operates luxury cruises from
Punta Arenas, via Ushuaia to Puerto Williams.
From Punta Arenas and Ushuaia, cruises sail
out into the Magellan Strait and beyond to
Antarctica and the South Atlantic Islands.

Catamaranes del Sur

*Pedro de Valdivia 0210, Providencia, Santiago
(02 2311902/www.catamaranesdelsur.cl).*
Open 9am-6.30pm Mon-Fri (also on Sat mornings
in high season). **Credit** AmEx, DC, MC, V.
Other locations: Hotel Loberías del Sur, José Miguel
Carrera 50, Puerto Chacabuco (067 351112/351115).

Navimag

*11th Floor, Avenida El Bosque Norte 0440, Las
Condes, Santiago (02 4423120/www.navimag.cl).*
Open *Apr-Aug* 9am-6.30pm Mon-Fri. *Sept-Mar*
9am-6.30pm Mon-Fri; 10am-1.30pm Sat. **Credit**
AmEx, DC, MC, V.
Other locations: Angelmó 2187, Puerto Montt (065
432300); Pedro Montt 457, Quellón (065 682207); Ignacio
Carrera Pinto 188, Chaitén (065 731570); Terminal de
Transbordadores, Puerto Chacabuco (067 351111);
Manuel Bulnes 533, Puerto Natales (061 414300).

Patagonia Connection

*Office 1006, Tenth Floor, Fidel Oteiza 1921,
Providencia, Santiago (02 2256489/www.
patagonia-connection.com).* **Open** 9am-6.30pm
Mon-Fri. **Credit** AmEx, DC, MC, V.

Skorpios

*Augusto Leguía Norte 118, y Don Carlos
(02 4771900/www.skorpios.cl).* **Open** 9am-7pm
Mon-Sat. **Credit** AmEx, DC, MC, V.
Other locations: Angelmó 1660, Puerto Montt (065
275613); General Parra 21, Coihaique (067 213756);
Turismo Lago Traful (Buenos Aires representatives),
Fourth Floor, Viamonte 377 (011 43112164).

Transmarchilay

*Angelmó 2187, Puerto Montt (065 270430/www.
transmarchilay.cl).* **Open** 9am-1pm, 3-7pm Mon-Fri.
Credit AmEx, DC, MC, V.

The ice box

You've travelled thousands of kilometres
to get in that prime position perched on
a rock staring at a wall of ice. Time for
contemplation – so here's a few facts:

How are glaciers formed?
When snow falls, it gets heavier and heavier
and becomes packed ice and the weight,
combined with a goo of rocks, earth and
melted ice below, help the ice-block move
along. It grows and grows so long as it's cold.

Why do they exist here?
Glaciers and ice fields are the last remnants
of the ice age, which drew to a close some
11,500 years ago. During the ice age about
32 per cent of the earth was covered by
glaciers – now it's about ten per cent.

Where else do you find them?
Greenland and Antarctica are the two
principal ice environments. There are also
glaciers in the Alps, the US, Canada and
on mountain tops in tropical regions.

Are they useful?
Chile and Argentina think so – they are
still arguing over who owns some of the
ice in the Patagonian Andes. Given the
general concern about global warming,
the vast resources of drinking water
(75 per cent of the world's fresh water
is glacial) might one day prove priceless.

Why do they look blue?
The spectrum of colours – blues, greens
and turquoises – trapped inside the ice
is caused by the dense, compacted ice,
which can only be penetrated by the short
wavelengths of blue light.

Will they eventually disappear?
The Perito Moreno glacier was growing
until 1988 – due to global warming or some
internal physics – but in general glaciers are
shrinking. The Upsala, the largest glacier
in Lago Argentino, has retreated 60 metres
(197 feet) a year over the past 60 years.

And then?
There will be more U-shaped valleys in
Patagonia, some of which will fill with
seawater. The sea would rise about 20cm
(8in) if all the glaciers outside Antarctica
and Greenland melted – or 70 metres (230
feet) if all the ice melted. If you want more
ice, you can visit Antarctica – while it lasts.

Chilean Patagonia

The Deep South 2

Where the Americas end. In style.

Chile's Región XII comprises the provinces of Magallanes and Ultima Esperanza and Chile's territorial claims to Antarctica. They make up 17.5 per cent of Chilean national territory but just a meagre one per cent of its population. The principal points of interest are on the mainland – **Parque Nacional Torres del Paine**, its access town the tranquil **Puerto Natales**, as well as livelier and more cosmopolitan **Punta Arenas**, the main settlement further south. Off the mainland, the coastline breaks up into hundreds of mostly uninhabited islands, lined with ice-walled fjords, that run all the way down to **Cabo de Hornos** (Cape Horn). By far the largest fragment is Isla Grande de Tierra del Fuego, separated from the mainland by the **Estrecho de Magallanes** (Magellan Strait). The more densely populated part belongs to Argentina and includes the city of Ushuaia (*see p158*), although nearly two-thirds of the land mass remains under Chile's jurisdiction. Mostly windswept steppe, the majority of Chilean inhabitants live in **Porvenir**, the only town and the capital of Chilean Tierra de Fuego. Founded in 1894 as a port to serve local sheep *estancias,* it flourished briefly during the gold rush, but has changed little with the years. Today Porvenir is home to 6,500 inhabitants, many of whom are of Croatian descent. A signpost in the town marks the distance to Croatia.

Also within Región XII is **Puerto Williams** on Isla Navarino, facing Argentinian Tierra del Fuego on the southern side of the **Canal Beagle** (Beagle Channel). It's the most southerly populated settlement in the world, boosted by the presence of a permanently staffed naval base and unspoilt save for the environmental havoc wreaked there (and in many other parts of Tierra del Fuego) by the non-indigenous Canadian beaver, introduced in 1946 to start a fur trade.

Cape Horn itself is a rocky outcrop marking the end of the Americas: beyond this point there is nowhere to go except Antarctica. It houses Chilean naval constructions and a lighthouse and is now a protected national park. A memorial honours the innumerable mariners who have perished there, and navigating the Horn is still a serious nautical challenge. The gentlest way to disembark is from one of the cruise ships that make brief stops when weather and tidal conditions allow.

Puerto Natales

Puerto Natales, capital of Ultima Esperanza province, is all about 'location, location, location'. Arrive in town on a rainy day and the town, with its not-quite-kitsch buildings and often deserted streets, is likely to inspire only the most ironically minded. However, dig a little deeper and some saving graces emerge, mainly in the form of good eateries and helpful local hosts, which make this a logical stopover en route to Torres del Paine, Chile's world-renowned national park, more than just tolerable. And you certainly shouldn't feel lonely: Puerto Natales sees its fair share of tourism, and lodging is often difficult to find in high season, when the town is bustling with travellers about to embark on a few days' immersion in wild Patagonia.

Puerto Natales was colonised comparatively late; European expeditions to the area took place from as early as the 1550s, though, due in part to resistance from the indigenous Tehuelche, it wasn't until 1893 that colonisation began. In that year German explorer Captain Hermann Eberhard built the first cattle *estancia* near Puerto Prat, the port that would later be replaced by Puerto Natales in a more accessible position to the south. The town was officially founded in 1911 and thanks to its slaughterhouse and meat factory – still in use at Puerto Bories, six kilometres (3.5 miles) north – became one of the world's leading beef exporters by the 1970s. Today, the main activities in town of around 19,000 inhabitants (less than one-fifth of the population of Punta Arenas to the south) are fishing, livestock raising and tourism.

The Sernatur tourist office, a smattering of hotels and restaurants and the ferry terminal can be found on the coastal road, Costanera Pedro Montt. Against this backdrop black-necked swans, flamingos and other bird life wander the **Canal Señoret** (Señoret Channel) shore line, where there are handsome views over **Seno Ultima Esperanza** (Last Hope Sound) to Península Antonio Varas. Up the hill on the main street, Manuel Bulnes, is the **Museo Histórico Municipal** which also houses the smaller municipal tourist office, with helpful staff. The small museum's clearly laid-out exhibits document the town's history. Its key curiosity is the boat used by Eberhard

View of Cerro Castillo from **Puerto Natales**. *See p210.*

Chilean Patagonia

Bruce and the giant sloth

As a child Bruce Chatwin was fascinated by the milodon. His genre-defining travel book, *In Patagonia*, was the result of his journey south in search of the story behind the mythical beast whose skin was on display in a cabinet in Chatwin's grandmother's dining room. 'Never in my life have I wanted anything as I wanted that piece of skin,' Chatwin wrote.

Every country, it seems, needs a monster to believe in. Claimed sightings of Nessie in Scotland, the simian-footed yeti in Tibet and Patagonia's own Nahuelito monster in Bariloche's Lago Nahuel Huapi have all generated acres of press over the years; and despite the unwillingness of these creatures to prove their existence to anyone other than a select number of believers and amateur documentary makers, countless folk still remain convinced of their existence.

In the case of the Chilean milodon, one crucial difference set apart the numerous professed sightings of this giant ground sloth in the 19th century. Although the hairy giant disappeared along with the woolly mammoth at the end of the Pleistocene era (or so killjoy naturalists would want us to believe), it did at least exist at one time.

In 1896 Captain Hermann Eberhard stumbled across a pile of dung, skin and bones in some caves north-west of Puerto Natales. Although belonging to a mammal that is now known to have expired some 10,000 years earlier, the remains were so well preserved by the cold that they appeared to be fresh. As a result, many wrongly believed that there were milodon still at large and that relatives of the 4.6-metre (15-foot) extinct creature could still be lurking in their subterranean lairs. A few years later more remains were uncovered during excavations led by the cousin of Chatwin's grandmother, who, after hawking his main find to the British Museum, sent back a small token to his family.

But even if the milodon had survived the ice age, there would have been no reason to fret. The giant herbivore would have far preferred a leaf salad with grub croutons over the blood of a German explorer. According to Chatwin, the milodon had a 'long extensible tongue, like a giraffe's, which it used to scoop up leaves and grubs.' Legend has it that the milodon was so tame that indigenous natives kept them as pets: until food became scarce, that is, when beasts would be killed and eaten.

that could be folded into a suitcase. At the **Museo de Flora y Fauna** in the same building you can familiarise yourself with the local wildlife before taking any trips out of town. Two blocks north-west from here is the quaint Plaza de Armas overlooked by the colonial bell-towered church, Iglesia Parroquial, and the Municipalidad (town hall) – a building carved in wood dating from the early pioneer days. In the centre of the plaza is an old locomotive engine once used in the meat factory in Puerto Bories, which, on Saturday nights, is now a focal point for groups of drunken teenagers.

EXCURSIONS

The point of a visit to Puerto Natales for most travellers is its proximity to what most people consider to be the finest national park in South America, 147 kilometres (91 miles) north (*see p214* **Parque Nacional Torres del Paine**). There are as many different ways to 'do' Paine as there are trekkers queuing up to do it. Many tourists come specifically to do the four- or seven-day trekking circuits, but there are almost infinite ways to get off these beaten tracks and you can also easily arrange a day trip out of Puerto Natales.

Scores of companies and private guides organise excursions in the area; alternatively, you can opt to use your own transport, the regular bus services or a taxi. Most major tour operators offer one-day guided treks to Glaciar Grey, or to the Torres themselves. **Comapa Turismo** (Bulnes 533, 061 414300, www. comapa.cl) offers trips to Torres by bus, or by boat along the Rio Serrano, with overnight options. For the more adventurous, **Big Foot** (Bories 206, 061 413247, www.bigfootpatagonia. com) runs one-day ice-trekking and climbing excursions to Glaciar Grey for US$120-$140 per person, as well as plenty of kayaking and horse-trekking trips, while **Chile Nativo** (Casilla 42, 061 411835, www.chilenativo.com) runs seven- to 12-day guided treks.

The Balmaceda and Serrano glaciers in the southern ice fields of the Parque Nacional Bernardo O'Higgins are also worth the day trip by boat through the Seno Ultima Esperanza, regardless of whether or not you intend to continue on to Torres del Paine. **Turismo 21 de Mayo** (Eberhard 560, 061 411978, www. turismo21demayo.cl) is a family-run outfit that's been following in Magellan's wake through these waters for more than three decades. Their well-equipped boats, *21 de Mayo*, *Alberto de Agostini* and *21 de Mayo III*, sail all year (round trips cost US$65; to Torres del Paine US$101 although trips are less frequent in winter).

A curious diversion on the way to the park is the **Monumento Natural Cueva del Milodón**, 24 kilometres (15 miles) north of Natales. It is made up of three caves and a rock formation known as the Silla del Diablo (Devil's Seat). A fibreglass model of the caves' former inhabitant poses for photo opportunities in its old home; the actual remains were shipped over to the British Museum long ago. There's a visitor centre with helpful staff and lots of information in English. Those preferring to saddle-up for the event can choose to take half-day horse treks to the cave for around US$70 (including lunch) with **Estancia Travel** (Puerto Bories 13B, 061 412221, www.estancia travel.com); they run the service between October and May only. Treks start from Estancia Puerto Consuelo, which was founded by Captain Eberhard in 1893.

If you're short on time and don't mind an epic bus journey, a number of agencies can take you on a day trip (15 hours round trip) to the unmissable Glaciar Perito Moreno, 440 kilometres (273 miles) away in Argentina (*see p150*). The trip will set you back around US$60. For information on boat trips north through the fjords, see *pp206-209* **Sea Routes South** or contact **Navimag** (*see p209*).

Monumento Natural Cueva del Milodon

Ruta 9 Norte (061 411438). **Open** Oct-Mar 8am-9pm daily. Apr-Sept 8am-4pm daily. **Admission** US$4; US$1 under-12s.

Museo de Flora y Fauna

Colegio Salesiano, Padre Rossa 1456, entre De Agostini y Tegualda (061 411258). **Open** 9am-noon, 2-6pm Mon-Sat. **Admission** free.

Museo Histórico Municipal

Bulnes 285, entre Magallanes y Barros Arana (061 411263). **Open** 8.30am-12.30pm, 2.30-6pm Mon-Fri; 3-6pm Sat. **Admission** US$1; US50¢ under-10s. **No credit cards**.

Where to eat

Although Natales is not famed for its culinary excellence, there are a few decent places to fuel up or wind down in. One good bet is **El Living** (Arturo Prat 156, no phone, www.el-living.com, $), a laid-back vegetarian café/bar serving quality coffee, home-made cakes, sandwiches, soups and curries, plus local wine and beer in the evening. English ex-pat owner Jeremy also runs Chile Nativo expeditions (*see above*). Next door at No.158 (061 413553, $$) is popular **El Asador Patagónico**, this time for the bloodthirsty, with its barbecued lamb and large steaks fresh off the *parrilla*. **Ultima Esperanza** (Eberhard 354, 061 411391, $$$) offers generous portions of the freshest seafood and meat; its '60s interior is in line with the rest of the town. The cosy restaurant at **Aqua Terra** (*see p216*; $$) serving freshly-prepared soothing soups and tasty hot snacks, is a handy respite when the unpredictable weather turns sour. And for higher-end dining, try **Paine** at the Hotel CostAustralis (*see below*; $$$), where you can sample traditional Patagonian dishes as you gaze across El Seno Ultima Esperanza.

Where to stay

One of the smartest places to stay in town is the **Hotel CostAustralis** (Pedro Montt 262, 061 412000, www.hotelesaustralis.cl, double US$83-$165). The building has large rooms and great views of the mountainous peninsula. Cheaper **Concepto Indigo** (Ladrilleros 105, 061 413099, www.conceptoindigo.com, double US$52), resembling a vamped-up fisherman's hut, has equally good views plus a lantern-lit, sociable restaurant and a climbing wall for practising those tricky ascents in perfect safety. Rivalling CostAustralis in terms of ambition and sophistication is newcomer **Hotel Charles Darwin** (Manuel Bulnes 90, 061 412478, www. hotelcharlesdarwin.com, double US$55-$110),

Parque Nacional Torres del Paine

Snow-capped mountains, glacier-fed turquoise lakes, meadows and Magellanic forests, rivers and waterfalls: it's the sheer variety of stunning landscapes, along with those famous granite peaks, which have made Chile's national park, declared an UNESCO Biosphere Reserve in 1978, world renowned. Still, even with a 600 per cent boom in tourism in the past decade, the park only receives around 80,000 visitors a year – 9.9 million less than its most visited equivalent in the US. The attention is well deserved – the park offers some of the best trekking in the world; and, despite being one of the busiest national parks in South America it's still possible to escape the crowds and find a sense of isolation.

Dodging herds of guanacos along the 120-kilometre (75-mile) gravel road from Puerto Natales to one of the entrances, the Paine Massif appears (if weather permits) towering above the prairies. One glimpse of the solid-granite spires and you'll agree with the verdict handed down in 1945 by Italian priest Alberto de Agostini, one of the first to explore the area, that 'the Paine massif is unrivalled... In its colours and forms it is without doubt one of the most spectacular sights that the human imagination can conceive.' The rocky outcrop, whose highest peak is the 3,248 metre (10,656 feet) Cerro Paine Grande, was carved with picture-perfect precision during the last ice age by the same sheet of ice that gave birth to Argentina's Fitz Roy massif and the Perito Moreno glacier. East of Paine Grande are the 2,600-metre-high (8,530-feet) Cuernos (Horns) del Paine, while just visible behind are the three polished granite towers, or Torres, to which the park owes its name. Paine (pronounced Pie-nay) is Telhueche for 'pale blue', a fitting tribute to the expanses of turquoise-coloured waters that speckle this unspoiled landscape. Upon arrival in the park, register your details with the guardaparques.

FLORA AND FAUNA

Until its creation in 1959, most of the park's 2,420 square kilometres (934 square miles) were used for sheep grazing, from which the lower grasslands are still recovering. Today, however, the biggest threat to the 150 different bird and 40 mammal species that call the park home is tourism. Many animals, however, seem positively to relish the arrival each summer of so many curious visitors. As a result it's not uncommon to see 100 guanacos in a single day at a few metres' distance or grey foxes snooping around your backpack for food at the park's entrance. The black-necked swans, upland geese and poorly camouflaged pink Chilean flamingo thrive on the park's many lakes, and the cool, open ñire and lenga (southern beech) forests are home to a variety of birds. The most impressive is the red-crested Magellanic woodpecker, an oversized version of its endangered, North American cousin. One species you'd be extremely lucky to see, other than in the captivating *National Geographic* video on display at the visitor centre, is the puma, larger here than in other wildcat habitats elsewhere in the Andes.

TREKS AND ACTIVITIES

The park's marquee trek is the seven-day Paine Circuit, which goes around the entire Paine range. The moderately difficult walk, a shoe-in to any top-ten trek list worth its salt, offers constantly changing views of the Paine massif as it leads you through bone-chilling glacial streams, boggy lowlands, gorgeous meadows, moist, green alpine forests and past mammoth-sized glaciers emptying into iceberg-spotted emerald lakes. Allow an additional three or four days for side trips, including the worthwhile hike up the Valle del Francés, which takes you to the inner heart of the Paine massif. Although the Paine Circuit requires a great deal of endurance, like most hikes in the park the trail is well marked, so guides aren't necessary and confident beginners shouldn't worry about getting lost.

For those with a little less time, the 'W' Circuit (four to five days) allows you to skip the 'duller' sections through the forest and pampas without missing the park's highlights. It includes an up-close visit to the Torres from the lake below it, which those rushing to finish the larger circuit often bypass. If your schedule is more leisurely, you can explore the less-trodden, but equally accessible, back country in almost complete solitude. The three-day, flat hike through forests to glacier-fed Lago Pingo is one alternative.

To disappear further, Big Foot in Natales (*see p213*) leads three-day kayaking trips down the winding Serrano River. Although you never see the Paine massif up close, it's almost always in view, and while you camp on still-virgin islands and play bumper cars with icebergs, you won't miss it anyway. They can also organise just about any adventure sporting activity you can imagine. See the website for more information.

FACILITIES

With the boom in tourism, authorities have made the park more accessible than ever. It's now theoretically possible to do the entire Paine Circuit without a tent, hopping from one *refugio* to the next. But the more fancy little lodges cost significantly more than pitching a tent (US$15-$20 per person per night) and fill up fast; book in advance if you want to go light. Although the *refugios* are privately run by several different companies, all of them can be booked through path@gone (Eberhard 595, 061 413291, www.pathagone.com), Andescape (Eberhard 599, 061 412592, www.andescapetour.com) or Comapa Turismo (Bulnes 533, 56-61 414300, www.comapa.cl). A number of pricier *hosterías* offer stunning bedroom views plus private guides and horses, the ultimate upscale experience being the smartly yet sensitively designed Explora Patagonia – Hotel Salto Chico, the preferred choice of the international jet set. Second best in terms of comfort is Hosteria Las Torres.

Basic provisions and cooking facilities are available at most of the *refugios*, while water from the flowing streams and rivers within the park is pure enough to drink.

CONAF – Corporación Nacional Forestal

O'Higgins 584, Puerto Natales (56-61 411438). **Open** 8.30am-6.30pm Mon-Fri.

Explora Patagonia – Hotel Salto Chico

Sector Salto Chico, PN Torres del Paine (in Santiago – no tel on site 02 11969682-6/ fax 02 11969687/www.explora.com). **Rates** from US$1,296 per person, all inclusive, 3 night min. **Credit** AmEx, DC, MC, V.

Hosteria Las Torres

(56-61 710050/www.lastorres.com). **Rates** US$149-US$209 double. **Credit** AmEx, MC, V.

Parque Nacional Torres del Paine

Entrances at Laguna Amarga, Laguna Azul & Lago Sarmiento, all 120km (75 miles) from Puerto Natales (Guardaparques 061 691931/torres_paine@hotmail.com). **Open** 24hrs daily. **Admission** *Apr-Sept* US$7. *Oct-Mar* US$12 (about US$17). **No credit cards.**

Chilean Patagonia

while for a more low-key yet equally comfortable affair try **Aqua Terra Lodge** (Manuel Bulnes 299, 061 412239, www.aqua terrapatagonia.com, double US$68-$95) next door to the Museo Histórico Municipal. Housed in a smart clapboard building, it has 15 very clean, nicely kitted-out rooms plus a North Face shop for that last-minute waterproof jacket. For a cheaper option try **Casa Cecilia** (Thomas Roger 60, 061 411797, redcecilia@entelchile.net, double US$35) a well-run hostel offering simple but pleasant rooms, each with private bath. It's very popular, so book well in advance if you're travelling in high season. Cecilia, who speaks fluent English, is the perfect host and problem solver. Within the national park, the classiest, most original and most eco-friendly lodging is the **Explora** (*see p215*).

Resources

Hospital
Hospital Puerto Natales, Carrera Pinto 537 (061 411306).

Internet
Rincón del Tata, Arturo Prat 236 (061 413845).

Police station
Rogers y Bulnes (061 411133).

Post office
Eberhard 429 (061 410202).

Tourist information
Sernatur *Pedro Montt 19, y Phillipi (061 412125/ www.sernatur.cl).* **Open** *Apr-Dec* 8.15am-6pm Mon-Fri. *Oct-Mar* 8.15am-8pm Mon-Fri; 8.15am-6pm Sat. **Oficina Municipal de Turismo** *Bulnes 285 (061 411263).* **Open** 9am-5pm Mon-Fri.

Getting there

By road
Puerto Natales is on Ruta 9, 247km (153 miles) or 3hrs from Punta Arenas, and 15km (9.5 miles) from the Argentinian border. Three passes cross the border into Argentina near Natales, connecting with RN40 to Rio Gallegos in the east, El Calafate in the north and nearby coal mining town Rio Turbio. Many road transport services are run by tour operators. There is no central bus terminal and in winter departures and prices depend on demand; check with the tourist office, agencies or your hotel. There are several buses daily year-round between Punta Arenas and Puerto Natales, regular service to Rio Gallegos and summer services to El Calafate.

By sea
Natales is the terminus for Navimag services, making the three-night journey to Puerto Montt via the fjords and archipelago. Departures every Fri. For details *see pp206-209* **Sea Routes South**.

Punta Arenas

Perched on the east coast of the Brunswick Peninsula at the foot of the Andes, Chile's southernmost city is Punta Arenas (meaning Sandy Point, a name given to it by legendary mariner John Byron, grandfather of the more legendary poet). It faces the island of Tierra del Fuego across the Magellan Strait, where the Atlantic and Pacific meet.

This lively and user-friendly city has been well thought out with all the most important attractions within walking distance of the pretty **Plaza Muñoz Gamero** (confusingly, most locals know it as Plaza de Armas). Statues and monuments on tree-lined grassy areas running down the main avenues make Punta Arenas an inviting place to discover on foot. The story of the city is told in its architecture, which ranges from modest colonial wooden houses and more majestic brick constructions, to belle époque and art deco.

In 1843 president Manuel Bulnes, fearing that his country's claims on lands by the Magellan Strait were not enough to deter others from helping themselves, sent an expedition south to establish a colony. It landed at Puerto de Hambre (Famine Port), so-called after a Spanish colonisation attempt in 1584 ended in the starvation of all the settlers. This time they were better prepared and began immediate construction of a small fort, **Fuerte Bulnes**. A replica of this historic fort was erected on the original site in 1940; this and Puerto de Hambre can be visited today.

Five hard years later, the settlers abandoned Fuerte Bulnes and moved 60 kilometres (37 miles) north to a more habitable spot on the shores close to the Rio del Carbón. Founded on 18 December 1848, Punta Arenas now has a population of over 115,000 inhabitants and is the capital of Chile's Región XII.

In the late 19th century Punta Arenas thrived as a refuelling port for maritime traffic from Europe bound for California and Australia. Although the opening of the Panama Canal in 1914 heralded an economic downtown, sheep farming was thriving after the 300 pure-breds, introduced from the Falklands/Malvinas, had multiplied tenfold. Today the main industries are methane gas exploitation, fishing and tourism. Punta Arenas claims the lowest rate of unemployment in the country at four per cent.

For a view over Punta Arenas and beyond, climb the gentle steps at the end of Waldo Seguel street to **Mirador Cerro de La Cruz**. Possibly the best view of the city, however, due to a lack of high-rise buildings obstructing your view is from the sixth-floor restaurant in the Hotel Finis Terrae (*see p220*).

Up close and personal with the glaciers around **Punta Arenas**.

Among the many prominent European immigrants who profited from sheep farming in the late 19th century was one José Nogueira, a Portuguese businessman who married local lass Sara Braun. Their opulent mansion, **Palacio Sara Braun**, an enduring testament to the wealth that once came from wool, is now the José Noguiera Hotel and Club de la Unión (*see p220*) on the north-west corner of the plaza. Just around the corner is the **Palacio Mauricio Braun**, home of Sara's brother, who married the daughter of Spanish entrepreneur José Menéndez. The Braun Menéndez descendants were one of Latin America's most influential dynasties. Mauricio's mansion was crafted between 1903 and 1906 using Italian marble, Belgium timber and fabrics and furniture from London and Paris. The ground floor of this exquisite home is open to view. The building also houses the **Museo de Historia Regional Braun Menéndez**, whose exhibits cover the discovery of the Magellan Strait, the building of the fort and Punta Arena's early development.

Six blocks north is the **Museo Regional Salesiano Maggiorino Borgatello**, considered to be one of the best museums in Chile. It has detailed displays on the work of the missionaries, and the Tehuelche, Selk'nam, Alacaluf and Yamana cultures – the very people who suffered when the sheep arrived. There are also intricate models on the second floor explaining oil exploration.

The other important museum in Punta Arenas is the **Museo del Recuerdo** at the local college, Instituto de la Patagonia, a short hop from the centre. Here you can meander in the open air among a well-maintained collection of industrial machinery used by early farming pioneers. Across the road is the bustling duty-free area **Zona Franca** (closed 12.30-3pm Mon-Sat), selling everything from brand-new cameras to used cars. The other main retail street, Bories, has numerous small shops selling crafts, clothes and chocolates.

At the well-laid-out cemetery **Parque Cruz de Froward**, on the way back to the centre, you can hunt out the names of European settlers on the colourful and ornate tombstones. Anyone who was anyone in Punta Arenas is buried here, including Sara Braun, José Menéndez and other family members. On Sundays you'll find crowds of locals here, visiting the glass shrines dedicated to their loved ones or paying their respects to Indiecito, a statue of the 'little Indian', honouring the extinct Selk'nam.

In summer Arenas is great for lovers of the outdoors with small parks and tables outside many cafés. There's a nine-hole golf course (closed Apr-Sept) five kilometres (three miles) south on the road to Fuerte Bulnes (closed Apr-Sept). Nine kilometres (5.5 miles) west, at **Cerro Mirador**, you can trek for two hours around a marked trail or hire mountain bikes. In winter buy a pass and hire skis or a snowboard for

Campfire blues

Meet Chile's public enemy number one, Jiri Smitak. On 17 February, 2005, the 31-year-old Czech hiker hunkered down in a prairie near Laguna Azul in the Torres del Paine national park and proceeded to boil some soup, knowingly in violation of park rules. After accidentally toppling his gas stove the fierce Patagonian winds did the rest. Two weeks of intense firefighting later, a full 143 square kilometres (55 square miles), 500-year-old forest were destroyed – eight per cent of the park's total area. The image of guanacos walking in a dazed stupor over the embers of their once Arcadian habitat was beamed across the world.

By then, however, Smitak had hotfooted it across the border to El Calafate: hardly in the Butch and Sundance category but a fugitive from the law nonetheless. Thankfully, he at least had the decency to report himself to the authorities. And the price for his carelessness? A slap on the wrist and a US$200 fine.

But matters didn't end there. As news of the event spread the Chilean public became outraged, the flames fanned, so to speak, as much by the token nature of the fine as the seriousness of Smitak's original mistake. A smear campaign was launched on the Internet and the shamed and repentant Smitak forked over his entire backpackers' life savings, a mere US$1,000. The Czech government, perturbed by the adverse publicity, pledged money and technical support in the recovery effort, which will take decades and cost at least US$5 million.

The real culprit, however, was Chile's fire prevention legislation, which is sorely out of step with the impact thousands of trekking tourists are having on Patagonia's slow-growing woodlands and fragile environment. Smitak was levied the maximum penalty Chile's authorities could apply. But the public quickly noted that the same act of negligence in Europe would have cost him millions and perhaps resulted in a spell in jail. As bad as the blaze was, it was symptomatic of the scant attention authorities in Chile – and even less so in Argentina – pay to fire fighting and prevention. Hopefully it won't take another catastrophe like this one to force them into action.

around US$30 per day from the **Club Andino** at the foot of the Cerro Mirador, and head up for some skiing. The novelty factor is looking down at the ocean while you glide down the short, though testing pistes. If you like to party, go during the winter carnival at the end of July when everyone hits the streets.

Located seven kilometres (4.5 miles) west of Punta Arenas on higher ground is the **Reserva Forestal Magallanes** (also known as Parque Japonés), 160 square kilometres (62 square miles) of pure lenga, coigüe and ñire forests.

EXCURSIONS

You can have a guide accompany you on excursions for US$35 a day and arrange mini-bus hire (US$80 per day to split with between as many as you can fit in) through the tourist office. Few destinations are accessible on public transport, so this is the best way to go, or on agency tours. Daily visits to **Fuerte Bulnes** (admission US$2) pause at the Obelisco, the halfway point between the north of Chile and the South Pole, and Puerto de Hambre. At the fort, cannons jut out from the continent's end towards a breathtaking vista of the Magellan Strait, Rawson Island and Tierra Del Fuego.

A trip to the **Reserva Forestal Laguna Parrillar** – even larger and older than the Reserva Forestal Magallanes – can be done in half a day. There's salmon fishing and self-guided nature trails, plus camping facilities if you want to stay overnight.

In November around 6,000 Magellanic penguins waddle onto dry land at **Seno Otway** 70 kilometres (43 miles) north and delight the crowds until March. The afternoon excursions organised by **Comapa Turismo** (Magallanes 990, 061 200200, www.comapa.cl, closed Sun) offer the best chance to see the birds on their return from the water to feed their young. An ever larger colony, with close to 150,000 birds, is a boat ride away on **Isla Magdalena**. Tours run from the pier in Punta Arenas between December and February. Inside the island's lighthouse you'll find a small museum with an exhibit on Chile's lighthouses. Comapa Turismo also runs cruises to the islands of Tierra del Fuego and can book you on to one of Navimag's boats from Puerto Natales.

While it is possible to visit Torres del Paine from Arenas, Natales is the logical base for visiting the park. Tough trekkers can organise trips from Punta Arenas to **Isla Navarino** to take on the 'Dientes' (Teeth) circuit. Check with the tourist office for travel options.

Cruceros Australis (02 442 3110, www.australis.com) launched smart *Mare Australis* in October 2002, a cruise ship running from Arenas to Ushuaia and Puerto Williams. It's one

of the few ways to see the main glaciers around **Parque Nacional Alberto de Agostini**. Trips are for three, four or seven days.

If that isn't enough to scratch your travel itch, ambitions to reach Antarctica, the Falklands/Malvinas or any other of the South Atlantic islands can also be realised from Punta Arenas. *See pp222-228* **Antartica & the Islands.**

Cementerio Parque Cruz de Froward

Avenida Presidente Carlos Ibáñez del Campo 07360 (061 222908). **Open** *Sept-Apr* 8am-6pm daily. *May-Aug* 9am-5pm daily. **Admission** free.

Club Andino

Cerro Mirador (tel & fax 061 241479/www.club andino.cl). **Open** *June-Sept* 9am-5.30pm Tue-Sun; 9am-6.30pm Sat, Sun. *Oct-May* 10am-5pm daily. **Credit** AmEx, DC, MC, V.

Museo de Historia Regional Braun Menéndez

Magallanes 949, entre Pedro Montt y José Menéndez (061 244216). **Open** *Apr-Sept* 10.30am-5pm daily; *Oct-Mar* 10.30am-2pm daily. **Admission** US$2; US$1 under-10s; free Sun. **No credit cards.**

Museo del Recuerdo

Instituto de la Patagonia, Avenida Bulnes 1890 (061 207056). **Open** 8.30-11am, 2.30-6.15pm Mon-Fri; 8.30am-1pm Sat. **Admission** US$2; free under-14s. **No credit cards.**

Museo Regional Salesiano Maggiorino Borgatello

Avenida Bulnes 374, entre Maipú y Sarmiento (061 221001/dirmusalbor@terra.cl). **Open** 10am-12.30pm, 3-6.30pm Tue-Sun. **Admission** US$2.50; US50¢ under-12s. **No credit cards.**

Where to eat & drink

La Leyenda del Remezón

21 de Mayo 1469, entre Boliviana e Independencia (061 241029). **Open** noon-3pm, 7pm-midnight daily. **Average** $$$. **Credit** AmEx, DC, MC, V. With its rustic decor, inviting fireplace and locally sourced Patagonian ingredients, Remezón is the star restaurant hereabouts, whose house speciality is game. Don't be surprised if the chef comes over to explain what's in the sauce.

La Luna Restaurant

O'Higgins 974, entre Pedro Montt y José Menéndez (061 228555/laluna@chile.com). **Open** *Apr-Sept* noon-3.30pm, 7.30-11.30pm Mon-Sat. *Oct-Mar* noon-3pm Mon-Sat; 6.30pm-11pm daily. **Average** $$. **No credit cards.** The decor at La Luna is a work in progress; ask for a flag to write your name on and pin it to your home town on one of the large wall maps. Highlights of the reasonably priced menu include the home-made desserts and the shellfish and crab soups. They also do a mean pisco sour.

Parrilla Los Ganaderos

Avenida Bulnes 0977, y Manantiales (061 214597/ www.parrillalosganaderos.cl). **Open** noon-3.30pm, 8pm-midnight daily. **Average** $$$. **Credit** AmEx, DC, MC, V. Waiters clad in gaucho get-ups await you in this popular grill, just a short taxi ride from the city centre. If the colour scheme of pink, orange and green doesn't spoil your appetite, you'll enjoy the hefty portions of Patagonian lamb.

Santino Bar-Restó

Avenida Colón 657, entre Bories y Chiloé (061 220511). **Open** 6pm-3am daily. **Average** $$. **Credit** AmEx, DC, MC, V.

More bar than restaurant, and one of the finest drinking dens in town. Pub grub from the kitchen goes down easily with the potent drinks and an fish tank embedded in the wall holds your attention.

Sotito's Restaurant

O'Higgins 1138, entre Roca y Errázuriz (061 243565). **Open** noon-4pm, 7-11.30pm Mon-Sat; noon-4pm Sun. **Average** $$$. **Credit** AmEx, DC, MC, V.

A smooth choice for the romantically inclined. This small, red brick restaurant offers intimacy, excellent seafood soups and stews and tasty meat dishes. Staff are efficient and eager to please and courteous enough to leave you in peace.

Where to stay

Hostal y Turismo Calafate

Magallanes 922-926, entre José Menéndez y Pedro Montt (tel & fax 061 241281). **Rates** US$16-$28 single; US$45-$55 double; US$50-$65 triple. **No credit cards**.

This central hostel is good for budget travellers. Choose from 18 comfortable rooms with private or shared bathrooms. There's a travel agency located within the hotel and discounted rates for net access.

Hotel Finis Terrae

Avenida Colón 766, entre Magallanes y Bories (061 228200/fax 248124/www.hotelfinisterrae.com). **Rates** US$98-$140 single; US$111-$160 double; US$130-$190 triple; US$137-$260 suite. **Credit** AmEx, DC, MC, V.

The most impressive aspect of centrally located, Alpine-style Hotel Finis Terrae is the spectacular 360° view of the Magellan Strait from its elegant sixth-floor restaurant and lounge. A luxurious lobby and second restaurant are downstairs, and the 64 rooms are well fitted.

Hotel Isla Rey Jorge

21 de Mayo 1243, entre Errázuriz y Balmaceda (tel & fax 061 248220/222681/www.hotelislarey jorge.com). **Rates** US$88-$119 single; US$110-$146 double; US$143-$172 triple; US$169-$199 suite. **Credit** AmEx, DC, MC, V.

25-room Hotel Isla Rey Jorge, just a block and a half from the Plaza Muñoz Gamero, occupies a quaint century-old building. A cannon protects the entrance, and inside you'll find a cosy lounge and friendly staff. The Farmer restaurant specialises in exotic meats such as rhea, beaver and wild goose.

Hotel José Nogueira

Bories 959, entre Plaza de Armas y José Menéndez (061 248840/fax 248832/www.hotelnogueira.com). **Rates** US$95-$149 single; US$115-$179 double; US$135-$255 triple; US$179-$298 suite. **Credit** AmEx, DC, MC, V.

The mansion inherited by Sara Braun from her husband is now home to the Hotel José Nogueira and the classy bar of the Club de la Unión (open also to non-residents). This magnificent, historical building looks stunning when lit up at night and some of the

25 rooms boast original furniture. The glass-domed restaurant Pérgola and indoor garden make lovely surroundings for breakfast, dinner or just a cocktail.

Hotel Tierra del Fuego

Avenida Colón 716, entre Magallanes y Bories (tel & fax 061 226200/tierradelfuego@entelchile.net). **Rates** US$89 single; US$98 double; US$118 triple; US$130 suite. **Credit** AmEx, DC, MC, V.

This classy, well-located hotel opened five years ago. Built in a European style with 26 sizeable rooms and a spa, there is also an elegant bar attached to the lobby concocting cocktails and special coffees.

Resources

Hospital

Hospital Regional, Angamos 180 (061 205000).

Internet

Austro Internet, Croacia 690 (061 229297).

Police station

Errázuriz 977 (061 241714).

Post office

Bories 911 (061 222796).

Tourist information

Sernatur, Magallanes 960, entre Waldo Seguel y José Menéndez (061 225385/248790/www.sernatur.cl). **Open** 8.15am-6pm Mon-Thur; 8.15am-5pm Fri.

Getting there

By air

Airport **Presidente Carlos Ibáñez de Campo** (Ruta 9, km21, 061 219131) is 20km (12.5 miles) from town. Flights daily from Santiago via Puerto Montt, plus connections to Porvenir, Puerto Williams and Antarctica (monthly); every Sat to the Falklands/Malvinas, every 2nd Sat of mth via Rio Gallegos.

By road

Punta Arenas lies at the southern end of Ruta 9, which comes down from Puerto Natales 247km (153 miles) to the north. Ruta 225, the continuation of RN3 from Rio Gallegos in Argentina, joins Ruta 9 north of Punta Arenas. Ruta 225 can also be joined from Chilean Tierra del Fuego on the ferry that connects with Punta Delgada on the mainland. There is no central bus terminal. Buses leave from company offices; several daily to Puerto Natales, daily service to Rio Gallegos, 4 per wk to Rio Grande and Ushuaia. The tourist office has lists of companies and services.

By sea

From **Embarcadero Tres Puentes** (end of Avenida Bulnes) daily crossings with **Transbordadora Austral Broom** (061 218100, www.tabsa.cl) go to and from Porvenir on Tierra del Fuego. There are irregular sailings to Puerto Williams, some via Ushuaia. Cruises and sailships dock on their way to/from Antartica and South Atlantic islands. See pp206-209 Sea Routes South.

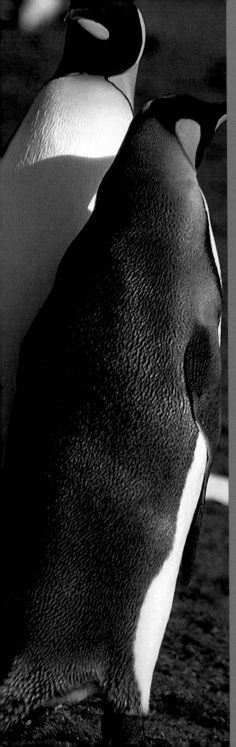

Antarctica & the Islands

Antarctica & the Islands   222

Antarctica & the Islands

Frozen wastes, sunken wrecks, isolated communities and ten million penguins.

For travellers feeling hemmed in by the beaten path of Patagonia, a two-day boat trip across the Drake Passage yields the icy frontier of Antarctica. Larger than Australia, this sparkling white mass of shifting ice and rock is experiencing a minor tourist boom – the wildlife, volcanoes, and glaciers calving huge icebergs into pristine waters lured over 15,000 people to make the 1,000-km (621-mile) trip from Ushuaia in 2005. But humans are still scarce and the wildlife is especially bold: pods of curious whales approach boats, and colonies of squawking sea birds 'pose' for ornithologists.

There are various ways to see Antarctica, none of which is cheap; but each provides a truly unique travel experience through the driest, windiest, coldest place on earth.

For a more diverse trip, tag a few days on to your cruise and head east to the Falkland Islands/Islas Malvinas or to South Georgia Island. The former are still associated with the senseless war of 1982 ('Two bald men fighting

over a comb' was the dry assessment of Jorge Luis Borges), but the reality is rather more soothing. Like turning back the clock on rural England, the residents here live the quiet life of isolated islanders. Beyond the small-town charm, the Falklands/Malvinas offer top-drawer birding, boasting unique species.

South-east from the Falklands/Malvinas is South Georgia Island, an Antarctic oasis with a surprisingly diverse environment. Mountains and fjords, penguins and seals, birds and caribou can all be found. There are even grasslands, and those passing through in January will have a chance to see wildflowers at the bottom of the world.

Antarctica

Roughly circular, with a diameter of 4,500 kilometres (2,796 miles) – though its surface area doubles in winter – Antarctica is divided by the Transantarctic Mountains, where the

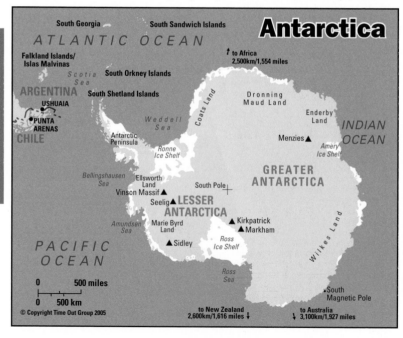

highest peak, Vinson Massif, stands at 4,897 metres (16,066 feet). Its ice sheets contain over 90 per cent of the world's ice and is up to 5,000 metres (16,404 feet) thick. Here the cold is harsher and winds wilder than anywhere else. Winter temperatures average between -40°C (-40°F) and -70°C (-94°F); throw coffee in the air and it turns to brown snow. Superlative, hostile, pristine – Antarctica gets to people.

For centuries its nature remained a mystery and source of debate. The ancient Greeks believed it to be populated and fertile; then a theory got about that passage to it was blocked by monsters. Opinions changed, as explorers returned to their monarchs with tales of icy winds; among early adventurers was Captain Cook who in 1773 breached the Antarctic Circle for the first time, yet somehow failed to find the continent. Although no official record stands, the first probable landings took place at the start of the 19th century, when sealers hopped from nearby South Shetland Islands to the mainland peninsula, the spike of land that juts north at the same longitude as Tierra del Fuego.

In the next century, other expeditions, driven by science, greed and sheer curiosity, ventured on to the continent. But no permanent foothold was established until 1943 when the British set up the first base on Wiencke Island. Four years later, with Russian/US relations cooling, the US sent 4,700 men, 13 ships and 23 planes to chart maps and prepare troops for Arctic conditions.

In 1957, in a more peaceful spirit, a world scientific body (the International Council for Science, ICSU) organised the International Geophysical Year (IGY),a programme dedicated to the study of astronomy. Following its success, 12 countries established 40 scientific bases across the continent. In 1961, the Antarctic Treaty came into force, declaring the continent free, borderless and non-political, dedicated to peace and science. These utopian principles haven't stopped Chile and Argentina marking their national maps with what both claim is their slice of ice (also claimed, albeit less vociferously, by Britain).

Lately, scientists having been making noises about the increasing loss of mass in nearly 90 per cent of Antarctica's ice bodies. Few of them claim to be ompletely certain of the causes and results of the melting. Global warming is a worry – the temperature on the Antarctic peninsula has risen 2°C in a brief span of 50 years. But studies indicate that other factors are also at play. Some scientists cite shifting ocean currents and a natural curtailing of a delayed ice age as contributing factors. One thing is certain: Antarctica is changing.

Cool cruising

'Good God, this is an awful place,' wrote Robert Scott in 1911. It was one of the last entries in his diary. The place in question was, of course, Antarctica, and within days it had lived down to Scott's assessment by claiming his life.

Would he have enjoyed Antarctica more from the comfort of a cruise ship? Probably not. Scott, Amundsen and their comrades did it the hard way, partly because they had to and partly because it was in their nature to do so; the thrill and the risk were indivisible. While modern travellers can take the thrill and leave the risk, the Antarctic continues to draw those with a thirst for adventure and an appetite for the unknown.

For an Antarctic cruise is unique. Those who crave permanent sunshine, dodgy cabaret and the occasional E. coli outbreak should go float somewhere else. The allure of the ice continent lies in its immaculate emptiness, the palpable absence of cities, factories, governments and all the other trappings of civilisation most people would gladly leave behind for a couple of weeks.

Unlike the pioneers, with their wooden schooners and dog-drawn sleds, you'll travel in research ships equipped with steel hulls and global positioning technology, with a warm bed awaiting you at the end of the day. But in common with them you'll need some dosh behind you to realise the dream: expect to pay a minimum of US$5,000 (flights not included), rising to US$20,000 if a plush cabin is important to you. (For details on cruise operators, see p225.)

So what do you get for your money? First, a visual experience that will haunt your memory for ever. Second, a crash course in Antarctic studies: most of the cruise ships carry scientists who give daily lectures to passengers. By the end of the trip you'll know the difference between fast and pancake ice, have no trouble distinguishing bergy bits from hummocks, and understand why humpback whales are able to belt out a tune for up to 45 minutes at a time.

Finally, and for some worth the cost alone, there are the bragging rights, redeemable for life. So if want to impress the grandchildren, and you can't get to the moon, get to the pole.

Bring a good camera and some thermal underwear to the **Antarctic Peninsula**.

Many people come solely for the wildlife. Of 17 types of penguin, the emperor is regarded as the signature species. These comical beings can grow up to one and a half metres (5 feet) high. Elegant in the water, they are hopelessly clumsy on land, waddling over snow and rocks, sliding across ice on their bellies. At the end of the long winter, millions of sea birds arrive. Giant albatrosses with a wingspan of four metres (13 feet), petrels, shearwaters and fulmars are among the 35 species found around the Antarctic. Pack a good pair of binoculars.

Sharing their time between the ice and the sea, seals, in the absence of polar bears, are particularly friendly. Out of the six species, Weddel, Ross, crab-eater and leopard are native to the Antarctic. Killer and sperm whales are the only toothed leviathans to visit these waters. Bigger but toothless species such as fin, humpback, Minke, sei, southern right and, the mother of them all, blue whales, are all to be found during the austral summer.

Nearly everything in Antarctica is stunning, but there are a few obvious musts that you will or won't see depending on the length and route of your cruise. For a start, check out the narrow waterways, glaciers and icebergs dotted around the Antarctic Peninsula. Equally thought provoking, but seen only on the pricey icebreaker tours, are the desolate ice-free **Dry Valleys**, where scientists estimate it hasn't

rained for two million years. The icebreakers continue around the western shoulder of the continent to the **Ross Island Ice Shelf**, a glistening marvel and ice factory that calves around 150,000 cubic metres (196,000 cubic yards) of icebergs each year. Close by, Mount Erebus, an active volcano, can be seen with a plume of smoke drifting lazily from its crater.

Most visitors arrive by ship, usually passing several of the South Atlantic islands en route before heading down to the mainland. Travelling via Ushuaia or Punta Arenas, a typical cruise lasts 10-14 days from the time it leaves either destination. Once past the tip of the continent, boats head south across **Drake Passage**. During this stretch, teams of naturalists and geologists give lectures elucidating the complex natural processes that continue to shape Antarctica. But it's not all school: the crew also runs zodiac forays on to the South Shetland Islands.

After a few days at sea, you'll visit spectacular **King George** and **Livingston Islands**, home to huge numbers of nesting penguins, sea birds and elephant seals. Further south, you'll slip through the fallen walls of a volcanic crater into the flooded caldera of **Deception Island**. Formerly a centre for whaling, remnants of beached vessels, huts and even a whalers' cemetery can be seen close to the shore station.

By the end of the week, you'll be at the **Antarctic Peninsula**, the easiest point of access and the liveliest in terms of seals and penguins. Here, you'll visit **Paradise Harbour**, which shelters glaciers and icebergs shaped by the winds. Just opposite, **Port Lockroy** – the most visited spot in Antarctica – has colonies of penguins and shags and a former British scientific station that is now a fantastic museum. **Cuverville Island** and **Rongé Island** are home to a large colony of nearly 5,000 pairs of Gentoo penguins, while a little further south is the stunning **Lemaire Channel**. Just 1,600 metres (5,249 feet) wide, this narrow waterway – nicknamed the Kodak Gap – runs between the cliffs of **Booth Island** and the peninsula. From here, cruises push on to **Petermann Island** before heading back home; unless, of course, you've spent a mogul's wad and are circumnavigating the continent.

Owing to the recent tourist boom, options in Antarctica are increasing. Keep an eye out for tour companies that provide more interactive outings. **Quark Expeditions**, for example, give passengers the chance to camp out on the ice – it's not Shackleton style, as they whisk you there and away, but few can claim to have slept a night on the Antarctic ice. Many companies also offer sea kayaking or, for the still more adventurous, scuba diving in the freezing waters. You may even be able to catch a flick. The M/V *Ushuaia*, one of the few vessels with bilingual staff and crew (great for those interested in working on their Spanish), makes a stop at the research station of Junaby, where the world's southernmost cinema was recently inaugurated. This incongruous picture palace, fully equipped with 50 seats and the latest technology, kicked off in April 2005 with a series of Argentinian films.

In summer, the only time when you can get near most of Antarctica, temperatures are a mean 0°C (32°F) to -5°C (23°F) on coastal areas. Take lots of layers rather than just a few heavy coats and pack rubber boots and waterproofs for the expeditions.

TRANSPORT OPTIONS

There are many types of boat to choose from. Luxury cruisers look grand but are alien to the spirit of the Antarctic. In contrast, icebreakers look plain, but fewer people means more attention from crew and lecturers. With a lower draught, you can also get closer to the sights, though in heavy seas the boat is more likely to roll. Cabins tend to be comfortable with shared or private bathrooms; food varies according to the boat, but is wholesome rather than exotic (no penguin). Some vessels have helicopters on board – useful for flyovers and excursions.

Some cruises, especially around the holidays, book up a year in advance, so plan ahead. Many operators offer more adventurous ways to travel: a combination of flights (for example, from Punta Arenas to Chile's Frei Base on the South Shetland Islands) and sailing boats. Antarctica flight veterans **Aerovías DAP** and **Antarctica XXI** have combined to offer more flight options, but keep in mind that air travel is subject to the vagaries of the weather and the presence of other takers.

Contacts

For cruises to Antarctica, check the operator is a member of **IAATO** (International Association of Antarctica Tour Operators, www.iaato.org), which promotes environmentally responsible tourism to the Antarctic. One recommended, experienced company is **Quark Expeditions** (US 1-203 656 0499, www.quarkexpeditions. com). Or contact Quark's accommodating, friendly and knowledgeable southern cone representative, Zelfa Silva (Buenos Aires 4804 9474, www.antarcticacruises.com.ar). **Aerovías DAP** (O'Higgins 891, 061 223 340, www.aeroviasdap.cl) in Punta Arenas has charter and scheduled flight options from Chile. Last-minute, cheaper deals are sometimes available at the end of February – if you are in Ushuaia, you might be lucky enough to get a last-minute space on an icebreaker for a lesser rate. There is a tourist office in Ushuaia – **Oficina Turística Antártida** (Tourist Pier, Maipú y Lasserre, 02901 15617078) – dedicated to information about the white continent.

Falklands Islands/ Las Islas Malvinas

For some, the Falkland Islands/Islas Malvinas (phone code +500, see www.falklandislands. com or www.tourism.org.fk) are a natural extension of Patagonia separated from the coast by just 644 kilometres (400 miles) of cold South Atlantic ocean. For others, this archipelago of two sizeable islands and countless islets is a universe away from South America.

The islands are usually promoted as a wildlife destination, home to thousands of penguins, albatross and seals plus a couple of thousand people… and thousands of sheep. You can get up-close views of unafraid species such as elephant seals and porpoise, and meet penguin after penguin after penguin at places like Volunteer Point. Yet the islands are more than just a photo op and they did exist before the 1982 war. You just need the money to explore and the weather to make it memorable.

Forgotten army

It has been more than two decades since Argentina and Great Britain waged war over the Falkland Islands/Islas Malvinas. But for many Argentinian veterans of the 1982 conflict, the end of hostilities signalled only the onset of a new battle – for recognition and renumeration.

The demands of veterans for greater governmental recognition of their plight have, however, repeatedly fallen on deaf ears. Unemployment, homelessness, addiction and mental illness have been the norms for the thousands of Argentinian ex-conscripts who, on their return home, found themselves traumatised by combat, stigmatised by defeat, and shunned by successive governments lacking the political will to prioritise their cause. The statistics are stark. More than 60 per cent of veterans are jobless and around 350 have taken their own lives since the end of the war – a figure that exceeds the total number of battlefield casualties suffered by Argentina during the conflict.

Now, for the first time, there is hope. President Néstor Kirchner's administration has recently upped war pensions by 130 per cent and made public guarantees on the introduction of new healthcare and housing schemes for all ex-combatants. Apparently intent on righting the bloody wrongs of Argentina's last military dictatorship, Kirchner, who has already agreed compensation plans for the children of Argentina's 'disappeared', is now said to be planning a similar reparations package for those conscripted to fight in the Malvinas. If implemented, such a move could finally signal an end to more than 20 years of unrelenting struggle for Argentina's veterans.

There's a human population of fewer than 3,000 on the islands, plus about 1,500 British soldiers at Mount Pleasant military base. **Stanley** (Puerto Argentino for Argentinians), the capital and where most civilians live, is situated at the end of the belt of low mountains that stretch across the rainy, blustery east. Here you'll find places to eat and drink, hotels and guest houses, a youth hostel, a plush community school complete with giant pool, a cute little museum and enough Union Flags to supply both Last Night at the Proms and the UK Conservative Party conference and still have some left over. But beneath all the 'land of hope and glory' symbolism lies a genuinely heroic story of settlement and survival. As the political needling continues, you'll find people who want little more than to be left alone with their very good standard of living intact.

Tourists' first port of call should be the **Jetty Centre** by the passenger dock. Just about everything you can see and do is advertised, and staff can help organise it – for a small population, there are a multitude of tour companies and travel agencies. Head west from the Jetty Centre, towards the hills, and you'll find the post office, police station, bank, supermarket, 1982 War Memorial, Government House, and finally the **Falkland Islands Museum** (Britannia House, closed Mon), all on Ross Road. Stanley is full of colourful cottages with manicured gardens and the occasional horse or sheep grazing nearby. The corrugated iron-clad timber box-houses are being overtaken by grander, imported Swedish kit homes – warmer to live in but harder on the eye.

Around Stanley, an important port of call during the sailing ship era, many shipwrecks languish in the harbour. Stanley was en route to the California gold rush and many ships lost out to the savage seas around the Cape (not to mention the occasional insurance fraud). At low tide, you can walk on a number of the ships and dive to see others. Rumour has it that wine salvaged from wrecks is still tasty after two hundred years, but as yet nobody has owned up to seeing any lost gold.

EXCURSIONS

It's worth taking the one-hour flight to the West Falklands (Gran Malvina) where you'll find the scenery spectacular and the weather better. The government air taxi service will fly you, for a cool US$150, to any guest house there. You'll be met by the owner at their grass airstrip.

If you can't afford onward air travel, journey out into 'the camp' (as in 'campo' or countryside – Spanish rural expressions and place names are still used) by road. Strike a deal with one of the many 4x4 tour operators that can drive you

Not many people, but plenty of gnomes and penguins on the **Falklands/Malvinas**.

anywhere on the east, and visit **Darwin**, a small settlement; or Goose Green, which used to be the largest working farm on the east island; or the vast, very Patagonian grasslands of **Lafonia**. At the first, the **Darwin House Lodge** (32255, darwin.h@horizon.fk.uk) is a hotel that also has self-catering lodging – the owners do a refreshing English tea.

Near Darwin, some 97 kilometres (60 miles) from Stanley, you can visit the Argentinian Cemetery. This sits alone on a bleak headland, a setting every bit as joyless as the history commemorated there. War-inspired tourists can contract local guides and visit the battle sites on the east. There you can still find pieces of clothing, shell craters, downed aircraft and pieces of tent flapping in the wind. Mines are well-marked and fenced-off, but be alert.

Where to stay, eat & drink

Arrange accommodation before arriving, as at the airport there are only immigration officials making sure you have enough money to stay for the minimum week. It's hard to spend less than US$50 per night on lodging. The newly remodelled **Water Front Hotel** (22331, thewaterfront@horizon.co.fk) is on Ross Road in Stanley and provides good harbour views. Other top-end options on Ross Road include **Malvina Hotel** (21355, www.tourism.org.fk /pages/malvina.htm) and the **Upland Goose Hotel** (21455, fic@horizon.co.fk). Otherwise there are cheaper guest houses like Scotia House (21191, bobstewart@horizon.co.fk); some even let you camp in the garden. If you haven't prebooked, go to the Jetty Centre.

For food, go to the **Globe Tavern** on Crozier Place, up the hill from the Jetty Centre, for good fish and chips, or the **Falklands Brasserie** on Philomel Street No.3 for classier seafood and lamb. Entertainment is usually 'bottle fed'; Friday and Saturday nights can get quite wild. Start at the Globe Tavern for a 'mixed' crowd of off-duty soldiers, party-goers, visiting 'around The Horn' sailors, the odd Spanish speaker and locals whose only voyages are to the bar and back. John Street is the main drinking drag. Everybody drinks as much and as quickly as possible. Bars close at 11.30pm, prompt.

Getting there

By air

Lan Chile flies to **Mount Pleasant** airport in Stanley, departing Santiago Sat morning. The flight stops in Puerto Montt and Punta Arenas going south, so you can join there. One of these flights goes via Rio Gallegos every 2nd Sat of the month, returning a week later. This is the only direct link to Argentina.

By sea

Small boats sail from Punta Arenas every 6-8 weeks, collecting wool and delivering stores and have space for six – it's 2 days to get to the islands and the same price as flying. For boat service contact **Byron Marine** in the islands at byron@horizon.co.fk.

Other South Atlantic islands

South Georgia lies approximately 1,000 kilometres (about 621 miles) south-east of the Falklands/Malvinas, crossing into the polar weather zone. On the way you'll pass **Shag Rocks**, an outcrop that is home to thousands of cormorants, sticking up out of the sea like a ship passing in the mist. South Georgia is less than half the size of the Falklands/Malvinas; it's a dramatic island of snow-covered mountains, complete with glaciers, turquoise-blue harbours and abundant wildlife.

The island is home to visiting scientists, a few administrative staff and the occasional yacht crew, usually totalling no more than 20-30 people. Skiing, mountaineering and photographing the wildlife (which includes king penguin colonies, nesting albatrosses and thousands of fur seals) are the main attractions. You can also visit abandoned whaling stations along the northern coast. South Georgia used to be one of the most productive whaling stations in the world and worked until the early 1960s mainly as a Norwegian enterprise. When whalers realised they had killed all the whales, they simply upped and left. Most of the rusting, iron stations are now home to rats scurrying through eerie, deserted boiler rooms. South Georgia's only permanent residents, Brits Tim and Pauline Carr, moved to the island 12 years ago and remodelled an old whaling station, which now functions as a museum. From there the Carrs give lectures and slide shows; they also sell copies of their book about the area, *Antarctic Oasis*. To get to South Georgia, contact Government House in Stanley, as there are no tourist facilities as yet.

The **South Sandwich Islands** is a group of nine islands. Despite obvious similarities with South Georgia – they are equally rich in wildlife – they have less lowland areas and are uninhabited by people. Closer to the ice, the South Orkneys, 600 kilometres (373 miles) north-east of the Antarctic Peninsula, comprise four main and a number of much smaller islands. They are usually only visited as part of cruises that continue on to Antarctica proper. Most cruises (and flights from Punta Arenas in Chile) use one of the **South Shetland Islands** – usually Deception Island – 120 kilometres (75 miles) north of the Antarctic Peninsula, as a stop-off point en route.

Directory

Features

Directory

Planning Your Trip

Getting started

The first decision to take in planning a trip to Patagonia is whether to go independently or with a tour operator.

Organised packages are time efficient, as transfers, entrance to attractions and guided tours are pre-planned. Getting around may also be smoother, as the tour operator will have contracted services specially to meet the needs of the group. If you want to see a lot of Patagonia you have to cover huge distances. Bus or air services may be infrequent between the destinations you wish to visit, and arranging internal travel can be very time consuming.

Yet despite its vast size, Patagonia is manageable for independent travellers, and initiatives like the introduction of **flight passes** (which you must buy before you travel; *see p236*) have made life easier still. Flexibility is the plus as you are not tied to an itinerary. Travelling independently is likely to give you a greater opportunity to get to know the locals, though that could depend on your choice of tour operator and the packages offered. Patagonia is an extremely hospitable place.

Tour operators

Free from the threat of terrorism, high on adventure and relatively easy on the bank account, Patagonia is today one of the world's hot travel destinations. As a result of the region's tourism boom, a number of general and specialist travel agencies now include Patagonia in their portfolios. Therefore, even if you travel independently, contacting tour operators once in the region, which you can use for particular trips, services or destinations, is also a good option. The companies recommended for excursions throughout this book can arrange local guides, transport and logistical services as well as sporting activities.

We list below a selection of companies that offer holidays to Patagonia. Apply the usual checks and criteria in selecting a holiday company before confirming any reservation.

In the UK

Audley Travel *01869 276210/ www.audleytravel.com.*
Established small group tours of the highlights of Patagonia.
Cox & Kings *020 7873 5000/ www.coxandkings.co.uk.*
High-end natural history tours, covering Patagonia and Antarctica.
Journey Latin America *020 8747 8315/www.journeylatin america.co.uk.*
Specialist in group tours; it's useful for flights to Chile and Argentina as well.
Last Frontiers *01296 653000/ www.lastfrontiers.com.*
A good source for riders, anglers and honeymooners – working with some of the top-end Patagonian *estancias*.
LATA *020 87152913/www.lata.org.*
The Latin American Travel Association online; a worthwhile first point of call for information on travel to the region.

In the US

Chile Discover *1-866 753 5668/ www.chilediscover.com.*
Cruises, flyfishing, rafting and mountain biking in Chilean and Argentinian Patagonia.
Ecoventures Nature Tours & Travel *1-800 743 8352/ www.ecoventures-travel.com.*
Eco-friendly tours from birdwatching to photography safaris, plus trekking on and around the glaciers.

Ladatco *1-800 327 6162/ www.ladatco.com.*
Creative packages covering all of Patagonia – Chile and Argentina – including *estancias* on Ruta 40.
Latin American Escapes *1-800 510 5999/ www.latinamerican escapes.com.*
Customised luxury itineraries, featuring trekking and *estancias*.
SATA USA *www.sata-usa.com.*
The South and Central American Travel Assocation's website. Not as many members as LATA, but has a useful online facility for sending questions about travel in the region to participating members.

Suggested itineraries

Where to go? What to do? How to travel? Be it a seven-day sprint or a month-long marathon, planning a trip to Patagonia – a region the size of Britain and France combined – can be a daunting business. Still, even with a week (though from Europe or the US it's the absolute minimum), you can see some of the south. Here are a few ideas to help you plan your time.

One week

If you've only got a week, make sure you add a night in either the Argentinian or the Chilean capital at the start or end of your trip (*see pp239-40*). With five or six days in the middle your best bet is to head to the Lake Districts: from there you can border hop for a broader Patagonian experience. In manageable distances you can visit a variety of town and smaller mountain villages and enjoy the outdoor life. The Ruta de los Siete Lagos in Argentina can be done in one day or over several. Chile's lakes are also worth seeing – the Bariloche–Peulla boat crossing gets you across the Andes without buses or footwork. Alternatively, you can Argentina's Atlantic coast, an ideal short-stop destination. Spend at least a couple of days spying the spectacular marine fauna on Peninsula Valdés and other spots around Golfo Nuevo, before exploring the Welsh villages of the Chubut valley. Then on to Puerto Madryn, from where, time permitting, of course, you can beach hop to other resorts along the coast. Then again, you could do a one- or two-destination hop: lakes and glaciers, or the end of the world and the Atlantic coast.

Two to three weeks

With a full two weeks you can hit three to four key destinations; with three you can add in extra stops and get further off the beaten track. Buy a flight pass (see p236) if you want a multi-stop itinerary. See pp234-40 **Getting There & Around** for information on travel options.

A logical itinerary is to head all the way south and then zigzag your way up. Getting down to Ushuaia means you can head out into the waters off the tip of the continent. Cross into Chile, via historical Punta Arenas, up to Puerto Natales for Torres del Paine national park – serious trekkers will want at least a week here to do the classic seven-day circuit. Then it's decision time.

There are three great options. Cross back into Argentina and head to PN Los Glaciares to see Perito Moreno and the Fitz Roy massif, then follow the Andes up to the Lake Districts, visiting some of the steppe en route. Or head to Río Gallegos and up the Atlantic coast to Peninsula Valdés to take in the marine wildlife. Even if you travel up the Andes, it's worth crossing over to the coast at the end. If you want a change from planes and buses, take the train from Bariloche to Viedma to reach the ocean. Option three involves actually taking to the sea: do the three-night Navimag boat through the fjords and ice fields of the Chilean archipelago. You need to plan your dates, though: departures are Fridays going south–north, and Mondays going north–south. The boat deposits you conveniently at Puerto Montt, capital of Chile's Lake District. Be sure to include a couple of nights on the secluded island of Chiloé.

Three weeks or more

Now you're laughing… With this much time, renting a car (or better still a 4x4) is the perfect way to see Patagonia (see p237 **By road**). Build in a few days on an estancia for some ranching activities. There's no need to worry about the borders: you can cross from one side of Patagonia to the other across the international passes. If you want to do it all, plot a circular route: either fly all the way down from Santiago to Punta Arenas or from Buenos Aires to Ushuaia – then from either destination head up one or other coast, cross the Andes via the lakes region, and track back down the other coast. You can't do all of the south of Chile by road: at some point you've got to hit the water. On wheels, pick up the Chilean Southern Highway at Coyhaique, Chaitén or Puerto Montt; in Argentina you can drive up the Atlantic coast or through the steppe.

Accommodation

The recent growth in tourism to Patagonia has inevitably led to a marked increase in accommoation options for visitors. That said, in towns and villages located well off the beaten track, choice is often limited to one or two places, the quality of which can be somewhat hit and miss.

Book ahead if travelling in peak periods: January and February or over any long weekends (see p233 **Public holidays**) and July winter holidays in ski regions. In far southern destinations, most hotels close for large periods of the year – May-Oct/Nov – and although everywhere there is at least one year-round option, it may not be your first choice. Periods of the year when establishments are closed are noted in this guide.

Pricing

There is a huge variance in prices across the region. The top-end private estancias and fishing lodges (whose facilities may include access to the best fishing areas, private guides, a helicopter or small plane, polo ponies and the like) are only for high-rollers. They charge up to US$750 per night, with everything you could ask for included. It can be argued that this compares favourably to hotel prices in many of the world's more expensive capital cities, but it's still a large chunk of change.

However, some places offer exceptional value. You can find gorgeous cabins or delightful hotels for around US$35 per person per night. At the bottom end, the cheapest (often extremely basic) hotels or very good hostels should not exceed US$10-$15 per night, subject to time and place. There's also a whole lot of space in which to camp for free.

In reaction to the 2002 Argentinian currency devaluation, many hotel owners – particularly in the higher categories – employ a differential pricing system for residents and foreigners, with foreigners paying more and being charged in US dollars. You can try to get around this by travelling in mixed groups with Argentinian nationals and having them book the room, since most rates are per room, not per person (excepting hostels).

In Chile a two-tier system has been in place for longer; it's usual for foreigners to be charged in dollars. Make sure the hotel displays tarifas diferenciales so you can see both rates. In Chile foreigners are not charged sales tax: show your passport and make sure you get a factura de exportación (tax-free bill).

Albergues

See p232 **Hostels**.

Apart-hoteles

In Argentina apart-hoteles have standard hotel features, but larger rooms with kitchenette and small living/eating area. In Chile it often indicates apartments for rent to tourists.

Cabañas

Cabin complexes are extremely common in the Lake Districts. Cabins have a master bedroom, living room and kitchen, secondary bedrooms or dorms

Directory

and can sleep four to ten people. They are grouped in complexes of three to 50 cabins, and facilities depend on the size of the centre, but often include a café, swimming pool or other sports facilities.

Camping

There are organised campsites in most national parks and towns in Patagonia, although facilities vary enormously. You can usually camp for free in the national parks, but must ask first at the Intendencia about where you are allowed to pitch your tent. Always respect rules about litter disposal and fire prevention. Many landowners are willing to let you camp on their property for free or a minimal sum; but again, ask first.

Estancias/fundos/ haciendas

The word '*estancia*' is most used in Argentina; it's more common to call private ranches *haciendas* or *fundos* in Chile. The terms denote working farms or places dedicated to tourism. Some can be visited on a day trip, including lunch and activities, and most offer accommodation, though of a varying standard. Every *estancia* has its attractions, and the price always includes all home-cooked meals, so represents fair value as well as a unique experience. *See pp62-3* **Ranching**.

Hostels

Hostels are also called *Albergues de la juventud* (youth hostels). Chile has a greater number under the aegis of the Youth Hostelling Association (RHI in Spanish) than Argentina, where most are independent. Standards are generally high. Set-ups vary from mixed rooms for 30 to rooms for two or six.

Hosterías

A *hostería* is a small hotel (three to 15 rooms) offering reasonably priced lodging.

Hotels

Hotel means the same in Patagonia as elsewhere and the standards on both sides of the Andes are largely comparable. The star rating system is not the best guide to quality: rules tend to be followed to the letter, so a hotel can have four stars because its hallways are the requisite width, but may be lacking in other key services.

Refugios

These refuges are located in and run by the national parks or by licensed concessionaries. They are often no more than a wooden shelter where you can bed down in your sleeping bag for a couple of dollars per night. In the most popular parks some are more sophisticated and charge a few dollars more.

Tourist information

These details direct you to tourist information in the UK, US, the Chilean or Argentinian capitals, plus main contacts for Patagonia's regional/provincial tourist offices.

The state Argentinian tourist board is the **Secretaría de Turismo y Deportes de la Nación**. Individual provinces of Argentinian Patagonia are also represented by Casas de Provincia in Buenos Aires and offices in provincial capitals.

In Chile the state-run tourist authority is **Sernatur** (www.sernatur.cl), which has its head office in Santiago.

Under each destination in this guide we have provided the details of the local tourist office and, in relevant boxes, the national parks offices.

In the UK

Argentinian Embassy

65 Brook Street, London W1 (020 7318 1300/fax 020 7318 1301/ www.argentine-embassy-uk.org). Open 9am-1pm, 2-5pm Mon-Fri.

Chilean Consulate

12 Devonshire Street, London W1 (020 7580 1023/cglonduk@ congechileuk.demon.co.uk). Open 9am-1.30pm Mon-Fri.

In the US

Argentinian Embassy

1600 New Hampshire, NW, Washington, DC (1-202 238 6400/ fax 1-202 332 3171/www.embajada argentinaeeuu.org). Open 9am-5pm Mon-Fri.

Chilean Embassy

1732 Massachusetts Avenue, NW, Washington, DC (1-202 785 1746/ fax 1-202 8875579/www.chile-usa.org). Open 8.30am-1pm Mon-Fri.

Argentina

Buenos Aires

Secretaría de Turismo de la Nación *Ground Floor, Avenida Santa Fe 883 (011 4312 2232/ freephone 0800 555 0016/www. turismo.gov.ar/info@turismo.gov.ar).* Open 9am-5pm Mon-Fri.
Administración de Parques Nacionales *Avenida Santa Fe 690, entre Maipú y MT de Alvear (011 4311 0303/www.parquesnacionales. gov.ar).* Open 10am-5pm Mon-Fri.
Aeroparque Jorge Newbery *Central Hall, Aerolíneas Argentinas terminal (011 4771 0104/4773 9805).* Open 8am-8pm daily.
Aeropuerto Ministro Pistarini *Central Hall, International Terminal (011 4480 0207).* Open 8am-8pm daily.

Provincial tourist information

Chubut *In BA 011 4383 7458/ in Rawson 02965 481113/www. chubutur.gov.ar.*
Neuquén *In BA 011 4326 9265/ in Neuquén 02994 486755/www. neuquentur.gov.ar.*
La Pampa *In BA 011 4326 0511/ in Santa Rosa 0295 4424404/www. turismolapampa.gov.ar.*
Río Negro *In BA 011 4312 2232/ in Viedma 02920 422150/www.rio negro.gov.ar.*
Santa Cruz *In BA 4325 3098/ in Río Gallegos 02966 422702/ www.scruz.gov.ar.*

Directory

Climate chart

Destination	Average temperatures	
	Jan max/min	*July max/min*
Argentina		
Bariloche	21°C (70°F)/7°C (45°F)	7°C (45°F)/-1°C (30°F)
Neuquén	31°C (88°F)/15°C (59°F)	13°C (55°F)/0°C (32°F)
Puerto Madryn	27°C (51°F)/13°C (55°F)	13°C (55°F)/2°C (36°F)
Río Gallegos	20°C (68°F)/10°C (50°F)	6°C (43°F)/-3°C (27°F)
Ushuaia	13°C (55°F)/5°C (41°F)	5°C (41°F)/-1°C (30°F)
Chile		
Temuco	25°C (77°F)/11°C (52°F)	12°C (54°F)/4°C (39°F)
Valdivia	23°C (73°F)/11°C (52°F)	11°C (52°F)/8°C (46°F)
Puerto Montt	20°C (68°F)/11°C (52°F)	10°C (50°F)/5°C (41°F)
Aisén	18°C (64°F)/11°C (52°F)	7°C (45°F)/2°C (36°F)
Puerto Natales	17°C (63°F)/6°C (43°F)	5°C (41°F)/-3°C (27°F)
Punta Arenas	15°C (59°F)/7°C (15°F)	4°C (39°F)/0°C (32°F)

Tierra del Fuego *In BA* 011 4311 0233/*in Ushua*ia 02901 421423/ www.tierradelfuego.org.ar

In Chile

In Santiago
Sernatur Calle Providencia 1550, 2nd Floor (02 731 8419/www. sernatur.cl). **Open** 9am-6pm Mon-Fri; 9.30am-1.30pm Sat.
CONAF (National Parks) *Avenida Bulnes 291, y Eleuterio Ramirez (02 3900125/www.conaf.cl).* **Open** 9am-5.30pm Mon-Thur; 9am-4.30pm Fri.
Aeropuerto Internacional Arturo Marino Benítez *International Terminal (02 601 9320).* **Open** 8.30am-9.30pm daily.

Regional tourist information
Región IX *In Temuco* 045 211969/ serna09@entelchile.net
Región X *In Puerto Montt* 065 259 615/sernatur@telsur.cl
Región XI *In Coihaique* 067 231 752/sernatur_coyhai@entelchile.cl
Región XII *In Punta Arenas* 061 225 385/serna12a@entelchile.net

What to take

Despite its proximity to the South Pole, summer does exist in Patagonia. For packing, you are advised to take a little of everything. Think layers, plus comfortable walking shoes, wind and waterproof gear (essential) and swimwear.

Remember that Patagonia is too close for comfort to the very large hole in the ozone layer. Good sun protection is essential, along with sunglasses and a hat. The good news is that the region is relatively mosquito free, due to the varying combinations of dryness, temperature and altitude. However, a repellent is always advisable for the greener, waterside locations.

When to go

Climate

All of Patagonia is in the southern hemisphere. The summer is from December to March, and the winter solstice is 21 June. The temperature range is huge: extreme winter temperatures can drop to as low as -15°C (5°F), and feel even colder when the wind is up, although the average is -2°C (26°F). In summer, the mean is 23°C (73°F) but in the northern areas can hit a stifling 40°C (104°F), though it stays cold at night at higher altitudes. Still, daytimes in the summer are beautiful and, on the

northerly coastal stretches and in the mountains, often warm enough for sunbathing.

Public holidays

Argentina's fixed national public holidays (*feriados*) are:
1 January (New Year's Day); **Jueves Santo** (Thursday before Easter); **Viernes Santo** (Good Friday); **1 May** (Labour Day); **25 May** (May Revolution Day); **9 July** (Independence Day); **8 December** (Day of the Immaculate Conception); **25 December** (Christmas Day).

The following holidays transfer to the Monday preceding if they fall on Tuesday or Wednesday, or to the Monday following if they fall on Thursday or Sunday:
2 April (Falklands/Malvinas War Veterans' Day); **20 June** (Flag Day) **17 August** (San Martin Memorial Day); **12 October** (Christopher Columbus Americas Day)

Chile's public holidays:
1 January (New Year's Day); **Viernes Santo** (Good Friday); **1 May** (Labour Day); **21 May** (Navy Day); **June** – varies (Corpus Christi); **29 June** (San Pedro y San Pablo); **15 August** (Ascensión de la Virgen); **First Monday in September** (National Reconciliation Day); **18 September** (Patriotic Fiestas); **19 September** (Army Day); **12 October** (Christopher Columbus Americas Day); **1 November** (All Saints); **8 December** (Day of the Immaculate Conception); **25 December** (Christmas Day).

Directory

Getting There & Around

Arriving & leaving by air

Any trip to Patagonia will necessarily take you via the Argentinian or Chilean capitals: Buenos Aires and Santiago. You can arrange to fly south straight away, but a night or two in either city at the start or finish of your trip is well worth it (see pp239-40).

Airports in Argentina

Aeropuerto Ministro Pistarini

Ezeiza, Buenos Aires, 35km (22 miles) from city centre. Recorded flight information or operator, plus listings of airline telephone numbers 011 5480 6111 (English & Spanish).
The official name of Buenos Aires' international airport is Aeropuerto Ministro Pistarini, but it's more commonly known by the name of the area in which it is located, Ezeiza.

All international flights arrive and leave from here – including flights to Santiago for going on to Chilean Patagonia – except for those between Buenos Aires and Uruguay (see p235 **Aeroparque Jorge Newbery**).

Allow 30-40 minutes to travel between the centre of Buenos Aires and Ezeiza in normal traffic and up to one hour 20 minutes in rush hour.

The airport has two interconnected terminals: A and B. Aerolineas Argentinas uses Terminal B; all other airlines operate out of remodelled Terminal A. Although not big by international standards, you'll find all the usual shops and facilities within the terminals – public telephones, banks, an ATM and bureau de change, newsstands, a pharmacy, souvenir shops, a bookshop, tourist information, restaurants, bars and cafés (the ones in Terminal A are better). Duty-free shops are in the pre-boarding sector; you can buy duty-free purchases on arrival and before leaving.

Arriving by air is straightforward, though often six international flights arrive at around the same time, making luggage collection and immigration lengthy processes. Before landing, you must complete arrival and departure forms; keep the departure form for when you leave (although you can complete another one at check-in if you've mislaid the original). Argentinian departure tax

is US$18 payable at the airport (cash: pesos, euros, dollars; credit: MC), plus US$12.50 usually included in the ticket, depending on the airline or travel agency.

Despite Argentinians' legendary unpunctuality, many arrive early for flight departures. As those leaving are often accompanied by numerous family members, the airport is busy prior to international departures, so allow plenty of time for check-in.

As you come into the arrivals area, you will be approached by people offering you taxi or *remise* (minicab) services. Never accept a ride; always use one of the approved companies that operate from the airport, or arrange transport with a company of your choice. For two to four people, it's worth paying for a *remise*. Unless otherwise stated, you have to pay road tolls (US$1, one-way) at the end of the journey.

Manuel Tienda León (4315 5115, freephone 0810 8885366, bus US$8, *remise* US$25) is a reliable company offering bus and *remise* services with desks inside the airport, a branch in town and English-speaking operators. Their buses run every 30 minutes, 5am-8.30pm. For an extra US$1 charge they will pick you up and drop you off within a defined area of the city centre; otherwise, journeys start and finish at the firm's office on Eduardo Madero 1299.

Remise firm **Transfer Express** (0800 4444 872, US$21) also has an airport desk and English-speaking operators. Otherwise, try one of several *remise* and radio taxi alternatives that can take you to or meet you at the airport. If you haven't arranged a pick-up, call on arrival and they'll send a driver within 15 minutes. Fares are to the city centre: for a *remise*, use **Blue** (4777 8888, US$15) or **Recoleta Vip** (4801 6655, US$13); for a radio taxi **Radio Taxi Premium** (5238 0000, US$13), **Mi Taxi** (4931 1200, US$12) and **Pidalo** (4956 1200, US$14).

You can take a city bus, though we recommend one of the services above. You should allow at least two hours for the trip to the airport. Bus 86 runs to/from La Boca and Avenida de Mayo.

Airports in Chile

Aeropuerto Comodoro Arturo Merino Benítez

Santiago, 20km (12.5 miles) from city centre. (Passenger information 02 690 1752/53/www.aeropuerto santiago.cl).

Santiago de Chile's airport's official name is Comodoro Arturo Merino Benítez, though locals often call it Pudahuel. All international and domestic commercial flights arrive and leave from here, including those to Buenos Aires for destinations to Argentinian Patagonia. Allow 30-45 minutes to travel between the airport and the centre of Santiago.

The airport has a food court and a series of small snack bars, as well as duty-free shops, newsstands, bookshops and a tourist information desk. There are shops selling Chilean products and souvenirs before and after immigration.

There are two terminals – domestic and international – in the airport. Arriving by air is straightforward; under normal circumstances it should only take you 15 minutes to get out of the airport. You'll be given a tourist card and a customs slip to fill in on the plane, which you need to present on arrival and keep to hand in again on departure. You can get a new one again at the airport if you lose it, free of charge, but it's a drag.

United States (US$100), Canadian (US$55) Australian (US$30) and Mexican (US$15) nationals are obliged to pay an entry tax as part of a reciprocal agreement with Chile. This does not apply to EU citizens. Chilean departure tax is US$26, usually included in the purchase price of your ticket.

In the International Terminal there's a *casa de cambio* for changing money near the baggage claim area. Outside customs there are kiosks for bus and taxi companies, as well as car hire agencies. You will be approached by people offering transport services when you leave customs. These are usually official services, but, for security, you should contract bus or taxi services at the kiosks themselves. A taxi to the centre will cost US$23-$31: **Taxi Oficial** (02 690 1381). **Tur Bus** (02 60 9573/601 9621, www.turbus.com) have buses running every 30 minutes daily, from the airport to the city centre from 6.15am to midnight, for US$2.5 one-way, US$4 return (and beyond that time they offer a tur-transfer to your hotel for US$7).

Airlines

Airline contact phone numbers in Buenos Aires and Santiago are given below, though not all the companies listed fly to both cities. BA and Santiago are also served by other European carriers, including Air France, Alitalia, Iberia and Lufthansa. For information on flying within Patagonia, *see p236.*

Aerolíneas Argentinas
BA freephone 0810 222 86527
Santiago 02 210 9300/690 1030
American Airlines
BA 011 4318 1111
Santiago 02 601 9272/601 9318
British Airways
BA 011 4320 6600/freephone 0800 666 1459
Santiago freephone 0800 207 207
Air Canada
BA 011 4327 3640/44
Santiago 02 337 0022/690 1115
Delta
BA 011 4312 1200
Santiago 02 690 1551/690 1555
LanChile
BA 011 4378 2200/freephone 0810 9999 526011
Santiago (56 2) 526 2000
Qantas
BA 011 4114 5800
Santiago 02 232 9562
United Airlines
BA only 011 4316 0777/freephone 0810 777 8648

Flying to Patagonia

Flights to Chilean Patagonia from Santiago leave from **Aeropuerto Arturo Merino Benítez**. To reach Argentinian Patagonia by air, you will leave from BA's **Aeroparque Jorge Newbery**.

If you are transferring from the international airport, it's a 50-kilometre (32-mile) trip. Manuel Tienda León runs shuttle buses (US$9 one-way) connecting the two airports; otherwise it's just ten minutes from the centre of Buenos Aires. Manuel Tienda León also runs bus (US$3 one-way) and car services (US$7 one-way) between the city centre and the Aeroparque.

Several city buses also serve the airport; the fare is US25¢. Bus numbers 37C (make sure that it says Aeroparque on the front), 160, 45 and 33 all run from the centre. There is a taxi rank at the airport entrance – only take one with a sign showing it is a radio taxi. A taxi or *remise* to a city-centre hotel costs US$3-$4.

Aeroparque Jorge Newbery

Avenida Costanera Rafael Obligado, entre La Pampa y Sarmiento, Costanera Norte (recorded flight information or operator, plus listings of airline telephone numbers 011 5480 6111, information available in both English and Spanish).

Arriving by other methods

By bus

International bus services into Buenos Aires arrive at the main bus terminal (**Estación Terminal de Ómnibus**), near a mainline train station, often just known by its area name, Retiro. International bus services into Santiago will arrive at **Estación Central Internacional de Ómnibus** on Alameda Ruiz Tagle.

Numerous long-distance bus companies operate from both terminals. In Argentina, reliable companies serving Patagonia are: **TAC** (011 4313 3632), **Vía Bariloche** (011 4315 3122) and **Andesmar** (011 4313 3650, www.andesmar.com) – all with booths in the bus station; in Chile, **Tur Bus** (02 270 7500), **Cóndor Bus** (02 680 69 00) and **Buses Jac** (02 7761582).

There are a number of daily services to provincial and regional capitals in Patagonia and other primary tourist destinations. Examples of one-way ticket prices and journey times from Buenos Aires are: to Bariloche 21.5 hours, US$35-$45; to Puerto Madryn 18 hours, US$35-$50; to Comodoro Rivadavia 24.5 hours, US$50-$75; to Río Gallegos 36 hours, US$70-$90. To go to Ushuaia, take a plane. From Santiago: to Temuco, 9.5hrs, US$22-$25; to Valdivia, 11hrs, US$21-$23; to Puerto Montt, 14hrs, US$24-$26; to Pucón, 11hrs, US$22-$24. To get to Punta Arenas or Puerto Natales, fly or use boat services.

Purchase tickets at the bus station. In high season (Dec-Feb, July), it's best to book in advance. In low season, you can usually buy your ticket a few hours ahead of departure. For tips on getting around by bus within Patagonia, *see p237.*

Estación Central Internacional de Ómnibus

Alameda Ruiz Tagle, Santiago. (Passenger information 02 376 1755).

Estación Terminal de Ómnibus

Avenida Ramos Mejía 1680, Retiro, Buenos Aires. (Passenger information 011 4310 0700).

By train

There are no international train services into Argentina or Chile. Travelling by train to Patagonia from the capital can only be done in Chile. The daily overnight service is run by **Empresa de los Ferrocarriles del Estado** (02 585 50 00, www.efe.cl) and goes from **Estación Central de Santiago** (Avenida Alameda 3170) via: San Bernardo, San Fernando, Curicó, Rancagua, Talca, San Javier, Linares, Parral, San Carlos, Chillán, Concepción, Hualqui, Bulnes, Cabrero, Monte Aguila, Yumbel, San Rosendo, La Laja, Renaico, Victoria, Lautaro, arriving after 11.5 hours in Temuco. Tickets cost US$12-$70.

By sea

Cruise ships, as well as boats arriving from nearby Uruguay, come to Buenos Aires. The passenger port – **Dársena Norte** – is a few blocks from the city centre at Avenida Córdoba and AM de Justo. The main destination in Patagonia for cruises is Ushuaia. Cruises also stop at ports in Chile: in Valparaiso near Santiago, and Puerto Montt and Punta Arenas in Patagonia.

Directory

Getting around Patagonia by air

The situation regarding the domestic flights service in Chile and Argentina looks a little confusing at first. In Chile, more than 80 per cent of internal flights are run by the national carrier, **Lan Chile**, although **Sky Airlines**, which also serves destinations in Patagonia, entered the market in 2002 to provide much-needed competition. In Argentina the main carrier is **Aerolíneas Argentinas** (whose domestic service was called Austral – you may still hear/see that name), though **Southern Winds** also fly a number of routes to Patagonia. (They are currently under investigation following a drugs smuggling scandal and are therefore best avoided.) The air force also has an airline, **Lade**, which runs commercial services between small destinations in Argentinian Patagonia.

FLIGHT PASSES

Flight passes are usually cheaper than buying several individual tickets in either Chile or Argentina but you can only get them outside these countries. Travel agencies have access to a number of 'flight pass' deals for South America or Mercosur, if you are going to be in more than one country. For Argentina only, Aerolineas Argentinas' **'Visit Argentina'** offers fixed low-fare options (see airline website) for domestic flights within Argentina. Reservation for the first flight coupon, total payment and ticket issue for the whole itinerary must be made at the same time as that of the internacional ticket.

The **'Visit Chile'** air pass is available to LanChile and Iberia passengers booking intercontinental flights into and out of Chile. At the time of going to press prices were:

US$270 for three one-way flights, and a further US$90 for each additional coupon (six maximum); children pay the same as adults. It includes all destinations in Chile except Easter Island.

Aerolíneas Argentinas

Perú 2, Buenos Aires (011 4320 2000/0810 2228 6527 telesales/ www.aerolineas.com.ar). **Open** 9am-7pm Mon-Fri; 9am-1pm Sat. **Credit** AmEx, DC, MC,V.

Aerolineas is the national carrier, rescued from bankruptcy in 2002. Its subsequent progress has been encouraging; prices are competitive and standards high and it has the biggest network. Aerolineas has offices in major cities around the country, sales desks in all destination airports and you can book over the internet. Prices are the same whether booking in person or by phone.

In Patagonia, Aerolineas flies (from Buenos Aires) to: Neuquén, Bariloche, Chapelco, El Calafate, Rio Gallegos, Trelew, Comodoro Rivadavia, Ushuaia, Rio Grande, Esquel, as well as to Santiago.

Lade

Perú 710/714, Buenos Aires (011 5129 9000/freephone 0810 810 5233/www.lade.com.ar). **Open** 9.30am-5.30pm Mon-Fri; 9.30am-4pm Sat. **Credit** MC, V.

Lade flies Fokker and Twin Otter military aircraft between 25 destinations, most of which are in Patagonia. It make so many stops en route that what would normally be a three-hour flight with another airline can take up to twice as long – but it's useful for flying between close destinations.

LanArgentina

Cerrito 866, Buenos Aires. (0810 9999 526). **Open** 9am-6pm Mon-Fri; 10am-1pm Sat. **Credit** AmEx, DC, MC, V.

Part of the Lan group, sharing an office with LanChile in Buenos Aires. Daily flights to Bariloche for US$281 return, bi-weekly to Rio Gallegos and Comodoro Rivadavia for US$207 and US$192 respectively.

LanChile

Huérfanos 926, Santiago (02 526 2000/565 6498/www.lanchile.com). **Open** 9am-6.30pm Mon-Fri; 10am-12.45pm Sat. **Credit** AmEx, DC, MC, V.

In Chile, LanChile runs nearly all scheduled domestic passenger flights. You can book via the internet on www.lanchile.com or www.lanexpress.com; special offers are posted on Tuesdays.

Lan has ticket sales points at airports and offices in Santiago, Buenos Aires and cities in the south. Destinations covered by Lan are: Temuco, Valdivia, Osorno, Puerto Montt, Balmaceda, Punta Arenas and Pucón (summer only). Flights originate in Santiago, other than for direct services between Temuco and Valdivia, and Puerto Montt and Punta Arenas. Lan also flies to Buenos Aires and has a once a week service (Sat) to the Falkland Islands/Las Islas Malvinas, stopping at Santiago, Puerto Montt and Punta Arenas on the way there and back.

Sky Airlines

Andrés de Fuenzalida 55, Providencia, Santiago (02 353 3169/600 600 2828/www. skyairline.cl). **Open** 9.30am-9.30pm Mon-Fri; 9am-2pm Sat. **Credit** V, MC, AmEx, DC.

Operating since mid 2002, Sky has provided some much-needed competition to Lan's domestic service. Runs daily flights to Temuco, Puerto Montt, Coyhaique and Punta Arenas and has sales offices in each destination.

Southern Winds

Avenida Santa Fe 784, Buenos Aires (011 4515 8600/ freephone 0810 777 7979 telesales/www.fly-sw.com). **Open** 9am-6.30pm Mon-Fri; 9am-1pm Sat. **Credit** AmEx, DC, MC, V.

Southern Winds introduced welcome competition into Argentina's domestic air travel – the fleet is modern and service good – but as this guide went to press, the company was under investigation over a drugs scandal. Check in advance with a travel agency.

By bicycle

The immense distances between destinations in Patagonia somewhat negate idealistic visions of a gentle cycling holiday – this isn't the Netherlands. Not only do you need to be in excellent physical condition, but along the coast things get even more complicated; two wheels versus the strong and unremitting southern winds is not a fair match. However, within each town, cycling is a good way of getting around, and there is always bicycle rental available. Ask at the local tourist office.

Passing over

These are the passes connecting Argentinian and Chilean Patagonia by road, ordered from north to south. 'Links' shows the nearest Argentinian and then nearest Chilean town or village to the pass. These border points all have immigration officials and are the only place you should cross over, unless you are with an organised excursion.

Paso de Pino Hachado Links Las Lajas–Paraje Liucura. **Open** 8am-9pm.
Paso de Icalma Links Aluminé–Melipeuco. **Open** 8am-9pm.
Paso Mamuil Malal Links Junín de los Andes–Cararrehue. **Open** 8am-8pm.
Paso Carirriñe Links Junín de los Andes–Liquiñe. **Open** 8am-8pm.
Paso Hua-Hum Links San Martín de los Andes–Panguipulli. **Open** 8am-8pm.
Paso Cardenal Samoré Links Villa La Angostura–Osorno. **Open** *May-mid Oct* 9am-8pm. *Mid Oct-Apr* 8am-9pm.
Paso Peréz Rosales Links San Carlos de Bariloche–Peulla. **Open** *May-mid Oct* 9am-8pm. *Mid Oct-Apr* 8am-9pm.
Paso Río Puelo Links Lago Puelo–Segundo Corral. **Open** 24hrs.
Paso Río Futaleufú Links Los Cipreses–Futaleufú. **Open** 8am-8pm.

Paso Río Encuentro Links Carrenleufu–Palena. **Open** 24hrs.
Paso Coihaique Links Aldea Beleiro–Coihaique. **Open** 8am-8pm.
Paso Huemules Links Lago Blanco–Balmaceda. **Open** 8am-8pm.
Paso Ibañez Links Perito Moreno–Puerto Ingeniero Ibañez. **Open** 24hrs.
Paso Río Jeinemeni Links Los Antiguos–Chile Chico. **Open** 8am-10pm.
Paso Rodolfo Roballos Links Hipólito Yrigoyen–Cochrane. **Open** 24hrs.
Paso Río Mayer-Rivera Norte Links Gobernador Gregores–Villa O'Higgins. **Open** 24hrs.
Paso Lago San Martín/Lago O'Higgins Links Tres Lagos–Cochrane. **Open** 24hrs.
Paso Río Don Guillermo Links Río Turbio–Cerro Castillo. **Open** 8am-midnight.
Paso Dorote Links Río Turbio-Puerto Natales. **Open** 8am-midnight.
Paso Laurita/Casas Viejas Links 28 de Noviembre–Puerto Natales. **Open** 8am-midnight.
Paso Integración Austral Links Río Gallegos–Villa O'Higgins. **Open** 24hrs.
Paso San Sebastián Links Río Grande–El Porvenir. **Open** *Apr-Oct* 9am-11pm. *Nov-Mar* 24hrs.

By boat

In Argentina, transport services by sea hardly exist. As in Chile, there are boat excursions and charter services in the Deep South into the Beagle Channel and around the islands of Tierra del Fuego, or even to Cape Horn or Antarctica. The key difference is that in Chile boat travel is part of the way of life; getting to Chiloé or heading south from Puerto Montt will almost inevitably involve you taking to the sea. *See pp206-209* **Sea Routes South**.

By bus

Bus is a viable and affordable alternative for getting around – if you can stomach long journeys – and between some destinations it's the only way if you don't have your own transport. International buses connect the Lake Districts of Chile and Argentina. But not every corner of Patagonia is accessible by road, though buses reach all the region's towns; in summer, competing bus companies offer several services daily. This is normally reduced to just one daily service, or just two or three per week, in midwinter between smaller towns.

The regional/provincial capitals are the main hubs, with buses heading out to other key cities. Only these and other large towns have central bus terminals – which are more common in Argentina than Chile. Otherwise each company has its own office (where buses stop), making selecting a service more complicated. In villages drivers will usually drop you where you want. Local tour operators with minibuses are a useful alternative. It pays to get a group together when contracting these kinds of transport, then split the cost.

By road

Car – ideally a 4x4 vehicle, and in summer – is a great way to get around Patagonia, provided you like driving long distances. In Argentina, only the main national highways – Ruta Nacionales or RN – are asphalted. Rutas Provinciales (RP) are usually *ripio* (dirt roads with loose gravel): avoid emergency braking and slow down through gear changes on this surface. For more advice on driving, *see p200*.

Directory

Breakdown services

Only members of automobile associations or touring clubs with mutual reciprocal agreements with other regions (FIA in Europe and FITAC in the Americas) can use the rescue services of the **Automóvil Club Argentino** or ACA (Information 011 4315 5678, freephone 0800 888 84253, freephone 24hr breakdown service 0800 777 2894, www.aca.org.ar) and of the **Automóvil Club de Chile** or ACC (information 02 431 1000/freephone 24hr breakdown service 600 6000 600, www.auto movilclub.cl).

This includes members of the British AA and RAC. You can use this facility in either country for 30 days. You will be asked to present the membership credentials of your local club, showing the FITAC or FIA logo, to the mechanic, who, under the scheme, will come to the rescue no matter how far you are from the closest city.

Petrol stations

The cost of petrol has risen steeply in Argentina over the past few years, but fuel in Argentinian Patagonia is still 40 per cent cheaper than in the rest of the country. '*Precios patagónicos*' start at Sierra Grande on RN3. Petrol in Chilean Patagonia costs only three per cent less than in the rest of the country. You can get a list of all Argentinian stations at www.aca.org.ar and of their Chilean counterparts at www.automovilclub.cl.

Vehicle hire

Legally you need to be over 21 (but some agencies require you to be over 23 or 25), with a driver's licence, passport and credit card to hire a car in Chile or Argentina. Car hire is available in most larger Patagonian towns (Comodoro Rivadavia has particularly good deals). In Chile, if you want to save money hire your car at a small local agency, though it may end up being a false economy because their insurance policies leave you largely uncovered.

Every agency has its own rates and special deals – but a rough guide for a standard category vehicle is US$40 per day in Argentina which is only a little cheaper than in Chile where the least you'll pay is US$50 per day, depending on mileage required. Extra mileage costs US14-22¢ (Argentina) and US22-30¢ (Chile) per additional kilometre. Some hire companies let you take the car across the Argentinian/Chilean border, but the paperwork is painful. You have to sign a contract in front of a public notary, which will set you back US$100-$200, and you'll have to let them know four days in advance. You can often return the car to a different office within Argentina and Chile. Most agencies will charge you a drop-off charge depending on the kilometres between the city where you rented the car and the one you hand it back: it's usually around US35¢ per kilometre. You must have at least third-party insurance (*seguro de responsabilidad civil*), but it's sensible to take out comprehensive insurance. If you hire a car in Santiago, take note that a pollution control system operates; only certain cars can be used in the city each day.

Argentina

ABA Rent a Car *First Floor, Mitre 437, entre Palacios y Bescheted, Bariloche (02944 461443/02944 15 60 4766/info@abarentacar.com.ar)*. **Open** 9am-8pm daily. **Credit** AmEx, DC, MC, V.
This is one of the few agencies which lets you take the car across into Chile for no cost whatsoever. You can drop it off in any Argentinian or Chilean city with a drop-off charge. Rental costs are from US$25 per day.

Dollar Rent a Car *Carlos Rodríguez 518, entre Salta y Jujuy, Neuquén (0299 4420875/ Reservation Centre 011 4315 8800/www.dollar.com.ar)*. **Open** 9am-1pm, 4-8pm daily. **Credit** AmEx, MC, V.
You're not allowed across the border with the car, but you can leave it in any number of branches located throughout Argentinian Patagonia for an extra fee of US13-32¢ per km. An economy model costs US$23 in Neuquén, US$28 in Bariloche.

Chile

Hertz *Andrés Bello 1469, Providencia, Santiago (02 496 1000/es.hertz.com)*. **Open** 8am-8pm Sun-Fri; 8.30am-6pm Sat. **Credit** AmEx, DC, MC, V.
Hertz does allow you to take the car across the Argentinian/Chilean border, but it must be returned to a Hertz office in Chile by the same driver. Three days' notice is required and an additional insurance charge of US$170 is incurred. Within Chile you may leave your car in a different city from the one where you arranged the rental, though a drop-off fee will be charged. The cheapest model costs US$41 per day with unlimited mileage, and a 4x4 model costs US$106, also with unlimited mileage. **Branches**: Airports and cities across Chilean and Argentinian Patagonia; check website for details.

Rosselot *Booth 9, Aeropuerto Tepual, Puerto Montt (065 430510/ www.rosselot.cl)*. **Open** 9am-9pm daily. **Credit** AmEx, DC, MC, V.
If you want to get across the border from Chile into Argentina, you'll have to pay US$200 extra (phone 4 days in advance); to leave the car in a different city within Chile costs US25¢ per kilometre's distance from the point of departure. The cheapest model costs US$23 per day with unlimited mileage, while a 4x4 costs US$55, also unlimited mileage. **Branches**: Aeropuerto Tepual, Puerto Montt (065 430510); Bilbao 2032, Santiago (02 381 3690).

By train

Although you can arrive by train in Temuco from Santiago, train travel as a primary means of transport is no longer an option in Patagonia; the once-proud rail network is virtually defunct. But train enthusiasts will enjoy a ride on the **Tren Patagónico** (*see p104*) along the one working section of track from the Atlantic coast to the Andes.

Buenos Aires

Buenos Aires, a city of collective obsessions represented by Maradona and Evita, tango and psychoanalysis, is slowly crawling out of the hole left by the catastrophic economic collapse of December 2001. Although prices have risen across the board, Buenos Aires is still affordable and the social climate of the city is more relaxed by the day.

The main areas of interest to the tourist are found near the brown waters of the Río de la Plata. Start your sightseeing in the mythical southern port district of **La Boca**, but stay close to the tourist trail as the proximity of *villas* (shantytowns) can make it dangerous. Then move on to the charming cobblestone streets of **San Telmo** for antique markets, cafés, bars and restaurants. From there head along the river to the booming and trendy **Puerto Madero**, where a clutch of new eateries and hotels has brought life to the once moribund port.

The **Plaza De Mayo**, home to the Casa Rosada (Balcarce 50), the pink government house where Evita and Maradona waved to adoring masses, is packed with history, palm trees and pigeons. From the plaza, stroll up the architecturally rich **Avenida de Mayo** or head up pedestrianised Florida Street to Plaza San Martín. Don't miss verdant and wealthy **Recoleta**, best known for housing one of the world's finest necropolises, the **Cementerio de Recoleta** (Junín 1760). Wander through the majestic tombs, then head to the adjacent Centro Cultural Recoleta and relaxing greenery of Plaza Francia, which fills with stands peddling arts, crafts, and clothing on the weekends. Further north, the city's cutting-edge arts scene is best expressed at the **Museo de Arte Latinoamericano** (MALBA) (Avenida Figuero Alcorta 3415).

Continue on to the attractive parks and residential areas of **Palermo**, where hipsters flock to the bars, restaurants and boutiques.

Where to stay

To pass your days in the city in high style, rub shoulders with BA's glitterati at the new **Faena Hotel + Universe** (Martha Salotti 455, Dique 2, 4021 5555, double from US$300), a ritzy funhouse in the trendy Madero Este neighbourhood. Close by, cheaper and still highly chic is the **Hotel Madero** (Rosario Vera Peñaloza 360, Dique 2, 5776 7777, double from US$170). For

boutique style, check out **NH Jousten** (Avenida Corrientes 240, 4321 6750 doubleUS$120). Smaller, friendlier and cheaper accommodation is at funky **Malabia House** (Malabia 1555, 4833 2410, double US$50) in Palermo Viejo, or youthful **Milhouse** (Hipólito Yrigoyen, 4827 3061, US$7 per person). There are many cheap hostels in the San Telmo neighbourhood.

Where to eat

Beef is everywhere, but a classic is sepia-tinted **El Obrero** (Agustín Caffarena 64, 4362 9912) in La Boca – go in company, by taxi. For a more modern, colourful take on the traditional Argentinian *parrilla*, try Palermo's **La Cabrera** (Cabrera 5099, 4031 7002). A classy joint is **Olsen** (Gorriti 5860, 4776 7677) themed along sleek and stylish Scandinavian lines, but with an international menu and gorgeous garden. For good pastas and Vegas style, try **Guilia** (Sucre 632, 4780 3603). For those looking for a break from Argentinian fare, there's good Morrocan food in an attractive atmosphere at **Bereber** (Armenia 1880, 4833 5662).

Nightlife

BA's nocturnal scene has few rivals. For cool cocktails in a lavish setting, head to the lovingly restored French-style mansion **Millión** (Paraná 1048, 4815 9925) or follow the beautiful people to Palermo Viejo's **Unico** (Honduras 5604, 4775 6693) or **Mundo Bizarro** (Guatemala 4802, y Borges, 4773 1967). The big night out – with regular visits from superstar DJs– is at **Pachá** (Avenida Costanera y Pampa, 4788 4288), or get down, dirty and decadent at **Niceto Club's** (Niceto Vega 5510, 4779 9396) Club 69 on Thursday nights. For a more down-to-earth evening, prop up the bar at cosy **Gibraltar** (Perú 895, 4362 5310) for a pint of Guinness. Or for old-style fun, go to the *milonga* – tango dance salon – at **Torcuato Tasso** (Defensa 1575, 4307 6506) or **Salón Canning** (Scalabrini Ortiz 1331, 4832 6753).

Getting around

Colectivos (buses) go everywhere in the city and cost US25¢ a ride. The Subte – a small but reliable subway network – is a fast alternative branching out from the centre (till 10.30pm only); a single fare costs US20¢. Otherwise take a taxi (use radio taxis only), or *remise* (licensed minicab).

Santiago

If you arrive by plane the Chilean capital city of Santiago is a stunning sight: the towering bank of the Andes pushes steeply down into a smudge of dark smog. For the city, this dynamic geography is both a blessing and a curse. Surrounded by impressive mountains, the city's emissions are often trapped in the valley, causing severe environmental problems. Smaller and calmer than Buenos Aires, Santiago de Chile is nonetheless unique, and this five-million strong metropolis has all you need to get back the urban rhythm after a trip south.

Climb to the elegant fort at the top of **Cerro Santa Lucía** (Calle Merced to the north, Avenida O'Higgins to the south, Santa Lucía to the west and Caseaux to the east), or take the cable car up higher still **Parque Metropolitano** (Avenida Pío Nono) for a view of the snow-capped Andes. They're visible beyond the shiny towers that symbolise Chile's recent economic success.

To distract attention from the smog, the city has a number of parks, palaces and a range of day- and night-time entertainment – servicing the large student population and an expanding nouveau-riche sector. Culture and hedonism are spread out but getting around is a cinch. From south-west to north-east you move from the historic and civic centre to racier Bellavista, on to Providencia and then Las Condes, the smartest of the city's residential districts.

Start your sightseeing with the edifying stuff: 18th-century **Casa de la Moneda** (Avenida Portales 3586, Estación Central, 02 680 5200) – the seat of government – and the **Plaza de Armas**, laid down in the city's foundation year, 1541. The plaza, fed by pedestrianised streets, is surrounded by listed buildings. Full of Chileans, foreigners and immigrants from Chile's poorer barrios, it's a good place to spend the evening observing the city's cast of characters.

Neruda fans will want to do some idolising in Santiago, and **La Chascona** (Fernando Márquez de la Plata 192, Providencia, 02 777 8741/737 8712), the poet's house at the foot of Cerro San Cristóbal, has lots of bookish things on display.

Where to stay

The París-Londres neighbourhood near the old civic quarter has some nice places all next to each other. **Residencial Londres** (Londres 54, 02 638 2215, double US$21) is a cheap and cheerful rabbit warren of a place; round the corner,the slightly smarter **Hotel París** (París 813, 02 664 0921, double US$26) has grand rooms with attractive fittings. **Vegas** (Londres 49, 02 632 2498, double US$47), in the same quarter, is the best of the lot. **Hostal Río Amazonas** (Rosas 2234, 02 671 9013, double US$40), in the central Barrio Brazil, is great for budget travellers.

Where to eat

To continue on the trail of Neruda, go to **Venezia** (Pío Nono 200, 02 777 4845), one of the poet's old haunts and a classic, serving hearty fare since 1937. For another eaterie steeped in history, try **El Rincón de las Canallas** (San Diego 379, 02 669 1309), forced underground during the dictatorship but now thriving. For a taste of more modern cuisine coming out of Santiago, try **Agua** (Nueva Costanera 3467, 02 263 0008, www.aguarestaurant.cl). Or if you're in Los Condes and want to avoid the typical fast food, try **Fast Good** (Isidora Goyenechea 2890) for pop atmosphere and hamburgers made by a gourmet Spanish chef. **El Toro** (Loreto 33, 02 737 5937) specialises in seafood dishes. And if you're desperate to drop some coin, try the highly touted French menu at **El Europeo** (Avenida Alonso de Córdova 2417, 02 208 3603).

Nightlife

There are several neighbourhoods for night jaunts but Bellavista leads the pack. **Tantra** (Ernesto Pinto Lagarrigue 154, 02 732 3268) is a pub-disco with a strong line in cocktails and techno; nearby **Punta Brown** (Recoleta 345, 02 217 0385) is one of the top neo-industrial dance joints. **Las Brujas** (Avenida Príncipe de Gales 9040, 02 273 1072) is the queen of the Santiago night, with pop, rock and Latin tropical sounds and room for a thousand sweating torsos.

Getting around

Santiago's Metro is clean, fast and comparatively calm. Single tickets are US50¢, or US40¢ off-peak. Buses cost US40¢ within the city and are very regular: the easiest way to move around is to jump on and off buses running along the main O'Higgins/Providencia drag. Taxis are metred, reasonably priced and safe.

Resources A-Z

Addresses

Small towns may not have house numbers – San Martín s/n or sin/n°, means San Martín street without a house number. In this guide, such addresses are denoted simply as San Martín. In larger towns, buildings are numbered, and it is useful to know the cross-streets or nearest corner: thus San Martín 232, entre Sarmiento y O'Higgins, is number 232 San Martín street, between Sarmiento and O'Higgins streets. When giving cross streets, you don't have to say 'calle', 'Avenida' or other prefixes. If a house or building is near a corner, give that one nearest cross street – San Martín y Sarmiento or, in Chile, San Martín con Sarmiento. In Chile, some street numbers have a '0' prefix.

In the countryside, there are rarely street names. Addresses are given as their distance in kilometres from the start of main roads. For example, RN23, km 80 means that a place is 80 kilometres along Ruta Nacional (main national highway) number 23. RP is Ruta Provincial (secondary road). Main national roads in Chile are just Ruta and a number, and secondary roads are identified by a letter and number, such as T253.

Where an address is even less precise – as in the case of the entrance to a national park, we have given the most useful indications: distance from nearest town, distance along a road, or which road to take.

Age restrictions

In Argentina the law says that to buy alcohol or have sex you must be 18 years old; to buy cigarettes you need to be 16;

and you have to be 17 (16 with parental consent) to drive. The law, at least in the first three cases, is broken. Chileans can drink, smoke and drive at 18, and while law-makers are firmer, sex and smoking do begin earlier. Also, regardless of age, drinking on the streets in either country is punishable with a fine or one to four days' voluntary work – not what you wanted on your holiday.

Attitude & etiquette

Meeting people

Argentinians are sociable and friendly, and always interested in meeting foreigners. Tactile and physically demonstrative, most exchange kisses (usually a single cheek-to-cheek kiss) on first meeting – men or women. If meeting a senior person, it's safer to shake hands, and when speaking Spanish, use the *usted* (formal) form rather than the *vos* (informal). In Chile, people are a tad more reserved, though equally friendly once they get to know you. Kissing between men is less common, so hands are best, and the ordinary Iberian Spanish informal *tú* is used between friends.

Personal contacts are highly valued. In business, if someone is proving difficult to reach, a quick name-drop can help, or, better still, use a third party for an introduction. When selling, it does no harm to lean heavily on the foreign side of your business background.

Start conversations with a '*buenos días*' (before noon) or '*buenas tardes*' (after noon) and a brief exchange of pleasantries if your Spanish is up to it. You will find most business people speak at least

some English, although this is not true in other environments. Any attempt to speak Spanish will always be appreciated, in all situations.

Don't sweat if delayed on your way to an appointment; punctuality is a phenomenon that barely exists, though Chile is said to be more 'Germanic' or orderly with respect to meetings. Most people turn up late. Out of politeness, as the foreigner, it's better to be on time, but expect to be kept waiting, always.

Dress & manners

Argentinians and Chileans are well presented. Threadbare jeans are thrown away or banished to intimate moments of housework. Best classified as casual but smart, the dress code is applicable from the pub to the boardroom.

Argentina's contradictory nature is apparent in aspects of the behaviour of its citizens. On the one hand, they are the champions of door-opening and good manners; on the other hand, they are great perpetrators of shoulder-barging and queue jumping. Chileans are less loud and gregarious and less effusive even when being friendly.

Business

Most business meetings take place in BA or Santiago, though Patagonian cities are popular for conferences. Four- and five-star hotels offer business services, from shipping to photocopying.

Business attire is formal for office meetings, but if you are out in the country or meeting at an *estancia*, informal is fine. In general, deals won't be closed after a single meeting, partly because of red tape, but also because hedging bets and haggling is part of doing business here. Patience, flexibility and a willingness to deviate from hard negotiating will usually be rewarded.

Couriers & shippers

See p246 **Postal services**.

Useful organisations

Argentina

Ministerio de Relaciones Exteriores, Comercio Internacional y Culto *Esmeralda 1212, y Arenales, Buenos Aires (011 4819 7000/www.mrecic.gov.ar).* **Open** 9am-6pm Mon-Fri.
Cámara de Comercio de los Estados Unidos *8th Floor, Viamonte 1133, entre Libertad y Cerrito, Buenos Aires (011 4371 4500/www.amchamar.com.ar).* **Open** phone for details.
Cámara de Comercio Argentino-Británica *10th Floor, Avenida Corrientes 457, entre San Martín y Reconquista, Buenos Aires (011 4394 2762/www.ccab.com.ar).* **Open** phone for details.

Chile

Cámara de Comercio Chileno-Americana *2nd Floor, Office 201, Avenida Kennedy 5735, Torre Poniente, Las Condes, Santiago (02 290 9700/www.amchamchile.cl).* **Open** 8.30am-6pm Mon-Fri.
Cámara Chileno-Británica de Comercio *Avenida El Bosque Norte 0125, Las Condes (02 3704175/www.britcham.cl).* **Open** 9am-5.30pm Mon-Fri.

Children

Most of the larger hotels and cabin complexes offer crèche and even kindergarten services, as well as spaces for playing in. National parks and ski centres offer special classes for kids and the visitor centres in Chile are particularly child-centred. Both countries are famously 'child-friendly'; eating out, travelling on public transport and visiting people with kids in tow are all encouraged. Long distances in Patagonia make journeys trying for all involved and some of the more arduous excursions aren't suitable for infants or young teenagers.

Customs

Entering Argentina, you can bring in the following without paying import duties: two litres of alcoholic drinks, 400 cigarettes, 5kg of foodstuffs, 100ml of perfume. If entering from a neighbouring country, these quantities are halved. The Argentinian province of Tierra del Fuego, and the city of Punta Arenas in Chilean Tierra del Fuego, are duty-free zones. You can enter Chile with: 400 cigarettes, 500g of tobacco, 50 cigars, 2.5 litres of alcoholic drinks, and goods with a value of up to US$1,500.

Disabled

The principal challenge for disabled travellers is getting around; a combination of air travel and taxis is usually the most workable option. Travel agencies organise minibuses between many destinations, which will be viable for wheelchair users. As a rule, hotels in higher categories have disabled adapted rooms and ramp access. Pavements in town have ramps, though often in poor condition – smaller towns or villages have fewer paved roads or pavements. Take spare parts; it may be impossible to get replacements if anything breaks. While facilities may be lacking in hostels or small hotels, people will try to make your stay as easy as possible.

Tour agencies in each location, however, can usually assist with travel planning. Chile's tourist board was not able to name any specialist agencies, but large firms like **Cocha** (56 2 464 1000, r5. cocha.com) are happy to give advice, and will adapt tours to meet needs. One Argentinian agency specialising in disabled holidays is **Barlan Travel** (5th Floor, Office A, Mitre 124, Bariloche, 02944 429999, www.barlantravel.com).

Drugs

All non-prescription drugs – hard or soft – are illegal in Argentina, whether they are for trafficking or personal consumption. Nonetheless, in southern campsites few log fires are to be found without a guitar and a spliff and the police seem to turn a blind eye. But if they do decide to nail you it could mean a night in jail, deportation, or the demand of a very hefty 'fine' to get yourself out of trouble. In Chile the laws are the same with respect to trafficking and possession and police are stricter. While grass is widely smoked, police and, especially, border guards will carry out thorough checks if you so much as look like a potential stoner, and won't let you off if found in possession.

Electricity & gas

Electricity in Patagonia runs on 220 volts. Sockets take either two- or three-pronged European-style plugs. To use US electrical appliances, you need a transformer and an adaptor; for UK appliances an adaptor only is required. Transformers (*transformador*) and adaptors (*adaptador*) can be purchased in hardware stores, known as *ferreterías*. Power cuts are occasional, though more frequent in bad weather. In Chile this won't affect rustic lodgings much, as wood burning stoves are used for cooking and heating in many homes and hotels.

Embassies & consulates

Buenos Aires

Australia *Villanueva 1400, entre Zabala y Teodoro García, (011 4779 3550/www.argentina.embassy.gov.au).* **Open** *Visas* 8.30-11am Mon-Fri. *Information* 8.30am-5pm Mon-Fri.

Canada *Tagle 2828, entre Figueroa Alcorta y Juez Tedín, (011 4808 1000/www.dfait-maeci.gc.ca/ argentina).* **Open** *Visas* 8.45-11.30am Mon-Thur. *Information* 8.30am-12.30pm, 1.30-5.30pm Mon-Thur; 8.30am-2pm Fri.
Ireland *6th Floor, Avenida del Libertador 1068, entre Avenida Callao y Ayacucho, (011 5787 0801/www.irlanda.org.ar).* **Open** 9.30am-1.30pm, 2-3.30pm Mon-Fri.
New Zealand *5th Floor, Carlos Pellegrini 1427, entre Arroyo y Posadas (011 4328 0747/www. nzembassy.com/buenosaires).* **Open** *Information* 9am-1pm, 2-5.30pm Mon-Thur; 9am-1pm Fri.
South Africa *8th Floor, Marcelo T de Alvear 590, entre San Martín y Florida (011 4317 2900/www. embajadasudafrica.org.ar).* **Open** *Information* 8.15am-12.30pm, 1.15pm-5.15pm Mon-Thur; 8.15am-2.15pm Fri.
United Kingdom *Dr.Luis Agote 2412, y Guido (011 4808 2200/ www.britishembassy.gov.uk).* **Open** *Mar-Dec* 8.45am-5.30pm Mon-Thur; 8.45am-2pm Fri. *Jan, Feb* 8.45am-2.30pm Mon-Thur; 8.45am-2pm Fri.
USA *Avenida Colombia 4300, entre Sarmiento y Cerviño (011 5777 4533/http://buenosaires.usembassy. gov).* **Open** *Visas* 7.30am-12.30pm by appointment only (4321 1100) Mon-Wed, Fri. *Passports & reports of births abroad* 8:30am-noon Mon-Fri by appointment only.

Santiago

Australia *12th & 13th Floors, Isidora Goyenechea 3621 (02 550 3500/www.chile.embassy.gov.au).* **Open** 8.30am-5pm Mon-Fri.
Canada *12th Floor, Torre Norte, Nueva Tajamar 481, entre Nueva Costanera y Vitacura (02 362 9660/www.dfait-maeci.gc.ca/chile).* **Open** *Visas* 9-11am Mon-Fri. *Information* 8.30am-5.30pm Mon-Thur; 8.30am-1pm Fri.
Ireland *8th Floor, Office 801, Isidoro Goyenechea 3162 (02 245 6616).* **Open** 9am-6pm Mon-Fri.
New Zealand *Office 703, El Golf 99, Las Condes, Santiago (02 290 9800/www.nzembassy.com).* **Open** 9am-1pm, 2-5pm Mon-Thur; 9am-1.30pm Fri.
South Africa *17th Floor, Avenida 11 de Septiembre 2353, y Fernández (02 231 2862/www.embajada-sudafrica.cl).* **Open** *Visas* 8.15am-1pm, 1.45pm-5.15pm Mon-Thur; 8.15am-2.15pm Fri. *Information* 8.30am-12.30pm Mon-Fri.
United Kingdom *Avenida El Bosque Norte 0125, y Don Carlos (02 370 4100/www.britemb.cl).* **Open** 9am-1pm, 2-5.30pm Mon-Thur; 9am-1pm Fri.

USA *Avenida Andrés Bello 2800, Las Condes, Santiago (02 232 2600/www.embajadaeeuu.cl).* **Open** 8.30am-5pm Mon-Fri.

Emergencies

The nearest hospital and police station are given under each destination. These are the national emergency numbers:

Argentina
Police 101
Fire 100
Ambulance 107

Chile
Police 133
Fire 132
Ambulance 131

Gay Patagonia

Argentina and Chile are countries with a strong and influential Catholic church and an historically strong military – two reasons why both have been relatively slow to adopt a tolerant attitude towards homosexuality. They are also patriarchal societies, and as a consequence, gay men enjoy considerably greater visibility, acceptance and choice of venues than lesbians, transgenders and transvestites. By law, all sexual practices are prohibited for those under 18.

Buenos Aires now has a progressive and open scene, regarded by many as the best in Latin America. For up-to-date information, check out *La Otra Guía* (distributed in pubs and clubs) or buy *NX* or lesbian publication *Fulanas* at newsstands. Argentina's most politically influential queer organisation is **Comunidad Homosexual Argentina** (www.cha.org.ar). In rural Patagonia you can expect a less progressive yet tolerant attitude. For organised trips in the south and general information, check out **Mix-Travel** (011 4312 3410, www.mixtravel.com) and **Pride Travel** (011 5218 6556, www.pride-travel.com).

Gays in Chile have long suffered; yet in the past few years, attitudes have relaxed and gay life has sprung out into a more accepting society. Gay bars and clubs coexist with activist organisations. Although the scene is a far cry from the streets of San Francisco – or even Buenos Aires – visiting gays in Santiago will find plenty of clubs and bars in and around the Bellavista barrio. Check out the very complete www.gaychile.com for up-to-date information on gay activities. According to one website, **Ventistur** (061 229081, www.ventistur.com) is a gay-friendly, English-speaking travel agency in Punta Arenas. Other useful websites for information on Chilean gay and lesbian life are www.gaychile.com – covering travel as well as health. social issues and education – and the political site www.movilh.org, run by the **Movimiento de Integración y Liberación Homosexual**.

Health

There are no tropical diseases, so there is no need to vaccinate against malaria, dysentery and the like. All Patagonian towns have clinics, hospitals and A&E facilities, though in the open country, you may be some distance from assistance.

If you are on medication of any kind, it's wise to bring a supply to last you the entire trip as you may not find the same brands or laboratories as back home, although standard pharmaceutical products and remedies for average aches and pains are widely available.

Tap water tastes good in Patagonia and is highly drinkable. Glacial spring water, rivers and lakes is pure and drinkable, though rogue microbes can cause diarrhoea – it's always safest to use purification tablets. In Chile

Directory

watch out for the infrequent *'marea roja'* (red tide) – you must not eat shellfish at these times as it can be fatally toxic.

Contraception & abortion

Public hospitals will supply the contraceptive pill after an appointment with a doctor, but brand names vary between Argentina and Chile. Abortion is illegal but available privately and off the record in hygienic, professional conditions, or – if it's a budget operation – in conditions involving serious health risks.

Doctors, dentists & opticians

Hotel concierges and pharmacists can recommend local GPs, dentists and opticians. If you have private insurance, the firm will have a list of selected practitioners. All towns have at least one optician. Wearers of hard or gas-permeable contact lenses should take solutions with them, as cleaning solutions for sale are almost exclusively for soft-lens wearers.

Hospitals

The closest hospital is listed in the **Resources** section under each destination in this guide. In an emergency, your best bet is one of these public hospitals, which have specialist doctors on duty 24 hours a day. Though there are no official reciprocal agreements between the health services of Argentina and Chile and those of other countries, state hospitals will usually attend to foreign patients, usually after a longish wait, and for a fee.

You are strongly advised to take out travel insurance that covers you in Argentina and Chile, to include any medical expenses and give you access

to private clinics or hospitals, which tend to have more personalised service and more modern facilities.

Pharmacies

Most chemist's shops (*farmacias*) open 9am-8pm, though there are also 24-hour outlets and *'farmacias de turno'* – shops that remain open late on a rota basis.

Prescriptions

For many drugs, and all antibiotics, you will need a prescription and therefore a visit to a doctor.

STDs, HIV & AIDS

Public hospitals and most private clinics offer experts in gynaecology, urology and sexual health, and in the cities there are HIV clinics. Any drugs for treating sexually transmitted diseases, HIV and AIDS require a prescription.

ID

By law, everyone must carry photo ID in Argentina and Chile. Checks are rare, but if you do get pulled over, you will be expected to show at least a copy of your passport or (photo) driving licence.

Insurance

Take out a policy that covers both health and accidents. As baggage can also go astray – and any local compensation will be meagre – it is also advisable to get protection for your luggage, during flights and on overland journeys.

Internet

Computers are expensive in Argentina, so many people converge on the privately owned *locutorios* call/internet centres to surf the net.

Telephone giants Telefónica and Telecom normally have at least one of these in each town, and even in large villages, though you will probably find a friendlier and better service at one of the cybercafés.

Legal help

If you have the misfortune to be arrested, the call you should make is to your embassy in Buenos Aires or Santiago.

Lost property

In general, if you've lost it, forget it. Recovering stolen or lost property depends on the good nature of the person who finds your belongings. If you've lost something on public transport, call the transport operator, which should, in principle, hold on to lost property – but don't hold your breath. It's another good reason to take radio taxis; call the operating company if you leave something in a cab.

Maps

Most bookshops in Bariloche, Comodoro Rivadavia and Temuco stock maps and you should also check the street newspaper kiosks and service stations, where road maps and guides are also sold. Towns near trekking centres also stock maps of the local area. As a rule, though, the best places to buy maps of Patagonia are outside Patagonia – bookshops in Buenos Aires and Santiago have large selections of maps. The popular **YPF** guide is comparable with a Michelin product; it's comprehensive, updated annually and comes with a CD-Rom.

The automobile associations ACA and ACC (*see p238* **Breakdown services**) produce quality maps and Turistel's Chile maps and guides are good for exploring region by region. Look out also for *Patagonia Ecomapa*, JUML's *Torres del Paine* map, Firestone's *Atlas de Rutas* (large format detailed road map of Argentina, Chile and other South American countries). Automapas have two useful maps: *Patagonia y Tierra del Fuego* and *Rutas de Chile* (Roads of Chile) available from kiosks in Buenos Aires and Santiago for US$3-$4.

Good online resources for ordering maps are: in the US, www.maps2anywhere.com; in the UK, www.stanfords.co.uk.

Media

The Spanish-language national newspapers are available throughout Patagonia, sometimes arriving in the afternoon; there are regional newspapers in many towns and provinces where you can catch up on the latest domestic crime, grain prices and local entertainment. Foreign publications are hard to come by and expensive. Cable and satellite TV are generally standard, even in the more remote places – about 60-plus channels, which usually include CNN or BBC World.

Chile

El Mercurio www.emol.com
Chile's heavyweight national paper, with a conservative bias.
La Tercera www.latercera.cl
Popular daily with more liberal angle and lots of sport and entertainment.

Argentina

Buenos Aires Herald
www.buenosairesherald.com
Long-established English-language daily; news summaries on Saturdays and stories from the *New York Times* on Sundays.
Clarín www.clarin.com
Mass-market daily paper that's fat with both local and international news. It somehow manages to be high-, middle- and low-brow at the same time, and so sells loads.
La Nación www.lanacion.com.ar
Argentina's grand old daily, beloved of the middle class and conservative on culture, art and lifestyle.

Money

Argentina's 2002 currency devaluation means dollars go further there than in Chile, though some hotels have kept prices at 'international levels' – for more information on hotel prices and policies, *see p231* **Accommodation**.

The large majority of hotels accept dollar payments, the general rule being that if you pay in dollars you should receive change in dollars. Smaller establishments, however, may advertise an exchange rate and give change in pesos. If in doubt, ask what rate they are offering and in what money you are going to receive your change.

The Argentinian peso ($) is divided into centavos. There are coins in one peso, 50, 25, 10 and 5 centavo denominations, plus 100, 50, 20, 10, 5 and 2 peso notes (in every kind of condition). You should beware of counterfeit money.

In Chile, the Chilean peso ($) is the currency, holding stable at present. There are $500, $1,000, $2,000, $5,000, $10,000 and $20,000 notes and coins of $1, $5 (rare), $10, $50 and $100. Currency is bought and sold freely – while dollars are widely accepted, it's best to have local dosh as the conversion maths make dealing in dollars a mess.

ATMs

International cards work in ATMs for cash withdrawal, but in moments of financial crisis you may find the machines are out of money.

You'll find ATMs in all but the tiniest of towns. The main networks in Argentina are Banelco and Link, in Chile look for the Redbanc symbol. ATMs provide pesos to anyone with a Cirrus or Visa symbol on their card and to credit card holders – that is, if you can remember your PIN.

Banks

The majority of banks in Argentinian Patagonia open at 7 or 8am and close at 1pm. Weekends and bank holidays, all banks close. Generally, banks in Chile open Monday through Friday, 9am to 2pm.

Bureaux de change

Throughout Patagonia *casas de cambio* offer the official exchange rate, are quick and queue-less and most open Saturdays as well as weekdays. There may be a siesta hour so go at 9am-2pm or 3-5pm.

Credit cards

Major credit cards are widely accepted, especially AmEx, Visa and Mastercard. There may be a charge for using plastic in Argentina (or more commonly you can ask for a discount if paying in cash), but this does not apply in Chile. Traveller's cheques are acceptable in major hotels, or can be changed to pesos or their original currency at banks and casas de cambio.

Lost/stolen credit cards

American Express (*In Argentina* 011 4310 3165/freephone 0800 777 3165. *In Chile* 02 230 1000).
Diners Club Contact your card issuer in your home country.
Mastercard (*In Argentina* freephone 0800 555 0507; *in Chile* freephone 1230 020 2012).
Visa Reverse charges (dial 000) to: +1 410 581 0120.

Tax

Local sales tax is called IVA: Impuesto al Valor Agregado. In Argentina it's 21 per cent, included in prices except for hotel rack rates (usually listed without IVA in more expensive hotels). We have quoted all Argentinian hotel prices with IVA included, so there's no

Directory

shock on the final bill. If you shop in Argentina, there is a not-entirely-reliable sales tax refund system, payable at the airport on departure for goods purchased during your stay. Look for the 'Global Refund' sticker, and ask for the necessary stamped form when you make your purchase, which explains everything.

In Chile, IVA is 19 per cent although foreign tourists are exempt from paying VAT on hotels – show your passport and ask for a *factura de exportación* to benefit from tax-free prices. Rates in Chile are quoted without tax (*'sin IVA'*). Sales tax must be paid on other purchases.

Natural hazards

Apart from a volatile economy, Argentina is largely free of natural hazards, while Chile has its famous volcanoes. Though the likelihood of one of these erupting during your holiday is remote, many are active and the sulphurous emissions are extremely poisonous. Mosquitoes are sporadically rife in the summer as are the tábano horseflies in the lake regions – they cause bleeding and a stinging sensation. There is no malaria or yellow fever, though there is a very low dengue fever risk in Argentina and a low cholera risk in Chile.

Opening hours

The relaxed pace of life in Patagonia is reflected in the opening hours. Many places shut in the afternoon, for a well-earned siesta. Bankers and postal workers kick off early but are scrambling for lunch by 1pm, and do not reappear till the next day. Chileans work more standard hours: 9am-6pm for most offices, banks, post offices and businesses. Shopping centres open later and stay open

longer (11am-10pm) and supermarkets have the longest hours (8.30am-10 or 11pm). Hours in Argentinian Patagonia tend to vary from province to province, but in general are: banks, 7am-1pm; offices, 9am-noon and 5pm-9pm; post offices, 8am- 2pm. Across the region, restaurants usually open noon-3pm and again from 8pm till close.

Police stations

As a tourist, with any luck, you won't have any dealings with the police. If you need a police station, the closest one is given under the **Resources** section of each destination.

Postal services

Correo Argentino (www. correoargentino.com.ar), the former state service which is now fully privatised, handles most post in Argentina. All towns have one or more offices, open normal office hours, and some call centres (*locutorios*) are authorised to issue stamps and handle post – look for the Correo Argentino sign. These tend to be open longer. Postal workers say the mail takes 13 days; off the record it is more like 20. The price of mail has risen steeply since the economic crisis of December 2001; at time of press a lightweight letter to Europe/ the US costs US$1.50/$1.70.

In Chile, **Correos de Chile** (www.correosdechile.cl) is the main company. A lightweight letter to Europe/the US costs US$35¢/40¢. In both countries, send letters registered – *certificado* – to ensure delivery.

Packages & parcels

Both Correo Argentino and Correos de Chile offer door-to-door (*puerta a puerta*) express international package services and **DHL** (www.dhl.com.ar) has offices in Comodoro

Rivadavia (0297 4444345), Puerto Madryn (02965 452 200) and Rio Gallegos (02966 430 156). It also has an office in Punta Arenas in Chile (061 228462, www.dhl.cl). **FedEx** currently has no outlets in Patagonia but can arrange for parcels to be collected if you call the office in Buenos Aires (011 4630 0300, freephone 0810 3333 339, www.fedex.com/ar) or Santiago (02 361 6000, freephone 0800 363 030, www. fedex.com/cl).

Post offices

The local post office is given under under the **Resources** section of each destination.

Religion

The majority of both populations is Catholic, but all religions are freely practised in Argentina and Chile. In the south, Christian churches dominate, though there are also synagogues, Muslim mosques and Greek Orthodox churches in some towns.

Telephones

Phone calls are possible from any Patagonian town or city, though you may have to go through an operator.

International calls

Argentina
International calls can cost a fortune, though phone cards for making international calls are providing more competitive rates. Avoid calling from your hotel; rates are a lot higher than from *locutorios* (call centres). *Locutorios* are found throughout the country. Their popularity is due to the fact that the phones work and you don't have to fuss around with coins – the bill is paid to the cashier. Public phones take coins or cards, the latter available at many kiosks. To call within the country, dial 0 before the number; to call overseas it's 00; Argentina's country code is 54. The international operator is 000. Mobile phone numbers have 15 between area code and number.

Chile

There are more public phones and fewer call centres in Chile, so the best thing is to have a magnetic card or a few 100 peso coins to make calls. Hotels hike prices significantly. All in-country area codes begin with 0 before the number; to call overseas dial 00; Chile's country code is 56. The international operator is 000. Mobile phone numbers start 09.

Mobile phones

Mobile phones in Chile use GSM technology, but you may still require an adaptor card. Argentina has three network technologies (GSM, AMPS/TDMA800 and CDMA800) in use and roaming with your own phone may not be possible across the country. Easiest is to rent locally: prearrange rental in Chile or Argentina with www.anywhere-phone-rental.com, or for a local supplier, www.altel.com.ar (who charge for calls made only, not rental). Many hotels have a cellphone rental service, and there are often firms at airports offering mobile rental. In some parts of Patagonia there are *only* mobile phones, since land lines don't cover the whole area. In very remote places, only shortwave radio or satellite phone communication is possible.

Time

In Argentina, clocks have been known to go back and forth at whim, but in recent years the time has stayed the same – GMT minus three hours, all year, with no use of Daylight Saving. Chile is GMT minus four hours, but from October to March, when Daylight Saving comes into effect, it is three hours behind GMT.

Tipping

Tips tend to be left in the same proportional quantities as is the case in most developed western countries. Workers in the restaurant trade are generally ill-paid. As a rule of thumb, ten to 15 per cent in a bar, restaurant, or for any delivery service is a decent tip. In a cab, simply round off the fare. In hotels, bellhops would expect US$1 for helping with bags. When checking out, it's normal to leave a small *propina* (tip) for the maids.

Visas & immigration

Information about longer-stay visas for students or business travellers can be obtained from your nearest Argentinian or Chilean Embassy.

Argentina

Entry visas are not required by members of the European Union or citizens of the USA. Immigration usually gives you a 90-day visa on entry that can be extended by a quick exit out of the country; from Buenos Aires most people choose a day trip to Uruguay; in Patagonia you can cross over into Chile. The fine for overstaying your visa is 50 Argentinian pesos (US$16.50); if you do overstay your official welcome, plan to arrive at the airport early so you have time to take care of the fine.

Chile

Very few travellers will need a visa to enter Chile; in most cases a valid, ten-year passport suffices. Visitors from the United States, Canada, Australia, New Zealand, the UK and most other Western European countries do not require a visa although US (US$100), Canadian (US$55), Australian (US$30) and Mexican (US$15) citizens have to pay an entry tax as part of a reciprocal agreement with Chile. These fees are subject to change and should be checked prior to travel. Standard tourist visas are for 90 days.

Crossing the border

To drive across the frontier, you'll need passports, a valid international driving licence, papers for the vehicle and if you're with kids, proof they're yours or that you have permission to take them across the border in the form of a birth certificate or a document signed by a notary. Do not cross with firearms, dope or even plants and fresh produce – the Chileans in particular are likely to strip you of your aspidistra and fresh peaches in order to keep foot and mouth at bay. Many border posts close at time so check the opening hours before driving. (*See p237* **Passing over**). You can cross the border on foot at these same border points, going through the usual immigration procedure (filling out an immigration form, showing your valid full passport and getting a 90-day tourist entry stamp).

Weights & measures

Argentina and Chile use the metric system, though a few old measures still apply in the countryside.

Women

It is generally safe for women travellers to move around in Chile and Argentina, and Patagonia is particularly safe. Alhough men in these countries have very different natures, they share a common need to flirt, stare, whistle and *piropear* (making a suggestive remark as you pass). Just ignore it and nothing will ensue. Both countries are very friendly to foreigners and people will help women travellers. Avoid hitch-hiking alone unless you're offered a ride with a family (though there's unlikely to be much room in the car).

Directory

Language & Vocabulary

Argentinians and Chileans living and working in tourist areas usually have some knowledge of English, but the more remote the area, the less you can assume that people will speak other languages. Thos who do generally welcome the opportunity to practise, but a bit of Spanish goes a long way and making the effort to use even a few phrases and expressions will be greatly appreciated.

As in other Latin languages, there is more than one form of the second person (you) to be used according to the formality or informality of the situation. The most polite form is *usted*, and though not used among young people, it may be safer for a foreigner to err on the side of politeness. The Argentinian variant of the informal, the *voseo*, differs from the *tú* that you may know from European Spanish. In Chile they use *usted* in formal situations, but *tú* for the informal as in Spain. All forms are given here: *usted*, then *vos*, then *tú*.

Pronunciation

Spanish is easier than some languages to get a basic grasp of, as pronunciation is largely phonetic. Look at the word and pronounce every letter, and the chances are you will be understood. As a rule, stress in a word falls on the penultimate syllable, otherwise an accent indicates stress. Accents are omitted on capital letters, though still pronounced. The key is to master the correct pronunciation of a few letters and vowels. Understanding isn't always so easy – locals talk fast, and in Chile seem to swallow sections of words, making life difficult. But any effort made will usually be rewarded by an attempt to communicate back.

Vowels

Each vowel is pronounced separately and consistently, except in certain vowel combinations known as diphthongs, where they combine as a single syllable. There are strong vowels: a, e and o, and weak vowels: i and u. Two weak vowels, as in *ruido* (noise), or one strong and one weak, as in *piel* (skin), form a diphthong. Two strong vowels next to each other are pronounced as separate syllables (as in *poeta*, poet).

a is pronounced like the **a** in army.
e is pronounced like the **a** in say.
i is pronounced like the **ee** in beet.
o is pronounced like the **o** in top.
u is pronounced like the **oo** in mood.
y is usually a consonant, except when it is alone or at the end of the word, in which case it is pronounced like the Spanish **i**.

Consonants

Pronunciation of the letters **f, k, l, n, p, q, s** and **t** is similar to English.
y and **ll** are generally pronounced like the French '*je*', in contrast to the European Spanish pronunciation.
ch and **ll** have separate dictionary entries. **ch** is pronounced as in the English **ch**air.
b is pronounced like its English equivalent, and is not distinguishable from letter **v**. Both are referred to as **be** as in English **b**et. **b** is **long b** (called *b larga* in Spanish), **v** is known as **short b** (*b corta*).
c is pronounced like the **s** in sea when before **e** or **i** and like the English **k** in all others.
g is pronounced like a guttural English **h** like the **ch** in loch when before **e** and **i** and as a hard **g** like **g** in **g**oat otherwise.
h at the beginning of a word is silent.
j is also pronounced like a guttural English **h** and the letter is referred to as **jota** as in English **h**otter.
ñ is the letter **n** with a tilde accent and is pronounced like **ni** in English on**i**on.
r is pronounced like the English **r** but is rolled at the beginning of a word, and **rr** is pronounced like the English **r** but is strongly rolled.
x is pronounced like the **x** in ta**x**i in most cases, although in some it sounds like the Spanish **j**, for instance in Xavier.

Basics

Where usage differs, variants are given: Argentinian Spanish/Chilean Spanish.

hello *hola*
good morning *buenos días*
good afternoon *buenas tardes*
good evening/night *buenas noches*
OK *está bien*
yes *sí*
no *no*
maybe *tal vez/quizá(s)*
how are you? *¿cómo le va?* or *¿cómo te va?*
how's it going *¿cómo anda* or *andás* or *andas?*
Sir/Mr *Señor*; **Madam/Mrs** *Señora*
please *por favor*
thanks *gracias*; **thank you very much** *muchas gracias*
you're welcome *de nada*
sorry *perdón*
excuse me *permiso*
do you speak English *¿habla* or *hablás* or *hablas inglés?*
I don't speak Spanish *no hablo castellano*
I don't understand *no entiendo*
speak more slowly, please *hable* or *hablá* or *habla más despacio, por favor.*
leave me alone (quite forceful) *¡déjeme!* or *¡dejame!* or *¡déjame!*
have you got change *tiene* or *tenés* or *tienes cambio?*
there is/there are *hay/no hay*
there isn't/there aren't *no hay*
good/well *bien*
bad/badly *mal*
small *pequeño/chico*
big *grande*
beautiful *hermoso/lindo*
a bit *un poco*; **a lot/very** *mucho/harto*
with *con*; **without** *sin*
also *también*
this *este*; **that** *ese*
and *y*; **or** *o*
because *porque*; **if** *si*
what? *¿qué?*; **who?** *¿quién?*; **when?** *¿cuándo?*; **which?** *¿cuál?*; **why?** *¿por qué?*; **how?** *¿cómo?*; **where?** *¿dónde?*; **where to?** *¿hacia dónde?*
where from? *¿de dónde?*
where are you from? *¿de dónde es or sos or eres?*
I am English *soy inglés* (man) or *inglesa* (woman); **Irish** *irlandés* or *irlandesa*; **American** *americano* or *americana/ norteamericano* or *norteamericana /estadounidense*; **Canadian** *canadiense*; **Australian** *australiano* or *australiana*; **a New Zealander** *neocelandés* or *neocelandesa*
at what time/when? *¿a qué hora?/¿cuándo?*

forbidden *prohibido*
out of order *no funciona*
bank *banco*
post office *correo*
services *servicios*
stamp *estampilla*

Emergencies

Help! *¡auxilio! ¡ayuda!*
I'm sick *estoy enfermo*
I need a doctor/policeman/
hospital *necesito un médico/un
policía/un hospital*
there's a fire! *¡hay un incendio!*

On the phone

hello *hola*
who's calling? *¿quién habla?*
hold the line *espere en línea*

Getting around

airport *aeropuerto*
station *estación*
train *tren*
ticket *boleto*
single *ida*
return *ida y vuelta*
platform *plataforma/andén*
bus/coach station *terminal de
colectivos/omnibús/micros*
entrance *entrada*
exit *salida*
left *izquierda*
right *derecha*
straight on *derecho*
street *calle*; avenue *avenida*;
motorway *autopista*
street map *mapa callejero*;
road map *mapa carretero*
no parking *prohibido estacionar*
toll *peaje*
speed limit *límite de velocidad*
petrol *nafta/bencina*; unleaded
sin plomo
side road *banquine/berma*
lane *carril/pista*

Sightseeing

museum *museo*
church *iglesia*
exhibition *exhibición*
ticket *boleto*
open *abierto*
closed *cerrado*
free *gratis*
reduced *rebajado/con descuento*
except Sunday *excepto los
domingos*

Accommodation

hotel *hotel*
bed & breakfast *pensión con
desayuno*
do you have a room (for this
evening/for two people)? *¿tiene*

una habitación (para esta noche/para
dos personas)?
no vacancy *completo/no hay
habitación libre*; vacancy
desocupado/vacante
room *habitación*
bed *cama*; double bed *cama
matrimonial*
a room with twin beds *una
habitación con camas gemelas*
a room with a bathroom/shower
una habitación con baño/ducha
breakfast *desayuno*; included
incluido
lift *ascensor*
air-conditioned *con aire
acondicionado*
to rent *alquilar/arrendar*

Shopping

I would like... *me gustaría...*
Is there a/are there any?
¿hay/habrá?
how much? *¿cuánto?*
how many? *¿cuántos?*
expensive *caro*
cheap *barato*
with VAT *con IVA* (21 per cent in
Argentina, 18 per cent in Chile)
without VAT *sin IVA*
what size? *¿qué talle?*
can I try it on? *¿me lo puedo
probar?*

Numbers

0 *cero*
1 *uno*
2 *dos*
3 *tres*
4 *cuatro*
5 *cinco*
6 *seis*
7 *siete*
8 *ocho*
9 *nueve*
10 *diez*
11 *once*; 12 *doce*; 13 *trece*; 14
catorce; 15 *quince*; 16 *dieciséis*; 17
dieciete; 18 *dieciocho*; 19 *diecinueve*;
20 *veinte*; 21 *veintiuno*; 22 *veintidós*
30 *treinta*
40 *cuarenta*
50 *cincuenta*
60 *sesenta*
70 *setenta*
80 *ochenta*
90 *noventa*
100 *cien*
1,000 *mil*
1,000,000 *un millón*

Days, months & seasons

morning *la mañana*
noon *mediodía*;
afternoon/evening *la tarde*
night *la noche*

Monday *lunes*
Tuesday *martes*
Wednesday *miércoles*
Thursday *jueves*
Friday *viernes*
Saturday *sábado*
Sunday *domingo*
January *enero*; February
febrero; March *marzo*; April
abril; May *mayo*; June *junio*;
July *julio*; August *agosto*;
September *septiembre*;
October *octubre*; November
noviembre; December
diciembre
spring *primavera*
summer *verano*
autumn/fall *otoño*
winter *invierno*

Others

In football-mad South America
you will undoubtedly at some
stage be asked '*¿Sos/eres
hincha de quien?*', meaning
'which team do you support?'
The word *hincha* means
supporter and breaker, thus
hinchapelotas is a pain in the
balls or a pain in the arse.

Many words can be used as
insults or, among friends, in an
affectionate way – everything
depends on tone and context.
In Argentina it's common to
hear friends address each
other as *boludo* or *pelotudo*
(big balls), or *huevón* in Chile,
which can be used in both
the masculine and (illogically)
feminine (*boluda, pelotuda* or
huevona). In Chile you'll also
hear *roto, cuma* and *picante*.

There's not much spirit of
political correctness and people
are given nicknames that refer
directly to their looks, origins
or other attributes. The word
gringo can be applied to just
about any foreigner, and is
particularly common as a form
of address in Chile. Be tolerant;
it's usually colloquial, not
racist. There's not much love
lost between Argentinians and
Chileans. Argentinians refer
to all Chileans as *chilotes*, and
Chileans use the Argentinian
che or the more derogatory
argentuzo. There are more
extreme jokes and insults –
just use your imagination.

Further Reference

Books

Alberto De Agostini *Andes Patagónicos* The bible for climbers, by a Salesian priest who scaled the highest of the Patagonian peaks.
Lucas Bridges *The Uttermost Part of the Earth* First-hand account of life among the Fuegian natives.
Jimmy Burns *The Land That Lost Its Heroes: Argentina, the Falklands, and Alfonsín* The essential analysis of *that* conflict.
Bruce Chatwin *In Patagonia* Fact meets fiction in what is still essential reading for first visits to Patagonia. Read it while you're there!
Charles Darwin *Voyage of the Beagle* Sea, sand, shells, wind, waders, homo sapiens... everything matters to Darwin's inquiring mind.
Miranda France *Bad Times in Buenos Aires: A Writer's Adventures in Argentina* Mainly on the city but some sardonic words on the south of Argentina too.
Graham Harris *A Guide to the Birds and Mammals of Coastal Patagonia* Fully illustrated guide to the richly varied fauna of Argentina's Atlantic coast. Suitable both for experienced naturalists and those who can barely tell their penguins from their pumas.
WH Hudson *Idle Days in Patagonia* Quasi-mystical account of the minute natural wonders found in the seemingly empty plains of Rio Negro.
Sylvia Iparraguirre *Tierra del Fuego: An Historical Novel* A novel about the Jemmy Button affair – from the perspective of one of his captors.
Colin McEwan (ed) *Patagonia: Natural History, Prehistory and Ethnography at the Uttermost End of the Earth* Original, profound essays on the ideas and realities of Patagonia.
Anne Meadows *Digging up Butch and Sundance* History of the outlaws' South American sojourn, with bits of travel and adventure, researched and penned by a husband-wife team.
Nick Reding *The Last Cowboys at the End of the World: The Story of the Gauchos of Patagonia* Arresting eyewitness chronicle of latter-day gauchos and their families in southern Chile.
Paul Theroux *The Old Patagonian Express* Classic travelogue that winds up memorably in Argentina.
Sara Wheeler *Terra Incognita.* Near-religious revelations on the big ice of Argentina's deep south.
Glyn Williams *The Welsh in Patagonia: the State and the Ethnic Community.* Standard text for the great Welsh adventure.

Film

Gregorio Cramer *Invierno Mala Vida* (*Winter Land*) Drinking his life away at the end of the world, Valdivia takes on odd delivery jobs – when he loses a weird cargo, things get beyond his control. Stars BA acting supremo Ricardo Bartis.
Lucas Demare *Plaza Huincal* (1960) A gritty story about oil workers grafting and striking on the windswept plains of Neuquén province, Argentina.
Héctor Olivera *La Patagonia rebelde* Chilling 1974 film based on Osvaldo Bayer's account of the murder of farm workers in 1921.
Claudio Remedi *Fantasmas en la Patagonia* Powerful docu about the end of mining and its consequences for the people of Sierra Grande.
Carlos Sorín *Bombón el perro* (*Bombon the Dog*) Middle-aged unemployed petrol station attendant hits the dog-show circuit after accidentally coming into ownership of a pedigree hunting hound. Unusually for a film set in Patagonia, it's as much about life as landscape.
Andrés Wood *La fiebre del loco* (2001) tells how southern fishermen go crazy every few years when the government allows them to catch the supposedly aphrodisiacal, but protected mollusc known as the *loco*. Wood's *Historias de fútbol* (1997) deals with the arrival of a Chilote boy in his hometown on one of the smaller islands – he comes to see a key World Cup game but finds himself cut off from the broadcast.
Walter Salles *Diarios de motocicleta* (*The Motorcycle Diaries*) Bio-flick chronicling the young Ernesto 'Che' Guevara's epic – and scenic – road-trip through Argentina and Chile.

Music

Bordermar *Sur de Chile* A very best of... compilation of this virtuoso outfit's stirring fusions of Bach and European folk with native rhythms.
Camerata Bariloche *Suite Argentina* The south's finest chamber orchestra, with respected Argentinian folker Eduardo Falú as guest guitarist.
León Gieco *De Ushuaia a La Quiaca* An exploration of Argentinian regional folk music, from a rock and human rights legend.
Beatriz Pichi Malen *Plata* An insightful introduction to the earthy, evocative and often spooky sounds of northern Patagonia – sung in Mapudungun, the Mapuche tongue.

Websites

www.andes.org.uk A climbing guide for all the top Andes walks from Venezuela to Isla Navarino. The site is commercial, but click on 'Free info files' for facts and figures.
www.bbc.co.uk/cymru/patagonia Excellent (we suppose) website about the Welsh in Patagonia. In Welsh.
www.chile.com News, features, services and, in the section 'A la chilena', food, dance and language tips on this Yahoo!-style portal.
www.chipsites.cl Loads of Chilean insights and hard news from the people who produce the English-language *Santiago Times*.
www.cruzadapatagonica.org Charitable organisation focusing on education and agriculture across Andean Argentinian Patagonia.
www.dinosaur.org Home of DNN (the Dinosaur News Network), with pretty pictures of large lizards.
www.hvra.com.ar/eninfoct.htm Roam *estancias* virtually, and fantasise about buying them; also has a great 20-page PDF article called 'Paradise Patagonia'.
www.interpatagonia.com All things to all wannabe Patagonians – loads of excursion information and esoteric stuff on legends. In Spanish and English.
www.mapuche-nation.org Site fighting for the rights of indigenous Americans, especially the Mapuche, by campaigners based in Bristol, UK.
www.monumentos.cl All Chile's national monuments, from Chiloé's churches to those long faces on Easter Island. In Spanish.
www.patagonia-argentina.com The most comprehensive online guide to Patagonia: lots of good info in English and Spanish.
www.patagonianatural.org Website of the Fundación Patagonia Natural, an NGO that campaigns for wildlife conservation in Patagonia.
www.patbrit.com Treasure trove of historical information about the British in southern Patagonia.
www.pbs.org/edens/patagonia /index.htm Educational service highlighting ecological challenges.
www.samexplo.org Useful website for travellers in South America and also a good place to find like-minded travellers.
www.surdelsur.com Music, nature, history and culture explained in English by Argentinian authors.
www.travellersguru.com Online version of the free quarterly backpackers' guide (in English), published by long-time Bariloche residents Alan and Ron.

Directory

Index

Note: page numbers in **bold** indicate section(s) giving key information on a topic; *italics* indicate photos.

Advertisers' Index

Please refer to the relevant pages for
contact details

| Aerolineas Argentinas | **IFC** |

In Context

| Gobierno de la Ciudad de
Buenos Aires (Tourism) | **10** |

Argentinian Patagonia

Argentina Hostels Club	**66**
Burco Adventure	**68**
Fueguito	**84**
Estancia Peuma Hue	**84**
Fundación Cruzada Patagónica	**84**
Correntoso Lake & River Hotel	**88**
Meridies	**92**
Tipiliuke Lodge	**92**
patagonia-argentina.com	**146**

| Time Out City Guides | **IBC** |